MEGABRAIN

New Tools and Techniques for Brain Growth and Mind Expansion

Michael Hutchison

BALLANTINE BOOKS • NEW YORK

ON THE CUTTING EDGE OF EVOLUTION: THE LAST FRONTIER

You sit down in a comfortable chair, don the electrical headgear, flip a switch on the small control console by your hand, close your eyes, and sink into a state of deep relaxation. A half hour later as you turn off the machine and remove the headgear, you feel extremely alert and lucid. Your brain is now functioning far more effectively than it was before. Your memory—your ability both to memorize new information and to recall information you have already learned—has increased dramatically. Your ability to think creatively, to solve problems, has expanded. The speed with which your brain cells pass messages among themselves has increased. In fact, many of your brain cells have actually grown—a microscopic examination would show that the brain cells have developed more dendrites, the branching filaments that carry messages from one cell to another, and more synapses, the junctures between brain cells across which impulses are transmitted. You are more intelligent than you were a half hour before.

Such devices now exist and are being used by increasing numbers of people.

MEGABRAIN

"A fascinating text on speculative science."
Booklist

TO CARRIE

ACKNOWLEDGMENTS

Among the many to whom I am grateful for the advice, assistance, encouragement, and expertise they offered me in the research and writing of this book, my particular thanks to: David Size, Dave Seefelt, and Charles Docherty of Tranquility Center in New York City; Joseph Light, David Abramson, Dr. Jeffrey Gmelch, Caroline Schneider, Maggie O'Bryan, Dr. Charles Stroebel, Dr. Denis Gorges, Philip Brotman, Jonni Winchester, and Chinmayee Chakrabarty.

CONTENTS

INTRODUCTION:
THE LAST FRONTIER

You sit down in a comfortable chair, don the electrical headgear, flip a switch on the small control console by your hand, close your eyes, and sink into a state of deep relaxation. A half hour later as you turn off the machine and remove the headgear, you feel extremely alert and lucid. Your brain is now functioning far more effectively than it was before. Your memory—your ability both to memorize new information and to recall information you have already learned—has increased dramatically. Your ability to think creatively, to solve problems, has expanded. The speed with which your brain cells pass messages among themselves has increased. In fact, many of your brain cells have actually grown—a microscopic examination would show that the brain cells have developed more dendrites, the branching filaments that carry messages from one cell to another, and more synapses, the junctures between brain cells across which impulses are transmitted. You are now more intelligent than you were a half hour before.

The machine sounds like a prop from a science fiction movie, but devices reputed to have the brain-boosting effects described now exist and are being used by increasing numbers of people. If you have not yet heard of them it is understandable, since they operate by exploiting brain capabilities that have been discovered so recently that they are not widely known or understood outside the world of neuroscience. This book explores some of those recent discoveries about the

1

brain, and the mind machines that are purported to stimulate the brain and enhance mental functioning.

NEUROSCIENTISTS AS EXPLORERS, HIGH PRIESTS, AND REVOLUTIONARIES

NEUROSCIENTISTS CLAIM THAT WE HAVE LEARNED MORE about the brain in the last decade than we learned throughout all the ages that went before. Much of what has been learned has been not only surprising but also, when considered in the light of the traditional views of the brain, almost unbelievable, contradicting long-standing assumptions. As one astonishing discovery follows another, neuroscience has become a glamour area, hot, exciting, what scientists call "sexy."

No wonder—these scientists claim they are investigating "the last frontier." That makes them explorers, and puts them in pretty heroic company—astronauts, moon walkers, adventurers, mountain men, intrepid characters like Columbus, Lewis and Clark, Magellan, and Captain Cook. Exciting stuff. Nobel prizes are up for grabs, as well as the satisfaction of finally comprehending the most mysterious and complex structure in the universe. You can catch a whiff of the neuroscientists' feverish passions by listening to their descriptions of the current state of brain research.

"It's difficult to try to responsibly convey some sense of excitement about what's going on," says UCLA neurophysiologist John Liebeskind. "You find yourself sounding like people you don't respect. You try to be more conservative and not say such wild and intriguing things, but damn! The field is wild and intriguing. It's hard to avoid talking that way. . . . We are at a frontier, and it's a terribly exciting time to be in this line of work."

"There's a revolution going on," says neurochemist Candace Pert of the National Institute of Mental Health. "There used to be two systems of knowledge: hard science—chemistry, physics, biophysics—on the one hand, and, on the other, a system of knowledge that included ethology, psychology, and psychiatry. And now it's as if a lightning bolt had connected the two. It's all one system—neuroscience. . . . The present era in neuroscience is comparable to the time when Louis Pasteur first found out that germs cause disease."

The scientists are talking not just revolution, but religion as well (curious how the two always seem so intertwined). Arnold Scheibel is professor of medicine at UCLA, his wife Marian Diamond a neuroanatomist at UC Berkeley. Scheibel explains their fascination with the brain: "We like to think that somehow the brain in a sense will become the religion of the future, largely because it is absolutely the instrument of humanity. It's the source of all human culture, and then, most excitingly, human culture plays back on the brain, and changes the brain."

"The study of the brain is one of the last frontiers of human knowledge," declares neuroscientist Colin Blakemore, "and of more immediate importance than understanding the infinity of space and the mystery of the atom."

"It is difficult to escape the conclusion that a new era in neurobiology is dawning," proclaim the editors of the magazine *Trends in Neuroscience*. "The flow of information through neural circuits is more dynamic than previously imagined."

Says neuroanatomist Floyd Bloom of Scripps Clinic in La Jolla, California, "A neuroscientist used to be like a man in a Goodyear blimp floating over a bowl game: he could hear the crowd roar, and that was about it. But now we're down in the stands. It's not too long before we'll be able to tell why one man gets a hot dog and one man gets a beer."

"It's just beginning to happen now," says UCLA neurophysiologist Alan Grinnell. "Everyone is very optimistic now that we're getting the tools to learn a great deal more about how it all works. . . . The next ten years are going to tell us an enormous amount about how the brain works. . . . With this big surge in understanding has mainly come a much better appreciation for the difficulty of what we're being asked to understand. In that sense, even though we have discovered the new land, it's a pretty formidable continent."

"This is a fun time to be doing neuroscience," says Michael Brownstein of NIMH. "A lot of good people see it as the last frontier."

INTERESTINGLY, THE EXCITEMENT OF THE NEUROSCIENTISTS is shared by the general public, historically a fairly rare occurrence. Many of the new discoveries, concerning what would ordinarily be thought obscure and highly specialized subjects, such as the differing functions of the brain's hemispheres and the properties of various brain chemicals such as those natural opiates the much-celebrated endorphins, are enthusiastically reported in daily newspapers, on television news broadcasts, and in an assortment of immensely popular mass-market science magazines, as well as in women's and men's magazines, health journals, and many other media outlets. What's all the excitement about?

Could it be that the general public has suddenly developed an overwhelming interest in science? I think not. Startling discoveries are being made in fields like nuclear physics, chemistry, biology, mathematics, and computer science without arousing widespread interest.

But brain research, most people seem to feel, is something different—not science so much as, well, romance, or that now-epidemic hobby "self-discovery." While the scientist may claim to be objectively studying a mere physical organ, the nonscientists know that what is really being scrutinized and analyzed is their most private and passionate self. Says UCLA psychologist Liebeskind, "Literally and figuratively, it's the sexiest organ we have. . . . It's where we live. That's why it's so sexy; I mean, that is us. You can't get any more private. You can't touch anything more private than the brain."

So when the neuroscientists make a new discovery about the brain, we are enthralled, not so much for the contribution the new discovery makes to the field of brain science, but for the light it casts into our own depths, for the insights it offers into our own emotions, memories, thoughts, and intelligence. When the scientists discover something new about the brain, we discover something new about ourselves.

What are these exciting discoveries? Among the most intriguing and important recent revelations about the human brain, whose implications we will investigate throughout this book, are the following:

BRAIN GROWTH. SCIENTISTS HAVE LONG ASSUMED THAT the physical size of the brain—weight, number of brain cells, thickness of cortex—is determined by heredity. But a series of astonishing studies has now proved that certain external stimulations of the brain, or "enriched environments," actually cause a pronounced increase in brain size, including the size of the neurons and the number of certain brain cells.

AGING AND THE BRAIN. IT HAS BEEN ASSUMED THAT after reaching maturity, not only does brain growth cease, but there is an inexorable, unavoidable loss of brain cells. Now studies have shown that with the proper stimulation, the brain does not lose cells with increasing age, that in fact parts of the brain can continue to grow, producing increased intelligence, more effective brain functioning, even after seventy, eighty, or ninety years.

BRAIN REGENERATION. ANOTHER SCIENTIFIC TRUTH THAT has gone largely unchallenged for decades has been that while other cells of the body can reproduce or regenerate themselves, the cells of our brain are incapable of regeneration. This means that the brain cells we have developed by the age of two must last us our entire life. Since it is known that there is a continuous loss of neurons, this has meant that humans are condemned to a slow but inexorable diminishing of neurons. In recent years, however, studies have shown that under the right conditions neurons *can* regenerate, suggesting that given the right type of stimulation the brain will continuously heal itself and replace lost cells, in much the same way as our skin can heal itself after it is cut.

BRAIN SYNCHRONIZATION. THE REVELATIONS OF BRAIN lateralization studies—that the left and right hemispheres of our cortex operate in different modes and in different rhythms —led scientists to conclude that humans generally emphasize half their brains at a time, dominance flickering back and forth between hemispheres depending on the task at hand. But studies by neurologists have now proved that in certain extraordinary mental states, such as deep meditation or intense creativity, both hemispheres shift into a single, coherent rhythm, operating in unison. Scientists call this state of whole-brain thinking *synchrony*, and it has recently become clear that certain brain-stimulation devices can rapidly boost the brain into this beneficial state.

THE ELECTROCHEMICAL BRAIN. SCIENTISTS ASSERT that every imaginable mental state is the result of a specific pattern of electrical and chemical activity in the brain. This brain activity, they have discovered, can be altered and shaped by external stimuli, including sounds, lights, electromagnetic fields, and physical movements. Mechanical devices that can direct these stimuli to appropriate areas in the brain can reliably trigger specific brain states: it is now possible, using these devices, to guide yourself into such brain states as euphoria, reverie, recall of long-past experiences, stimulation of memories, sexual excitement, deep concentration, and heightened creativity.

BRAIN SELF-REGULATION. SCIENTISTS LONG ASSUMED that most aspects of brain operation, including the rhythms of the brain's electrical activity and the secretion of brain chemicals, were, like much of the human nervous system, beyond conscious control. Then, in the 1960s, discoveries in biofeedback proved that humans can learn to take conscious control of any *physical* system of which they can be made aware. Using biofeedback, we can quickly learn to alter such "involuntary" systems as our blood pressure, heart rate, and secretion of hormones. But recent technological advances have now made possible extraordinarily sensitive machines that can monitor and feed back to us what are essentially *mental* states. By sensing the brain's electrical activity and simultaneously "feeding back" to us that activity in easily understandable images, these machines enable users to observe their brain states and change them. In effect, you can learn to alter and control your own thoughts, emotions, moods, and mental states, at will.

SUPERLEARNING AND THE BRAIN. RECENT STUDIES INDICATE that the human brain is capable of far greater feats of learning, remembering, and creating than had previously been imagined. Under the proper conditions, normal humans can absorb, store, process, and recall vast amounts of information.

OF MACHINE AND MIND

THE IMPLICATIONS OF THESE RECENT DISCOVERIES ARE QUITE clear: the brain is much more powerful, capable, and complex than had previously been imagined. What we think of as normal intelligence is probably just a pale shadow of the brain's actual powers and faculties. It's as if we've all been given superbly engineered sports cars in which we've been putt-putting about without ever shifting out of first gear, never realizing that there were higher gears.

But the newfound brain capabilities described above suggest that there are ways the brain can be shifted into higher gears, that brain functioning can be substantially improved, *provided* the brain receives the right type of stimulation. There is increasing evidence that this essential brain stimulation can be supplied by mechanical devices of various sorts.

In the past, the only accepted uses of machines in conjunction with the human brain have been for diagnostic or therapeutic purposes: electroencephalographs to analyze brain waves in search of potential epilepsy or tumors, electrical brain stimulation to alleviate pain, CAT and PET and NMR scanners to get accurate images of what is happening inside the brain, and so on. Today, however, more and more scientists are becoming interested in using machines not only to help sick people get well, but to help normal, healthy people increase their ability to learn, think, imagine, remember, create.

Can a machine actually make you smarter? Enhance your mental functioning? In this book I will examine a number of machines now being used to stimulate the brain and will evaluate the available scientific evidence of their influence on mental abilities. As you will see, the evidence includes studies showing that experimental users of various mind machines responded with dramatic improvements in (depending on the machine in question) IQ, neuro-efficiency quotient, long-term memory, serial memory, attention, reaction time, recall, sensory acuity, hemispheric synchronization, brainwave amplitude, and other capacities. If any of the instruments could consistently and reliably produce increases in brain functioning across the range of abilities listed above, it would be a potentially revolutionary device, perhaps even, as one inventor has claimed, the most significant development in learning since the invention of writing. We will investigate the validity of these studies.

In Part I we will look at some of the ideas and discoveries that have led to our new, revised, and expanded vision of the brain as an enormous and virtually untapped reservoir of powers and skills. We will see why these discoveries have inspired a number of imaginative scientist-inventors to construct devices intended to tap those hidden reserves, to trigger the ordinarily dormant mental powers.

In Part II we will take a close look at nine mind machines, each one taking advantage of a different facet of brain physiology to produce its mind-altering effect. I will give a firsthand account of how the machines work and what it feels like to use each of the devices, discuss what the inventors and manufacturers claim to be the benefits of each device, and, through interviews with frequent users, the inventors, scientists, and others, discover whether the machines live up to the claims made for them. I will alert you to any possible harmful effects the machines might have.

In the Afterword, I discuss new devices and developments in the field, and provide an address for those seeking more information or interested in experimenting with, renting, or buying any of the machines. The Bibliography that follows the Afterword is numbered; corresponding superscript numbers entered in the text refer the interested reader to the sources of quotations and research projects described.

PART I

Everyone is familiar with the phenomenon of feeling more or less alive on different days. Everyone knows on any given day that there are energies slumbering in him which the incitements of that day do not call forth, but which he might display if these were greater. Most of us feel as if a sort of cloud weighed upon us, keeping us below our highest notch of clearness in discernment, sureness in reasoning, or firmness in deciding. Compared with what we ought to be, we are only half awake. Our fires are damped, our drafts are checked. We are making use of only a small part of our possible mental and physical resources.

Stating the thing broadly, the human individual thus lives far within his limits; he possesses powers of various sorts which he habitually fails to use. He energizes below his *maximum*, and he behaves below his *optimum*. In elementary faculty, in co-ordination, in power of *inhibition* and control, in every conceivable way, his life is contracted like the field of vision of an hysteric subject—but with less excuse, for the poor hysteric is diseased, while in the rest of us, it is only an inveterate *habit*—the habit of inferiority to our full self—that is bad.

—WILLIAM JAMES

The finitude of *Dasein*—the comprehension of being—lies in forgetfulness. This forgetfulness is nothing accidental and temporary but is constantly and necessarily renewed. All construction relevant to fundamental ontology, construction which strives towards the disclosure of the internal possibility of the comprehension of Being, must in its act of projection wrest from forgetfulness that which it thus apprehends. The basic, fundamental ontological act of the metaphysics of *Dasein* is, therefore, a remembering.

—MARTIN HEIDEGGER

I reckon I got to light out for the Territory ahead of the rest, because Aunt Sally she's going to adopt me and sivilize me and I can't stand it. I been there before.

—MARK TWAIN,
Adventures of Huckleberry Finn

1

LIGHTING OUT FOR THE TERRITORY

THE OUTLOOK WASN'T BRILLIANT FOR ENLIGHTENMENT AND tranquillity that morning. I'd arranged with a magazine editor for us to have a demonstration of an odd machine, something called a Whole Brain Wave Form Synchro-Energizer. Several people had told me in awed tones that the device, which supposedly "synchronized" the electrical waves of the two brain hemispheres, induced states of deep relaxation, serenity, and trancelike visions, and did so even in people who were ordinarily resistant to such states. Its inventor claimed it increased intelligence, improved memory, accelerated learning, increased creativity, stimulated problem-solving, facilitated retrieval of subconscious memories, and sharpened perceptions, among other effects. It had sounded weird and interesting, and I wanted to do a piece on it for the magazine. The editor had reserved judgment until he could see the machine in action. I had called the inventor/manufacturer of the device, and he had agreed to have two of his associates come by the editorial offices for a demonstration.

But the morning had suddenly turned wintry, with icy rains whipping through the streets as the photographer and I had raced about midtown in search of a certain type of light she needed. In a frantic scramble we made it to the magazine offices on time, only to discover that the Synchro-Energizer authorities had been delayed in Boston. The editor had waited awhile, grown impatient and irritable, and gone off to an editorial conference. When the Synchro-Energizer people arrived, we were installed in a room which opened onto the magazine's busy reception area. The room felt like a refrigerator, my clothes were still damp from the rain, I felt wired from having sloshed down six cups of coffee and no breakfast, and as the technicians set up the machine an endless stream of people kept peering in crying, "What the hell is that?"

The editor, not a placid sort in even the best of times, seemed more than usually frantic as he rushed in. "This is it?" He gestured toward the machine. In truth, it didn't look impressive—a small electric console about the size of a hardcover book, covered with dials, to which were attached ordinary stereo headphones and some goggles. With a skeptical look implying that something so small could hardly have much effect, he sat down and donned the headphones and goggles, and the machine was turned on.

The small light bulbs surrounding each eye inside the goggles began to flicker rhythmically. As the technician turned a dial, the light patterns changed, first flashing in each eye alternately, then both eyes simultaneously, then in more complex patterns around both eyes. We couldn't hear what the editor was hearing through the headphones, but the technician demonstrated the various sounds by turning another knob, saying, "This is a heartbeat . . . here's the ocean sound . . . and this is an electronic hum." With each change, the editor nodded a bit, a smile playing across his lips.

"Nice sounds," he said to us. In the room people milled around, commenting on the machine, cracking jokes, asking questions of the technicians. The photographer was snapping away, flashbulbs popping, automatic film advancer whirring. But the editor seemed unaware of the chaos. "I'm hearing women's voices," he said in a far-off voice, "now chanting, like monks chanting." He had settled back in the chair, his body melted into a posture of deep relaxation.

"Now it's a violin, and a woman singing. Also I hear a

male announcer, like a talk show, and a chanting chorus." He swayed and tapped his foot in time to the music he was hearing.

Astonished, the watching technician shook her head from side to side. "This is a new one for me," she said. "The only real sound he's hearing is an electronic hum. The rest is hallucinations!"

"Now it's piano music," said the editor. "Now it's guitar, voices chanting—I think I'm picking up every radio station in the city!"

The technician adjusted the dial, and the pattern of flashing lights changed. "Ah, striking visual effects," said the editor. "An insect furiously flapping its wings, a black insect, but the vibration of the wings is purple and yellow. Hey, I can change it! I thought I was seeing what I was supposed to see, but now it's occurred to me I can change it. I feel extraordinarily open and receptive," the editor was saying. "I'm experiencing euphoria." He laughed to himself with pleasure.

"Yellows, oranges, reds flashing by like a merry-go-round. Oh wow! It's flickering, like a fan, except instead of seeing the fan, I *am* the fan. I'm looking into the sun. It's spinning now—sound waves, spiraling in oranges and yellows and purples. In the middle is a star." He gasped. "Oh, that's fabulous. A shift from red to black except that as it shifts it goes through a number of colors so fast that I can't see them, except I have! It's like somebody just dropped me in the sun. A white light . . . a prism letting off colors in front of the white light. And now the radio stations have come back on . . . all the radio stations in the world. With yellow amoebas going through, and every flash changes the radio station. . . ." A blissful smile filled his face. This, I thought, must be some machine.

WHEN MY TURN CAME, I SAT DOWN TO THE DEVICE WITH SOME trepidation. The irritations of the day had jangled my nerves, and I was shivering with cold and fatigue. I was acutely aware of the people watching, and would rather have tried it out alone somewhere, at my own pace. Putting on the headphones, I heard a bland electronic hum, and wondered how on earth the editor could have imagined he'd heard a celestial variety show. As I donned the goggles the tiny white lights surrounding each eye flickered annoyingly. I noticed by the digital readout on the console that the current rhythm was about 20 cycles per second—the rapid beta waves of ordinary waking consciousness. I turned the frequency dial downward, which caused the lights to flash more slowly, and watched the digits decrease through the teens and stop at 5 cycles per second—the slow theta waves that accompany deep reverie, meditation, and mental imagery. The brightness of the flashing lights increased and suddenly I saw. . . .

I knew the tiny flashing lights were plain white, and yet the visions that appeared to me were vivid, spectacular, of bright primary colors—jagged alien landscapes, narrowing tunnels of swooping looping light, swirling multicolored checkerboards, a realistic view across the gray surface of a pond being stippled into fragmented light patterns by a gentle rainfall, sleek fish moving below the surface.

I felt my attention drawn irresistibly inward. My tension was melting away. I was aware there were people in the room, but it was of no interest—they were in another world, far away. I experimented with different frequencies and patterns of stimulation, and with each twist of the dials the visions would change. I noticed that some visions would call up vivid memories. I dialed back to the pond, and suddenly I was a kid again, stalking frogs, feeling the sun hot on the back of my neck, smelling the green algae and mud of the pond.

At times I had the feeling that I had suddenly been placed at the controls of some immensely powerful machine. It was as if my brain had been given a tune-up and was now working in new ways, presenting me with new thoughts, new ways of thinking, new capabilities. What if you could wear this machine while you were reading, I wondered, or playing the piano, problem-solving, creating? A swarm of ideas buzzed around in my brain, all of them having to do with the human brain and ways it could be influenced, ways the function of the brain could be enhanced and its powers boosted, by means

16

of external stimulation. Hey, said the voice in my head, this thing really works!

MIND MACHINES AND THE WEASEL'S EYE

THE IDEA THAT YOU CAN ACTUALLY CHANGE THE BRAIN—NOT simply emotions and thoughts but the actual physical structure—simply by altering the type of external stimulation the brain receives had intrigued me since the early '70s, when, for reasons not entirely clear to me at the time, I was living alone in a small log lean-to I'd built on a mountainside in the wilderness. I would go long periods without speaking to another human. During my first winter up on the mountain I found some strange things happening to me.

I was surrounded by blankness: the mountains around me were white; the valley stretching away for miles below was a pure white snowfield; the winter sky was a featureless slate; I spent much time trekking out across the drifts in snowshoes searching for standing deadwood to chop down for firewood, or sitting on a log staring into my fire. I began to see things— exotic colorful cities, rows of marching nuns, flickering faces in the fire. In the midst of the silence I carried on long conversations with a voice inside my head. I heard voices coming out of the nearby stream, shouting to me or talking with each other, just loud enough for me to hear but not loud enough for me to make out what they were saying. I was swept with vivid memories of my childhood, and sat for hours doing nothing, detached and serene.

When I did suddenly encounter a patch of color, or sudden movement—the red blood of a freshly killed deer, a raccoon's pink tongue—it seemed electrifying, magically intense. I learned to sit still for long periods. Once I was sitting on a boulder overhanging a rushing stream and was so motionless that a weasel came slinking by and sat down only a couple of feet away before he even noticed me. Then our eyes locked— his glittering eyeball became the center of the universe, everything else grew white and faded away, and I stared into the eye

17

for what seemed like hours, hypnotized, full of some vast wisdom.

I'd been given a copy of Dr. John Lilly's recent book *Center of the Cyclone*, in which the neuroscientist, famous for his work in mapping the pleasure and pain centers of the brain and in trying to establish communication with dolphins, described his attempts to understand the workings of the brain by means of sensory deprivation. At the National Institute of Mental Health he set up a tank in which he could float suspended in total darkness and silence in body-temperature water. Freed from ordinary external stimuli, he experienced many states of consciousness, discovering that the brain had numerous powers of which he had been unaware until they creativity, and even transcendence and revelation. He found that simply by entering the the tank—that is, altering his external stimulation—he could boost his brain into states of extraordinary lucidity, deep meditation, concentration, and contemplation.

As I sat reading of Lilly's self-exploration, it struck me what I was doing on the mountain. I saw that I was undergoing a sort of half-assed but effective experiment in sensory deprivation. Except, of course, that what had taken me months of wilderness isolation Lilly was able to accomplish in just an hour. It was a bit like making a cross-country trek on foot, reaching your goal after weeks of plodding, to find upon arrival that someone else has made the same journey by jet in a few hours.

The secret to Lilly's shortcut, I realized, was imaginative use of state-of-the-art technology and scientific information. In this case, Lilly used a saturated solution of Epsom salts to provide buoyancy, heating devices to warm the water to body temperature, air pumps, water filters, and a specially designed chamber to shut out sound and light. The result was a "machine" that rapidly induced the sort of mental changes that ordinarily had taken long periods of isolation, meditation, or contemplation to achieve.

RANDOM PARTICLE PROPELLED BY ALPHA WAVES TO GUATEMALA

MY FIRST CHANCE TO TRY OUT A BRAIN MACHINE CAME A FEW years later when, sweating in the sauna of my local Y, I heard someone tell his friend about a scientist at New York University—just a few blocks away—who was looking for volunteers for a study of biofeedback. "He hooks you up to this gizmo," the guy said, "and gets you to generate these alpha rays, and afterward you feel, like, zonked for hours!"

"Sounds weird to me," said his friend; but it sounded interesting to me. Eavesdropping shamelessly, I noted the name of the scientist, called him up, and asked if I could join the experiment. It turned out to be a study comparing the effectiveness of various techniques for learning to generate alpha *waves*, not rays. The researcher put me in the control group; while other groups were carefully instructed in meditation, deep breathing, progressive relaxation, or other techniques, my group was given no instructions at all. It was like learning to swim by being tossed in the ocean: the scientist stuck electrodes on my skull and said to try to make the clicker (which was activated by alpha waves) go faster. I did, it did, and I found I had a knack for it. All I had to do was think of sitting in the snowy wilderness gazing into the eye of a weasel.

The researcher was puzzled, since I totally disrupted his statistics by producing more alpha than the groups that were learning specific techniques for doing it. I could never understand exactly *how* I did it, but I could always tell *when*—the feeling was immediate and unmistakable, something like idly twisting a radio dial, when suddenly all the static disappears, and there are all those lovely alpha waves clicking like mad. Each time I emerged after the experiment I felt fine-tuned—like a superb motorcycle humming along a smooth highway at about 95 mph ticking like a clock.

I asked the scientist why making a clicker click faster would make me feel so good, and he explained that in ordinary waking consciousness the dominant brain waves are *beta* waves—rapid and relatively weak. But when we become more relaxed, the dominant brain waves become the slower, more powerful alpha waves. Thus, he explained, the reason I felt so good was that I was simply more relaxed. This made sense, and yet I sensed something more. I wasn't just relaxed, I felt truly different; and not just different but, well, *better*, even *more intelligent*.

It occurred to me that until then I had accepted my various mental states as natural events: if I felt depressed, angry, befuddled, why then that was the way I felt, and it was something to be lived with, until somehow it changed. Now I realized that ordinary consciousness was not just a given, but the product of something called brain waves, and that these brain waves could be altered at will: if you don't like what's going on in your head, then *change* it. It was a revelation.

Interestingly, the mental clarity I felt after working with the click machine stayed with me for days, making me not only feel different but act different. From nowhere I found myself writing a series of bizarre short stories. They were exciting and funny but seemed to have emerged full-blown from the ozone, since the characters and plots were things I never would have imagined. I sat and watched entranced as my fingers flew over the typewriter keys, and wondered what would emerge next.

Then, like a character in one of the stories, I surprised myself by packing up my bag and departing for the south, where I ended up living on the side of a volcano near a small Indian village in Guatemala. The writing poured out, and I studied, traveled, worked, picked up Spanish. I felt energized, with a new sense of mental clarity that came in part, I felt, from the experience of being hooked up to the alpha machine and learning to take some control of my own brain waves, that is, my state of mind. I felt it made me smarter, more creative, more productive, wiser.

Before that I would have scoffed at the idea that some machine could actually enhance mental powers. After all, everyone knows that innate intelligence is determined by heredity; that our characters are molded by the experiences we've had by the age of five; that creativity, imagination, sense of self are products of the way our inborn genetic potential is nurtured or thwarted by our early life experiences. By the time we reach our twenties we are, for better or worse, what we are, something that no machine can alter. The contraption you hook up to your skull that suddenly makes you smarter or more creative, or sends you off to Guatemala, was the stuff of science fiction, right?

But now I was beginning to wonder. Dr. Lilly's experiments with the isolation tank and my experience in the wilderness had shown me that mechanical devices can enormously accelerate normally slow mental processes. The alpha device had convinced me that machines can stimulate the brain into taking control of usually unconscious processes, such as the type of brain waves it generates. And the idea that machines can influence, even radically alter, so-called reality was not far-out. Physicists were doing it constantly with their powerful cyclotrons. These machines, accelerating and bombarding matter, caused bizarre subatomic particles to reveal new potentials, new elements, new realities. Here, teased out of hiding by machines, were odd particles that ran backward in time, passed through dense matter like ghosts, or had some sort of negative existence. Perhaps machines directed at the brain, "psychlotrons," devices to accelerate and bombard the elementary particles of mind, could reveal new mind potentials, create new mind realities. The cyclotrons of nuclear physicists caused subatomic particles to perform in unpredictable ways. Maybe the alpha machine had sent the random particle that was me accelerating off to Guatemala to write novels and live on the side of a volcano with the Indians.

VOODOO TECHNOLOGY ENTERS THE SCIENTIFIC MAINSTREAM

THE QUESTION IS, CAN CERTAIN MACHINES MAKE US BETTER—smarter, wiser, more capable, more creative? I had a gut feeling that that had happened to me, but feelings don't constitute

21

proof. I began to investigate—reading, talking with scientists
—and I found out that my interest in mind-machine interactions
was shared by increasing numbers of mainstream
scientists. In fact, the development of brain-exploring technology
has become a hot spot in brain research, with scientists
from all disciplines, from psychology to neuroscience, in the
midst of projects that only a few years ago would have
sounded like pure science fiction—memory transfusions,
brain transplants, computer-brain interfaces, electrical stimulation
of brain pleasure centers, electromagnetic sleep machines,
"rewiring" of faulty brain circuits, electrically
triggered brain growth and neural regeneration, vastly accelerated
learning in controlled environments, brain mapping with
the entrancingly named SQUID (Superconducting Quantum
Interference Device—an ultrasensitive detector of the brain's
magnetic patterns).

While many of the mind-machine studies going on today
would have sounded like so much voodoo technology only a
decade ago, they now have not only credibility (for example,
funding from the government and reputable educational or research
institutions), but also prestige and the excitement that
comes from being on the cutting edge of scientific advance.
The source of this newfound respectability is a steadily increasing
accumulation of rock-hard evidence compiled by
highly respected scientists, evidence that challenges longstanding
assumptions about the limitations of the human
brain, evidence that certain machines can be tools not just for
sharp increases in mental power, but for stimulating actual
growth of the physical brain.

In the remaining chapters of Part I, I will describe and
discuss many of the recent discoveries and ideas that have
revolutionized the field of brain studies. Neuroscientists now
see the brain as a challenging frontier. And just as the discovery
that the world is round made possible the exploration of
the New World, with adventurers, pirates, rogues, priests, free
spirits, soldiers, loonies, and politicians pushing into the frontier,
stumbling onto scenes of unimagined grandeur and vast
unexplored territories, so the new discoveries about the elec-

trochemical nature of the brain make possible the exploration of an entire new world of hitherto unsuspected capabilities, mind states as yet unmapped, by a variety of colorful, ambitious, and at times bizarre mind pioneers.

My discussion of these new insights into the brain has a specific purpose: in each case the brain research will cast some new light on the way machines—i.e., devices or techniques for stimulating the brain—can increase or enhance the functioning (and physical structure) of the human brain.

2

GETTING SMART: BRAIN EXPANSION THROUGH STIMULATION

FROM PUMPING IRON TO PUMPING IDEAS

STRENUOUS PHYSICAL EXERCISE CAUSES THE BODIES OF healthy people to get stronger. The exercise can be focused on very specific parts or systems of the body. For example, a weight lifter who does biceps curls but nothing else will develop large biceps but little else. Marathon runners focus on developing their cardiovascular system, with the result that they often have extraordinary endurance, powerful hearts and lungs, and the torsos of ninety-eight pound weaklings, with arms and legs like rubber bands. But body building does work, and it works the same way in every case, from weight lifters to distance runners: select that part of your body you want to grow in size and strength and *use* it. And, most important, use it against increasingly arduous challenges, for it is the steady increase in difficulty, whether through lifting ever heavier weights or running longer or faster, that stimulates the target muscle to grow.

Now, imagine that all this is true of the brain as well as the body. Substituting "brain" for "body," the above paragraph states, in effect, that strenuous intellectual exercise causes the brains of healthy people to get stronger. This brain-building exercise can be focused on very specific parts of the brain— simply select that part (or *quality*) of the brain you want to grow in size and strength and *use* it, against increasingly difficult challenges.

Imagine further that just as we now have devices to stimulate the body to healthy growth, and to speed up the slow process of body growth—barbells, Nautilus and Universal machines, treadmills and bicycles, rowing and cross-country skiing machines—so we also have devices to stimulate brain growth and to speed up the process of brain building enormously.

"Nice pipe dream," I hear someone scoffing, "but pure fantasy—everyone knows that the anatomy and physiology of the brain simply can't be changed by sensory stimulation or experience."

The scoffer is voicing what was, until recently, an undisputed scientific truth. Long ago scientists established that absolute brain size has little to do with intelligence—when they weighed brains during autopsies, they found that the brains of idiots were sometimes larger than those of great intellects, and geniuses at times had comparatively small brains.

And if brain size seemed irrelevant to intelligence, the idea that either brain size or intelligence could be changed by experiences seemed absurd. First, it was an accepted fact that intelligence was genetically determined—people with high intelligence are born that way, and while life experiences may nurture or thwart that inborn genetic potential, experiences can't increase or decrease that innate intelligence; that is, experiences can't change the structure of the actual brain. Freud and his followers had demonstrated clearly that experiences we have in early childhood largely mold our characters, but whether someone born with a brain of a specific anatomical structure goes through experiences that mold him into a bold, creative leader or timid follower, that person's brain anatomy and chemistry remain unchanged.

And finally, it was commonly accepted that the growth in the total *number* of brain cells we have is completed by age two. As techniques of microscopic examination of brain cells were developed, scientists made the discovery that apparently brain cells, called *neurons*, do not reproduce themselves. In other words, the absolute number of one's brain cells is determined from infancy, and no matter what experiences or stimulations the brain receives, the number of brain cells could not increase. In this the neurons are unlike the other cells of the body, which can reproduce many times—if a muscle cell is damaged or destroyed it can be replaced by a new cell; it is this capability that is exploited by body builders, whose large muscles are the result of the repair and regeneration of muscle cells damaged or destroyed by strenuous exercise. No wonder scientists found it hard to conceive of any way brain structure and function could be changed by sensory input. No wonder our scoffer finds it hard to believe in brain machines that can be used like body-building devices, stimulating the brain and triggering brain growth and increases in mental powers.

HOW TO DEVELOP VERY SMART RATS

THEN CAME A SERIES OF EXPERIMENTS BY BIOLOGICAL PSY-chologists Mark Rosenzweig and colleagues at the University of California, Berkeley, that were so unexpected in their implications that they were, for many scientists, unbelievable. When it became clear that the controversial studies were being widely replicated by numerous independent researchers, initial disbelief and skepticism turned to universal acceptance, yet the studies remain revolutionary and astounding in their implications.

The studies started out innocently enough. Back in the 1920s, a Berkeley psychologist had noticed that some rats were better at running mazes than other rats. He had specifically chosen and bred generation after generation of "maze-bright" rats, and another strain of genetically bred "maze-dull" rats. Some forty years later these strains of rats were still reproducing in the Berkeley labs. Mark Rosenzweig and associates David Krech and Mark Bennett, who were interested in the relationship between brain chemistry and learning, asked themselves, "If the rats run mazes differently, do they have a different brain chemistry?"

More generally, they wondered how the brain's chemistry was changed by various types of mental activity. They hypothesized that mental activity, particularly learning and memory, would result in higher levels of a certain brain enzyme (acetylcholinesterase, or AChE). To test this, they took laboratory rats with different levels of AChE in their brains and compared how they performed on problems that required mental activity (such as maze running). They found that the rats with higher levels of AChE learned better than those with low levels: the maze-bright rats had higher levels of AChE than the maze-dull rats.

Then they decided it would be interesting to approach the problem from the opposite direction, by making rats perform problems that required mental activity, and seeing whether different types of performance produced different levels of AChE. In other words, since there was a chemical difference in the brains of bright and dumb rats, could you change that chemistry by designing the rats' environment in a different way? That is, could you alter brain chemistry and structure by altering the environment?

To perform this experiment, they needed to have groups of rats whose lives had required of them differing levels of mental activity. Thus, the researchers took a pool of rats which through many years of controlled laboratory breeding had been made genetically equal, and divided them randomly at weaning into three different groups. Each group was placed in a different environment. The first group was placed in ordinary laboratory cages, three rats to each plain wire-mesh cage. This was called the *standard environment*. The second group was placed in isolation, each rat held in solitary confinement in a cage with three opaque walls, dim lights, little noise, a minimum of stimulation, and no chance to interact with other rats. This was called an *impoverished environment*. The third group was raised in "play groups" of ten to twelve rats, in a large, well-lit, multileveled cage filled with swings, slides, ladders, bridges, an assortment of toys, frequently changing stimuli, and a variety of challengers. This was called an *enriched environment*.

After certain periods ranging from days to a number of months, the brains of the rats were removed and analyzed. The researchers discovered that rats raised in the enriched environment showed higher levels of AChE activity in their brain cortex than did rats raised in the standard and impoverished environments. (The cerebral cortex is a layer of nerve cells forming a convoluted outer shell over the brain, the "thinking cap" or "gray matter" atop the brain, in which much of the thinking or higher intellectual activity of the brain takes place.) Says Rosenzweig, "Rather than cortical AChE activity being a fixed individual characteristic, as we had supposed, it could apparently be altered by experience!"[281]

Since AChE activity was related to learning *ability*, that is, the ability to process information, this meant that the rats in the enriched environment had more learning ability—were "smarter"—than the other rats, despite the fact that they had all started out as equals. Somehow, experiences had altered intelligence.

HIGHLY STIMULATED EINSTEINIAN RATS WITH BIG BRAINS

THIS WAS PRETTY STARTLING IN ITSELF, BUT NOTHING COMpared to what the researchers stumbled onto next. The way AChE was measured was as enzymatic activity per unit of tissue weight. "Fortunately," recalls Rosenzweig, "we had to record the weights of our brain samples in order to measure chemical activity per unit of tissue weight. After about two years of contemplating the chemical effects, it finally dawned on us that the weights of the brain samples also changed."[267] What they discovered was so astonishing that even the researchers, after checking and rechecking their figures found it almost incredible: the cortex of the enriched-environment rats was much heavier than the cortex of the other rats! Somehow, stimulating experiences had caused the rats' brains to grow.

"The changes in brain weights were even more astonishing at that time than were the neurochemical changes," says Rosenzweig, "because it had become a dogma by the start of the present century that brain weight remains stable in the faces of challenges that affect many other bodily measures." So astonishing, in fact, that many scientists claimed the results were impossible. According to Rosenzweig, "skepticism or frank disbelief were the initial reactions to our reports that significant changes in the brain were caused by relatively simple and benign exposure of animals to differential environmental experience."[281]

The revolutionary findings and the doubts of their peers triggered a new series of studies by the Berkeley group. With the collaboration of neuroanatomist Marian Diamond, they set about to find out what was happening anatomically to make the cortex of the enriched rats heavier. These studies resulted in a succession of discoveries which were even more amazing. In all cases, the rats raised in the enriched environment showed:

—increased thickness of the cerebral cortex or "gray matter,"

—a 15 percent increase in the actual size of individual neurons in the cortex,

—increases in protein in the brain paralleling the increases in cortical weight, proving that the growth effect was on tissue and not just on fluid content of the brain,

—an increase in the amount of dendritic branching (dendrites are the hairy branching fibers which project in large numbers from the body of each neuron, and which receive inputs from other neurons and conduct them to the cell body; thus, an increase in branching means a greater number of potential inputs, and a greater amount of potential information available to each neuron),

—an increased number of dendritic spines per unit length of dendrite (spines are the small projections that cover the surface of dendrites by the thousands, each one marking the site of a synapse, the point where another neuron makes a junction with this neuron; thus increased numbers of spines indicates a potential for a greater richness of interconnection between neurons),

— increases in the number of synapses and in the size of synaptic contact areas (synapses are the spots where different neurons are connected and by means of which communication among neurons takes place; thus, the increase in their number and size means increased richness of communications in the cortex),

— an increase in the ratio between the weight of the cortex and the weight of the rest of the brain (thus the enriched environment does not simply stimulate and trigger generalized growth throughout the entire brain, but is specifically beneficial to that area of the brain devoted to thinking, learning, and memory),

— a 15 percent increase in the number of *glial cells*, the "glue" cells that are the most numerous cells in the brain, and which hold together, support, and nourish the brain neurons, act as guides for neural growth, assist in learning, and seem to form some mysterious communicating network of their own.*[88, 281]

---

*Many have recently come to suspect that one key to intellectual ability is the ratio between glia and neurons in the cortex, a ratio which is about ten to one in humans. The human brain is about five times as large as that of a chimpanzee, yet contains only about 30 to 50 percent more neurons—the intellectual abyss dividing man from chimps seems to come from the larger numbers of glial cells in the human brain. As a result of newly developed research technology, scientists have been able to detect a variety of hitherto unsuspected activities in the glial cells. Research by neurophysiologist Gary Lynch of UC at Irvine has shown that "in the period before there is any axon sprouting, before any axon growth, the glial cells go crazy in terms of activity. The glial cells divide and they move through the intact tissue of the brain. They migrate through big sections of the brain to get to the active site. And the ones that are already there undergo incredible reactions. They send out branches that become very large. All this is going on before there is any axonal growth. None of these findings have been incorporated in textbooks yet. . . . It's a strange, bizarre system," he says. "You know, the thought of these things crawling through your head, it gives you a different vision of the brain."[65] There is also evidence that the glia are electrically sensitive, and some believe they may act much like semiconductors, picking up faint electrical charges from the nervous system or surrounding electrical fields and amplifying them just as transistors amplify electrical signals. A recent study by Brian MacVicar of the University of Calgary in Alberta shows that under certain conditions the glial cells become electrically excitable and behave like neurons. He has detected the occurrence in glial cells of action potentials, the self-propagating

As Diamond continued her autopsies with rats exposed to enriched environments for various periods, she made the further discovery that brain changes could take place with startling speed—she soon learned they could bring about changes in the chemistry and structure of the cortex in only four days. Studies later lowered that estimate to forty-five minutes, and now have proved that significant structural changes in response to stimulation take place almost instantaneously.[101,102] Study has followed study, with results that have been replaced or advanced by work in other laboratories, not only with rats, but with gerbils, squirrels, and monkeys. These studies, while trying different approaches and examining different variables, have consistently supported one conclusion: in some way an enriched environment, that is, increased brain stimulation, not only produces a growth in size and weight of the cortex, but completely alters and enriches the quality of the entire cerebral cortex.

---

electrical changes characteristic of nerve, muscle, and endocrine cells. "A new function may be added to the postulated actions of glial cells," says MacVicar. "It may be possible for glial cells to cause widespread excitation of neurons."[2] Thus, a system which is as yet little understood. However, it's clear that the increase in number of glial cells resulting from mental stimulation, which means an increase in number of glial cells nourishing and supporting each neuron, somehow assists in higher mental functioning. In fact, as this is written, word arrives from Marian Diamond that a high ratio of glial cells to neurons may play a part in the intellectual superiority of certain geniuses, like Albert Einstein. Diamond obtained samples of Einstein's brain from the pathologist who performed the autopsy on Einstein in 1955 and examined sections of the neocortex to determine the ratio of glial cells to neurons. Since her work shows that animals in environments that stimulate mental activity have more glial cells per neuron, says Diamond, "we hypothesized that if Einstein's brain was more active in some areas, we would find more glial cells there." She found that indeed Einstein's brain contained more glial cells per neuron in all four of the brain areas studied, compared with samples from the brains of eleven normal males ranging in age from forty-seven to eighty. "We don't know if Einstein was born with this or developed it later," Diamond points out, "but it tells us that in one of the highest evolved areas of the brain, there is evidence that he had greater intellectual processing."[225]

STIMULATING THE THINKING CAP

THE IMPORTANCE OF THIS QUALITATIVE AND QUANTITATIVE change in the cortex as a result of environmental enrichment can be seen when we consider a few facts about the cerebral cortex (also called the *neocortex*). Whatever evolution "means," perhaps its most tangible result is the cortex: it is the end result of the tendency of creatures to develop their nervous system as they increase in complexity. In the case of vertebrates, this has meant a steady shift to the top, or the uppermost part of the nervous system. In the earliest vertebrates this meant a swelling of nervous tissue at the top of the spinal cord. As creatures evolved, this swelling increased in size and complexity, including first a hindbrain, then a midbrain or limbic brain, then a forebrain. Only in higher mammals does there develop a new evolutionary structure, the cerebral cortex, which gains in size and importance as we go up the evolutionary ladder.

In rats, the cortex is fairly smooth, and quite small in proportion to the lower parts of the brain. In cats and dogs the cortex grows in size, and in order to pack more cortex into the available space there appear crumples and folds called convolutions. The relative size of the cortex and its amount of convolutions increase in apes, and in humans it is deeply convoluted and makes up about *83 percent of the total brain weight*.

The neocortex can be visualized as a sheet about two and a half square feet in area (in the case of humans) and less than an eighth of an inch thick, containing about 100 billion neurons, supported and nurtured by many billions of glial cells. Remarkably, these neurons, with their unimaginably rich numbers of interconnections (each neuron with its hundreds or thousands of axonal and dendritic extensions is as complex as a small computer, and each is linked to thousands of other neurons), are virtually all linked only to other neurons in the cortex, with relatively few neurons connecting the cortex to the lower brain structures. As brain expert Dr. Eric

Harth points out, this means that the incredible interweaving of neural connections largely represents "*cortex talking to cortex*. This remarkable fact . . . points to the highly *reflective* mode of operation of the neocortex. If we were to compare it to a government, it would be analogous to a group of people in lively dispute with one another, but virtually isolated from the outside world."

The cortex is, then, in evolutionary terms, something very new, very different; it is the seat of our so-called *higher functions*. These functions include, in Harth's words, "detection of features in all sensory systems; learning and association of new features and learning of all kinds; memory and recall of sequences of events perceived in the past; patterning of elaborate programs of voluntary muscle actions from tying shoelaces to playing Liszt; formation and understanding of speech; creativity and appreciation in all forms of art, and of course all sensations and consciousness."[138]

So when we consider the importance of the cortex to everything that makes us human, the implications of the studies of Rosenzweig, Diamond, and their colleagues are staggering. Those studies clearly indicate that environmental enrichment, that is, *stimulation*, or *sensory experience*, leads to enlargement and other structural changes in the cortex. Since the cortex is the seat of intelligence, then it makes sense to conclude that environmental enrichment, stimulation, or sensory experience leads to increased intelligence.

Intelligence is, of course, a slippery concept; an animal can prove intelligent when tested for one quality, less intelligent when tested for another. But there are clear indications that there is a strong connection between sensory stimulation and intelligence. Berkeley psychologist David Krech, who with Rosenzweig pioneered the studies of the relationship between mental activity and brain chemistry using rats from different environments, has made a number of studies of the relationship between intelligence and experience.

In one experiment he took the two groups of rats which had been selectively bred for many generations, one group for "maze dullness," the other for "maze brightness." It's important to stress that these rats were genetically different, with quite different brains—different levels of brain enzymes, different ratios of cortex to subcortex. Krech set out to discover whether environment could change these hereditary differences. A group of maze-bright rats were placed in an impoverished environment, while a maze-dull group were given an enriched environment. The differences in their brains virtually disappeared. Similarly, when a maze-bright group was given an enriched environment while maze-dulls were given an impoverished environment, the differences doubled.

Krech also tested the rats for another type of intelligence—the ability to learn that rules can change. On this test of "reversal discrimination" the gifted rats always were far superior to the maze-dull rats. However, when the bright rats were raised in an impoverished environment and the dull rats were given an enriched environment, the dulls proved far superior in performance on the test! Krech's resounding conclusion: "We can now undo the effects of generations of breeding. Heredity is not enough. All the advantages of inheriting a good brain can be lost if you don't have the right psychological environment in which to develop it."[267]

TEACHING OLD RATS NEW TRICKS

WELL, ALL THIS IS INTERESTING, YOU SAY, BUT WHAT DOES IT have to do with me? These studies all have to do with mammals who are raised in distinct environments from the time they're babies. I'm already an adult, so my brain has already taken on whatever cerebral growth it's ever going to have.

Not so. This assumption that the brain somehow becomes set, like concrete, after a period of youthful plasticity, has been widespread. Rosenzweig and colleagues even based their early experiments on it. According to Rosenzweig, "Our initial studies were of animals placed in the differential environments at weaning . . . because we supposed that the brain would be more plastic at weaning than in older rats."[281] Says Marian Diamond, "The general conception in the 1960s, and of course before, was that the brain did not change—that it was a stable structure—and after it developed, it retained its size and eventually decreased."

Soon, however, they began to wonder. If an enriched environment can alter the brains of young rats, isn't it possible it could also benefit even mature rats? They set about investigating. In one experiment they kept the rats in a standard, non-enriched environment until they were the equivalent of seventy-five years of human age. As Diamond describes it: "The rat has the potential to live 1,000 days, and the human being has the potential to live 100 years. So at 766 days, when we moved some rats to enriched environments, we were three-quarters of the way through the animals' lives. . . . We found that when they were exposed to an enriched environment between 766 and 904 days of age, even these very old rats showed thickening of the cerebral cortex."[225] In test after test the Berkeley researchers found that, in Rosenzweig's words, "The capacity for plastic neural changes was found to be present not only early in life but throughout most if not all of the life span."

While some of the studies have shown that the amount of growth in the cortex is somewhat less and takes more exposure to the enriched environment to bring about with advancing age, all the evidence indicates that cortical growth can take place even at extremely advanced ages. What a stunner. Rosenzweig puts it a bit more soberly: "The findings of brain plasticity in adult rats challenged the assumptions of many psychologists and neuroscientists that the brain assumes adult values early in life."[281] In fact, the findings met much resistance in the scientific community. And no wonder. They seem to challenge not only scientific dogma but even common sense—we have all noticed how as people age they become more set in their ways, resistant to change; how adults find it more difficult to open their minds to new ways of thinking than children, as for example in learning a new language.

The implications of the Rosenzweig findings are so vast they're hard to grasp fully. For after all, what they mean is that, provided an environment that is sufficiently enriched (i.e., challenging, stimulating, complex), growth and qualitative enrichment of the cerebral cortex can continue throughout adult life. And since the cortex is the seat of the higher functions, such as intelligence and creativity, we can suppose that, given the right experiences, intelligence, creativity, and brain size can continue to increase even into extreme old age.

PRESTO CHANGO: THE BRAIN AS QUICK-CHANGE

WE MUST REMEMBER, OF COURSE, THAT THESE ARE STUDIES OF animals other than humans, so it's possible that their conclusions can't be applied generally to humans. However, as the studies have progressed from rats to squirrels to monkeys, whose brains are very similar to human brains, the results have remained consistent. Also, it's significant that the part of the brain altered by an enriched environment is the cortex, which grows not only in absolute size, but in its ratio to the rest of the brain. While rats have small cortex-to-subcortex ratios, some 83 percent of the total weight of human brains is in the cortex. So it makes sense to think that the relative effects of environmental enrichment compared to lack of stimulation would have even more pronounced effects in humans than in rats—after all, the cortex plays a much greater role in human affairs than in rat affairs. We don't know what effect varied environments like those the Berkeley rats experienced have on rat creativity, rat philosophy, rat wisdom, rat intuition, and so on; but since human life is powerfully influenced by these products of our "higher," which is to say cortical, faculties, substantial cortical growth could have an enormous impact on human consciousness and human evolution.

But, you point out, these rats experienced cerebral development as a result of being raised, or spending large amounts of their life, in this so-called enriched environment. Granted that an enriched environment or increased environmental complexity, challenge, and stimulation might lead to human brain growth—the whole point is moot, since no human would agree to being confined for long periods of time to a controlled environment, no matter how "enriched."

If it were the case that the enrichment effect required long periods of exposure, this would be true. However, the research of Rosenzweig and his colleagues at Berkeley has proved that cortical change can happen much more easily and rapidly than they had initially thought. First they found that keeping the rats in the enriched cage for only two hours a day resulted in just as much brain growth as keeping them in the cage all day.

Argentinian researchers created a "super-enriched" environment and found that it caused as much brain growth in four days as took place in thirty days in the ordinary enriched environment of the Berkeley group. Later they found that four daily one-hour periods of enriched exposure significantly increased cortical growth. Then they went on to find that four daily exposures of *only ten minutes* to an enriched environment brought significant increases in cortical weight![101] Other investigators found that a single forty-five-minute session of learning to choose lighted alleys to avoid shock has resulted in significant brain changes, such as increase in the number and shape of some synapses.[281] As researchers become increasingly sophisticated, they are discovering that even very short exposures to an enriched environment can have significant and long-lasting effects on the cortex. And what's more, these brain changes can happen rapidly—in some cases structural changes in the brain are evident within seconds of sensory stimulation!

In another series of experiments, scientists demonstrated that when neurons in the brains of lab rats are electrically stimulated, new synapses are formed within seconds, dramatically increasing the number of synapses per neuron. Neurobiologist William Greenough of the University of Illinois at Champaign-Urbana is one of many brain scientists intrigued by these experiments. "This is the most extraordinary case of structural plasticity encountered so far in the brain sciences," says Greenough. He asked himself if there was a relationship between increased brain capacity, represented by a growth of new synapses, and memory. To answer this question he decided to see if this almost instantaneous brain growth can happen not only in response to electrical stimulation but also in response to learning and experience. He taught a group of rats to master a number of mazes over a period of three and a half weeks, then microscopically examined their brains. He found pronounced increases in their cortical dendrites, compared to no increases in control rats.

Next, he fitted rats with tiny opaque contact lenses. By covering one eye and then teaching them to run mazes, he was able to compare the growth of one side of the brain with the other. He found increased dendritic branching and increased synapses in the brain hemisphere that received the sensory input from the eye with vision. The equation was clear: more information, more synapses. What's more, experiments with infant, adult, and even very old rats showed this same rapid-brain-growth effect. Greenough's work suggests that an individual's experience can cause new neuronal connections to spring up quickly and systematically, exactly where they are needed: "synapses on demand."

"We can offset and even reverse late brain aging in rats by providing changes in experiences on a regular basis," concludes Greenough. "It's known that old rats lose synapses, and old people do, too. Are they lost because they're forming fewer connections? There's a good possibility that experience can govern the number of synapses that are born and the number of synapses that survive."[135]

If this kind of significant structural change can happen as a result of brief stimulation in a rat's cortex, surely the much larger, more responsive, more powerful human cortex should similarly respond to certain types of "enrichment," that is, stimulation, or challenge, or complexity, with significant structural changes—i.e., growth—in the cortex. These structural changes should result in increases in the functioning of the cortex, which means increases in intelligence, creativity, and all those other higher faculties that reside in the cortex.

WHEN WE USE THE FRUITS OF THIS RESEARCH TO THINK ABOUT the human brain, with its much more powerful and important cortex, it make sense that humans who are exposed to enriched environments—that is, humans whose brains are challenged and stimulated—should experience changes in the shape, size, and structure of the cortex. These changes should result in enhanced cortical function, including increased intelligence, creativity, and so on. Very short exposures to stimulation can bring about these changes. That is, it's likely that short periods of intense brain stimulation can increase brain complexity and capacity for humans of any age. As David Krech predicted with characteristic audacity more than fifteen years ago, "I foresee the day when we shall have the means, and therefore, inevitably, the temptation, to manipulate the behavior and the intellectual functioning of all people through environmental and biochemical manipulation of the brain."[65]

And how could this environmental manipulation of the brain take place? One possibility is by using any of a variety of machines designed by scientists to expose the human neocortex to stimuli and experiences which are novel, changing and challenging, and which provide the brain an opportunity to exercise itself by means of self-observation, self-transformation, and learning. These mind machines, many scientists now believe, can be the adult human counterpart to the swings, slides, bells, ladders, and flashing lights of the lab rats' enriched environment.

3

THE WISDOM OF AGE: LEARNING THE SECRET OF LIFELONG GROWTH

OLD GRANDAD AS TEST PILOT

WHEN I WAS A BOY, OLD PEOPLE ACTED LIKE OLD PEOPLE— they kept their false choppers in a glass of water beside their bed, hung around on front-porch swings; when they walked they shuffled their feet and they moved very slowly. No wonder—their bodies were just *worn out*, like machines that had been operating so long the parts simply wore away and the whole shebang started to creak, groan and fall apart. What you didn't see back then was some eighty-year-old codger cutting for the finish line of a marathon race, or a rosy-cheeked grandmom putting on a final kick at the end of a triathlon.

Of course, we all know times have changed. Everywhere you look you see old gents as healthy as hounds, pounding out their daily ten miles, twenty svelte grandmoms in skin-tight Danskins moving like chorus-line sweeties as they do their daily aerobic dancing at the local spa, elder statesmen climbing Himalayan peaks and diving out of planes while white-haired duchesses pump iron and sweat like steel-workers or pop into the water for a quick swim across the channel. Doctors are spreading the word—bodies don't wear out and deteriorate from overuse but instead decline from *underuse*. As everyone has heard by now you've got to *use it or lose it.*

But even as more and more aging people were discovering that hard exercise could not only keep them healthy but actually get them in better physical shape than ever before in their lives, sports physiologists and other medical professionals still assumed that despite intense exercise there was an unavoidable drop in fitness of about 10 percent every decade. Now a ten-year study at the University of Wisconsin Mount Sinai Medical Center indicates that regular intense exercise can virtually eliminate this decline. The investigators, led by Dr. Michael Pollock, tested the aerobic capacity (called the VO_2 max) of a group of Masters runners in the early '70s. Ten years later he retested them (all were men, now aged from fifty to eighty-two) to see how much their aerobic capacity had declined. The researchers were surprised to find that the runners who still ran stiff workouts—nearly half the total group—had absolutely no drop in aerobic capacity! Among the ones who had let up a bit but still trained vigorously, there was a slight decline, but the men were still in the top percentile of their age groups. Marveling over the physical vigor of the men, many of them in their seventies and eighties, Pollock said, "If you put bags over their heads you'd think they were twenty-year-olds."

This kind of thing has never happened before. Like those test pilots with the Right Stuff who were trying to "push out the edge of the envelope" to discover the limits of their experimental planes, humans are now like test pilots of their own bodies, pushing the envelopes to find out what their limits might be. Records for events like the marathon continue to fall regularly for racers into their nineties, and physiologists admit that the upper limits of the body's capacity in old age remain to be discovered.

METHUSELAH AGAINST ENTROPY

BUT WHILE OUR ATTITUDES ABOUT AGING AND PHYSICAL FIT-
ness have changed, many have not recognized that the brain is
a part of the body, similarly capable of lifelong fitness. Like
the popular image of old people in the past—shuffling,
creaky, withered—the assumption that old age means inevitable mental decline—forgetfulness, senility, confusion, and
boredom—hangs on.

In part this assumption is based on the long-standing belief
that brain cells, unlike other cells in the body, lack the ability
to regenerate or reproduce themselves, and that therefore the
X billions of brain cells we're born with must last us for the
rest of our lives. A companion piece of accepted wisdom is
that we lose thousands of brain cells every day. Then there are
the claims that every drink of liquor wipes out large quantities
of brain cells. These and similar assumptions lead to an inevitable conclusion: after we reach maturity we are condemned to
a slow ride downhill to senility as our brain cells inexorably
diminish.

Fortunately, this bleak vision of mental entropy simply
isn't true. UC Berkeley neuroanatomist Marian Diamond was
puzzled by the widespread belief in inevitable cell loss. Along
with her colleague Mark Rosenzweig and others, Diamond
was a key figure in the Berkeley experiments described in the
last chapter, and knew that rats exposed to an enriched environment could experience brain growth even when exposure
took place in old age. So she was understandably interested in
tracking down the source of the belief in unavoidable cell loss.
However, after an exhaustive search through all the scientific
research, Diamond could not find a single definitive study
proving it. Says Diamond, "In many studies showing losses of
neurons, the animals were in isolation—they were simply left
alone. Environmental factors were not taken into account. A
few other studies had failed to find such a loss, and we successfully replicated those findings."

Dr. Diamond conducted studies of her own to measure cell

loss with aging, and found that "while there is some cell loss, the greatest decrease is early in life and subsequent losses are not significant even into late life."[125] Says Diamond, speaking of her studies with rats and aging, "In a nonenriched environment, the normal rat brain does decrease in size and age, but it is not necessarily losing brain cells. It is just the dendrites coming down so the cells get more compact." And what is "coming down"? "When I lecture," says Diamond, "I show my hand—my palm is the cell body and my fingers are the dendrites. With use, you can keep those dendrites out there, extended, but without stimulation, they shrink down. It's quite simple: you use it or lose it. . . . The main factor [that constitutes an enriched environment] is stimulation. The nerve cells are designed to receive stimulation." Diamond has concluded that, provided reasonable stimulation, "there is good evidence that drastic structural changes do not occur in the mammalian brain with aging."[225]

Other studies of aging and the brain indicate that many areas of the brain suffer no cell loss whatsoever, and in the areas that do experience a loss of neurons, there is also an offsetting growth of dendrites (the filaments that receive messages from other nerve cells). Research shows that the total dendritic length of an entire cell system in rats is maintained, with no loss, because of continuing dendritic growth.[61] Studies such as those of neurologists Stephen Buell and Thomas McNeill of the University of Rochester indicate that at any given time, there are two populations of neurons—one is dying and the other is undergoing dendritic growth. "In aging without dementia," says Buell and McNeill, "it is the latter which predominates."[338] Longer dendrites mean more dendritic spines, more synapses, more possible points of linkage and communication with other neurons, and a greater number of potential mental states—that is, richer and more complex mental capabilities. Thus, any minor loss of neurons in healthy aging people is offset by the increasing enrichment of neural connections.

Scientists at the National Institute of Aging recently used a brain scan to study the brain chemistry of men aged twenty-one to eighty-three and found that "the healthy aged brain is as active and efficient as the healthy young brain," as indicated by direct measurement of the brain's metabolic activity.[125] This echoes the conclusion that Marian Diamond has drawn from her widespread research in the field: "We can absolutely keep our brain as resilient and young as it was when we were eight or ten years old."[49]

This continued growth of brain cells throughout life has important implications, since there is much evidence that, as we have seen, this brain growth, in areas such as the cerebral cortex, can be directly linked to growth in such higher faculties as intelligence and creativity. Supporting the laboratory studies showing that brain cells continue to grow into old age are the accumulating data from numerous studies showing that intellectual growth can continue well into the eighties and nineties. That is, healthy people can just get more and more intelligent throughout life.

Whatever intelligence is, many experts agree that one key aspect is the mental faculty called *crystallized intelligence*, which psychologist Daniel Goleman describes as "a person's ability to use an accumulated body of general information to make judgments and solve problems. In practical terms, crystalized intelligence comes into play, for example, in understanding the arguments made in newspaper editorials, or dealing with problems for which there are no clear answers, but only better and worse options." University of Denver psychologist John Horn has done extensive research into crystallized intelligence and asserts that the studies show this kind of intelligence does not diminish but rather *steadily increases* with age (though the rate of increase slows somewhat in old age). Says Horn, "The ability to bring to mind and entertain many different facets of information improves in many people over their vital years."

A related type of intelligence, made up of information that people pick up throughout life—ranging from how to fix a flat tire to who is the mayor of Chicago—has been called *world knowledge*. Roy and Janet Lachman of the University of Houston tested this world knowledge in different age groups and found that it steadily increased through the seventies; most important, they found that the oldest group recalled this information *more efficiently* than groups in middle age or their twenties. Gerontology researcher Warner Schaie has found that many brain functions that were long assumed to decline with age of necessity are quickly reversed through stimulation; according to Schaie, "The use-it-or-lose-it principle applies not only to the maintenance of muscular flexibility, but to the maintenance of a high level of intellectual performance."

Summarizing recent research on how people maintain mental capabilities through old age, Daniel Goleman concluded that the key factors included "being mentally active. Well-educated people who continue their intellectual interests actually tend to increase their verbal intelligence through old age." Also essential is "having a flexible personality. A longitudinal study found that those people most able to tolerate ambiguity and enjoy new experiences in middle age maintained their mental alertness best through old age."[125]

These are, of course, the same factors that Rosenzweig and associates found led to increased brain growth in rats of all ages. Being "mentally active" and able to "tolerate ambiguity and enjoy new experiences" is a fair description of the type of life led by the rats who were exposed to an enriched environment, where the objects in their cage were constantly changing, where they were challenged by ladders and swings, numerous social interactions, and novel experiences. In other words, while it doesn't constitute direct proof, the accumulating evidence that human brains and human intelligence can continue to grow throughout life *provided* the human lives a life of new and challenging experiences seems to link directly to the studies of rats, squirrels, monkeys, and other mammals indicating that an enriched environment causes dramatic growth in brain size, in the size of individual brain cells, and in at least many types of intelligence.

Clearly, if we continue throughout our lives to assimilate new information, if we continue to tackle challenges and to welcome change and new, unpredictable experiences—i.e., to provide ourselves an enriched environment—then the enchanted loom of our brain will continue to weave an ever richer, more subtle, and more complex tapestry of neural connections, leading to increasing numbers of possible brain states. In other words, brain scientists are providing actual proof of something well known in the orient and other traditional cultures—age can bring increasing wisdom. The evidence the scientists are providing also indicates that it is not age itself which is the essential factor in increasing wisdom, but the enriched environment.

In the light of these studies we can see that the creative humans whose brains continued to develop, grow, and produce fine work far into old age—Bertrand Russell, Picasso, Yeats, Shaw, Buckminster Fuller, Michelangelo, Toscanini, Stokowski—were not superhuman exceptions, but simply representative humans fulfilling the ordinary human potential for continued mental growth. The crucial factor, as their biographies show, was that they never let themselves get kicked out of the cage marked "enriched environment" and into the one marked "standard environment."

No doubt many aging people today and in the past have suffered from declining mental capabilities. We now know, however, that this is not a natural or inevitable part of aging. "The belief that if you live long enough you will become senile is just wrong," according to psychiatrist Robert Butler, founding director of the National Institute on Aging. "Senility is a sign of disease, not part of the normal aging process."

The widespread belief that age means mental decline is a self-fulfilling prophecy. "What can happen," according to Dr. Jerry Avorn of the Division on Aging at Harvard Medical School, "is that an older person who is admitted to a hospital for something like a broken hip or heart attack can become confused as a side effect of drugs or simply from the strangeness of the hospital routine. The condition is reversible, but the family, or even the physician, doesn't recognize that fact. They assume this is the beginning of senile dementia, and pack the person off to a nursing home. . . . No one knows what exact proportion of people in nursing homes needn't be there

. . . but we have ample clinical evidence that the numbers are large."[125]

Frequently people who have been active all their lives reach retirement age. Suddenly they are cut off from the stimulation of work and work companions. Often their social connections are reduced. Another frequent occurrence is the death of a spouse, which has a similar effect of reducing stimulation and cutting the survivor off from social networks, often resulting in isolation and loneliness.

All these cases—nursing homes, hospitals, retirement, death of a spouse—are human examples of the "impoverished environment" faced by rats who were put in cages alone, cut off from challenges, change, companionship, and other sensory and intellectual stimulation. We have seen the results in the rats—stunted brain growth and accompanying mental dullness or retardation as shown by response to various tests. So it's no wonder that humans placed in similarly impoverished environments show some loss of brain cells or diminished mental sharpness.

Most important, scientists discovered that the rats who were isolated and mentally impoverished were able to reverse their conditions when placed in an enriched environment. For example, in one study rats that had been isolated for 535 days (in other words, until they were in the rat equivalent of middle age) quickly responded to an enriched environment with brain growth equivalent to rats that had been exposed daily to the sensory stimulation, demonstrating unequivocally that even an isolation-stunted brain maintains the potential for sharp and rapid development, that even severe environmentally caused dullness is reversible.

Similarly, studies of aging humans who have shown mental deterioration in areas such as reaction time, memory, and spatial orientation showed that when the subjects received various types of environmental enrichment, including tutoring or playing with computer games, they exhibited immediate and significant gains in their scores on tests in these areas.

WHAT THIS CHAPTER IS REALLY ABOUT

WHILE THIS CHAPTER HAS FOCUSED ON AGING, THE REAL SUB-ject has not been old people but the importance of exposing the brain to stimulation, challenge, change, ambiguity, nov-elty—an enriched environment. All evidence indicates that whether we are twenty, forty, or eighty our brains have the capability of growing, and we have the ability to become more intelligent. In fact, the evidence indicates that the more you learn, the greater is your capacity for further learning. The more you put into your memory, the more powerful your memory becomes. Without sufficient stimulation, however, this growth will not happen; in fact, our minds and brains will deteriorate, no matter how young or old we are.

When the Berkeley researchers first began studying the re-lationship between sensory stimulation (or learning) and phys-iological brain growth, they put their rats in three environments. Later research with a "super-enriched" environ-ment produced even greater brain growth than the enriched environment. This raised a question. Just how much can a rat's cortex grow? Where are the limits? Researchers created a "seminatural" outdoor environment and found that the rats raised there showed even greater brain increases than in the super-enriched environment. Recent studies of squirrels raised in a feral or fully natural environment indicate that in many brain measures, such as brain RNA per unit of brain weight, the feral squirrels are significantly higher than squirrels raised in an enriched laboratory environment. Where will it end?

In each case, increases in environmental complexity lead to increases in brain growth. We can imagine the possibility of devising some sort of "super-mega-enriched" environment that would produce even greater brain growth in rats and squirrels than their natural wild environment. What the scientists are beginning to do, step by step, is *learn how to make a superior brain*.

There can be no doubt that this research has important im-plications for humans. We know that environmental factors are enormously important in brain development. For example, University of Arizona professor Samuel A. Kirk claims that given a certain amount of brain at birth, a person's intelligence may vary up to 40 IQ points as a result of different environments. Recent studies have shown that adults with low IQs, "retarded" since birth, when given challenging educational or life experiences can "outgrow" their low IQs and gain average or above average intelligence.[262]

And just as the octogenarians who are cruising through marathons are constantly challenging our concept of the limits of the human body, these humans who continue to grow mentally into old age are reminders that we—and scientists— have yet to discover the limits of human brain growth. Surely, like those rats placed in the "super-enriched" environment that showed as much brain growth in four hours as the enriched environment rats showed in a month, there must be some human super-enriched equivalent. Could the mind machines, by subjecting the brain to intense amounts of stimulation, have that sort of hothouse effect, force-feeding enrichment to our neurons and triggering rapid brain growth?

Interestingly, one technique used with enormous success to reverse aspects of brain decline in old people has been machines. Aging people challenged by computer video games like Pac-Man and Space Invaders have been found to show significant mental improvements. Other machines, a number of which I will describe, have been used to stimulate directly the brains of humans with a variety of neurological problems, including Down's syndrome, mental retardation, and learning disabilities; the subjects have responded with astonishing recoveries of mental abilities or sharp increases in a variety of brain values.

The thrust of this book is to examine these machines not as therapeutic devices capable of bringing subnormal or sick brains to a state of normality or health, but rather as tools for stimulating already healthy brains and spurring them into greater-than-normal growth, higher-than-ordinary capabilities. What are the limits to brain growth? No one yet knows. As author George Leonard expressed it in his words of awe at the incredibly vast potentials of interaction between neurons, "A brain composed of such neurons obviously can never be 'filled up.' Perhaps the more it knows, the more it can know and create. Perhaps, in fact, we can now propose an incredible hypothesis: *The ultimate creative capacity of the brain may be, for all practical purposes, infinite.*" [195]

4

EVOLUTION AGAINST ENTROPY

RUNNING NAKED THROUGH THE STREETS: THE EUREKA EVENT

THE TALE OF SAUL OF TARSUS ON THE ROAD TO DAMASCUS IS one of our culture's most powerful stories of mental transformation. Like some impetuous, driven district attorney, Saul had made a name for himself with his zealous persecution of the hated Nazarenes, who were springing up in and around Jerusalem in the years after the death of Jesus. So obsessed was he with eradicating this sect that he even went to his employer, the high priest, and asked for authority to journey out of his usual bailiwick—Palestine—to distant Damascus, to seek out these cultists, so that "whether they were men or women, he might bring them bound unto Jerusalem," and have them put to death.

But while he's on the road to Damascus something unexpected happens: suddenly he's hit with a light so bright it knocks him down, blind and bewildered, and he hears the voice of God. His traveling companions lead him off to Damascus, but for the next three days he's blind, and just sits in a stupor, without eating or drinking. Then one of the very Nazarenes he has been so determined to persecute appears, calling him Brother Saul, and claiming he has been sent by God. Instantly Saul's eyesight returns, and he knows exactly what he must do: he becomes a Nazarene, and does the exact thing he was persecuting Nazarenes for, going into the synagogues and preaching this new religion. Having changed his name from Saul to Paul, he becomes the most influential and charismatic of all the early Christian apostles, traveling all over the known world to preach and convert.

I retell this story as a clear example of a mental process all of us have experienced, though probably in a far less dramatic and soul-searing form. It is an example of that moment when some problem that has been bothering us suddenly and spontaneously solves itself; when the pieces of some puzzle that have been shifting and sliding back and forth inside our heads causing a feeling of vague discomfort or dissatisfaction suddenly all fall into place.

It has been called the *Eureka event*, after the tale of Archimedes, the Greek thinker who had been trying to figure out how he could determine the amount of gold in a precious crown without melting it down. He had pondered the problem from all angles, but could find no answer. Then one afternoon while taking a bath, he noticed how the water in the tub was displaced by his body. Suddenly he saw the answer to his problem: measure how much water the crown displaced. Everything fell into place, and he ran into the streets still naked crying "Eureka!" ("I have found it!").

Whatever we call this experience—the Aha! moment, the flash of insight, creativity, having a brainstorm, turning on the light bulb in the brain, the "felt shift," wordless knowing—our gut feeling is that in some way the contents of our brain have been rearranged, or perhaps that our brain itself has been reconstructed. As we shall see, scientists have discovered that this is exactly what happens. During those moments, the pattern of electrical waves that sweep throughout the brain is altered, the type of electrical waves the brain generates changes, and individual neurons in the cerebral cortex alter the number and shape of their dendrites, dendritic spines, and synapses, so that the network of other neurons they are linked with is altered, creating new patterns of electrochemical message transmission, new states of mind: a way of seeing reality that is totally new.

THE BENEFITS OF GIVING RATS BRIGHT IDEAS

IN FACT, THESE FLASHES OF INSIGHT, RANGING FROM LOW-wattage inner light bulbs like "Say, square pegs do not fit into round holes!" to high-intensity mental lightning flashes like Einstein's $E = mc^2$, are what constitute the process we call *learning*. And to return to our Berkeley rats in enriched or impoverished environments, what Rosenzweig and colleagues first set out to investigate was the relationship between learning and brain chemistry. What if, they wondered, we could cause one group of rats to have a whole bunch of Eureka events, or flashes of insight, while another group had almost none whatsoever—what would the difference be in their brain chemistry?

As we saw, there were great differences. The brain chemistry of the Eureka (i.e., enriched-environment) rats was much higher in brain enzymes associated with learning. And what's more, the brains of the Eureka rats were larger and heavier and had qualitatively more complex cerebral cortexes. So, when we speak of feeling "new connections" being made in our brains during our moments of insight, we are not using a metaphor but being literally descriptive: in those moments we learn, our brains actually undergo structural change with incredible speed.

The question, of course, is *why*? Why does some external stimulation cause the brain to alter so radically while a similar stimulation will hardly affect the brain at all? One person driving his car passes a red neon light and barely notices it. Another person, an astrophysicist, say, who's working on some problem about the expanding universe, sees the red light, is reminded perhaps of something having to do with the red shift, or a specific red in some spectrogram, and it suddenly triggers a full-blown Eureka experience, leading him to the solution of his problem. A third person, having recently experienced certain personal traumas, sees the light, is reminded of the red skirt of the woman who has left him, and is immediately thrown into such an extreme emotional state he loses control and goes mad. Same red light in all cases.

Why can such simple stimuli have such extraordinary transforming effects in the brain? Why can such stimuli lead in some cases to brain states that produce higher levels of order, beauty, complexity, and in others to disorder and destruction? Why is it that the brain even needs the input of an external stimulus to be spurred or boosted or triggered into making new connections, forming new ideas, experiencing Eureka moments?

These are important questions; but they are doubly important in this context because if we can answer them, we can perhaps discover something of momentous consequence: *how to intentionally direct specific stimuli to specific areas of the brain and trigger new ideas or Eureka moments at will*. In fact, users and designers of some of the machines we will look at claim that this is exactly what they do. What an idea! Creativity on command! Flashes of insight at the push of a button! Is this possible?

WHY THE UNIVERSE IS RUNNING DOWN

AN ANSWER TO ALL THESE QUESTIONS CAN BE FOUND IN THE theories of an extraordinary Russian-born Belgian theoretical chemist, Ilya Prigogine. For the last half century, Prigogine has devoted himself to the study of thermodynamics. This science of "heat dynamics," that is, the relationship between mechanical energy (or work) and heat, developed during the industrial revolution of the late eighteenth and nineteenth centuries, as engineers and physicists studied the workings of thermal engines.

As scientists pondered the workings of the steam engines

that powered the factories of emerging industry they discovered that there is an interesting relationship between heat and work. First, they noted that work and heat can be converted into each other. If, for example, someone applied work to a piece of metal by rubbing a file against it, the friction would produce heat; and heat applied to water in the boiler of a steam engine would cause the piston to move and produce work. Scientists then discovered that this interchangeable relationship existed not only between heat and work; chemical, mechanical, thermal, and electrical energies can all be converted into one another.

On the heels of this discovery came another, with powerful implications. While an engine can transform energy into work, no engine can ever yield as much work as the energy it consumes. So whenever work is done, energy is irretrievably lost. In a steam engine, for example, the heat is transformed to mechanical work by causing a piston to move; however, no matter how well the engine is designed and built, there is always a certain amount of friction between the piston, cylinder, and other parts of the engine, and in this friction energy is lost.

Not only is this energy loss inescapable, the scientists discovered, but as a corollary the machine or system itself necessarily becomes increasingly disordered in the process of transforming energy to work. In the case of the steam engine, the friction inevitably wears away the metal engine parts; fine tolerances become loose, rubs turn to knocks and clanks, and more energy is lost; the engine grows even less efficient. Unless more energy is put into the system in the form of new parts or an overhaul, the clanking, shuddering engine will eventually crash into a great heap of twisted rubble. In plain terms, all machines must eventually run down, a conclusion which remains unshaken as the second law of thermodynamics: in any energy interchange, there is a decrease in the amount of energy available to perform useful work.

Since the scientists have verified that the law which governs the exchange of energy in a machine can be expanded to include all the matter and energy in the universe, what the second law of thermodynamics dictates is that the universe is moving irreversibly toward increasing decay and disorder. Most of us have a fair layman's grasp of this idea in what has become known as the law of increasing entropy: like some vast industrial machine the universe is running down.

One way of defining entropy is as a measure of the amount of randomness in a system. The less entropy there is in a system, the less randomness—in other words, the more order, the less entropy. A new steam engine, with exact tolerances, correctly assembled, has its maximum amount of internal order. But as it begins wearing down, disorder—randomness —increases.

In molecular terms (the machine consists of molecules), heat causes increased molecular motion; as the moving molecules collide with each other, they are knocked out of their normal course into essentially random paths. As the collisions between the molecules continue, the randomness of the paths of the molecules increases until finally all molecules are bouncing around totally at random. Total randomness is chaos. What was once a system of organized structures has become an inert, featureless fog; that is, the system has reached a state of maximum entropy that scientists call *equilibrium*. In universal terms, this state of equilibrium—popularly known as "heat death"—is like a tepid, homogenous soup of random molecules and atoms.

If order and structure must become disorder and chaos, if the universe tends toward ever-increasing randomness, then how did life develop? This process of evolution is a process of ever-increasing order and complexity—atoms become molecules become amino acids become proteins become cells become complex organisms, which themselves become ever more complex in response to environmental challenges, organizing, growing, evolving. Life, it seems, moves toward increasing order, while the second law of thermodynamics demands that it should gain entropy, decaying into the lifeless soup of equilibrium. Is this a paradox? A contradiction? An illusion? What's going on?

THE POET OF THERMODYNAMICS

SCIENTISTS AND PHILOSOPHERS HAVE BEEN WRANGLING OVER this mystery for centuries, but everyone remained stumped until Ilya Prigogine came up with a startling conclusion, one that was backed up by unassailable mathematical proofs. Order, he said, arises *because* of disorder, not *despite* it; life emerges *out of* entropy, not *against* it.

A driving force behind Prigogine's lifelong efforts to understand how order could emerge from chaos was his realization while still a student that the second law of thermodynamics only applied to *closed systems*, systems which are totally self-contained, with no flow of matter of energy between the system and its environment. Such a system might be some sort of container so tightly sealed and densely armored that nothing—no air, no light, no magnetism, no sound, no subatomic particles—could enter or affect it. In that sense, then, a true closed system is an ideal concept and can never actually exist.

However, there are systems which are for all *practical* purposes closed systems, systems in which the constituents have reached a state of near equilibrium, such as a stone, a cup of coffee that has gone cold, a crystal, a motionless steam engine. In these systems, the interchange of energy between the system and the environment remains virtually constant; the exchange between heat and work is clear and unchanging; nothing new or unexpected enters or leaves the system. It was to such closed systems, Prigogine asserted, that the second law of thermodynamics could be applied.

However, Prigogine pointed out, living systems are always *open systems*, always exchanging matter and energy with the outside environment (the open system known as a human being, for example, is always taking in energy and matter from the outside, in the form of food, light, oxygen, information; and is always sending matter and energy back into the environment, in the form of carbon dioxide, waste, heat, art, and other excretions). These open systems had been virtually ignored by thermodynamics; and no wonder—while one can usefully apply the laws of thermodynamics to a steam engine, a stone, or any other near-equilibrium system, these laws aren't much use when applied to living systems, since they are *far from equilibrium*: they constantly adjust to all sorts of unpredictable outside forces and changes, are extremely unstable, grow in unexpected ways, reproduce, fix themselves when they get out of whack, learn to operate in new ways when part of the system is lost or altered.

So classical thermodynamics had confined itself largely to closed or near-equilibrium systems, viewing the universe and its constituents in mechanical terms, as a system with a coherent structure, an automaton, made up of changing substances such as atoms and molecules that acted upon each other in a chain of causality. The randomness and instability of nonequilibrium systems were, to these scientists, something negative and even vaguely disturbing—some sort of decay or error occurring in the orderly structure of reality.

Prigogine, however, was drawn to nonequilibrium systems, seeing them not as something negative, but rather as creative, vibrant with energy, unstable but fertile: the source of order, organization, evolution, life itself. He decided that by studying the dynamics of far-from-equilibrium environments he could perhaps discover the answer to the age-old puzzle of how order emerges from chaos, how life evolves from lifeless matter. He focused his studies on a number of physical and chemical systems that somehow spontaneously developed ordered structures, such as certain mixtures which, when heated, begin to "self-organize" into structures of extraordinary complexity and beauty, at times taking on patterns that resemble living cells. Prigogine thought such self-organizing systems might represent a link between nonlife and life.

One specific far-from equilibrium chemical process fascinated Prigogine. Known as the Belousov-Zhabotinsky reaction, it occurred when four chemicals were mixed in a shallow dish at a specific temperature. Very quickly, the mixture began to self-organize into a structure of concentric and spiraling waves which spread and pulsated with clock-like regularity and changed colors at precise intervals. The process is entirely chemical, and yet very much like animate matter, remaining stable and secreting more and more "cells" in a self-renewing and self-transforming process that is like the growth of a living system. Clearly here was a case where internal order increased without such order being fed into the system from the outside. Superficially, it appeared to contradict the second law of thermodynamics, as a system that decreased entropy. However, Prigogine ascertained that while the reaction itself decreased entropy, it did so *only by exporting entropy to the environment*.

His studies of the Belousov-Zhabotinsky reaction, and his mathematical analysis of the process, gave Prigogine the experimental evidence he needed to substantiate his theory that order emerges not against but because of entropy; that ordered structures are an *inevitable* product of far-from-equilibrium situations. It was a process Prigogine called "order through fluctuation," and the structures that emerged he called *dissipative structures*. It was for this startling theory of dissipative structures that Prigogine was awarded the Nobel Prize.

It is the nature of dissipative structures that they are open systems in far-from-equilibrium environments—they are continuously taking in energy and matter from the environment. Now according to the second law of thermodynamics, this energy interchange must produce entropy: the energy flow into the dissipative structure should cause increasing molecular chaos, increasing randomness. In a closed system, such a continuous flow of energy would create such entropy that the system would eventually run down, wear out, or fall apart. Dissipative structures, however, are self-organizing, and maintain their structures by constantly dissipating entropy into the environment. By maintaining their order, such structures demonstrate a *decrease* in entropy within the system; but this decrease in entropy is only maintained by exporting or dissipating the entropy to the environment, so the net entropy of the whole system (the dissipative structure and its environment) actually *increases*, just as the second law of thermodynamics dictates.

REVOLUTION, SPORTS CARS, CHAOS, AND SELF-ORGANIZATION

PRIGOGINE'S THEORY OF DISSIPATIVE STRUCTURES EMERGED from his study of chemical reactions, but as he expounded his ideas it became clear that the theory had relevance to all open systems in which a structure exchanges energy with its environment: a seed, a society, a town, a living body, an ecosystem, a highway network. All such systems take in energy from the surroundings, the energy is used to maintain the structure of the system, and the entropy produced is expelled to the environment. As Prigogine points out, this process constitutes a sort of "metabolism" (from the Greek words *meta*, beyond, and *ballein*, to throw). A word usually restricted to zoology and biology, metabolism refers to the sum of all the processes involved in the building up, maintaining, and destruction of protoplasm; that is, metabolism is the process of *life*. Prigogine's discovery that systems like a highway network, a town, or a society have a metabolism of their own reveals that in many ways they are quite like living things, with the potential to grow, evolve, and develop what can only be called "intelligence." What's so exciting about Prigogine's insight is that it offers new ways of understanding the dynamics—or life—of such systems.

According to Prigogine, dissipative structures can maintain their structure *only* by a continuous dynamic energy flow from outside. Think of a windsock, filled by the whipping breezes that funnel through it—its structure is unpredictable, unstable, created, shaped and maintained by the energy (the wind) which passes through the system; but if the energy/wind ceases, the windsock droops, ceasing to exist as a three-dimensional, open system.

The more complex the structure, the more entropy it must dissipate, since complex structures are more susceptible to the decay of entropy than simple ones (just as a complex sportscar engine is more susceptible to breakdown than a simple steam engine). But the only way it can dissipate entropy is with a constant input of new energy and matter (just as the only way the roaring sports-car engine can continue to propel its driver along at 140 mph is to continuously force more fuel through the carburetor and the rest of the system, thus forcing out the already combusted fuel and its by-products). Dissipative structures, that is, are largely formed by the energy and matter flowing through them, just as our bodies are not simply preexistent structures that pass energy and matter through them in the form of food, water, oxygen and so on—they literally *are* the energy and matter that flow through them. Dissipative structures, that is, are *flow*.

Dissipative structures are created by and thrive in a far-from-equilibrium, high-energy, unstable, even volatile environment—you can't imagine a whirlpool forming in, say, a cup of cold coffee. Since dissipative structures must remain open to a flowing exchange of matter and energy with the environment, and since their environment is so volatile and unstable, the structures must pass fluctuating amounts and kinds of energy and matter through themselves, which causes the structure itself to fluctuate. Up to a certain point, the structure can absorb these fluctuations, dissipate the entropy, and still maintain its internal organization. For example, the human body can absorb a certain amount of electrical current with no real damage; it can cope with the loss of a limb or two; it can withstand a certain amount of impact or vibration without serious damage; it can suffer certain damages and still heal itself through its self-organizing capacity. A society is able to absorb the disruptions and instability caused by a minor war; it can suffer a moderate famine or drought and still "heal" itself.

Such fluctuations in a dissipative structure can, within limits, be absorbed. At a certain point, though, the fluctuation begins to grow too great to be absorbed and healed, and the structure becomes more and more unstable. As the fluctuations increase, the structure reaches a critical point. It is highly unstable, like a complex machine that is on the verge of flying apart, maintaining its structure by the barest of margins. Perturbed by fluctuations, the elements of the system

61

have increased interactions as they are brought into contact with other elements of the system in new ways. This razor's edge is the point where the system has the potential to move in an almost infinite variety of unpredictable directions, like an unstable society on the verge of revolution or a human at the crisis point of a severe disease. Like Saul of Tarsus on the road to Damascus.

At this point even a small fluctuation can be sufficient to push the elements of the system beyond the point where they can heal themselves. Then suddenly the entire system seems to shudder and fall apart. In some cases the system may be destroyed. But if the system survives, it survives by emerging from this point of collapse (what Prigogine calls "the bifurcation point") in a new pattern. The elements of the system, having increased their interactions with each other and been brought into contact with each other in novel ways, reorganize in a different form, create a new organization. This recombination of the elements of the system is essentially *nonlinear*, and the new level or organization is able to handle the energy flow that was too much for the preceding system to handle; it is able to dissipate the entropy to the environment and maintain its new higher level of internal organization.

The nation that has undergone a revolution, with different levels of the society having been brought into contact with one another in new ways, creates a new government that is somehow able to absorb and dissipate the energy that had created the revolution in the earlier order of the society. The human body creates new antibodies that are able to overcome a disease. Tormented, fanatical Saul of Tarsus is knocked to the ground by a blinding light and is transformed into Paul, certain of his new mission in life. Out of chaos emerges a transformed system; the dissipative structure has, in Prigogine's words, "escaped into a higher order."

This higher order, once established, is stable, and resistant to further structural change or fluctuation, unless and until the energy flowing through it alters sharply and causes the system to undergo an intense new fluctuation. At this point, the structure might fall into a new phase of chaos and then once again escape to a higher order. Since each new level of order is more complex than the one before, each is more fragile than its predecessor, each more open to fluctuation, each more susceptible to collapse, chaos, change, creation.

Prigogine's vision of a universe of dissipative structures replaces the mechanistic view of a cosmos of "things" with a cosmos of "process." The entire process, with structures transforming themselves into new structures of greater complexity and diversification, is unpredictable, self-organizing, and evolutionary. The process is what scientists call *saltatory*, that is, characterized by a series of leaps and bounds, or discontinuities, rather than a gradual, incremental progression. In fact, as applied to the origin and evolution of species, Prigogine's theory of dissipative structures offers a clear description of how life evolved on our planet, with various species remaining relatively stable over long periods, then altering rapidly and evolving into different species, usually as a result of rapid environmental changes (i.e., increased fluctuations). This view of evolution, called *saltationism* or *punctuated equilibrium*, is supported by the fossil evidence and is now coming to be widely accepted. In a more universal way, Prigogine's ideas explain how, without contradicting the second law of thermodynamics, complex systems can grow and evolve in a universe of entropy. The importance Prigogine gives this idea can be seen in the title of his most recent book: *Order out of Chaos*.

Prigogine's ideas have had an impact in virtually every field of human inquiry, and the concept of dissipative structures has been fruitfully applied to understanding such phenomena as the process of sugar metabolism by which living cells transform food into energy, the moment an audience breaks into applause, the growth of plants, the organization of a variety of social structures including slime molds, bee swarms, termite colonies, and human cultures, economic patterns, the psychology of altered states of consciousness, the nonlinear interactions of nerve cells, the origin and development of cancer cells, social and behavioral change, the process by which musical instruments are developed, and artistic inspiration. The U.S. Department of Transportation has even used it to analyze and predict traffic-flow patterns (crowded freeways turn out to be a fine example of dissipative structures).

For many people, Prigogine's ideas seem profoundly optimistic, offering a message of continuing order, progress, and evolution, against the hopeless determinism of the message of entropy. By demonstrating that periods of instability, perturbation, upheaval, collapse, and chaos are not to be seen as absolute evils but instead as absolute necessities, as phases through which every structure must pass in order to evolve to higher levels of complexity, the theory of dissipative structures clarifies how out of political and economic upheavals we can evolve new social orders, how the volatile and disordered process of artistic creation can lead to new artistic forms and visions, how psychological suffering, conflict, and collapse can lead to new emotional, intellectual and spiritual strengths and how confusion and doubt can lead to new scientific ideas.

Prigogine himself at times supports this essentially optimistic view. "Within the framework of the second law," he says, "irreversible processes can have a constructive, positive role, rather than a destructive one. They give rise to dissipative structures. . . . Now, looking at biology, social behavior, ecology, and economics, we begin to have a meeting point between the various concepts of evolution. . . . Near equilibrium you always go to the most banal, the most uniform state. The general idea of classical physics is that we progress toward the running down of the universe. What we see here on Earth, on the other hand, is just the opposite of that. Instead of going to heat death, we see successive diversification. And so, in spite of the fact that the second law is probably satisfied in the universe as a whole, we are not going toward equilibrium, basically because we receive a constant infusion of energy from the stars, the galaxy, and so on. . . . With the paradigm of self-organization we see a transition from disorder to order. In the field of psychological activity this is perhaps the main experience we have—every artistic or scientific creation implies a transition from disorder to order."

However, Prigogine's ideas are not necessarily optimistic. The key to the development of dissipative structures is what he calls the bifurcation point, when the structure can move in a variety of directions, not all of them beneficial, including total collapse and destruction. Comparing his ideas to those of Teilhard de Chardin, Prigogine points out that Chardin "was sure that every change, every new bifurcation, was going in the right direction—in the direction of increased spirituality. On the contrary . . . a bifurcation can lead us to the best or to the worst. We are participating in an evolution whose outcome isn't clear to us."[367]

Today more than ever before, humans seem to be at a crucial and potentially disastrous bifurcation point. The dissipative system of our society is experiencing an enormously increased flow-through of energy and matter, as we consume fuels, food, natural resources, and other materials at a skyrocketing rate. At the same time we are experiencing increasing entropy as general disorder, conflict, social disintegration, and environmental depletion send perturbations through the fragile human system. Increasing energy flow combined with increasing entropy in a dissipative structure result in major destabilizing fluctuations. We seem to be nearing the point at which the fluctuations are too powerful to be damped, the bifurcation point that will, in Prigogine's words, "lead us to the best or to the worst." The outcome is not yet clear to us.

5

ASCENT TO A HIGHER ORDER: BRAIN AS DISSIPATIVE STRUCTURE

PLANNED EVOLUTION: GETTING SMARTER BY LEAPS AND BOUNDS

SO, HAVING TAKEN A QUICK TOUR THROUGH THE THERMODY-namics of far-from-equilibrium systems, we have come full circle, back to Saul of Tarsus being slammed into enlightenment on the road to Damascus, and Archimedes leaping from his bathtub and crying "Eureka!" as he pads naked through the streets. And we come full circle back to the questions with which we began the tour: why does the brain operate as it does, with the same stimulus—a red light, say—triggering in one brain a new idea, in another a collapse?

And as we contemplate these questions once more, it should now be clear that the brain, as an open system constantly exchanging energy with the environment, far from equilibrium, is a dissipative structure *par excellence*: enormously complex, swept and transformed by oscillations and chemical and electrical waves, self-organizing, and structured of networks that are so sensitive that, according to neuroscientists, they can be completely destabilized by a change in permeability of just *two* of its billions upon billions of cells.

This being the case, Prigogine's insights into the workings

of dissipative structures shou'd provide us with important new information about how the brain operates. And, most important for the purposes of this book, Prigogine's theory of dissipative structures gives us compelling reasons to believe that, given the appropriate influx of energy, the brain as dissipative structure can be destabilized, made subject to internal fluctuations, and these fluctuations can be amplified until the structure spontaneously shifts, like a kaleidoscope falling into a new pattern, and the brain spontaneously transforms itself into a new state, more ordered, more coherent, more complex, more interconnected, more *highly evolved* than before.

Perhaps by proper use of certain devices that somehow increase the flow of energy to the brain—whether by means of stimulating the brain with flashing lights or phased sound waves, revolving the brain through an electromagnetic field, or floating the brain in a gravity-free environment free of external stimuli—it might be possible to amplify the brain's fluctuations and cause it to "escape into a higher order."

The question is, then, can any of the brain-stimulation devices we are going to examine in this book be used to trigger the inherent self-organizing potential of the brain and stimulate the brain to become more complex and more coherent— that is, larger, smarter, more creative, wiser? If this is the case, we are talking about devices with revolutionary potential, devices that can spur the brain within a short time into a sort of growth that for all of human history has been thought to be of necessity extremely difficult and slow.* And we are talking about being able to spur this kind of growth con-

---

*In fact, the evidence supports the "saltatory" or leaps-and-bounds view of evolution, indicating that human brain growth can happen very rapidly—so rapidly that in a matter of a few hundred thousand years or so (a mere flash in evolutionary history) the brain of our ancient ancestors actually doubled in size, a growth so rapid it has come to be called "the brain explosion." Interestingly, anthropologists now link this explosive growth in brain size, most of it in the neocortex, to the moment humans began manipulating tools. Tools, of course, are, essentially, machines. So we see that the possibility we are exploring here—that a machine or device can interact with the brain in such a way as to stimulate the brain to grow—is nothing new or extraordinary, but simply the application of the central impetus of human evolution.

sciously and intentionally, rather than as a by-product of other practices and disciplines, such as meditation. We are talking about something that could change the way we all live: conscious, intentional mental growth. Planned evolution.

First, let's look at the proposal that the brain is a dissipative structure. In his researches, Prigogine found that for a system or structure of some sort to become a dissipative structure it must be:

—*open*. A dissipative structure can exist only by remaining constantly open to a flowing interchange of matter and energy with the environment.

—*far from equilibrium*. A high-energy environment, with a constant influx of new energy, is necessary for the process of self-organization, subjecting the system to fluctuations and allowing it to dissipate the resulting entropy into the environment. Near equlibrium the system would become like a closed system, subject to increasing entropy, tending toward bland uniformity.

—*autocatalytic*. From the words "auto" (self) and "catalyst" (an agent that helps change other things while not becoming changed itself); that is, elements of the system enter a cycle that helps them to reproduce themselves—elements of the system are self-reproducing, or self-reinforcing. An example of this is, in living systems, the ability of cells to reproduce themselves.

There's no doubt the brain fulfills these requirements. It is certainly an open system; energy and matter are constantly flowing into the brain in the form of light, sound, sensations, information, and oxygen and other nutrients in the blood (in fact, while the brain is only about 2 percent of total body weight, it uses more than 20 percent of all oxygen taken into the body, which makes the brain the most prodigious energy consumer/transformer in the body). This influx of energy is transformed in the brain and flows back into the environment, as carbon dioxide and other waste products in the bloodstream, as heat, and as action.

Unlike equilibrium or near-equilibrium systems, with their clearly defined parts, their tendency toward uniformity, their predictability, their lack of anything new or volatile entering or leaving the system, the brain is clearly far from equilibrium. Instead of clearly defined parts with fixed functions, the brain is, as scientists are now discovering, incredibly flexible, flowing, plastic, constantly transforming itself, its neural networks moving and changing with experience and in response to the energies flowing through the system.

That is, neuroscientists are now discovering that the brain does not, as they once believed, operate like a machine, based on the on-off electrical pulses generated by individual neurons, but rather by Nonlinear cooperative interactions sweeping across and interconnecting millions and hundreds of millions of neurons. The brain, they find, does not respond to the energy that flows into it in a linear, mechanistic, predictable way, but instead transforms that influx into emotions, ideas, and drives. The input triggers results that are spontaneous, unpredictable, creative.

The third characteristic of dissipative structures, autocatalysis, self-reinforcement or self-reproduction, is another of the brain's most obvious means of maintaining its structure, shape, and flow. On the physical level, we have seen that at least some of the brain's cells, the glial cells, are capable of reproducing themselves, as did the glial cells of the rats raised in enriched environments at Berkeley. There is also increasing evidence that even neurons, in response to certain energy fluctuations, are capable of regeneration.

But where the real autocatalysis takes place in the brain is in the sweep of energy through the neural networks, the sweeps that we experience as emotions, desires, ideas. We know, for example, that even the smallest, subtlest thought can enter the brain and there, through a process of self-reinforcement, grow stronger and even stronger in a self-perpetuating cycle, as when a hope, a fantasy, or a fear insinuates itself into our brain, and then, feeding upon itself, grows greater and more powerful, until it has seized control of our brain and become a ruling obsession.

It is, in part, this autocatalytic nature of the brain (and of all dissipative structures) that accounts for the fact that when the structure is at a critical point, even the most infinitesimal impulse can be sufficient to destabilize the whole system and cause it to reorganize at a higher level, or having failed to reorganize, to experience chaos. Thus, a simple red light, passed through the brain and reproduced and reinforced, feeding upon itself autocatalytically, can become powerful enough to trigger an escape into a higher order, a new vision of reality—or to drive an already disturbed brain into total disorganization.

THE ADVENTURES OF PAUL IN AN ENRICHED ENVIRONMENT

KNOWING THAT THE BRAIN IS A DISSIPATIVE STRUCTURE IS USE-ful, since it allows us to apply to the brain certain facts known to be true of all dissipative systems. First, we know that dissipative structures must constantly dissipate entropy: for order to develop within the system, entropy must be externalized so that the net entropy of the system and its environment will increase, thus satisfying the second law of thermodynamics, and so that the entropy does not increase within the system itself, and thus "kill" it by causing it to run down, wear out, or approach equilibrium. We also know that the only way entropy can be dissipated is for the system to have a constant input of energy and new materials. An example is the whirlpool or vortex that can form in flowing water: it must dissipate entropy, which it does by the centripetal force of the whirling vortex; but to do this, to maintain its existence, it must have a continuing flow of water *into* the vortex. If the influx of energy were to stop—that is, if the vortex were to be suddenly placed in a motionless lake—the vortex would cease to exist.

What this means for the brain is that the only way it can maintain itself is by receiving a constant input of energy and new materials. And in fact scientists have found this to be true. For example, the rats that Rosenzweig, Diamond, Krech, and their colleagues placed in enriched or impoverished environments showed enormous differences in brain weight and size and in the actual complexity of the brain structure, while rats placed in a nonenriched environment showed an almost immediate decrease in brain size and complexity.

Another thing we know about dissipative structures is that, as open systems in far-from-equilibrium environments, they receive unpredictable and widely varying kinds of energy input. High-energy influxes set up fluctuations in the system. Within certain limits, the structure can absorb or "damp" these fluctuations, but if the jolts and jars become too violent the structure may be broken out of shape and "escape to a higher order." In the case of the brain, this escape to a higher order is experienced as having a new idea: the Eureka event, the Aha! moment, the light bulb going on in the brain. This movement or "leap" to a higher level of complexity and connectedness is what we mean by "learning."

Again, lest someone assume that I am speaking metaphorically when I speak of a higher level of brain complexity as "learning," it's essential to remember that, as Rosenzweig and associates discovered, not only did rats from enriched environments have thicker cortical layers and heavier brains, but the areas of their brains that grew in size also grew in richness, density, and complexity: larger neurons, longer dendrites, more dendritic spines, more glia, more connections between neurons. These same rats, when tested with various laboratory measures of intelligence, such as maze-running, were superior to nonenriched rats—they were smarter, and "learned" more. That is, the increased structural complexity accompanies higher levels of intelligence and learning.

Relating this to the brain as dissipative structure, we can say that the brain is able to accept certain amounts of energy input (such as ideas or events) and assimilate them without any serious challenge to the internal organization of the brain. "Yes, yes," we say in response to certain ideas or stimuli, "this all makes sense." However, at a certain level of intensity, the external events or stimuli become too intense, the brain's fluctuations become too great to be damped, and the brain will escape from its old pattern into a new organization of higher order and coherence. First, things no longer make "sense," then, with a shock of recognition, they make a new type of sense, sense of a sort we had never before imagined.

Here we have one explanation for the extraordinary thing that happened to Saul on the road to Damascus. From the bits and pieces we learn about him in the New Testament, Saul must have been in some way unsatisfied with the internal organization of his brain—nagging uncertainties, perhaps, vague longings for something that would satisfy his deepest yearnings. In any case, it seems a sure bet that the wild ideas of the Nazarenes—talk of a Messiah and so on—stirred up a lot of perturbations and fluctuations in the dissipative structure of his brain. For a while Saul was able to absorb the fluctuations, damp the perturbations. Soon, however, the inner turmoil became too much, and the only way Saul could resist was to fight actively against the disruptive ideas. Thus he became known as a merciless hounder of the Nazarenes, bragging of how many he had executed.

And yet all the time, the far-from-equilibrium system of his brain was becoming more and more fragile. He was driven to more flagrant actions to struggle against the threatening chaos he felt in his head. He asked the chief priests if he could take his anti-Nazarene campaign clear outside of his normal territory of Jerusalem and chase the subversives way up in Damascus. By this time he must have been growing desperate, the perturbations in the brain reinforcing and amplifying themselves maddeningly. To this volatile and obsessive inner state, add the uncertainties of traveling into strange territory, the pure physical stress of walking and riding for long distances, and we can see that Saul was ripe for a fall.

The outcome is classical dissipative-structure thermodynamics: order out of chaos, escape to a higher level. Saul's brain, no longer able to maintain its inner organization against the violent fluctuations, is destabilized, torn loose from its moorings. He is at Prigogine's bifurcation point, capable of falling into total disorder and madness, or of reorganizing at a higher level. He goes for days without eating or drinking, totally blind. Then, suddenly, the pieces are all put together, but in a new way—more coherent, more interconnected, more complex, more able to bear the energies passing through, more evolved. Saul becomes Paul, and sets out on a lifelong mission to preach the very religion he had so passionately despised—which is to say, Paul found a new way to dissipate the entropy in his system; instead of allowing the entropy to build up in his brain and destroy it, he forced it into the environment, dissipating his entropy in the expended heat and energy of his ceaseless travels all over the known world, thus fulfilling the requirements of the second law of thermodynamics.

If somehow we were able to dissect his Paul-brain in a laboratory and compare it to his Saul-brain, would we find that the Paul-brain, like that of a rat in a super-enriched environment, had denser and richer neural connections? The laboratory evidence, in which the brains of rats given learning experiences are found to show immediate and permanent structural changes, suggests that we would. As neurobiologist Gary Lynch of UC at Irvine puts it, when you give the brain a momentary stimulation of the right type, "just bip!—literally that long, the nerve circuits change and don't go back."[112]

And such transformations are not limited to mystics and oddballs like Paul: we have all had the experience of having our brain structure (which we might call our "preconceptions" or our "rational minds" or our "vision of reality") challenged by new ideas, new ways of looking at life, events that somehow don't fit into our ordered way of seeing things or challenge our sense of ethics. Often we resist these challenges completely; often we can fit them into the dissipative structure of our brain without causing fluctuations or perturbations that are too violent. And sometimes the whole house of cards comes falling down and we see things afresh, with what Blake called a cleansing of our doors of perception, which is to say, a reorganizing of the neural connections.

WHY ARTISTS ARE A LITTLE NUTS

THIS BRINGS US TO ANOTHER CHARACTERISTIC OF DISSIPATIVE structures that is important in our understanding of brain stimulation: for transformation or evolution to take place, there must be either a lot of instability and fluctuation within the system, so that even a small stimulus can bring about dissolution and reorganization; or, on the other hand, if the structure is stable, there must be some extraordinary influx of energy into the system, something powerful enough to destabilize a structure that is strong enough to resist most fluctuations.

In the first case, we can see that the greater the instability of the system, the greater the number of interactions among its various parts, the greater its susceptibility to fluctuations and disorder, and the greater its potential for evolution, transformation, diversification, evolution, and (in the case of the brain) wisdom. Thus, the theory of dissipative structures supports the long-standing assumption that artists, creative thinkers, and others who are constantly seeking to open themselves up to "new" ideas are on the whole more mentally fluid, more susceptible to turmoil, chaos, and disorder in the brain. Lest this sound forbidding, remember that on the positive side of the ledger, creative thinkers also probably have a richer and denser neural network, with greater numbers of interconnections between their neurons (and thus a great number of potential mental states; that is, a wider range of ideas, feelings, sensations, intuitions). And, as Prigogine always emphasizes, it is out of the chaos, turmoil, and disorder that higher levels of order and wisdom emerge; thus if the creative thinkers have less mental stability than some people, they also experience higher levels of mental connectedness, complexity, evolution.

On the other hand, we can also surmise that people who are set in their ways, who resist any new idea, who hate to try any new experience, who refer every idea or experience to their past, attempting to fit it into the structure of their brain without causing fluctuations or perturbations, who are always sure they are right and never experience self-doubt—these people, whatever their feelings of self-satisfaction, are trying to eliminate the influx of new energy and matter into their brains. Since, as we know, open systems cannot exist without a constant flow-through of energy, what the people are essentially trying to do is turn their brains into closed structures—like a steam engine, a cup of coffee that has gone cold, a stone. Certainly these closed systems are never threatened by chaos or disorder, but who wants a near-equilibrium brain? Such a brain, like a rock, would never be destabilized, but then again it would never have a new idea or feeling either. In any case, physiologically, such brains will probably have far fewer neural connections and less-developed cortical layers than the brains of people who remain open to stimulation, to energy. And it is unlikely they will experience any significant mental evolution, transformation, or reorganization after they reach maturity.

We have been talking about different types of brains subjected to the same intensity of external stimulation: one system being complex, in a state of fluctuation, wide open to new materials and energy, will be more susceptible to being altered by X amount of energy; the other, crystallized, solid, largely shut off to new materials, will be less susceptible to being altered by X amount of energy. However, we can approach the problem of brain change from the other end, by altering the amount of energy influx: if the energy or matter flowing into the brain has enough force, it can transform even brains that are stable and strongly resistant to change. This offers one explanation for the mind-altering powers of the devices described in this book. All of them make use of types of energy that flow through the brain in everyday life—sound, light, motion, electricity. However, the mind machines make use of state-of-the-art technology to focus and intensify these types of energy to a degree that is rarely if ever encountered in daily life. The result is a powerful energy influx to which the brain can respond only by altering in some way.

Many readers will share my willingness to challenge their brains and send some fluctuations through their gray matter.

However, many people are not so eager; many people are quite determined to hang on to their present structure, thank you, and have no desire to escape to a higher order. For such people, the mental destabilization some of these devices can bring can be frightening. For this reason I want to emphasize here that the machines I describe should be used only by people who are fully willing, who understand that the devices can have and often are intended to have a somewhat disruptive effect on the brain. People with rigid personality structures, with a strong need to feel in control, should approach these devices carefully, at their own speed.

BEYOND BOREDOM AND ANXIETY: THE LINK BETWEEN PEAK EXPERIENCES AND LEARNING

SINCE I'VE DESCRIBED ESCAPE TO A HIGHER ORDER AS SOME process involving chaos, disorder, instability, perturbations, and collapsing like Paul on the road to Damascus in a state of total if temporary derangement, it's likely some wary reader is muttering, "Who needs this? These brain machines sound like something Dr. Frankenstein cooked up; you'll never get me in one of those things without a fight!"

But what we're talking about, after all, is simply a process of increasing brain coherence. It's a process that most people experience as one of the most pleasurable in life. It happens when making love, watching our child sleep, absorbing a work of art or being moved by music, perceiving beauty, feeling the birth of a new idea, and at all moments of self-realization, fulfillment, achievement, illumination, peace, and joy—the process of our brain's components rearranging themselves to accommodate themselves to reality in a new way. It's an occurrence psychologist Abraham Maslow devoted his career to exploring, and which he called having "peak experiences."

One characteristic of peak experiences is that they feel good. They feel so good that most of us would willingly have peak experiences as frequently as possible, and one of the most powerful human drives is toward peak experiences. Much of the energy and time we expend in our lives—in seeking or using sex, drugs, money, prestige, power, wisdom—is devoted to confused or misdirected attempts to have peak experiences. How nice if we could have them at will!

Unfortunately, peak experiences are not easy to come by. Throughout history there have been many attempts to devise techniques that would enable humans to trigger peak experiences, but these techniques (including types of yoga, meditation, tantricism, trance-inducing dance and music, fasting, drugs, and religious practices) sometimes have harmful side effects, and virtually always demand discipline and long arduous practice. Discipline and practice are good things, in general, but in our skeptical and impatient culture, many people seek shortcuts. Too often these shortcuts, ranging from voracious materialism to mindless occultism, end up leaving the seekers dissatisfied, even more needful of peak experiences than they were when they set out on the shortcut. The end result is a loss of faith in the existence of peak experiences and higher states, a sneering dismissal of such levels of mental development as pure self-delusion by willowy souls too weak to face the facts about the cold, hard, brutal, peak-experience-less world.

Can people intentionally boost themselves into a higher order and induce authentic peak experiences? One way of approaching the problem is to find out what are the components of peak (or, at the least, pleasurable) experiences; once these elements are known, we might be able to induce peak (or pleasurable) experiences by creating the necessary components. One scientist who has done this is Mihaly Csikszentmihalyi of the University of Chicago. He concluded that such experiences are *intrinsically rewarding*—that is, we participate in them not for external rewards, "not as compensation for past desires, not as preparation for future needs, but as an ongoing process which provides rewarding experiences in the present."

To study this intrinsically rewarding behavior, Csikszentmihalyi interviewed and studied chess players, rock climbers, surgeons, and others who did things not for external rewards but simply because they enjoyed them. He found that the underlying similarity of all these activities is that "they all give participants a sense of discovery, exploration, problem solution—in other words, a feeling of novelty and challenge." The outcome of these activities, he discovered, is uncertain ("like exploring a strange place") but "the actor is potentially capable of controlling it."

Csikszentmihalyi noticed that his informants often described their experiences by using the same word: *flow*. He concluded that the essential element of all peak experiences was this "flow." He found that while many sought their flow experiences in games and play, flow was also the key element in such activities as creativity, love, and religious experiences. "In a variety of human contexts, then, one finds a remarkably similar inner state, which is so enjoyable that people are sometimes willing to forsake a comfortable life for its sake."

To further define this enjoyable inner state of flow, Csikszentmihalyi places all human activity along a scale of increasing challenge or difficulty. At one end of the scale are activities which present no challenges or difficulties whatsoever. At the other end of the scale are those activities which are so challenging or difficult that they are impossible for the person engaged in the activity to perform. An example of the first activity might be waiting in a long and slow-moving line. An example of the second kind might be (depending on who you are) hang gliding from a high mountain, taking an examination in a course you can't comprehend, or charging an enemy machine gun. At one end of the scale is boredom; at the other, anxiety. Thus the title of Dr. Csikszentmihalyi's book: *Beyond Boredom and Anxiety.* For an activity to produce flow, says Csikszentmihalyi, there must be an even match between the difficulty of a challenge and a person's ability to meet it. A person whose personal record for a marathon is four hours will receive as much flow from running in 3:50 as a world-class runner will get from running 2:09. Both are meeting the challenges and are capable of overcoming the challenges.

Here we have a fascinating confluence of ideas and terms. First, religion, love, creativity, peak experiences, games, and all such intrinsically pleasurable events are linked by the fact that they give participants a sense of "flow," and this flow experience, while enjoyable, is not necessarily comfortable, since people will forsake comfort for its sake. Rather than comfort, flow has to do with "problem solution" and "challenge," "novelty," and "exploring a strange place."[83] It is not boring, or easily mastered, nor is it so extraordinarily difficult as to cause overwhelming anxiety.

SMART RATS AND THEIR PEAK EXPERIENCES

"FLOW" SEEMS TO BE QUITE THE SAME THING THAT WE HAVE been describing as "learning." Indeed, Rosenzweig and the other Berkeley scientists, when trying to define what constituted an enriched environment—in other words, what was the contributing factor to brain growth and increased intelligence in the enriched rats—continually use the very same terms: an enriched environment, they say, is one that presents "challenge," "novelty," the necessity of "solving problems and exploring strange places."

Other tests, however, have found that when rats are placed in an environment that is too frighteningly challenging and stressful (the rats were subjected to shocks), the rats do not enjoy the enrichment effect; in fact, they suffer mental problems. In other words, as Csikszentmihalyi points out with his boredom-to-anxiety scale, not only too little but also too much challenge can be damaging. The impoverished environment was, in a word, boring. The enriched environment presented challenges that were capable of being mastered by the rats: the enriched environment, then, is one that produces "flow," and lies "between boredom and anxiety." While the researchers have ascertained that the enriched rats had larger, more complex brains, and were more intelligent (as far as rat intelligence can be measured), they have never examined the amount of pleasure experienced by the enriched rats as compared to the impoverished rats, but it seems clear that the enriched rats were enriched to the extent that their lives were filled with almost constant flow. Surely, we must believe, these were fun-loving peak-experiencing rats.

Finally, the boredom-to-anxiety scale brings us back to the idea of the human brain as dissipative structure. If the structure receives insufficient energy input (which is, in Csikszentmihalyi's terms, boredom), it ceases to grow and begins to deteriorate. But if the energy flow through the structure is much too great, the fluctuations grow too violent to be absorbed or damped and the structure is destabilized (what Csikszentmihalyi calls anxiety). Between these two extremes is a range of energy input that is sufficient to challenge the structure and induce change. Thus, Csikszentmihalyi's concept of flow can be seen as a statement in psychological terms of Prigogine's ideas of dissipative structures.

The Berkeley rats in an enriched environment learned because they were challenged but not challenged too much, because their environment was between boredom and anxiety, because the flow of energy and matter to their brains was enough to cause their brain structures continually to escape to a higher order without being torn apart. The connections are clear—flow is learning is pleasurable is brain-enriching is mind-expanding. And mind expansion is accompanied by flow, in an endless upward spiral of brain evolution through escape to higher order.

6

RELAXATION AND
THE BRAIN

RECALL THE STRESSFUL DAY I FIRST TRIED THE SYNCHRO-Energizer. The magazine editor who tried the machine melted in his chair, oozing into a state of blissful relaxation. When I put on the device I was almost rigid with cold and tension, but within a minute or two I was dreamy and relaxed—and the feeling of relaxation stayed with me all day.

The Graham Potentializer, a device that gently moves the user in a horizontal circle through an electromagnetic field, causes most users to become so relaxed they fall asleep or into a near-sleep state.

Scientists had used the EMG (electromyograph) to measure the electrical activity of the body's muscles (i.e., muscular tension) and found that a short session in a flotation tank spontaneously produces a more profound state of whole-body relaxation than such techniques as progressive relaxation, autogenics, meditation, and stretching—techniques specifically designed to relax the muscles.

These mind machines, and other devices described in the coming chapters, put most users into a state of profound relaxation. The relaxation occurs rapidly and spontaneously. In the last few chapters, however, the words I've used to describe the effect of the machines have been "challenge," "exploration," "novelty," "fluctuations," "increased energy input," "instability," and "structural disorganization." Such words refer to a process that is, as we discovered in the last chapter, highly enjoyable, but still, you might think, full of perturbations and vaguely disquieting. What does all this have to do with profound relaxation?

STRESS AND THE BONEHEAD EFFECT

MOST OF US ARE AWARE THAT HUMANS, LIKE ALL MAMMALS, have an efficient evolutionary mechanism for enabling them to deal with a threat to their security. This mechanism is called *the fight-or-flight response*, and it works as follows. Some external event is interpreted by the brain as being a threat; certain parts of the brain release neurochemicals that have a wide range of effects throughout the body, all directed toward mobilizing the body's energies toward fighting or fleeing the perceived threat: sugar pours into the bloodstream for quick energy, the heart rate speeds up to pump more blood, breathing becomes more rapid, blood pressure rises, blood flow is shifted away from the digestive system, body periphery, and brain to the heart and trunk muscles, muscles become rigid and tight, sweating increases, oxygen consumption increases, body temperature rises, and we experience the well-known "adrenaline rush." The threat or demand that triggers the response is a *stressor*, and the response itself is *stress*.

This response is a most excellent thing when we need to run in mindless terror from a saber-toothed tiger or tear out someone's liver with our bare hands. On the other hand, it's pure hell on coherent thinking. After all, who needs to entertain deep and elegant thoughts while being pursued by a wild beast? With blood and oxygen directed toward the muscles and away from the brain, the brain simply does not operate very well, which is the reason people have been known to make incredibly knuckleheaded moves when under pressure, running to the wrong end of the football field and so on.

This "bonehead reaction" has been proved in laboratory

tests and in numerous real-life situations. Statistics show, for example, that basketball players mess up more free throws in "pressure" game situations than in nonpressure situations. Many people have experienced "test anxiety" when under the pressure of having to perform for an examination. One's fight-or-flight responses kick in and suddenly the brain becomes a Tasmanian tarpit.

Extreme stress has the same ruinous effect on the ability to learn as on the ability to think. Rats put under great stress— by having shocks delivered to their tails, or by being put in cages where the floor periodically delivered an electric shock —found it hard to learn anything compared to rats who learned under more serene circumstances.

The fight-or-flight response can be an automatic reaction to a single stressful event, but it can also be longer-lasting. Since the stress-inducing events most of us confront in modern society consist not of saber-toothed tigers but of subtle, insidious, or indirect pressures which we can't directly confront or flee from—jobs, a technological society, generalized fears of crime, pollution, and so on—most of us are never able to fully turn off our fight-or-flight response. As a result, we live in a constant state of low-grade, nonspecific arousal. And if single stressful events can cause us to become boneheads, crippling our ability to think and learn, perpetual stress has a similar deleterious effect on our brain functions. For example, in a recent study of four thousand schoolchildren, conducted at Georgetown University, the children were tested to determine the amount of stress they were experiencing in their lives; physical handicaps, parents' marital problems, the recent loss of a job by a parent, ill health, and poor eyesight were some of the major causes of stress for the children. The study concluded that high stress reduced scores on IQ tests by a full 13 percent. That is, the students under the greatest stress scored 13 percent lower than the students under the least stress.[340]

So, whether as response to a single stressful event or to chronic, nonspecific, low-grade stress, the activation of our fight-or-flight response cripples our ability to think and to learn, and, at least as measured by IQ tests, it lowers our intelligence.

RELAXATION AND THE LOOSE-GOOSE EFFECT

ON THE OTHER HAND, HUMANS HAVE A SECOND INNATE RE-flex that is almost the mirror image of the fight-or-flight response. Instead of mobilizing our bodies for outward activity, this second system mobilizes our bodies' resources for *inward* activity. The effects of this response include reduced heart rate, blood pressure, and sweating, increased functioning of the gastrointestinal tract, relaxation of muscles, and increase in the percentage of oxygen and blood flowing to the brain. Also, the predominant type of electrical activity in the brain changes from the low-amplitude, rapid-frequency *beta waves* indicative of external attention to the slower, higher-amplitude, more strongly rhythmical *alpha* and *theta waves*, which characterize attention to inner experience and are found in such states as meditation and contemplation. This reaction has been called the *relaxation response* or the *quieting reflex*.[341, 31]

The relaxation response is an innate human (and mammalian) characteristic—one thinks of how cats and dogs, for example, can quickly go from states of extreme arousal to deep relaxation, yawning, stretching, curling their tails about themselves, and instantly falling into a state of absolute rest. Unfortunately, perhaps because of increasing evolutionary pressures caused by urbanization and industrialization, humans seem to have largely lost the knack of instant relaxation. They have, however, sought to develop many techniques or disciplines to bring on this beneficial state, including meditation, controlled breathing, progressive relaxation, biofeedback, and so on. Interestingly, study after study has concluded that this state of relaxation is not only pleasant and stress-relieving, but also leads to superior performance on both mental and physical tests. We know this instinctively when we talk about the value of being "cool-headed" in solving problems, when we describe superior performers as being cool as a cucumber or loose as a goose and claim that they "make it look easy."

Recently, scientists have tried to find the common roots of all such techniques. One of them, Dr. Herbert Benson of Harvard Medical School, who popularized the term "relaxation response," concluded that the essential preconditions for eliciting the response are:

—a "constant stimulus—e.g., a sound, word, or phrase repeated silently or audibly, or fixed gazing at an object. The purpose of these procedures is to shift from logical, externally oriented thought."

—a "passive attitude." Any distracting external events or thoughts that occur during the practice "should be disregarded and one's attention should be redirected to the technique."

—"decreased muscle tonus. The subject should be in a comfortable posture so that minimal muscular work is required."

—a "quiet environment with decreased environmental stimuli."[31]

The mind machines described in this book are all quite relaxing. One explanation is that they all provide the four elements Benson says are essential components of the relaxation response. In general they produce a "constant stimulus" that is either light, sound, body movements or vibrations, an electromagnetic field, or some combination of these elements. The users are encouraged to have a "passive attitude," to assume a comfortable posture so that they have decreased muscle tonus and to use the devices in a quiet environment. Thus, since stress hinders mental functioning and relaxation enhances it, the simple fact that the mind machines rapidly induce deep relaxation can explain some of the increases in mental functioning experienced by users of the devices.

But there is an additional aspect we must take into account. We started out by asking how it could be that the mind machines could simultaneously induce deep relaxation in the user and, by increasing fluctuations and instability, cause the dissipative structure that is the brain to escape old patterns and reorganize at a higher level of order, coherence, and complexity. That is, how can deep relaxation coexist with increased fluctuations and instability in the brain? Now we have the elements necessary to answer that question.

HOW YOUR BRAIN IS LIKE A BUNCH OF PEOPLE CROSSING A BRIDGE

ONE CHARACTERISTIC OF THE RELAXATION RESPONSE IS THE rapid shifting of brain-wave patterns from low-amplitude, rapid beta waves to higher-amplitude, slower alpha and theta waves. These brain waves do not represent the electrical activity of individual neurons; instead, they reflect the cooperative electrical patterns of networks of millions of neurons—fluctuations of energy sweeping across the networks of the brain. To say that beta waves are low-amplitude means that there is very little difference between their highest and lowest point: think of a very fine sawtooth pattern. But the slower, more rhythmical alpha and theta waves, being of higher amplitude, have much larger differences between their highs and lows: think of a great jagged sawtooth pattern (see Figure 1). That is, beta waves, characteristic of external attention and "ordinary" states of consciousness, show virtually no fluctuations. The high-amplitude alpha and theta waves, however, indicate large brain fluctuations. It is such fluctuations or perturbations, as we know, that trigger alterations in unstable systems: increased fluctuations lead to organizational changes in dissipative structures.

An illustration of this is the effect of thousands of people walking across a bridge. If each person walks at an individually determined rhythm, the sound of the footsteps will be a continuous (i.e., high-frequency) shuffling and the vibrations of the bridge will be continuous but very slight. Like the

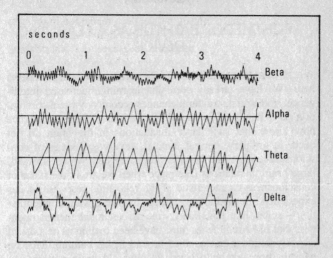

brain's beta waves, the fluctuations of the bridge will be high-frequency/low-amplitude. However, if all of the thousands crossing the bridge were to march to a single rhythm, the sound of the footsteps would be a series of separate (i.e., low-frequency) *tromp tromp tromps*; the vibrations of the bridge would be discontinuous and rhythmic, and would tend to become augmented and increase into self-reinforcing (auto-catalytic) fluctuations. Like the brain's alpha and theta waves, the fluctuations of the bridge would be low-frequency/high-amplitude. Ultimately these perturbations could exert such a powerful destabilizing influence on the bridge that it would be unable to dissipate the entropy and it would "escape" from its pattern of organization. In the case of the bridge, such escape would mean collapse; in the case of the brain, it can mean reorganization at a higher level of order and complexity.

ARCHIMEDES' BATHTUB AS A LEARNING DEVICE

WELL, CLEARLY THERE ARE SOME INTERESTING IMPLICATIONS here. We have already seen that learning, increased intelligence, and actual structural changes accompany brain stimulation as a result of increased fluctuations. What's more, we now know that such large fluctuations in the brain do not occur in ordinary, normal, typical, "everyday" states of consciousness, when the brain is producing beta waves. Instead, large brain fluctuations take place when we are in the states of consciousness characteristic of the relaxation response, states experienced in meditation, trance, intense inward contemplation—states like that floaty, free-associational mental openness that old Archimedes must have been feeling as he sloshed and daydreamed and noodled around in his bathtub. That is, we are more likely to learn, to alter old brain patterns, to trigger our brains to new growth, when we are in "nonordinary" states of consciousness, states which increase the brain's fluctuations.

This conclusion might sound odd to some, since it contradicts the accepted notion that learning is something that comes through practice and repetition: that learning has to do with conditioning. But in fact, it's a conclusion supported by research in virtually every discipline of human studies. Educators, psychologists, and other scientists of the brain are now exploring a variety of techniques for enhancing the ability of both children and adults to learn, among them the use of drawing, guided imagery, meditation, autogenics, rhythmic breathing, singing, storytelling, dancing, music, and relaxation. Studies show that all these techniques can lead to dramatic increases in the ability to acquire and remember and make creative use of information and ideas; which is to say such techniques lead to dramatic alterations in brain chemistry and structure and human behavior. The common denominator is that each technique augments brain fluctuations by increasing brain-wave amplitude and/or decreasing brain-wave frequency. Among the most interesting studies documenting the beneficial effects of boosting brain fluctuations:

FOCUSING. University of Chicago psychologist Eugene Gendlin has devised a mental technique called *focusing* that enables practitioners to manipulate their brains in such a way that they reach new insights that lead to dramatic and beneficial behavioral changes. It is, in other words, a technique for learning. In focusing, one tries to get a "felt sense" of the problem, and through a series of focusing steps that turn attention away from the external environment and increase awareness of subtle emotional states and physical sensations, one reaches a point at which one experiences a "felt shift," an experience marked by a sudden release of tension, a feeling of deep physical relief, a sense that the problem or unclear feeling has been understood.

We've all experienced both focusing and felt shifts. One elementary example: you leave your house and soon have an uneasy feeling you have forgotten something. You "focus," trying to identify the problem: have you left the gas on? the water running? In each case you know that's not the correct answer because you feel no inward release. Finally you get the correct answer: with a "felt shift" a feeling of understanding, release from tension, and satisfaction sweeps over your body. It is, in other words, the Aha! moment we've discussed earlier.

Curious about what was happening in the brains of people who were experiencing a felt shift, Norman Don of the biophysics division of the American Dental Association wired them up to a machine that recorded their brain waves and made a computer analysis of over 8,432 EEG readings (the EEG, or electroencephalograph, records the dominant brainwave frequencies). He discovered that just before the subjects experienced a felt shift, their alpha and theta waves shifted. In each case, the insights were preceded by peak periods of the dominant alpha waves (10 cycles per second) and its subharmonics (5 and 2.5 cycles). Opposite periods—when the person engaged in focusing felt "stuck" or "blocked"—the alpha rhythm and its subharmonics collapsed. According to Don, these felt shifts indicate "reorganization at a higher level of integration." Evidently a felt shift represents that breakthrough from conflict to clarity when the dissipative structure of the brain, having been shifted by the fluctuations of the alpha and theta peaks that immediately preceded it, falls into a more comprehensive framework, escaping to a higher level. [109, 147]

CREATIVE THINKING. In a study of learning at Texas A&M, chemistry professor Thomas Taylor monitored the EEG of students in the process of what he called "synthesis thinking," that is, taking information they had just acquired and synthesizing it in an original and creative way to solve a difficult problem. According to Taylor, "An EEG recording during the chance moment in which a difficult technical concept suddenly 'made sense'" to the subject "showed an abrupt change in brain-wave patterns" that took place "in the theta range." The EEG recording Taylor appends to his study indicates a series of powerful fluctuations taking place throughout the subject's entire brain. [356]

BRAIN SYNCHRONIZATION. Scientists studying meditators have found that when the meditators reach a state of deep awareness and intense mental clarity, the two hemispheres of their brain—which ordinarily generate brain waves of different frequencies and amplitudes—become synchronized, both hemispheres generating the same brain waves. It's important to consider the relationship between the wave patterns of the two hemispheres. It is possible to have two identical wave patterns that are not synchronized; that is, the peak of one wave happens just when the valley of the other wave happens. In such a case, the two frequencies cancel each other out, and the amplitude is greatly decreased. However, when the peak of one brain-wave pattern exactly matches the peak of the other wave pattern, it is as if the amplitudes of the two waves are *combined*—the two waves are added together to produce a waveform *twice the height of the original waveform*; that is, the amplitude is doubled. So when the brain hemispheres operate in synchrony, the amplitude of the wave pattern throughout the entire cortex is powerfully increased.

This represents forceful whole-brain fluctuations, with the resulting potential for brain reorganization at a higher order.

Probably the world's leading authority on brain synchronization is Dr. Lester Fehmi, director of the Princeton Biofeedback Research Institute. His careful observations of the relationship between brain-wave activity and behavior have convinced him that hemispheric synchronization "is correlated experientially with a union with experience, an 'into-it-ness.' Instead of feeling separate and narrow-focused," he told me, "you tend to feel more into it—that is, unified with the experience, you *are* the experience—and the scope of your awareness is widened a great deal, so that you're including many more experiences at the same time. There's a whole-brain sensory integration going on, and it's as if you become less self-conscious and you function more intuitively."

It makes sense then that one of the sessions that aroused the greatest interest at a recent convention of the American Educational Research Association was a demonstration by a research group of how students can learn to focus their attention by synchronizing EEG activity in both hemispheres, using biofeedback equipment. Biofeedback researcher Jean Millay pointed out that after the intense quiet focus that accompanies brain synchronization, subjects in her studies frequently reported flashes of intuition or creative insight. Said Millay to AERA researchers, "Instead of measuring how bright or dumb students are, perhaps we should be teaching them how to focus their attention," by teaching them how to synchronize their brains.[38] Clearly students who can learn to synchronize their brain waves at will can enormously increase the potential of their brain for learning and growth.

This assumption is borne out by recent studies conducted by teachers in the Tacoma public school system. These teachers, under the direction of psychologist Devon Edrington, made use of "Hemi-Sync" tapes that used phased sound waves of specific frequencies designed to create brain-wave synchronization; they found that students who were taught, studied, and took tests while the Hemi-Sync tapes were playing did significantly better than students who were taught the same material by the same teachers without the benefits of the Hemi-Sync tapes.[94]

SUPERLEARNING. A number of techniques combining deep relaxation with information input to achieve rapid learning have aroused considerable interest in recent years, among them Bulgarian psychiatrist Georgi Lozanov's "Suggestopedia." Hundreds of schools and universities around the world had adopted the Lozanov method of rapid learning, and a vast amount of research has confirmed that this technique can result in astounding increases in the ability of students to absorb, process, store, manipulate, and recall information. Lozanov and other researchers have found, for example, that using his technique language students can easily learn five hundred new words per day (selected groups have learned up to three thousand new words per day), with only a few hours of learning. In most language courses, one hundred new words a day would be considered excellent, and students in these courses have a rapid loss of recall of the new words. Lozanov's students, on the other hand, had (in one reported study) a retention rate of 88 percent after six months. Reports of such superlearning feats arrive from Lozanov institutes around the world, and while educators argue about the magnitude of the learning increase brought about by the technique, there can be no doubt that the method dramatically enhances the brain's functioning.

The essential elements of the Lozanov technique are deep relaxation combined with synchronized rhythms in brain and body. After preliminary instructions in whole-body relaxation techniques, students relax in comfortable chairs while listening to strongly rhythmical but soothing music (the largo movements of concerti by such Baroque composers as Vivaldi, Telemann, Handel, and Bach are favored, as they move at a stately tempo of about 60 beats per minute that seems to synchronize with and stabilize the pulse and breathing rates). Physiologists found that simply listening to this music not only causes the heart rate and breathing to slow down, but also causes a decrease in blood pressure; in the brain, the low-amplitude, lower-frequency alpha waves increase and become dominant. To increase the body-brain synchronization, students are instructed to breathe rhythmically. The material to be learned is then presented to the students by the instructor in rhythmic bursts of information that are synchronized with their breathing.

The brain-boosting mechanisms at work in the Lozanov technique, as well as the other methods of superlearning, are based on Prigogine's idea of extreme fluctuations of energy driving a system into new, more coherent, more intricately interconnected order. The brain-body synchronization results in brain fluctuations much the way thousands of people marching in step can cause fluctuations in a bridge: the various elements of the brain are destabilized, able to release old patterns and programs, open to receive new information and reorganize in a new way. In this state of "ripeness" caused by the body-brain synchronization, vast amounts of new information can be assimilated.

TWILIGHT LEARNING. Biofeedback expert Thomas Budzynski of the University of Colorado Medical Center has done extensive research with the effects of suggestion and learning when the brain is in a theta state (theta waves, at about 3–7 cycles per second, are of even greater amplitude and lower frequency than alpha waves, and thus indicate greater energy fluctuations in the brain). Usually we produce large quantities of theta waves only in those movements between waking and sleep when we have vivid images, called *hypnagogic imagery*. Budzynski has devised a biofeedback-based device that notes when the user has entered his theta state and only then begins playing the material to be learned. Says Budzynski, "We take advantage of the fact that the hypnagogic state, the twilight state, between waking and sleep, has these properties of *uncritical acceptance of verbal material, or almost any material it can process.*" It is in such "altered" states of consciousness, Budzynkski says, that *"a lot of work gets done very quickly."*[59, 58] Again, as in Gendlin's focusing and Lozanov's brain synchronization, what Budzynski seems to be describing is the brain as a dissipative structure and its incredible ability to reorganize virtually instantaneously.

TOTAL RECALL. Many scientists now believe that a large part of everything we see or hear or otherwise sense—including things that are only unconsciously processed by our brains and never actually enter our awareness—is permanently stored away in the brain, ready to be instantaneously recalled. There have always been rare humans who have exhibited unbelievable powers of memory, being able, for example, to memorize long lists of numbers or nonsense words and then recall them perfectly fifty years later.

Then in a series of now-classic experimental brain operations, Canadian researcher Dr. Wilder Penfield, of McGill University, stimulated human brains with mild electrical currents. Since the brain itself has no pain receptors, Penfield was able to stimulate various sites while the patient was conscious and ask what feelings or reactions were evoked. Patients described a variety of startling perceptions, instantly recalling past events as if they were actually reliving them. When the electrode was moved slightly, totally different experiences were recalled. Said Penfield, "Every patient reported a word-for-word 'playback' of long-forgotten conversations, songs, jokes, childhood birthday parties—things that had only been spoken *once* in their entire lifetimes—all perfectly recorded." He concluded that virtually every experience is recorded permanently in the brain.[261]

Lozanov agrees, contending that his techniques don't trigger some abnormal "supermemory," but simply facilitate recall: we all have almost everything we've ever experienced or learned stored away; the problem is to recover the material. Says Lozanov: "The human mind remembers a colossal quantity of information, the number of buttons on a suit, steps on a staircase, panes in a window, footsteps to the bus stop. These 'unknown perceptions' show us the subconscious has startling powers."[252]

Other evidence of our powers of perfect recall of all or nearly all past events had been put forth by Dr. David Cheek, a gynecologist at Children's Hospital in San Francisco, who has done extensive work with subjects placed in deep hypnotic trance. Cheek hypnotized individuals who had undergone surgery during which they were anesthetized and supposedly totally unconscious, and discovered that they could repeat exact phrases spoken by the medical personnel in the operating room. Further, he found that such operating-room chatter could have a profound effect on the later recovery of the patients. So if a surgeon had perhaps muttered, "I don't know if this guy's going to make it," the patient, with subconscious recall of that prognosis, would be less strongly motivated to recover. Cheek recommends strongly that surgeons be very careful of what they say during operations, and suggests that positive or supportive statements can speed postoperative recovery significantly.

In his studies of deep hypnotic trance, Cheek also found that many hypnotized subjects are able to recall past events with lifelike clarity, even as far back as the moment of their birth. One subject, for example, recalled something the doctor had said when he was delivered. Though his mother did not remember it and thus had never told him, the doctor confirmed the accuracy of the subject's memory.[269] The researches of Cheek and other investigators of hypnosis, including a number of Russian researchers, indicate that subjects can recall astonishing amounts of information, such as the number of telephone poles passed while walking to first grade, statements made by some long-forgotten aunt while they were infants in the cradle—all those "unknown perceptions" Lozanov mentions.

THETA WAVES AND MEMORY

WHAT AN ENORMOUS WEALTH OF INFORMATION WE COULD call on if only we could gain access to this storehouse of "forgotten" knowledge we carry around in our heads. Imagine, for example, having perfect recall of all the books you have read. How do we gain access to our inner encyclopedia? One intriguing method scientists have been exploring is using that mysterious mind state we've already spoken of, that elusive time when our brains are generating large quantities of theta waves—the hypnagogic state or theta state. Interestingly, the theta state also is the period when our brains produce vivid memories. Budzynski and others studying this state have found that when subjects enter the theta state, they frequently find themselves mentally reliving or recalling events which had long been forgotten.

This quality was first stumbled onto by psychobiologist Dr. James McGaugh, of UC at Irvine while studying memory and learning in rats. It was known that electroconvulsive shocks could make rats forget what they had just learned, so McGaugh wondered if certain drugs could counteract that effect. Amazingly, he found that the drugs could actually bring back memories that had apparently been completely erased by the electroconvulsive shock. Further investigations showed that the shocks prevented new protein synthesis in the brain. Apparently, memory formation depends on the formation of new protein in the brain. (Thus, one explanation for Rosenzweig's findings that rats in enriched environments increased the size and complexity of their brains, and dramatically improved their memory, is that the increase in brain weight and neural size is a result of the increased protein synthesis in the brain associated with memory formation.)

Then McGaugh and his associates discovered that during the post-shock amnesia the rats showed virtually no theta waves in their brain. Focusing on this, the researchers discovered that, in the words of science writer Maya Pines, "the more theta waves appeared in an animal's EEG after a training session, the more it remembered. This was true in all cases. . . . Apparently, the best predictor of memory was the amount of theta waves recorded in the animal's brain. McGaugh now tells his students that 'if you want to learn, and you're a rat, it's a good idea to have some theta.' But he does not believe the theta waves are a sign of memory as such. Rather, they show that the brain is in the right state to process and store information."[267, 218]

Following up on this research, a number of investigators of biofeedback began training people to produce theta waves voluntarily, in hope of improving their memory. Among these researchers were Elmer and Alyce Green of the Menninger Foundation. They found theta "to be associated with a deeply internalized state and with a quieting of the body, emotions, and thoughts, thus allowing usually 'unheard or unseen things' to come to the consciousness in the form of hypnagogic memory." Unfortunately, large quantities of theta waves are difficult to produce: usually we only experience the state in those brief moments between wake and sleeping. Even if you intentionally try to produce theta waves you will in most cases quickly fall asleep. The Greens set out to train people—using special biofeedback machines—to enter the theta state without falling asleep. This accomplished, they discovered that the subjects frequently reported vivid memories of long-forgotten childhood events: "They were not like going through a memory in one's mind," write the Greens, "but rather like an experience, a reliving." They also found that those producing theta waves frequently had "new and valid ideas or syntheses of ideas, not primarily by deduction, but springing by intuition from unconscious sources."[130] Here we are reminded of the Texas A&M experiment indicating that when students suddenly arrived at the Eureka event, the Aha! experience, their brains were in the theta state.

As a result of their work the Greens are convinced that the theta state not only is conducive to memory and learning, but is the source of creative thinking. We only have to remember all the tales of great ideas and seminal discoveries—and even our own flashes of insight—that occur as the thinker is drowsing before a fire, walking alone upon a beach, gazing pensively into the distance: in other words, in that state of near-sleep reverie when the vivid memories and "syntheses of ideas . . . springing by intuition from unconscious sources" characteristic of the theta state are free to emerge. One explanation for this, we can assume, is that since theta waves are of even higher amplitude and lower frequency than alpha waves, they represent greater energy fluctuations in the brain, which can rearrange the neural connections, leading to new, richer, more complex intercommunication between the brain's cells, causing the dissipative structure to reorganize and escape to a higher order.

Since a major effect of the machines we will explore is the production of a profound state of relaxation and, in many cases, of the elusive theta state that dramatically boosts our ability to acquire new information and is the source of memories and creative thinking, it is possible that in this way such machines can enhance our learning abilities, thrust us into higher levels of creative thought, and provide access to that vast fund of information and memories we have stored away in our brains and "forgotten." Perhaps it's too much to expect that these machines will enable us to turn our memories on or off at will, or to pinpoint certain events or information we once acquired but now only vaguely recall and allow us to switch on our powers of total recall. But many scientists believe such abilities are possible; moreover, they are actively devising and experimenting with machines and drugs that will soon make them possible.

7

IN SEARCH OF THE WILD MIND MACHINE

I'VE DESCRIBED THE ACCIDENTAL WAY MY OWN EXPERIENCES aroused my curiosity about how certain stimuli intentionally introduced into the brain could apparently enhance mental functioning. A bit of isolation in a mountain lean-to, a few clicks on an alpha-wave biofeedback machine, and suddenly I began wondering how far this could go. If such simple techniques and devices could have such powerful effects, wouldn't it be possible to devise far more elegant, specialized, technologically advanced machines that would have even more intense and dramatic brain-boosting powers?

In investigating some of the literature available on the subject, I found that the use of machines to stimulate and alter the human brain is seen by many scientists as the most exciting and potentially revolutionary development in modern neuroscience. It's a development made possible and triggered by the synthesis of sudden and enormous advances in two diverse areas. On one hand are the quantum leaps in our understanding of how the brain works, including the revelations about the virtually instantaneous growth of dendrites and synapses in response to experience, and the discovery of hundreds and perhaps thousands of new brain chemicals. On the other hand are the enormous technological advances being made, including increasingly sensitive and sophisticated computerized devices, lasers, neuroelectric stimulators, microelectrodes that can monitor the electrical activity of a single neuron. The simultaneous developments have seemed to fuse and feed off each other, with each discovery about the brain spurring the invention of more sophisticated devices with which to study that new aspect of the brain, and each leap forward in the technology providing tools that generated still more surprising revelations about the brain.

Happy that my curiosity had led me into a hotbed of scientific activity, I began to read the literature more systematically, to talk with scientists engaged in brain research, and found what seemed to be an extraordinary unanimity of opinion and interest. Scientists in virtually every discipline concerned with investigating the brain—electroencephalography, biophysics, neuroendocrinology, neurochemistry, neuroanatomy, bioelectricity, psychiatry, psychobiology, psychology—were excited by the wealth of new ideas and information (including much of what we have discussed in the preceding chapters) and were enthusiastically exploring the potentials of brain-machine interaction.

However, as I delved deeper it became clear that underlying the apparent unanimity was a serious division, that the investigators of the mind-machine connection were split into two factions. In the first faction were those scientists who want to use new machines for medical and therapeutic purposes. They are interested in how the devices can be used to treat schizophrenia, depression, anxiety, Parkinson's disease, epilepsy, Alzheimer's disease, mental retardation, Down's syndrome, and so on. When they speak of using machines to enhance brain functioning or mental powers, their main concern is with restoring normal brain functioning to those who have suffered brain damage or loss of mental powers because of sickness, stroke, accident, or birth defects.

The second faction comprises experimenters who are eager to explore the possibilities of using mind devices on perfectly healthy, psychologically fit people, expressly for the purposes of stimulating mental excellence. One research foundation with this orientation has recently undertaken a study of "The Neurobiology of Excellence," with the stated purpose of seeking tools for developing "extreme proficiency in performing selected tasks," and improving "such 'higher-brain-function' skills as information processing (e.g. extremely rapid mathematical calculation, conducting a symphony orchestra) memory (short-term/'encyclopedic'/photographic), and concentration."[338]

TOM SWIFT AND HIS MAGNIFICENT MIND MACHINE

A PROBLEM FOR THE SECOND FACTION IS THAT RESEARCH IS enormously expensive, and virtually all money now being provided to psychobiological research by the U.S. government and other sources is given to research projects intended to have medical/therapeutic value. Thus, while scientists in institutes such as the NIMH might have personal interests in discovering how to induce extraordinary mental abilities, their projects are by necessity directed to what are deemed more socially useful—i.e., therapeutic—ends. This makes sense, since it is the duty of a democratic society to ensure the welfare of all its citizens, and all of us share an interest in seeking to eliminate illness and disabilities. However, the mind-machine creators insist that a society's welfare also depends on improving the intelligence of all its citizens and nurturing the original, creative ideas of its finest minds, since those are the ideas that spur the society to higher levels of achievement.

In addition, the ideas of the scientific establishment about what constitutes even legitimate "medical" research often seem shortsighted and even self-serving to many who labor in the fields of brain stimulation. Dr. Robert O. Becker, for example, is the most widely known and deeply respected researcher in the field of electrical stimulation of living tissue. He stunned the scientific world with his well-documented experiments proving that electromagnetic energy could cause the regeneration of the amputated limbs of certain animals, and his research has led him to surmise that electrical stimulation is the key to remarkable human healing and growth potentials. Says Becker, "I believe that, in time, we can induce total regeneration in man, not only in his limbs, but also in his heart and other vital organs." Among the vital organs capable of such regeneration, he believes, is the brain. "In my opinion," says Becker, "this is the most important area of medical research today. For the first time since Hippocrates, the medical scientist has the ability, to a degree, to control the growth process. This is an enormous quantum jump in medical technology." However, Becker grumbles, "We have the electrical . . . technology and we have the evidence. But we don't have the funding. NIH [the National Institutes of Health] won't even give us a twenty-cent stamp to take a look at this. The establishment is too busy cutting and burning and charging huge fees to do it, while thousands continue to suffer."[140]

So while the psychobiologists doing their research in the institutes and universities have access to funding, the investigators of brain improvement are for the most part left out in the cold, scraping up funds wherever they can find them. Often they must subsidize their research with money they earn from working second jobs. Like the ex-NASA engineer who recently gained a bit of fame by single-handedly constructing in his garage a rocket and space capsule which experts believe could successfully launch a man into space and bring him back to earth (he scavenged junk heaps and used government-surplus parts that had cost the government millions to build and that he bought for a few dollars), these brain investigators put together their devices with whatever materials they can afford to buy. Naturally, the "establishment" scientists are sometimes suspicious of them, particularly since the innovators in the mind-enhancement area often have one foot in the scientific world and one foot in the marketplace.

The rationale of these mind-machine entrepreneurs is that if the scientific establishment won't fund the necessary research, they will find the money by selling their machines to the public. If perchance they happen to get rich in the process, so much the better—in fact, it's a grand old American tradition, exemplified by Thomas Edison and Tom Swift, that inventiveness in the service of humanity combined with initiative and an understanding of commerce will be rewarded with wealth.

As I spoke with them, a pattern quickly emerged: they all believe their machines hold enormous potential benefits for humanity. Many of them have medical degrees or academic training as scientists. All of them were well versed in the latest brain research, and claimed that their devices made use of this research—they all produced heaps of research papers by mainstream brain scientists that laid down the foundation or explained the principles on which their machines were based. And in every case they expressed their eagerness to validate the efficacy of their devices through rigorous, controlled scientific studies.

But despite their eagerness for scientific approval, the makers of these machines sometimes operate under different rules than accepted science. True scientific research is founded on value-free studies that are under intense scrutiny by others in the scientific community and that can be replicated by other researchers. Most studies make use of control groups, often using double-blind studies (in which neither the subjects nor the researchers know which is being subjected to the phenomenon being studied and thus are not influenced by their expectations). Most studies use large numbers of subjects, administer a variety of pre- and post-study tests, and use long-term follow-up studies.

The mind-machine entrepreneurs, on the other hand, say they have neither the money nor the resources for such expensive and time-consuming studies. With many of the devices it is impossible to do double-blind testing, since it's impossible to disguise from either the researcher or the subject that the subject is indeed wearing a device emitting flashing lights and odd noises. Also, the aspects of the brain being studied— things like creativity, intuition, intelligence, serenity—are not easily reduced to statistics. Says one such entrepreneur, Robert Monroe, who has created a system for synchronizing the brain by means of a patented process he calls "Hemi-Sync,"

"Pure science simply likes to find out and doesn't like to apply its findings. . . . My great joy is making something of value out of this discovery. I know the phenomenon exists, but I don't know the scope. To do the real science is the province of others. Why does Hemi-Sync work? Sometimes I get into the morass of that question, though I prefer not to. If something works, I always say, use it!"[277]

When I investigated the machines described in the next few chapters, the inventor/researchers generally provided me with many studies of the effectiveness of the devices; and while impressive, the studies were often based on small samples, sometimes with no control groups, and no follow-up procedure. This doesn't mean the studies were wrong or misleading—in fact, in most cases the studies clearly indicated that *something* powerful was happening to the subjects using the devices. But they simply don't constitute scientific proof. The researchers provided me with even greater numbers of case histories, in which individuals who had used the devices attested to their effectiveness, describing remarkable and sometimes astounding transformations as a result of their experiences. But while such "anecdotal evidence" is fascinating, impressive, and, in large quantity, compelling, it does not constitute scientific proof.

Even "pure" scientists who deeply believe certain types of brain enrichment can produce unprecedented growth in brain cells and mental powers remain hesitant about encouraging the widespread use of machines that purport to be brain boosters. One such is Robert O. Becker, who cautions, "Scientific evidence may indicate that there are specific and important effects of certain of these fields on the operation of the brain, but rock-hard scientific facts are needed. If someone uses one of these machines and something bad happens, the entire technology could go down the drain, or seem like the kind of charlatanism that abounded in the 1880s."[140]

NINETY-SEVEN-POUND WEAKLING SETS FORTH UNDAUNTED TO EXPLORE THE LAST FRONTIER

STILL, DESPITE THE LACK OF IRONCLAD PROOF OF THE TOTAL safety of these machines, I was eager to give them a try. I was convinced by my research that the human brain has a capacity for growth that remains undiscovered and untapped. I knew from my talks with scientists that brain growth can happen with astonishing speed, and that the most effective ways of inducing such growth are through what the scientists called "super-enriched environments," "intense sensory stimulation," "forced challenge," and "energy fluctuations leading to reorganization at a higher level of coherence." It seemed clear that the most efficient tools for such growth and transformation were devices specifically designed by brain experts to cause an influx of energy—whether in the form of flashing lights, phased sound waves, negative ions, alterations in gravity in the cerebellum, fluctuations in brain waves—to those parts of the brain most susceptible to such influxes.

I strongly suspected as a result of my own experiences— my flame-gazing and weasel's-eye visions on the lonely mountaintop, and my energy infusion from the alpha-wave machine—that high-tech brain stimulation can tremendously enhance mental capabilities. I had no doubt that there were things lurking inside my skull that were eager to come out, that my ninety-seven-pound weakling of a brain could pump mental iron and emerge as a slab-muscled two-hundred pound heavy thinker capable of kicking sand in the face of any bully metaphysician on the beach. And besides, I was ready for a bit of exploration.

But mostly there was a gut feeling. I was ready. Ever since my first encounter with Jim Hawkins hiding in the apple barrel in *Treasure Island* I'd felt I was destined for adventure on the high seas, pieces of eight, flagons of grog, and buried treasure chests. Cultural analysts tell us that where once the uncivilizable, the criminals, crazies, and seekers had set out for unknown savage lands to find cities of gold, two-headed cannibals, maze-dwelling Minotaurs, fakirs on flying carpets, and paradisiacal tropic isles, now the unknown lands lie within. "We're exploring the last frontier," say the brain scientists. Says Hemi-Sync inventor Monroe, "In creating my blend of sound vibrations I can possibly let [people] experience something beyond their normal five senses. This then becomes an exciting opportunity for exploration. Most of us would love to be an Admiral Byrd or Marco Polo. Well, we can, and those deep explorations into other states of consciousness can be as adventurous as any space exploration."

So I was ready to set out, ready to risk the great desert of the limbic system, cross the mountains and canyons of the neocortex wilderness, explore the rank, dense jungles of intertwined neurons, axons, and dendrites, leap death-defying across the yawning synaptic gaps, confront the monsters and demons of hypothalamic secretions, all in hope of finding tropic isles of gentle breezes where the fruit is sweet.

What follows is an account of my experiences with some of these brain boosters. As I mentioned earlier, most of these machines, while commercially available, are advertised and sold as "stress-reduction" devices—largely because of government regulations that forbid their makers to make any claims of healing or therapeutic effects. Most of them are in fact being used as therapeutic devices, and have been found effective for alleviating a variety of ills including high blood pressure, anxiety, depression, pain, Down's syndrome, autism, schizophrenia, learning disabilities, and sexual dysfunction. I will not deal with the therapeutic uses of these devices except now and then to mention them in passing. My interest is in the aspects of these machines their makers and supporters speak of in private with fervent belief: brain enhancement. Can these machines stimulate growth of brain tissue? Can they spur you to new levels of mental achievement? Can they boost creativity and enhance your problem-solving abilities? Can they make you smarter? Wiser? Better?

PART II

It is only by means of the sciences of life that the quality of life can be radically changed. The release of atomic energy marks a great revolution in human history, but . . . the really revolutionary revolution is to be achieved, not in the external world, but in the souls and flesh of human beings.

—ALDOUS HUXLEY

Nothing makes sense in biology except in the light of evolution.

—THEODOSIUS DOBZHANSKY

Consequently: he who wants
To have right without wrong,
Order without disorder,
Does not understand the principles
Of heaven and earth.
He does not know how
Things hang together.

—CHUANG TZU

What if you slept, and what if in your sleep you dreamed, and what if in your dream you went to heaven and there plucked a strange and beautiful flower, and what if when you awoke you had the flower in your hand? Ay, what then?

—SAMUEL TAYLOR COLERIDGE

8

WE SING THE MIND ELECTRIC, PART ONE: TENS

ZAPPING THE CRANIAL WHEATFIELDS WITH MR. LIGHT. "What we have here,'" said Joseph Light, "is a Transcutaneous Electro-Neural Stimulator—a TENS unit." He placed a black box about the size of a cigarette pack on the table between us. It had a dial on it, and two long wires were attached, each ending in a small flat metal slab covered with moist terry-cloth pads. "Those two slabs are electrodes," he said. "Put them inside your socks, one against each ankle, and we'll turn you on." He chuckled.

We were sitting in a fast-food restaurant, right beside the salad bar, and as the patrons browsed through the bean sprouts they cast sidelong glances at the odd black device, and the obviously deranged character sticking wires inside his socks. "Contact," said the appropriately named Mr. Light, turning on the switch. "I'll turn this up a bit." He adjusted the dial. "Can you feel it now?" My ankles began to hum, an odd, rather pleasant tingling sensation.

Wondering if perhaps I might commence to glow like an electric light or begin transmitting a radio talk show of my own thoughts to the nearby burger munchers, I asked Mr. Light, who has done extensive research into the effects of electromagnetism on the human nervous system and owns

111

Biomedical Instruments, Inc., a company that sells biofeedback and electromedical equipment, to explain what was happening to me. The battery-powered TENS unit sitting between us, he said, was producing an extremely mild pulsating current (from 5 to 200 microamperes—by comparison, a common 60-watt household light bulb draws about 0.5 amp, or thousands of times more current) which was passing through my body and brain.

Essentially, he explained, the brain is an electrically powered and electricity-generating organ. It is composed of an estimated 100 billion neurons—more neurons than there are stars in the universe—each as complex as a small computer, each producing and transmitting electrical impulses. These electrical impulses travel from the cell body down long fibers called axons until they reach a junction, or synapse, with another neuron. At this point, the electrical impulses fire chemical messengers, called neurotransmitters, across the synaptic gap to receptors on the next cell. The receiving neuron then generates its own electrical impulse, which again is sent to other neurons to which it is connected. Since each neuron can be connected with thousands of other neurons, each simultaneously sending and receiving electrical impulses to and from thousands of other neurons, a single signal from one neuron can quickly reach, and electrically alter, millions of other neurons.

Since each of these millions of neurons is unique, displaying slightly different response patterns, the brain is an unimaginably complex electrical network with billions of electromagnetic impulses flying in all directions every second. According to the National Academy of Sciences, "A single human brain has a greater number of possible connections among its nerve cells than the total number of atomic particles in the universe."

In addition to the neurons, the brain contains billions of glial cells—by some estimates as many as ten times more glial cells than neurons. According to Light, recent research has indicated that these glial cells are also electrically sensitive, acting much like liquid crystals, resonating in harmony with the surrounding electrical fields. What this means, Light pointed out, is that the glial cells may act as semiconductors, picking up faint electrical impulses from the nervous system and the environment and amplifying them thousands of times, much the way transistors amplify very faint signals in electronic circuits. Thus, while the neurons can be sending signals over networks of interconnected cells (something like an enormously complex telephone system, in which all individual telephones are connected, however indirectly, by wires), the signals are also amplified and carried throughout the brain by the glial cells (something like radio and television signals being broadcast over great areas), to be received by any neurons "tuned in" to the proper frequency.

And what is more, scientists are now finding that while individual neurons generate their own unique signals, they also tend to act cooperatively in networks of thousands or millions of cells, humming and throbbing simultaneously to the same electrical signal. Clearly, then, said Light, all our thoughts and perceptions essentially consist of the interactions of complex electromagnetic fields that constantly sweep across the brain.

Imagine a vast field of wheat, the millions of individual stalks of wheat being blown about and buffeted by powerful winds sweeping through the field in odd, unpredictable patterns. As we watch from a nearby hilltop we see areas where whole sections of wheat are being bent to the north, other areas where circular gusts of wind are forming whirling vortexes of swirling wheat. In a way, explained Light, the brain is like the wheatfield. The individual stalks of wheat are the neurons. The patterns of energy we see sweeping through the field are like our thoughts and perceptions, and the unpredictable winds that swirl through the field causing those thoughts and perceptions are the energy that is constantly flowing into and through the brain. That energy is electromagnetic: by blowing an electromagnetic wind through our brain, we can make the neural networks blow in certain patterns, and those patterns are thoughts and perceptions.

But of course, Light pointed out, this metaphor is a vast

oversimplification. For not only do electrical patterns constantly blow through our brains like a big wind, each individual wheat stalk is itself generating electrical energy, so that the vast patterns we see from our hilltop are also patterns generated by the cooperative action of the millions of wheat stalks. In fact, our brains generate so much electrical energy we can detect it clear through the thick bone of our skull simply by pressing sensors known as electrodes against our scalp to get a readout of the electrical waves called an EEG. Decades of scientific investigation of the brain's electrical activity have proved that alterations in the EEG represent alterations in thoughts and perceptions. When these electrical waves change, either in frequency or in amplitude, our state of mind changes too: one pattern of waves for doing arithmetic, say, another very different one for daydreaming. So, explained Light, it makes sense that shooting an electrical current through the brain should directly, at times radically, alter one's mental state.

As we have already noted, different brain-wave frequencies can, in a general way, indicate what sort of activity the brain is engaged in. The rapid beta waves (which vibrate at a frequency ranging from about 13 to 30 hertz—abbreviated Hz, and meaning cycles per second) are associated with a "normal" level of mental arousal, with attention directed externally. The slower alpha waves (8-13Hz) can indicate relaxation. The very slow theta waves (4-7 Hz) are often indicative of deep reverie, mental imagery, and access to memories. The ultraslow delta waves (0.5-4 Hz) generally accompany deep sleep. An explanation for this association between brain electrical activity and mental states is that certain electrical frequencies cause individual neurons or collections of neurons to release certain neurochemicals. These electrically triggered brain chemicals are the controlling factors of our mental states and the behaviors that result from them: fear, lust, depression, ecstasy, craving, love, shyness, all are the effects of combinations of certain neurotransmitters. Precise mixtures of these brain juices can produce extraordinarily specific mental states, such as fear of the dark, or intense concentration.

The important point, said Light, is that certain very specific electrical frequencies trigger the release of certain precise types of neurochemicals. The electrical frequency Light's machine was turned to was 7.83 Hz. This frequency, he claimed, is the same as that of the electrical field resonating between the earth and the ionosphere, and thus has unique powers, seemingly integrating and harmonizing one's body and brain with the earth's electromagnetic energy. It's as if, he said, the earth were resonating like a great bell, and suddenly your brain begins to vibrate at the same frequency, seeming to become in tune with—almost one with—the ambient frequency. Such an integration or resonance, said Light, causes the brain and body to operate with great coherence, and can produce states of elevated consciousness. In fact, he said, when meditators experience samadhi, or a feeling of oneness and harmony with all creation, researchers find that the EEGs of the meditators show their brain waves to be in this same frequency range. While Light talked, I seemed to feel my eyes bulge out slightly—a pleasurable sort of bulging—and felt a great desire to laugh wildly. The idea that I was resonating in tune with the earth was bizarre but somehow delightful. My mind seemed extraordinarily alert, and I shot rapid-fire questions at him.

Could it be so simple? I wondered if simply by sending a specific current through my brain I could call forth, for example, my exact mental state at the instant I hit a home run in a baseball game twenty years ago. "The frequency of the wave is important," said Light, "but even more important is the *shape* of the wave." A single frequency, such as 7.83 Hz, can be delivered in an infinite number of waveforms, ranging from the familiar regular rolling *sinusoidal* pattern, to jagged, irregularly shaped sawtooth waves, to waves that are rectangular or squared off, flat on top and flat on the bottom. And each different waveform at each different frequency will have a different effect on the user's brain, causing the release of a different combination of neurochemicals. One Japanese TENS researcher, it seems, discovered that the best waveform for producing a certain type of pain relief was Vivaldi's *Four*

Seasons as synthesized by computer and translated into an electrical signal.

"Some waveforms are very good for people who want to stop smoking, a different frequency and waveform will help someone withdraw from heroin, and another will make you extraordinarily alert," said Light. Drawing the particular waveform he was using for this TENS, a spike-tipped mountain-range shape, Light explained that this waveform and frequency had its own unique effect. Theoretically, he claimed, one could design a device to induce a specific wave form and frequency that could cause the user to experience utter terror, visionary imagination, violent nausea, or oceanic bliss.

Yes, yes, I cried. I felt as if I were bursting at the seams. Full of wonder and excitement, I told Light some of my feelings about brain research. I told him about an article I was in the process of writing about the brain. I told him how I had become interested in the brain. At that moment a series of studies I had read about a variety of subjects, including the relation between protein synthesis and memory and the biochemical basis of addiction, all flew together in my skull and I understood something new. Gesturing wildly and scribbling on a paper napkin, I began to explain my new insight. . . . Suddenly I stopped, with my mouth hanging open in wild surmise. People seated in nearby booths were peering at me with great interest. "Listen to me talk!" I said to Light. "Jabbering like a wired-up monkey!"

Light gave me a demonic grin and pointed his finger at the black gizmo on the table, and I realized that all this while subtle little electrical waves had been insinuating their way into my brain. I burst out laughing, filled with immense pleasure. I felt that my brain was working faster and more efficiently than ever before—ideas were tumbling into place so fast I could hardly capture them.

Light chuckled again and explained that the machine was causing my brain to release large quantities of painkilling, euphoria-causing *endorphins* as well as some other brain chemicals associated with increased mental activity. "Once I had to drive to meet someone for a conference," he said. "The guy lived six hundred miles away. I hooked myself up to this device and wore it while I drove. I made it the whole way, had my conference, turned around, and drove the whole way back, getting lots of mental work done all the while, and when I got back I wasn't even tired."

STUMBLING ONTO THE SECRET STRUGGLE FOR ELECTRICAL WORLD DOMINATION

IF THE DEVICE WORKED BY STIMULATING THE RELEASE OF SPE-cific neurochemicals, I mused, and since scientists now believe there are neurochemicals mediating such mind states as love, hate, fear, courage, serenity, and deep concentration, then it should be possible to electrically stimulate each of these emotions and more. All you would have to do is find the right waveform and frequency. "Just think," I joked, "you could zap someone with a love wave!"

Light nodded, and smiled at me. "Yes," he said, "in fact some researchers are working on that project already." As my jaw dropped, he spoke of other projects even more bizarre, arcane and top-secret projects conducted by the U.S. and Russian governments as well as by private researchers: devices that could send electrical signals into the brain without direct contact by electrodes (making it possible to aim the device at someone from a distance and alter his brain waves); projects for altering the consciousness of whole populations by bouncing specific electrical waves off satellites, off the moon! It seemed there was a vast underground network of bioelectricians busily tinkering away with electromagnetic devices that could potentially change the world. This is crazy, I said, I've never heard any of this stuff! Light looked over both shoulders to make sure no one was eavesdropping.

"There are important elements in the scientific community, powerful people, who are very much interested in these areas," he said *sotto voce*, "but they have to keep most of their work secret. Because as soon as they start to publish some of these sensitive things, they have problems in their lives. You see, they work on research grants, and if you follow the research being done, you find that as soon as these scientists publish something about this, their research funds are cut off. There are areas in bioelectric research where very simple techniques and devices can have mind-boggling effects. Conceivably, if you have a crazed person with a bit of technical background, he can do a lot of damage."

Light leaned across the table, speaking with excitement. "There are certain frequencies you can transmit onto a city that can render people useless, make them nauseous." He told me of the visionary, eccentric electrical genius Nikola Tesla, inventor of flourescent lighting, the alternating-current generator, wireless radio, and much more, who one day in 1898 hooked up a simple electrical oscillator the size of a small alarm clock to an iron pillar in his Manhattan workshop, switched it on, and caused a shimmying resonance so powerful that it was carried through the substance of Manhattan like an earthquake, shattering windows, shaking buildings, and causing panic across the entire lower part of the island.

"Electrical vibrations," whispered Light. "We're talking about powerful stuff, and it's a supersensitive area for the government. Because they've done intensive research since the 1940s, and basically we do have psychic warfare existing between us and the USSR. So we're getting into an area where they want to keep the information confidential and hushed-up, because it can be dangerous if it gets into the wrong hands. I'm not talking about simple TENS units. But when you start applying the technology to the mind, you get into things like mind control, moving objects with mind power, and this means the potential for mentally shutting down computers, missile-guidance systems, satellites . . ."

I nodded, convinced I had stumbled onto another one of those outcroppings of pure paranoia you find so often along the borders and fringes of the scientific world. This is all science fiction, I thought, weird scientists tinkering away in dank basement laboratories. Delusions of persecution, mad fantasies of magical forbidden powers, electro-Manichean struggles between good and evil. It was lunacy. But it was *damned interesting* lunacy, and I was eager to hear more. I turned up the TENS device a bit, enjoying the delicious resonant shimmying in my anklebones, as Joseph Light talked earnestly and excitedly about love guns, battery-powered intelligence boxes, fear-shooters, and memory machines. Electrical perturbations stormed through my neurons and my brain circuits hummed.

FROM EGYPTIAN EEL STOMPING TO SKULL SEISMOLOGY

THE ENERGIZED FEELING STAYED WITH ME ALL THAT EVENING, and lingered a bit on the next day. I resolved to read more about bioelectricity and to speak with scientists in the field to understand more clearly how this phenomenon worked. In the following weeks I pursued these investigations, and discovered how ignorant I had been of this subject. What was chastening was that the stories Joseph Light had told me were verified or supported by almost everyone else in the field with whom I spoke. What I had seen as paranoid fantasies were accepted by electronics experts as facts of life. I found that a number of government security and defense agencies *were* supporting this type of research, and that much of it was indeed classified. I heard rumors of a great Mind Race between the superpowers, battles for psychic powers generated by bioelectrical fields. I heard how the Russians had bombarded the American embassy in Moscow with a nasty variety of electrical waves, causing workers to come down with a variety of illnesses, including cancer. I heard of attempts to alter the consciousness of certain heads of state at a distance using electronic transmitters. Everywhere I turned, someone else seemed to have another story more weird than the last. So weird, at last, that I decided to limit myself to the verifiable facts, and try to understand how electricity could influence brain function.

First, I discovered that the use of electrical stimulation is far from new. The ancient Egyptians apparently used natural electrical stimulation quite frequently, zinging themselves with the Nile electric catfish, which can be seen on Egyptian tomb reliefs. Some two thousand years ago a Greek physician, Scribonius Largus, was known for his "seashore treatment," which he prescribed for sufferers of pain (particularly gout). The patient was advised to put one foot on an electrical torpedo ray and the other foot on wet sand: the electrical circuit was completed, the patient got zapped, the pain was alleviated. Similar electric-eel treatments have been widely reported throughout history, and are still used in some primitive cultures.

By the nineteenth century the use of a variety of devices that generated continuous or pulsating electrical current was widespread, and people were fascinated with the almost mystical powers attributed to electricity. Many saw electricity as a key to life itself, like Mary Shelley, who wrote of a doctor who put together parts of cadavers and was able to spark the dead flesh (and the dead brain) to life with a powerful zap of electricity. (Unfortunately Dr. Frankenstein's experiment had a few unforeseen complications.) Electrical-stimulation devices were most frequently used for therapeutic purposes, and the literature is full of electrical cures for such conditions as epilepsy, nervous debility, rheumatism, diabetes, impotence, and neuralgia. Interestingly, there were also persistent reports of electrical stimulation having remarkable effects on the brain, or at least on mental states—subjects would enter trancelike states, experience euphoria, mental imagery, elevated mental states. There are reports of people suffering from what we would today call depression and anxiety returning to normalcy after electrical stimulation. (The electrotherapy devices of the time used mild currents and had little similarity to modern electroconvulsive or "shock" therapy [ECT] that explodes such a powerful electrical jolt into the brain that the subject is sent into convulsions.)

Unfortunately, it was so easy to put together a device that

would send an electrical current into a willing subject that the field was soon full of charlatans, electro-snake-oil salesmen with traveling medicine shows, demonstrating "galvanic miracle cures" and "Voltaic Mesmerism" at the sideshows of county fairs, in theaters, and in the drawing rooms of gullible subjects. Since the type and strength of the current, waveform, and frequency used varied wildly, some of these devices were clearly dangerous. Inevitably, folks got zapped, sizzled, fried, and shocked. The medical establishment became so concerned that a commission to investigate electrotherapy was appointed, and the commission's widely publicized report, issued in 1910, was so critical of the practice that it disappeared from legitimate medical practice almost overnight.

But while medical practitioners shunned the use of electrical stimulation, research scientists became increasingly intrigued by the physiological and psychological effects of electricity, particularly in conjunction with the electrical activity of the brain. By the late 1920s scientists had discovered that by placing electrodes against the skull, they could detect and record the electrical activities of areas of the brain. This brain-wave activity, the electroencephalogram, was recorded in squiggly lines on long pieces of paper. But while the EEG patterns provided some information about what was happening in the brain—certain frequencies indicated attention, sleep, excitation, drowsiness—much of the information remained maddeningly indecipherable.

One problem was that EEG electrodes were separated from the brain by the thick barrier of the skull. The scientists were like seismologists, measuring subtle tremors on the surface of the earth and trying to infer from them what activity was taking place in the earth's interior. The solution was obvious: if the EEG from outside the skull didn't provide the necessary information, then the scientists would have to drill into the skull and implant the electrodes directly in the brain tissue.

LEARNING TO PUSH THE PLEASURE BUTTONS

AS EARLY AS THE MID-1920s A SWISS PHYSIOLOGIST, WALTER Hess, had begun investigating the effects of electrically stimulating certain areas deep inside the brains of cats. Surgically implanting thin electrical wires that were completely insulated except at their very tips, Hess found that extremely mild electrical currents could cause a cat immediately to undergo dramatic changes in behavior—stimulation of one area would cause the cat to fly into a spitting, howling rage; current directed to another nearby area triggered fear and terror. Hess found that any behavior that appeared to be the result of powerful emotion could be triggered if the right area of the brain was stimulated. But was what the cat was experiencing true emotion, or simply some mechanical response? Was it really possible that emotions themselves—those things we often believe are most truly *us*, our loves, fears, dreams—could be triggered as automatically as causing our knee to jerk by striking it with a small rubber mallet? Were we little more than robots, susceptible to emotional changes at the twist of a knob sending electrical current into parts of our mental machine?

Dr. Wilder Penfield's discovery that electrical stimulation of the human brain evoked perfect memories of long-forgotten events seemed to indicate that much of what we experience, even material that we have never been conscious of experiencing, is stored away in the brain in such a way that it can be precisely recalled (or called into consciousness for the first time ever) at any future time. Penfield concluded, "A synaptic facilitation is established by each original experience. If so, that permanent facilitation could guide a subsequent stream of neuronal impulses activated by the current of the electrode even years later."[261]

If we understand Penfield's idea of "synaptic facilitation" to be taking place on the level of thousands or millions of interconnected neurons, then clearly the contents of our brains—memories, emotions, images, ideas—are stored away in the form of vast but quite distinct neural networks connected by neuronal impulses. The networks for similar ideas or perceptions—say, the subtle difference in taste among wines of the same type—would be made up of almost all the same neurons, except for a few thousand here or there that would distinguish one wine from another. This would explain why a simple low-impulse electrical current applied to one highly specific group of neurons could, by "synaptic facilitation," activate a richly intertwined group of memories, perceptions, sensations, in the same way a simple sniff of a beloved wine can light up an entire neural memory network in a wine connoisseur.

While Penfield was stimulating various areas of the brain and trying to map out which areas seemed to control language, memory, speech, and specific emotions and sensations, another scientist, James Olds, with associate Peter Milner, was taking a different approach. Implanting electrodes in a certain area of the brains of rats, he found that electrical stimulation seemed to cause the rats to feel intense pleasure. Electrodes implanted in slightly different spots seemed to cause rats to experience rage, fear, and distinct displeasure when those centers were stimulated. What would happen, Olds wondered, if rats were permitted to trigger their own pleasure or "reward" centers?

After implanting the electrodes, Olds attached the wires to a device that allowed the rats to turn on the juice and give themselves a short jolt of joy by pressing a foot pedal. The rats were ecstatic, reveling in a tireless orgy of self-stimulation. They attacked the foot pedals with such hoggish verve they seemed possessed, pressing the levers as often as five thousand times an hour, and gladly underwent all sorts of arduous experiences, like crossing painfully shocking electrical grids, for the chance to press the pleasure pedal. Obsessed with pleasure, they would pass up food, drink, and rest, and literally starve themselves to death, stimulating themselves until they passed out with exhaustion. And when they awoke they would begin again.*[245]

Everyone was fascinated with Olds's research. The problem was that none of the scientists could understand the mechanism at work. What could be so pleasurable about a jolt of electricity in the brain? The scientists were to remain baffled by this pleasure effect for many years.

However, while the cause remained a mystery, many scientists of the 1950s were beginning to suspect that electrical stimulation of the brain was perhaps the most powerful technique for altering consciousness and behavior that had been discovered. Dr. Robert Heath, head of the neurology/psychiatry department at Tulane University School of Medicine, created a firestorm of controversy when in 1950 he became the first scientist to implant electrodes in the human brain and leave them in place for long periods. He used such electrodes both to record and stimulate: he made recordings of the EEG in the depths of the brains of people who were experiencing rage, seizures, hallucinations, sexual arousal; and by stimulating various sites in the subjects' brains he found he could trigger outbursts of joy, pleasure, fear.

His patients were all sufferers of seemingly incurable mental diseases—severe schizophrenics, homicidal psychotics, suicidal depressives—and Heath's research forced him to the conclusion that the unifying characteristic of all these mental disorders is that the subject has "an imbalance between pleasure and pain," with little or no ability to experience pleasure, and conversely a greatly exaggerated ability to experience pain, anguish, loneliness. These severe psychotics, Heath realized, were like Olds's rats being constantly tormented by electrodes stimulating their pain/displeasure centers. Why not actually implant working electrodes in their pleasure centers

---

*Interestingly, the wired-up rats turned into extraordinary learners. Mazes that took ordinary rats long periods of trial and error to learn the wired rats learned with astonishing speed. They also remembered longer and more clearly than did the nonstimulated rats. Curious. It also seemed as if the electrical stimulation itself was making the rats smarter. But of course, as all brain scientists knew in those days, that was impossible. We will return to this curious side effect later.

124

instead, and give them the pleasure they'd never been able to experience?

Heath began implanting electrodes in patients' brains, and allowing them to self-stimulate themselves to produce pleasure. He found that many of his most violent or intractable cases experienced immediate transformations and recoveries. Some of his cases he provided with small control boxes so they could stimulate their pleasure centers at will. Not only did such self-stimulation make depressions, delusions, violent rages, hallucinations, and some epileptic seizures go away, it also alleviated pain in subjects who had experienced chronic, intractable pain for many years. According to Heath, "Each system of the brain (pleasure and pain) is seemingly capable of overwhelming or inhibiting the other. Activation of the pleasure system by electrical stimulation or by administration of drugs eliminates signs and symptoms of emotional or physical pain, or both, and obliterates changes or recordings associated with the painful state."[276]

In the 1950s the reigning technique for approaching mental disorders was psychoanalysis. The great master was Freud, with his message that psychological problems could be traced to childhood traumas and unresolved complexes. Heath burst into this world like a Mad Hatter at a staid tea party. "I never thought that mental disease was anything other than biological," he has said. At that time such thoughts were pure heresay, reductionism of the worst sort. The Freudians had apparently forgotten that the master himself had written, "In view of the intimate connection between things physical and mental, we may look forward to a day when paths of knowledge will be opened up leading from organic biology and chemistry to the field of neurotic phenomena."

Through the 1960s and early 1970s, scientists continued to experiment with electrical brain stimulation. It was discovered that it was possible to alter the electrical activity of the brain and nervous system without direct stimulation (i.e., by implanted electrodes), but by applying the electrical current at the skin surface. This technique of transcutaneous nerve stimulation (TENS) was found to be particularly effective in reducing pain, and by the mid-1970s everyone from doctors to dentists to sports trainers was using TENS devices to alleviate pain. Things had come a long way from the ancient Egyptians and Greeks with their electrical-eel cures. Or had they? Scribonius knew that the electrical torpedo ray would relieve pain, though he didn't know how. And in the mid-1970s, millions were using TENS devices for pain relief. Yet despite extensive research, no one was able to explain exactly how electricity had such a dramatic pain-reducing effect.

ELECTRICALLY ACTIVATED KEYS TO PARADISE

THEN IN THE MID-1970S SCIENTISTS DISCOVERED THE EXISTENCE of endorphins, the body's own opiates. We all know that opiates, such as heroin, morphine, and opium, have profound effects on the human brain, not only relieving pain but producing such euphoria that millions of humans have become addicted to them, destroying themselves for these precious pleasurable substances. The reason for this fatal attraction between humans and opiates, it seems, is based on a bizarre coincidence: the molecules of opiates have the same shape as a group of molecules naturally produced in our bodies and brains, those now-famous endorphins (from *endogenous morphine*, morphine produced within ourselves). These neurochemicals, dubbed the "keys to paradise," serve a variety of purposes in our bodies, including reducing pain, alleviating stress, giving us pleasure, rewarding behavior that is conducive to our survival, enhancing or suppressing memories, and determining what information we allow into our brains. When triggered by some appropriate stimulus, our brains secrete endorphins. They then flow from neuron to neuron, like neurotransmitters, but also sweep through our nervous system, like hormones. In the brain, they are accepted by appropriate neurons at what are called *receptor sites*. These are areas which have a molecular structure appropriately shaped to receive the endorphins, as a lock receives a key. Once accepted by the receptor site, the endorphins cause electrical changes in the neuron, which are then passed along to other neurons.

Oddly enough, there is a drug that is virtually identical in molecular structure to the opiates but has none of the effects of opiates. This drug, *naloxone*, is called an opiate antagonist, because it fits right into the opiate receptor sites and keeps any true opiates from fitting into the sites. The result is that naloxone blocks the effects of both external and natural opiates. What makes it of such interest to us here is that with the discovery of endorphins in 1975 some of the scientists experimenting with using electrical stimulation for the relief of pain began to wonder if somehow this stimulation was working by causing the body to release its own opiates. If this was the case, then an injection of naloxone into the subject receiving the electrical stimulation should keep the electrical stimulation from working, i.e., should eliminate the pain relief. The scientists injected naloxone, the electrical stimulation ceased to reduce the pain, and the mystery of how electrical stimulation relieved pain was solved at last: it worked by triggering endorphins. [3, 316]

In fact, as laboratory techniques were developed that enabled researchers to measure the amounts and trace the pathways of endorphins in the brain and cerebrospinal fluid, studies showed that electrical stimulation of appropriate parts of the brain caused endorphin levels to increase sharply. [1] Among these studies was one by Yoshio Hosobuchi of UC San Francisco and Nobel laureate and pioneer endorphin researcher Roger Guillemin of the Salk Institute, which found greatly increased concentrations of endorphins in patients who received electrical stimulation. [131, 151, 285] Such a flood of endorphins could produce a powerful sense of euphoria, so it was no wonder that many who had been using electrical stimulation to alleviate pain had also found the experience quite enjoyable. And no wonder I had experienced such a warming flood of pleasure as I sat talking with Joseph Light with his TENS device tickling my ankles and my brain pouring out the juices of good cheer.

9

WE SING THE MIND ELECTRIC, PART TWO: THE ALPHA STIM

AFTER MY FIRST EXPERIENCE WITH THE TENS, AS I PLIED Light with questions about his little black box, he had shrugged. "Really," he'd said, "this thing is nothing much. Anyone who knows a bit of electronics could put it together with about nineteen dollars' worth of parts from Radio Shack. If you want to try something powerful, check out the Alpha Stim. It's something really new, a quantum leap beyond these TENS devices." That in itself was a fairly startling thought. I'd said I was interested, and Light had provided me with a heap of scientific studies from bioelectrical journals as well as some descriptive material about the Alpha Stim. And so a few weeks later, brain awash with tidbits of bioelectric lore, I sat down before an Alpha Stim machine—a device about the size of a typewriter and covered with dials, wires, gauges, and flashing lights—clipped soft electrodes to each of my earlobes, and waited for the technician to turn on the juice.

I knew that it would be a tiny amount of juice, since that was said by bioelectric experts to be one of the most revolutionary aspects of the device. While conventional TENS units delivered current at an intensity in the *milliampere* range (a milliampere is one one-thousandth of an ampere), the Alpha Stim's current was in the *microampere* range (a microampere is one one-millionth of an ampere; a common 60-watt light bulb draws approximately a half ampere, or 500,000 microamperes). In other words, the current emitted by the Alpha Stim is hundreds of times *less* than is emitted by most TENS units. According to recent bioelectric research, this current is much closer to the natural current produced by the body's cells than that produced by the more powerful TENS units, and is thus able to stimulate the cells in a more natural way.

Also different from most TENS-unit current is the waveform—it is a square wave, which experts claim allows the current to be delivered more effectively and naturally to the cells. And unlike most TENS units, which deliver their current at comparatively high frequencies (from the "slow" 7.83 HZ range of Joseph Light's device up into the hundreds and thousands of Hz), the Alpha Stim operates at extremely low frequencies (generally ranging from 0.5 to 1.5 Hz).

Like TENS units, the Alpha Stim is most widely used for pain relief—when the area of pain is electrically stimulated at appropriate frequencies and amplitudes, the body responds with a flood of endorphins, alleviating even severe and chronic pain for hours or days. According to numerous reports, including controlled studies and case histories, conducted in the three years since the machine was invented by California neurobiologist Dr. Daniel Kirsch, the Alpha Stim is far superior to ordinary TENS units in delivering pain relief. Like the TENS, the Alpha Stim is, by order of the FDA, available to laymen only by prescription from a doctor, dentist, psychiatrist, osteopath, or other health professional.

However, pain relief is hardly the only use for the Alpha Stim. Increasing numbers of psychiatrists and others have discovered that one of the operational modes of the device, known as *transcranial electrotherapy* (TCET), in which the electrodes are attached to the ears or the temples and the electrical currents sent directly into the brain, rapidly produces as state known as *electronarcosis*, characterized by deep relaxation, heightened awareness, and a sense of well-being or euphoria. In fact, many use the device exclusively for TCET, and much of the current research being done with the unit is in exploring the potentials of TCET. Psychiatrists and other mental-health professionals have found that TCET is remarkably effective in reducing anxiety and generalized stress. For example, Mitch Lewis, athletic trainer and conditioning coach for the Olympic men's rowing and judo teams, initially used the Alpha Stim for pain reduction, but soon found that the TCET mode was even more useful. Says Lewis, "I have used the transcranial electrostimulation as a relaxation/restorative modality with great results. The athletes report a good night's rest before an important competition. They also report that they have a more relaxed attitude toward the stress of competitions."[201]

In a controlled study of cocaine addicts, Los Angeles psychiatrist Dr. Alan Brovar found that those given TCET completed detoxification and rehabilitation programs more successfully than controls, had fewer relapses, and were less likely to seek readmission. Brovar speculated that by releasing endorphins, the TCET reduced the characteristic dysphoria, or lack of ability to feel pleasure, that addicts experience when undergoing withdrawal. "It may also produce hemispheric synchronization in the brain," said Brovar, "making addicts more willing to accept recovery-oriented concepts." The TCET had a sedative effect, he said, inducing "a state of relaxed alertness that decreases physical craving for the drug."[46]

Studies have also shown that the deep relaxation and calm alertness produced by TCET increases suggestibility and hypnotizability, and many psychologists and dentists who use hypnosis in their practice now use the Alpha Stim to assist in hypnotic induction. Some psychiatrists use TCET prior to or during treatment sessions to relax the patient and induce a state of openness and heightened awareness, allowing new ideas, memories, and subconscious material to come to the surface. Many regular users claim TCET enhances their creativity and sharpens their perceptions and sensitivities.

BOOSTING THE BRAIN TO A HIGHER ORDER OF COHERENCE

THE IDEA THAT ELECTRICAL STIMULATION MIGHT BOOST CREA-tivity and other high-level mental functions becomes plausible when we understand how the electricity is interacting with the neurons in the brain. This interaction is explained by Dr. William Bauer of Case Western Reserve University School of Medicine and Chief of Otolaryngology, VA Medical Center in Cleveland, Ohio:

> Basically, absorption of electromagnetic energy increases the kinetic energy of molecular constituents of the absorption medium. There is much evidence that the molecular organization in biological systems needed to sense stimuli, whether thermal, chemical or electromagnetic, may reside in joint functions of molecular assemblies or subsets of these assemblies. These assemblies form complex flow patterns that can undergo sudden transitions to new self-maintaining arrangements that will be relatively stable over time. Transformation of complex flow patterns into larger hierarchical patterns is saltatory. . . . Because these patterns are initiated and sustained by continuing inputs of energy, they are classed as "dissipative processes." For this reason, they occur far from equilibrium, meaning there is an organizing and building process. . . . In summary, the mechanism of tissue interactions with electromagnetic fields may be as follows: an electromagnetic field of the correct magnitude and frequency causes a "perturbation" or repositioning of the molecular plasma membrane of cells. This in turn may influence membrane enzyme systems by favorably altering stereoscoping configurations of molecules in much the same manner as a chemical catalyst holds molecules in the correct orientation for chemical reactions. The best known cell-membrane enzyme is adenelyate cyclase which converts ATP (adenosine triphosphate) to cyclic-AMP (adenosine monophosphate) which then acts as a *second messenger* intra-cellularly. In other words, an electromagnetic field may act in the same way as a hormone upon the cell membrane.[25]

That is, electromagnetic fields, provided they are of the correct magnitude and frequency, can act on the brain cells in the same way as many brain chemicals do, causing them to alter and grow in size and dendritic length (the process of converting ATP to cyclic-AMP Bauer mentions above is the key to cellular growth). Which is to say, according to Bauer, that electromagnetic fields of the correct magnitude and frequency act as an energy influx upon a dissipative structure—setting up fluctuations that cause the brain to reorganize at a higher level of complexity and coherence, to grow, to escape to a higher order.

If this was the effect of TCET, then it sounded like something both interesting and desirable to me, which was why I was sitting there beside the Alpha Stim with those electrodes clamped to my earlobes. I recalled Marian Diamond's response when asked, regarding her experiments showing that animals raised in enriched environments became more intelligent, what exactly constituted an enriched environment. "The main factor is stimulation," she said. "The nerve cells are designed to receive stimulation." The Alpha Stim sounded like about the most direct sort of stimulation available.

The machine was turned on, and I felt a tingling sensation of tiny pinpricks in my earlobes, as a few microamps of biphasic square waves at a frequency of 0.5 Hz passed into my brain. The tingling was not strong enough to be unpleasant. Unlike the sensations caused by the TENS device, which had crept upon me without my noticing them, the shift in consciousness was quick and unmistakable. My body immediately felt heavier, as if I were sinking down into myself. I realized I was becoming extremely relaxed, and all of a sudden, there I was. It was that feeling you get when all at once you blink your eyes and realize that you're awake. Not that you had literally been sleeping, but you hadn't been paying attention to things as carefully as you might, you had been sleepwalking through your day, and now you're awake and things are very, very clear. It was not a feeling of being in some strange stoned or otherworldly state, but rather a feeling of being exactly as you should be, at home in yourself—a feeling that your brain was operating correctly, efficiently, clearly.

I was intensely aware of everything that was going on

132

around me—the noisy office of a busy biofeedback instrument company, jangling phones, a variety of conversations—and simultaneously intensely aware of everything going on inside my head. My body was no longer heavy, but very light, full of energy. The feeling was one of openness, clarity, as though I had been wearing sunglasses for weeks and had suddenly taken them off. It was no big thing. Nothing special, really, except I couldn't help but feel that *this is the way we're supposed to be all the time*.

SPICING UP THE BRAIN SOUP: LEARNING, MEMORY, AND ELECTRICITY

AS I CONTINUED TO READ ABOUT AND EXPERIMENT WITH THE Alpha Stim and other electrical stimulation devices,* I found myself asking questions. There was no doubt that these devices, particularly the Alpha Stim, were effective in causing my brain to pour out endorphins—there is now a wealth of hard evidence linking electrical stimulation to release of endorphins. My question was, so what? Granted, electrical stimulation can increase endorphin levels; this can relieve pain, depression, anxiety; it can make me feel good; but what does this have to do with the subject of this book, enhancing mental functioning? Aside from their therapeutic applications, can such electro-stim devices benefit healthy people? Can they be used to stimulate brain growth, to boost the mind to higher levels of awareness, concentration, creativity? Can they make me smarter or help me think better? That is, can such devices

---

*One such device seems to fall somewhere between a TENS unit and the TCET mode of the Alpha Stim. Called the Alphapacer, this small Walkman-size unit uses an ultralow current (10 microamps, a bit more current than the Alpha Stim, but far less than ordinary TENS units) delivered in the form of a sine wave, and at a variable frequency ranging between 4 and 14 Hz, so that the user can select the desired frequency. The signal is introduced into the brain via a small electrode placed on the mastoid bone behind each ear. EEG tests by a neurophysiologist indicate that the machine can rapidly alter brain-wave patterns, slowing them and increasing synchrony, though so far no tests have been done to determine its influence on the production of neurochemicals such as the endorphins.

actually serve as learning tools, leading to increased intelligence and memory?

Whatever these words mean (and scientists still disagree about the specific physiological activities that produce such things as "learning," "memory," "intelligence," and "thinking"), there is now virtually unanimous agreement among neuroscientists that the general processes they refer to are, in essence, *chemical* events, depending on alterations in the amounts of certain juices in the brain.

This widespread acceptance of the biochemical basis of higher mental functions represents a dramatic shift. Well into the 1960s many scientists were convinced that such cognitive functions as memory relied on lasting electrical impressions in the brain, patterns known as *engrams* (though no scientist ever succeeded in actually "capturing" or detecting any of these elusive engrams). And until that time it was still debated whether neurons sent signals across synapses by means of electrical or chemical signals.

A key factor in the widespread acceptance of the link between cognitive functioning and neurochemicals was the seminal and controversial studies by Mark Rosenzweig and his colleagues of the brains of rats raised in enriched or impoverished environments. These experiments clearly demonstrated that there was a correlation between learning and brain chemistry: rats that had received greater stimulation and demonstrated greater learning, memory, intelligence, and ability to process information showed higher levels of the brain chemical acetylcholinesterase (AChE). This enzyme is an indicator of higher levels of the neurotransmitter acetylcholine. Increases in levels of AChE are linked to increases in intelligence and learning ability; rats with naturally high levels of AChE were more intelligent than rats with lower levels of this chemical.

As the result of such studies, scientific interest in the brain chemicals intensified. Once it was recognized that learning and memory were chemical processes, researchers began to sort through the chemical soup of the brain to discover precisely which chemicals were involved in which processes.

However, it was not until the late 1960s and early 1970s that laboratory equipment and techniques sophisticated enough to map the exact locations of specific brain chemcials were developed. With that began what many now look upon as "the neuroscience revolution."

NEUROTRANSMITTERS. The first chemicals the neuroscientists scrutinized were the most obvious and abundant ones, the simple molecules called neurotransmitters. These substances are held in hundreds of little sacs clustered around the tip of the axon. When the neuron sends an electrical charge down the axon, the bundles of neurotransmitters are released from the vesicles, cross the synaptic gap, and interact with receptors on adjacent neurons, fitting into the receptors like a key into a lock. There the neurotransmitters alter the cellular membrane in such a way as to generate an electric potential, which is then carried up to the cell's central body. The message carried can be one of only two types, excitatory (stimulating electrical current in the adjacent cell) or inhibitory (reducing the capability of the adjacent cell to produce an electrical current).

Early on, scientists discovered that the brain's most abundant neurotransmitter was acetylcholine. This substance, they found, is essential to such higher mental processes as learning and memory.[199] (Its importance can be seen in the changing amounts of the chemical in the brains of different animals along the evolutionary scale: greater brain size is associated not only with a greater number of neurons in the cortex, but with a greater density of acetylcholine, with humans having the highest density. Rosenzweig's studies of the brain growth of rats focused on this neurotransmitter by measuring the amount of the enzyme associated with it, AChE—the experiments showed a direct connection not only between acetylcholine and intelligence, but also between the neurotransmitter and brain size; so the chemical is associated with larger brain size both over the course of evolution and in short periods of the life of individuals.) Recent studies show that insufficient acetylcholine causes memory loss and reduces learning and intelligence.[108] Also, the confusion and loss of memory asso-

135

ciated with Alzheimer's disease has now been linked in part to a lack of acetylcholine in certain areas of the brain—when acetylcholine is injected into those areas, or the subjects are given acetylcholine-boosting drugs, sufferers of the disease respond with dramatic gains in memory and other mental abilities.

Even healthy people with "normal" levels of acetylcholine profit from higher levels of the neurotransmitter. Studies of normal subjects indicate that when these individuals are given substances that increase the amount of acetylcholine in the brain, they show significant increases in their scores on memory tests and other intelligence tests. At the National Institute of Mental Health, human subjects given substances to increase their acetylcholine learned serial lists (such as a series of names or numbers) more quickly than a control group. When these subjects were given a drug that reduces acetylcholine levels, their learning abilities were impaired, with the young subjects showing a pattern of memory loss similar to that found in senile old age.[314, 315] A research team at the Veterans Administration Hospital, Palo Alto, found that a group of normal human subjects showed great improvement in long-term memory when given a substance that increases acetylcholine in the brain. In another study, MIT students taking an acetylcholine enhancer had improved memory and increased ability to learn lists of words.[231] As one recent article concluded, "Like finger paint spread across a piece of paper, this chemical helps neurons in the cortex retain the imprint of incoming information."[152]

Another neurotransmitter, norepinephrine (also known as noradrenaline), also plays a key role in memory and learning. Precursor of adrenaline, NE has an arousing, sharpening effect in the brain. We've all noticed how things we experience at moments of heightened arousal—times of great joy, terror, crisis, or love, when we're riding the wave of an adrenaline rush—are remembered with particular intensity and vividness, and are, in fact, virtually impossible to forget. The drug amphetamine is structurally similar to NE, and works by increasing the effects of NE in the brain. Amphetamine—speed

—has long been favored by students cramming for exams, who claim it induces a state of intense mental alertness, enabling them to digest and remember large amounts of information. Some have discounted this "learning" effect, claiming it's only the result of the arousal and general nervous-system stimulation created by the drug, rather than a true increase in ability to process information. However, numerous laboratory studies have shown that the memory-enhancement effect of these pep pills is real. Even when the arousing effects are eliminated (by cutting out the adrenal glands), the increase in NE caused by the amphetamine directly enhances learning and memory processes.

What amphetamine can do, pure NE apparently does better. In experiments in which NE levels in the brain were reduced, memory and learning decreased. When NE levels were increased in certain parts of the brain, memory and learning were enhanced.[333] Cornell researchers found that inhibiting the synthesis of NE in rats' brains interrupted their ability to remember for more than twenty-four hours. The researchers conclude, "The synthesis of norepinephrine seems to be essential to the formation of memory."[274] It has been suggested that NE acts as a "Print it!" command, telling the brain to write in indelible ink the information that it is processing or receiving.

ONE-EYED CATS AND PLASTIC BRAINS.   Recent studies even indicate that NE not only enhances memory and learning, but seems to return the brain to a state of youthful flexibility and plasticity. In one experiment, kittens who were prevented from using one eye during the early months of their life later could not develop depth perception (stereopsis) when both eyes were permitted to function. This is a common occurrence, and scientists had assumed that certain developmental functions are completely dependent on timing—if the brain is not allowed to develop the function while in a state of youthful plasticity, it will not be able to alter its structure when it reaches maturity. This is the reason four-year-olds can pick up new languages better than thirty-four-year-olds: their brains are more susceptible to being changed by experience.

However, Takuji Kasamatsu of Caltech injected the brains of the cats with NE, and they quickly developed stereopsis! Kasamatsu also performed the experiment in reverse, temporarily sewing shut a normal adult cat's eyelid and injecting it with NE—the cat rapidly developed monocular vision, which remained even when the second eye was allowed to function normally; the adult cat's brain became "imprinted" with the monocular experience as easily as if it had been a kitten. Somehow the NE caused the brain to become extraordinarily receptive and plastic, allowing well-established neural pathways to be discarded and new neural connections to be developed. This has led NE to be termed "the brain's fountain of youth." "That's our dream," says Kasamatsu, "to make your brain young again."[148]

Another neurotransmitter, glutamate, has been little studied and less understood, but recent work by Gary Lynch of UC Irvine (for more than a decade a leading figure in the field of memory research) indicates that it is a key to memory formation. In experiments with rabbits and rats, he has found that memory formation is related to long-lasting increases in the number of glutamate receptors.[122] A variety of other studies have shown that other neurotransmitters, including serotonin, are also involved in memory formation or learning.

In this context, we can see the considerable implications of studies proving that electrical stimulation of the brain, at the proper frequency, waveform, and current, can quickly and sharply increase the levels of these and other neurotransmitters in the brain. You'll recall the studies by James Olds in which he implanted electrodes in the pleasure centers or reward centers of rats and allowed them to stimulate themselves by pressing a pedal. When Olds stumbled onto this phenomenon in 1954, no one had any idea why electrical stimulation of these areas could be so pleasurable. You'll also remember that Olds's self-stimulating rats were superlearners, mastering mazes with amazing speed and accuracy. Over twenty years later, with the discovery of endorphins, part of the mystery was explained—the rats were triggering the release of endorphins in their brains.

Then in 1979, neuroscientist Aryeh Routtenberg of Northwestern University discovered that the electrical stimulation was also triggering the release of large amounts of the neurotransmitters known as catecholamines (including NE and dopamine). According to Routtenberg, much of the pleasure of the electrical stimulation of the reward centers comes from this increased flow of catecholamines (very similar to the effect of cocaine in the brain, which also works by stimulating the catecholamines in the same areas; according to Dr. Solomon Snyder, professor of psychiatry and pharmacology at Johns Hopkins, and a discoverer of the opiate receptors, NE is in itself so pleasurable that if a drug could be devised that stimulated only NE, without dopamine, it would produce pure, undiluted ecstasy[267]). Routtenberg noted that catecholamine enhancing drugs facilitate learning, and that the centers and pathways of brain reward are also the centers and pathways of memory consolidation. He concluded that when something is learned, the learner is rewarded, and the activity in the reward centers and pathways facilitates the formation of memory. Said Routtenberg, "The improved learning may be due to the fact that the animals self-regulate the amount of stimulation, thereby self-reinforcing their behavior."[286]

More recently, research by neuroelectric-therapy pioneer Dr. Margaret Patterson in collaboration with biochemist Dr. Ifor Capel at the Marie Curie Cancer Memorial Foundation Research Department, Surrey, England, has proved that simple low-frequency currents induced by external electrodes from machines quite like the TENS, Alphapacer, and Alpha Stim can dramatically speed up the production of a variety of neurotransmitters, with different brain juices being triggered by different frequencies and waveforms (for example, Patterson and Capel have found that a 10-Hz signal boosts the production and turnover rate of serotonin). According to Capel, "as far as we can tell, each brain center generates impulses at a specific frequency based on the predominant neurotransmitters it secretes. In other words, the brain's internal communications system—its language, if you like—is based on frequency. . . . Presumably, when we send in waves of electrical energy at, say, 10 hertz, certain cells in the lower brain stem will respond because they normally fire within that frequency range. As a result, particular mood-altering chemicals associated with that region will be released."[215]

THE MUSIC OF THE HEMISPHERES

AS WE HAVE SEEN EARLIER, THERE IS NOW EVIDENCE THAT neurons function cooperatively, with various subpopulations linked together in networks of millions of cells, each subpopulation responding to vibrations in a certain frequency, much the way a spider's web will vibrate throughout its entire structure when a single strand of it is touched, or the way a crystal goblet will resonate to a specific pure tone. Memory, thought, consciousness itself are products of a complex, intricate arrangement of all these neurons and neuron subpopulations firing together in a sort of orchestral harmony. The various neuron groupings and centers are like different musical instruments in the orchestra, each vibrating within its own characteristic frequency range, together producing the tune we hear as consciousness, the rich, subtle, infinitely expressive symphony that is the whole brain in operation. And by stimulating specific brain centers or neural subpopulations with electrical current of the proper frequency and waveform, it is possible to act as conductor of the orchestra, causing, for example, the trumpets of norepinephrine to dominate with their brassy fortissimo, or the strings of acetylcholine to come to the front.

Many investigators of electrical stimulation believe that in addition to the specific effect certain waveforms and frequencies have on individual neurotransmitters, some electrical currents, such as the very slow 0.5-Hz wave of the Alpha Stim, can act as a "toner," resonating and stimulating all the brain's cells and bringing them into balance. As with the instruments of a symphony orchestra, there is evidence that neurotransmitters function best when their quantity is within a certain range.

140

For example, too much NE can lead to anxiety, tension, and hyperactivity, while too little can impair memory and cause depression. Too much acetylcholine leads to lethargy, too little to weakness and hallucination. Too much serotonin causes hallucinations and sleep, too little brings depression, aggression, and insomnia. That is, our brains function at their best when the various neurotransmitters are within their optimal range, just as the orchestra sounds best when no instrument plays so loud its sound is distorted and the other instruments drowned out.

However, many students of the human brain now believe that large areas of the brain are not functioning within their optimal range, not producing sufficient quantities of neurotransmitters. In one sense, this is what the scientists are talking about when they throw out the cliché that humans use only 5 percent or less of their brains. Rather than having a huge orchestra playing a grand symphony within our skulls, most of us have allowed the majority of the orchestra members to take a break, leaving rows of empty seats, while the few remaining musicians play with out-of-tune instruments. But there is increasing evidence that electrical stimulation of the brain can tune up or activate malfunctioning or underfunctioning neurons, causing them to begin operating at peak or optimal levels. This would in turn cause an overall increase in the amount of various neurotransmitters in the brain, while no neuron or neural network was producing more than the optimal amount. One of the foremost experts in the field of electromedicine, Dr. William Bauer, has noticed this tuning or balancing effect. When asked about the influence of electrical stimulation on neurotransmitters, he replied, "What I think is happening . . . is that by sending out the proper frequency, proper waveform and proper current . . . we tend to change the configuration of the cell membrane. . . . Cells that are at suboptimal levels are stimulated to 'turn on' and produce what they're supposed to produce, probably through DNA, which is stimulated through the cell membrane. I believe that normal tissue simply resonates with the electrical impulses we send in because there is nothing to turn on . . . they're already doing their job. But diseased cells will take up this energy and literally be turned on. You're 'charging' the cells through a biochemical process that can possibly balance the acetylcholine or whatever neurotransmitter needs to be turned on. . . . You're literally getting the body back into balance."[140]

PASSING INVISIBLE AND UNDETECTED THROUGH THE BLOOD-BRAIN BARRIER

THE PROSPECT OF INCREASING CERTAIN NEUROTRANSMITTERS through electrical stimulation has exciting potentials for those interested in enhancing mental functioning. As we've seen, increased levels of neurotransmitters such as NE and acetylcholine in normal, healthy subjects produce striking improvements in a variety of intellectual skills, including memory and learning. However, in many of these cases, the way the levels of the neurotransmitters were boosted was by giving the subjects drugs, either orally or by injection. The problem is that before a drug can have any influence in the brain at all, it must pass through the "blood-brain barrier," a dense thicket of filtering capillaries that protect brain tissue from harmful substances in the bloodstream. While all the chemicals that enter the bloodstream circulate past brain tissue, very few of these chemicals will actually make it through the maze of capillaries into the actual brain tissue. Thus, when a drug or any substance is taken by mouth, very little of it will ever end up in the brain. But if only 1 percent of the drug gets into the brain, the other 99 percent is carried to other parts of the body, where it can create a variety of potentially dangerous side effects, such as dry mouth, liver damage, heart failure, or cancer.

Electrical stimulation, however, goes directly into the brain tissue, unaffected by the blood-brain barrier, thus eliminating the possibility of side effects in other parts of the body. This raises the possibility of using such devices as the Alpha Stim to boost learning, memory, and other mental processes by increasing the synthesis of specific neurotransmitters in the brain.

142

EXTRACT OF FOUR THOUSAND
DARK-FEARING RATS

WHILE NEUROSCIENCE WAS INTRIGUED BY THE DISCOVERIES being made about neurotransmitters in the early 1970s, it was becoming clear that neurotransmitters themselves could not explain the most subtle phenomena and mysteries of consciousness. Neurotransmitters, scientists found, are very short, simple molecules. Molecules are constructed of building blocks called amino acids. In the case of neurotransmitters, often they are composed of only one or two of these building blocks. These small molecules travel extremely short distances, crossing the synaptic cleft between adjacent neurons in milliseconds, causing brief changes in the excitability of a specific receiving neuron. Scientists could understand how these simple molecules could carry messages such as "become more sensitive" or "become less sensitive." But it didn't seem possible that neurotransmitters could encode the complicated messages that seemed necessary to control such complex, subtle states as moods, thinking, and creativity.

A study by Dr. Georges Ungar of University of Tennessee Medical Center cast some light on this question and aroused an enormous amount of controversy when it was first reported in 1970. Ungar had taken some four thousand rats (creatures that ordinarily prefer dark areas to light) and trained them with electrical shocks to fear the dark. Ungar then took extracts from the brains of the dark-fearing rats, injected the material into ordinary untrained rats, and they too immediately feared darkness! Somehow it seemed that Ungar was transferring a fairly complex, unnatural (learned) behavior pattern from one group of rats to another—but by what means can behaviors be transferred?

Ungar painstakingly analyzed the brain extract and finally was able to narrow it down to a molecule made up of amino acids joined together in an eleven-link chain. He called this molecule *scotophobin*, from the Greek *skotos*, dark, and *phobos*, fear. He then created an analogue of scotophobin—a

143

synthetic equivalent made from pure laboratory chemicals—and injected it into another group of untrained rats. They too reacted with a sudden fear of the dark. What Ungar's experiment suggested was that specific memories or behaviors could be created synthetically, from ordinary chemicals. At the time this discovery sounded like some bizarre idea from a science fiction novel, and most scientists scoffed at Ungar's conclusions.

Then, a few years later, came the discovery of the endorphins amid much fanfare and granting of Nobel prizes. Until then, scientists had believed that there were two separate chemical systems coordinating brain and brain-body activity—neurotransmitters and hormones. Neurotransmitters, as we've seen, are small molecules (made up of only a few amino acid links or building blocks) that act rapidly across short distances from one neuron to a single specific target neuron. Hormones, on the other hand, had traditionally been seen as complex molecules—long chains with many, sometimes hundreds, of links or building blocks—that are secreted by groups of cells called endocrine glands (e.g., adrenaline from the adrenal glands, thyroxine from the thyroid gland). These complicated molecules are released into the bloodstream (instead of across the synaptic gap like neurotransmitters) and carried to one or more distant target areas. They do not act in milliseconds, as do neurotransmitters, but require time ranging from seconds to hours to reach their target. And unlike neurotransmitters, which cause brief changes in the excitability of the target neuron, hormones cause complex changes in the target cells that can be quite long-lasting (such as male hormones' increasing growth of facial hair, etc.).

But with the discovery of endorphins, and several related substances, suddenly this strict division began to break down. Endorphins at times could act like neurotransmitters, traveling from one neuron to the next across the synaptic cleft, at other times like hormones, carried through the bloodstream and in cerebrospinal fluid, traveling long distances, causing changes in target areas that are long-lasting and quite complex. They are like hormones secreted in and operating directly on the brain. Scientists dubbed these complex molecules *neuropeptides* or *peptides*, and unlike the neurotransmitters, which could only carry messages of "on" or "off," or "more" or "less," they seemed to be capable of conveying very specific ideas, moods, memories, emotional states, and behaviors. To return to a metaphor Joseph Light used, it seems that neurotransmitters operate like lines connecting individual telephones with one another, while peptides are more like a television broadcast, which can be picked up by anyone with the right receiver.

Just how specific and numerous these various mental states conveyed by peptides could be is mind-boggling. Each peptide is a string of amino acids. There are twenty main amino acids that can exist at any point and in any order along the chain. That is, the same amino acid can and often does appear in several places along the molecular chain of the peptide, just as the same letter can appear·in several places in a single word. And, as with letters, it is the order in which the amino acids are arranged that determines the "meaning" of the peptide—"god" means something very different from "dog," though they contain the same letters, and similarly, just a few amino acids can be arranged into many peptides that carry quite different messages. Consider that the genetic code has but four amino-acid "letters" and yet is able to carry a genetic message so complex and unique it can create and maintain our entire physical structure. So, in a molecular chain with two dozen or more links or units, each of which can be any of the twenty different amino acids, the potential number of combinations is virtually incalculable. When only two units are linked together, for example, using any of the twenty different amino acids for each link, one could create 20×20, or four hundred, different peptides. Three building blocks or links, using any of the twenty amino acids for each link, can be arranged into eight thousand distinct peptides. A combination of fifteen amino-acid links can result in 33.66 quintillion different peptides, many, many times more peptides than there are neurons in the brain. And these are relatively simple amino-acid chains compared to the fascinating 263-amino-acid chain called *pro-opiomelanocortin*, which is the subject of intense study by neuroscientists, since it is this peptide that contains within it the shorter peptides of endorphin (thirty-two links) and enkephalin (six links) and another peptide called MSH-ACTH 4-10 that apparently triggers sharp increases in learning and memory in human subjects. And compared to complex proteins, which may be several thousand links long, even such peptides seem relatively insignificant.

Given the vast variety of peptides possible, it seems possible that there are peptides that can carry messages triggering virtually any mental state or behavior pattern conceivable. Again, the twenty amino acids can be compared to the twenty-six letters of the alphabet: just as the letters can be arranged into an infinite variety of messages, consisting of short words, long words, and groups of words arranged into sentences, so the amino acids can be arranged into a variety of peptides as vast as the English language. A peptide of a hundred linked amino acids can encode a message that is the equivalent in information of three or four sentences. Thus, when a peptide is released and carried to individual neurons, it is as if a message several sentences long were communicated to the target neurons.

Using new laboratory techniques, scientists have now succeeded in creating a number of these peptides synthetically, including synthetic endorphins. And since peptides are so much more specific in their effects than neurotransmitters, it is probable that scientists may soon synthesize peptides that can do anything from increase your ability (or your desire) to read or to remember melodies, or cause you to feel elation at the sound of a bell, to avoid the color of blue, or to be attracted to redheads. Which brings us back to Georges Ungar's 1970 discovery of scotophobin, for it's now clear that this is simply another, relatively simple (eleven-link) peptide with a specific message: fear the dark.

Since then Ungar has gone on to create other peptides, including one which causes rats to become habituated to a sound (only a buzzer, however, not a gong), and two which cause goldfish to avoid the colors of green and blue respectively. Other scientists have extracted a peptide from rats that causes other rats to remain on a platform rather than climbing down. It's becoming apparent that peptides can have almost infinite variety and unlimited specificity.

SMART PILLS, OR BETTER LEARNING THROUGH CHEMISTRY

WHAT MAKES PEPTIDES SO EXTRAORDINARILY INTERESTING IS that they are clearly involved in and perhaps directly control those complex states—moods, emotions, thoughts, behavior patterns, habits, attitudes, tastes—that we ordinarily think of as our "mind" or our "self." "Neuropeptides are involved in acquisition and maintenance and new behavioral patterns," says Dutch pharmacologist David de Wied, a pioneer of peptide research. "They facilitate registration, consolidation, repression, and retrieval of information, which makes possible the selection of adequate behavior."[65]

Peptides, that is, seem to be at the root of the mystery of how we learn, how memories are formed, stored, and recalled in the brain. Somehow peptides appear to control the brain's ability to concentrate, think, and absorb information. This has been proved in many recent studies, including double-blind experiments in which a control group was used, with neither the subjects nor the researchers knowing whether the substance being administered was active (one of a number of endorphinlike synthetic peptides) or a neutral, impotent placebo. In each of these studies, the subjects taking the peptides showed clear improvements in various tests measuring learning and memory.

For example, one peptide called *vasopressin*, very closely related to endorphins, has been synthesized and administered in a number of studies. In one study, men in their fifties and sixties taking vasopressin showed significant improvements in memory and learning and actually decreased their reaction time (became quicker). In another experiment, sixteen normal healthy subjects of average intelligence were given vasopressin several times, after which there was a dramatic improvement in their ability to learn and remember, which lasted from ten days to two weeks. Dutch scientists have found that vasopressin has a long-term "cementing" effect on consolidation and information.[65] For example, when people receive the peptide they are able to remember long lists of objects much better. At NIMH, research has indicated that vasopressin boosts memory, enabling subjects to "chunk" (i.e., group large amounts of information of memories together into more easily remembered chunks) and "encode" things better, while decreased vasopressin is associated with memory deficits. The peptide also enhances production of theta waves, which are associated with increased access to memories, increased ability to remember, and increased creativity. The NIMH studies also indicate that vasopressin stimulates the release of endorphins, while endorphins in turn stimulate the release of vasopressin. In other studies, vasopressin has restored memory in amnesia victims.[190,192]

Another naturally occurring peptide which has been synthesized, MSH-ACTH 4-10, mentioned above, dramatically increases attention span, as well as visual memory in males and verbal memory in females. The peptide, which is a fragment found in beta-endorphin and other peptides, seems to enhance communication between cells, according to Boston University School of Medicine researchers, thus speeding transmission of signals in the brain and improving learning and memory. Users become alert while remaining deeply relaxed.[149] In Sweden, researchers found that this same peptide fragment improved visual attention and retention and reduced anxiety in healthy human subjects, and improved the brain's information-processing ability. They also discovered that small amounts of the peptide, like vasopressin, increase the brain's theta activity. Similar findings have been reported by Dutch researchers, who claim the peptide enhances motivation, excitability, vigilance, selective attention, and memory retrieval. When amnesia was induced in lab animals after they had learned a task, this peptide, administered twenty-four hours later, reversed the amnesia. Old animals, when given this peptide, had their ability to retain memories restored to the level of young animals. In human subjects, this peptide retards the development of habituation to a reaction-time task, as measured by EEG readings. Also, the peptide improved maximum performance levels and decreased errors on a number of sensorimotor and intelligence tests. Like vasopressin, the peptide has been synthesized and is available in a pill form for experimental use (vasopressin is available as a nasal spray, and can be obtained with a doctor's prescription).

The best-known peptides, the endorphins, have also been found to have a powerful strengthening effect on learning and memory. In one study, minute doses of some of the endorphins (beta-endorphin and Leu- and Met-enkephalin) were injected under the skin of rats. It's significant that the injections were under the skin and not into the brain, since because of the blood-brain barrier only minuscule amounts of the endorphins could have made it into the brain. Yet the tests of these rats showed that even such tiny amounts of endorphins in the brain had a strong anti-amnesia effect.

In studies by David de Weid in which rats were injected with tiny amounts of certain endorphins, the length of time the rats remembered things they learned was increased. Andrew Schally, winner of the 1977 Nobel Prize in Medicine, along with a group of colleagues, ran a test in which rats were forced to run a complex maze in order to get fed. Before confronting the maze, the rats received injections of two different endorphins, and both drugs improved their maze-running abilities. Interestingly, morphine had the opposite effect, though both morphine and endorphins reduce pain and cause euphoria. Larry Stein and James Belluzzi of Wyeth Laboratories taught a group of rats that wire mesh at the bottom of their cages would electrically shock them, then divided them into two groups, one receiving injections of endorphin. The electrical shocks were then stopped for a period. Afterward, the rats who received the endorphin forgot quickly about the shocks, while the rats with endorphin had heightened memories. A number of other tests have shown improvements in learning and memory in endorphin-boosted rats. These improvements are triggered by very small doses of the peptides, compared to the relatively huge doses required to get the analgesic effect.[84]

LEARNING ON THE PLEASURE PATHWAYS

BUT HOW COULD ENDORPHINS, KNOWN MAINLY FOR THEIR physical effects and "opiates," such as relieving pain and producing euphoria, have such powerful mental or cognitive benefits? One answer, neuroscientists now believe, is that in humans the places in the brain that produce most endorphins and contain the largest concentration of endorphin receptors are the same areas of the brain involved most intimately with learning and memory.

Three decades ago, James Olds, inserting electrodes into rats' brains and allowing them to simulate themselves, discovered that there were specific "reward centers" that seemed to produce so much pleasure that the rats preferred self-stimulation to food, drink, sex, or sleep. With the discovery of endorphins, as we have seen, numerous researchers confirmed that electrical stimulation of these pleasure centers caused sharp increases in endorphin production. In 1978, Aryeh Routtenberg of Northwestern University located these pleasure centers and found they were connected by what he called *pleasure pathways*. These pathways, according to Routtenberg, are more extensive than previously thought, extending from deep in the brain stem, the earliest part of the brain to evolve, far forward into the cortex of the frontal lobes, the most recent part of the brain to evolve. As he traced these pleasure pathways, Routtenberg found that they were connected with the pathways in the brain associated with the neurotransmitters called catecholamines (norepinephrine and dopamine) as well as the pathways and areas with the greatest concentrations of endorphins and endorphin receptor sites.

Further, Routtenberg noted that these pleasure pathways are closely associated with the areas of the brain known to be involved in learning and the formation of memory. He cited experiments by Olds and others that showed a connection between stimulation of the pleasure centers, or "reward," and learning, and concluded, "the evidence clearly shows that the brain-reward pathways play an important role in learning and memory." How? Says Routtenberg, "I have speculated that the pathways of brain reward may function as the pathways of memory consolidation. By this I mean that when something is learned, activity in the brain-reward pathways facilitates the formation of memory. . . . Evidence for the reward effects of localized electrical stimulation . . . and for the association of reward paths with memory formation indicates that the neutral substrates of self-stimulation play a vital role in the guidance of behavior."[286]

THE SELFISH GENES OF THE ROBOT DUCK

Learning and pleasure, memory and reward; they are, it seems inextricably intertwined. It's a truth we've all experienced: as we try to understand something, solve some problem which has been troubling us, stretch our minds to accommodate new ideas, we feel a vague sense of strain and effort. Then, suddenly, with a thrill, we understand, the problem is solved, the new ideas become clear, and we are filled with a sense of pleasure, a sensual feeling of satisfaction as our body flows with warmth.

Why are learning and pleasure so interrelated? Neuroscientists see this combination as an evolutionary development, a system that developed in animals over millions of years to increase their chances for survival. Decades of research with both laboratory animals and with humans have proved that one of the most effective ways to teach something is to provide the subjects with a reward when they learn. The endorphins, according to neuroscientists, serve as the body's "natural reward system," providing us with a rush of pleasure whenever we learn something or act in some way that is conducive to our survival as a species.

Neuroscientist Candace Pert, of the NIMH, startled the scientific world in 1973 when, still a young graduate student, she discovered the opiate receptor. Since then she has studied the actions of endorphins extensively, and sees them as a key to survival-oriented behavior. If the ability to survive as an individual and as a species can be equated with "intelligence," she suggests, then the endorphins could be said to be intelligence enhancers. Says Pert, "If you were designing a robot vehicle to walk into the future and survive, as God was when he was designing human beings, you'd wire it up so that the kinds of behavior that would ensure the survival of that species—sex and eating, for instance—are naturally reinforcing. Behavior is modifiable, and it is controlled by the anticipation of pain or pleasure, punishment or reward. And the anticipation of pain or pleasure has to be coded in the brain." This system of natural reinforcement, says Pert, is the endorphin system.

A key to this view of endorphins as stimulating intelligence by rewarding behavior that helps a species to reproduce and survive has been stated effectively by Richard Dawkins in his book *The Selfish Gene*: each creature on earth is a finely evolved device to reproduce and survive. A duck is simply a robot vehicle carrying around the duck's genes for the propagation of more duck genes. Says Pert, "A human being is a robot vehicle for the propagation of human genes. Yet *somehow it seems to be requiring greater and greater intelligence for human genes to propagate. We're evolving toward perfect knowledge*. Remember, all human beings alive today are the offspring of a long chain of ancestors, each of whom was smart enough to survive." (Emphasis added.)

In addition to rewarding us with pleasure for learning, endorphins also help us to learn and to survive by deciding what information we allow into our brains. According to Pert, the human brain acts as a "reducing valve," filtering out an infinite number of possible perceptions, so that we are able to become conscious of only a certain number of selected or filtered perceptions. One example she points to is the electromagnetic spectrum. "Each organism," she points out, "has evolved so as to be able to detect the electromagnetic energy that will be most useful for its survival. Each has its own window on reality. Humans can perceive the part of the color spectrum between infrared and ultraviolet. Bees can't see red at all. They can see up through several shades of purple. We cannot." Such a filtering process is, of course, essential for our survival: if all the possible information coming to us in the form of light, sound, taste, smell, emotion, thought, and so on were constantly to battle for attention in our conscious brain, we would soon be driven mad.

Pert and her team at NIMH have proposed "that the endorphins, our natural opiates, are a filtering mechanism in the brain. The opiate system selectively filters incoming information from every sense—sight, hearing, smell, taste, and touch—and blocks some of it from percolating up to higher levels of consciousness. . . . Everybody's version of the world is significantly different." Says Pert, "as incoming information travels from the senses up through higher and higher levels of the nervous system, it gets processed at each stage. Some is discarded; some is passed on to the higher regions of the brain. There's a filtering—a selecting—based on emotional meaning, past experience, and so on."[367]

What the endorphins filter out, claims Pert, is information which is not essential or helpful for our survival; when confronted by a life-and-death situation, such as a potential car accident, for example, all our attention is focused on that situation. Our senses seem to gain incredible intensity, with time slowing down, while other information available to us, such as what music is playing in the background, or what billboards are by the side of the road, seems to disappear from consciousness, filtered out as irrelevant to our survival. In other words, the endorphins choose what reality we experience, and they do so on the basis of what is "best" for us, like neurochemical mommies running around in our brains. And when we act in a way that is best for us, we are rewarded with a flood of pleasure. Since survival requires increasing amounts of intelligence and learning, then intelligence and learning are "good" for us as a species, and are rewarded by pleasure. Endorphins act as filters and determiners of "reality," and as rewards for survival-oriented—i.e., intelligent—behavior seem to be favoring and guiding us toward what Pert calls "perfect knowledge."

THE GOOSE-BUMP QUOTIENT

THERE ARE MANY TYPES OF LEARNING, AND SURVIVAL MEANS more than simply staying alive. While many of the studies mentioned above measure the amount endorphins and other peptides boost memory and learning in cold quantitative terms—relative ability to memorize long lists of words or numbers, reaction time, speed with which rats learn to run a maze—such measurable elements are not the only components of memory and learning. As we all know instinctively, the key to meaningful memory and learning is emotional involvement. Thus actors find they can memorize their lines more effectively when they try to become the character they are playing, finding the emotional meaning within the lines and connecting them to a feeling response within themselves. Thus we remember more vividly past events which aroused our emotions, and we learn more from a college course or a book whose subject matter we strongly value and respond to emotionally. It is in this type of learning through emotional involvement that the endorphins play a key role.

One study casts some light on the relationship between endorphins and highly charged emotional experiences, and suggests how this might be connected to increased learning abilities. Avram Goldstein, head of the Addiction Research Center in Palo Alto, California, and professor of pharmacology at Stanford, has long been a pioneer in the field of endorphin studies. Goldstein was fascinated by "musical thrills," the shudders, back-of-the-neck tingles, and chills up the spine we feel when listening to music that moves and involves us emotionally. He suspected that these sensations might be caused by the release of endorphins. To test this, he allowed experimental subjects to select music that gave them these thrills, then let them listen to it while signaling him when they were thrilled and how strongly. Then he divided them into two groups, injected one group with the endorphin antagonist naloxone, and injected the other group with an inactive placebo, in a double-blind situation. He found that the drug blocked or disrupted the thrill response in a significant number of subjects.[123] This suggests that the musical thrills were a result of endorphins released in response to the music.

This thrill response is not limited to music. Most of us feel it as a natural part of any experiment that is deeply moving or emotionally involving. In fact, it would be possible to use this response as a scale to measure just how strongly we were responding to a situation, be it a poem, novel, mathematical equation, landscape, film, philosophical disquisition, or song. The more strongly our response registers on the scale, which we'll call the goose-bump quotient, the more powerful is our involvement with the material being experienced. And to explore the implications of Goldstein's study of musical thrills, we might say that the greater the goosebump quotient, the greater the amount of endorphins being released in our bodies.

Most important, the goose-bump quotient can also be used as a rough indicator of one type of learning; the thrill comes in response to a sudden *understanding*, a feeling of *knowing* which is not coldly logical and rational but instead is visceral, intense, emotionally highly colored, and capable of altering your life. And, in the long run, it is this type of gutlevel learning that is long remembered, in fact is virtually unforgettable, and is in the truest sense learning that is "survival-oriented." The fact that the endorphins reward and favor this type of emotional response indicates that these aesthetic experiences, including music, art, philosophy, and the perception of beauty and order, are extremely beneficial and valuable, and perhaps even essential to intellectual and emotional growth. By inducing and mediating this type of learning through emotional response, the endorphins seem to be encouraging us to expand and enlarge those parts of our brains and minds which are uniquely human.

ENDORPHINS AND MENTAL EVOLUTION

WE HAVE TALKED SEVERAL TIMES ABOUT THE MENTAL LIGHT bulb, the Eureka event, the Aha! instant. We can now see it in a somewhat different light, as the moment when learning takes place, when the "reality" that has been selected and filtered by our endorphins is suddenly apprehended by our brains in such a way that we learn something new, and this learning is rewarded by a flood of endorphins along our pleasure-learning pathways.

We have earlier seen the Eureka event or moment of learning as the conscious result of a reorganization taking place within the brain: the influx of energy (in the form of information, electricity, etc.) has caused increasing fluctuations or perturbations in the finely balanced dissipative structure of the brain, until the fluctuations grow too great to be absorbed, and the brain is forced to abandon its present structure and reorganize at a higher level of complexity and communication. This evolution into new structures of greater coherence is perceived as something extremely pleasurable and rewarding, a "felt shift," when uncertainty and confusion are transformed into a new mental clarity, an expansion of understanding, a feeling that things make sense. We can now see that this feeling of rightness we get during those learning moments is a result of the flood of endorphins released along the pleasure-learning pathways of our brains.

The equation is clear. Endorphins reward behavior that contributes to our survival as a species. Survival now requires increasing intelligence. Therefore learning and increasing intelligence are rewarded. That is, mental development and growth, *mental evolution*, are rewarded.

ELECTRICAL-POWERED PEPTIDE PUMPING

THE INTIMATE CONNECTION BETWEEN LEARNING AND REWARD suggests that machines like the Alpha Stim may have potentials for increasing human learning abilities and intelligence that have not even begun to be explored yet. It has been proved beyond any doubt that these machines stimulate the release and production of endorphins in the brain. Thus far this capability has been used mainly for pain reduction. But it is also probable that, by increasing endorphins, that is, by activating the brain's reward system, these machines simultaneously activate the brain's closely related learning and memory systems. We can speculate that by giving users a feeling of reward and positive motivation, a feeling of being engaged in some essential activity, a palpable sense that the information now being filtered upward through their brains is important and therefore to be allowed to enter consciousness and be stored permanently in the brain, such electrical stimulation machines could increase our abilities to learn, remember, think, and create.

As numerous studies of electrically triggered endorphins have shown, the electrical stimulation does not have to be direct (i.e., from implanted electrodes)—studies of advanced TENS devices, such as that devised by Joseph Light, show that even stimulating the brain from electrodes placed against the skin outside the skull causes increased secretion of endorphins. For example, Dr. Ifor Capel of the Marie Curie Cancer Memorial Foundation Research Department in Surrey, England, used a TENS device and found that it caused a threefold elevation of endorphin levels.[215]

What this suggests is that by hooking yourself up to an Alpha Stim or a TENS device tuned to the proper frequency, amplitude, and wave form, you can activate your brain's learning pathways and enhance your ability to think, to absorb new information, to combine ideas in new ways, to consolidate facts into memory, and to recall or remember information already stored away in your brain. In practice, this might mean that devices like the Alpha Stim could be used as practical tools to increase learning. Users might, for example, present to their brains the information to be learned (in the form of audio or video tapes, books or articles, images, ideas) while they were hooked up to the electrical-stimulation device, or during the hours immediately after using the device (when evidence indicates the levels of endorphins and other peptides triggered by the device remain high).

In speaking of endorphins, I am using a general name for a variety of related peptides—scientists now know of at least seven chemicals in the endorphin family that have effects on memory and learning. Also, as we have seen, there are other quite similar or closely connected peptides, such as vasopressin and MSH-ACTH 4-10, that can dramatically enhance certain aspects or components of memory and learning. We know that there is a virtually infinite number of potential peptides, perhaps a specific peptide that is most appropriate and beneficial to every type of behavior pattern or information to be learned. It's possible that there are individual peptides that are ideal for learning math, reading Kant, creating vivid and colorful mental images, grasping quantum mechanics, experiencing transcendent love, or observing a hurricane passing through a patch of undisturbed azaleas.

It is possible that each specific type of electrical stimulation, made up of a unique combination of waveform, frequency, amplitude, and current, triggers the release of a specific peptide. Which suggests that in the future, as electrostim devices are built that allow the user to adjust wave-form, frequency, amplitude, and so on, users might be able to adjust the device to put them into the proper mental state for their chemistry class, another to study for their law exams, a third to listen to music, and another to construct a computer program.

It is possible that devices such as the TENS and Alpha Stim are not only boosting levels of endorphins but also stimulating our brains to produce vasopressin, MSH-ACTH 4-10, or other mind-enhancing peptides. At this point we simply don't know, because no one has yet tested the effects of electrical stimulation on these peptides. Because the whole field is still new, scientists understand little about the peptides and the studies that have been done so far hardly begin to scratch the surface. Thus far the only work done with electrical stimulation of peptides has been with the endorphins.

But while the brain-boosting potentials of electrical stimulation remain largely unexplored, there's no doubt that such stimulation does increase levels of endorphins as well as a number of key neurotransmitters. So the question becomes not whether electrical stimulation devices can enhance mental function, but how much and in what ways. Since several types of these devices are now available either in the open market or by prescription, such questions can be investigated by individuals interested in increasing their abilities to learn, think, create, imagine, and explore.

10

THE VIDEO GAME OF THE BRAIN: CAP SCAN

ALTERING THE TOPOGRAPHIC MIND MAP

YOU SIT IN A COMFORTABLE RECLINING CHAIR WATCHING A color television, entranced. What you are seeing is the top view of a human brain. You know this because on either side of the roughly oval shape are pink objects that are obviously ears. Between the ears, the brain looks like the topographical map of some exotic desert island—red and orange peaks tower to the left, light-blue plains spread through the right side of the island, cut by deep blue ravines. Scattered here and there are patches of deep green—forests? But there is something odd about this topographical map. The colors continually shift about, as if the island were in constant seismic upheaval.

"Now," says the calm voice, "visualize yourself at the seashore, hear the surf, feel the salt winds, the sands. . . ." Instantly the colors shift, the blue areas growing, the red and orange diminishing. Instantly you realize that this is not the image of just anyone's brain, but *your* brain, right now, reacting to your inner images of the peaceful seashore. With this realization—you're watching your own brain as it thinks!—the colors shift again, red and orange peaks rising suddenly out of blue plains, and you watch the image of your brain in the process of realizing, your own brain changing as it watches itself changing because it sees itself changing. . . .

It all seems quite simple. You are sitting in the easy chair with a simple "electrode cap" on your head. This cap presses the electrodes that pick up the brain's electrical activity against your skull; the cap can be fitted with as many as eighteen different electrodes. The electrodes beam the information they have received about the brain's electrical activity into a small box called a Biocomp Sensor module, and they do so without wires, by means of telemetry (the same technique with which you can switch channels on your television with a remote-control device), and using the same type of infrared-light link the module sends the information into a computer. You are free to turn your head, even get up and walk around if you feel like it, and your brain activity will continue to be beamed to the computer and presented on screen. The mind-opening device, called a CAP scan (Computerized Automated Psychophysiological scan), combines recent breakthroughs in computers, computerized electroencephalography (brain-wave measurements), and biofeedback.

THE INSCRUTABILITY OF SQUIGGLY LINES

SINCE THE LATE 1920S SCIENTISTS HAVE BEEN ABLE TO RECORD the electrical activity of the brain: electrodes are placed against the scalp, and the electrical waves are recorded as a jagged line by a stylus moving across a long roll of graph paper. Since electrodes can be placed virtually anywhere on the human skull, with each site producing squiggly lines that are different from those produced by all the other sites, to get a picture of the whole brain in action it is necessary to use many electrodes, each scrawling out its own distinctive squiggly line. The results are enormously complex and difficult to interpret, since sometimes certain squiggly lines seem related to certain other squiggly lines, either by producing similar patterns, or mirror images, or seeming to pass a rhythm on from one brain area to another. Different and totally unrelated

patterns are often detected by electrodes as close as a milli-
meter apart, while other parts of the EEG can be constant over
wide areas. At the same time, each line is subject to "noise"
and "artifacts"—random electrical waves generated by the
movement of scalp muscles.

With so many variables and uncertainties and such a mass
of information on the long strips of paper covered with eighteen or twenty squiggly lines, EEGs remained largely incom-
prehensible, though invaluable for revealing certain
pathological brain states (such as types of epilepsy). Until the
development of computers powerful enough to process all the
information from multiple EEGs—to compare, to average out
the highs and lows, to discard the abnormal or random activity—the ability of neurologists to interpret EEGs remained on
the rudimentary level of today's archaeologists trying to de-
cipher Mayan hieroglyphs. As neuroanatomist Floyd Bloom
of Scripps Clinic in La Jolla, California, puts it, it used to be
that a scientist using an EEG to try to figure out what was
going on in the brain was "like a man in a Goodyear blimp
floating over a bowl game: he could hear the crowd roar, and
that was about it."

MIND AS ELECTRICAL FIELD, BEETHOVEN'S FIFTH AS HYPERNEURON

FOR MANY DECADES, MOST NEUROSCIENTISTS BELIEVED THE
human brain was an enormously complex switching network
made up of the tens of billions of individual neurons, communicating with one another through electrical impulses. One
frequently used metaphor compared the brain to a vast telephone system: at any given moment phone calls are flying
throughout the world in a complex net of information passing
along the lines, yet at any point, we could theoretically tap
into someone's line and find out exactly what information was
being conveyed between the two people talking on those two
phones. (Though we must remember that this brain-as-tele-
phone-system metaphor, even seen as a vast oversimplifica-

tion, can hardly hint at the incredible complexity of the brain's communication system, with its tens of billions of neurons interconnected by more than ten trillion synapses and far more than 100,000 miles of dendrites: it's said that the telephone system of the entire world is equivalent to about one gram of the human brain—a tiny chunk about the size of a pea!)

Since the development of the EEG over fifty years ago, most neuroscientists, swayed by this vision of brain as electrical switchboard, have assumed that the squiggly wave patterns of the EEG were simply the random summation of the electrical impulses of the individual neurons—in a sense, the EEG was seen to be simply the combined noise of the individual neurons, much as if we could hear at one time all the billions of phone calls taking place all over the world.

Recent computerized research, however, has suggested that the EEG does not arise from the summation of individual nerve impulses, which are individual voltage spikes, firing in an on-off pattern; but from slow, graded electrical potentials produced by the bodies of the nerve cells. These slow-wave potentials often seem to sweep across thousands or millions of neurons—like that wind through the wheatfield—causing these vast areas of neurons to synchronize their slow-wave potentials. These changing patterns of electromagnetic fields, not the impulses of individual neurons, are what make up the "waves" of the EEG. These large groups of neurons working —or vibrating, or resonating—together form patterns that sweep through parts of the brain, at points reinforcing each other, at other points interfering with each other; again, much like a number of blustery winds sweeping through the wheatfield, at times combining to flatten the stalks in one direction, at other times interfering with each other and causing the wheatfield to be filled with odd patterns and vortexes of wheat stalks swept in different directions.

Using computers to analyze EEG patterns, scientists have found that the patterns can be directly correlated to specific cognitive processes: the changing patterns of electromagnetic fields that sweep the brain are the actual shape of thoughts and perceptions. Experimenter Robert Chapman and colleagues at the University of Rochester, for example, showed their subjects words divided into six groups with different connotations (such as "good" words like "beautiful," and "bad" words like "crime"). Different subjects were shown such words over and over, and their gross EEG patterns were analyzed by computer. The computer data demonstrated that each word type created a distinctive EEG pattern, and that the pattern was quite similar in the different subjects, suggesting that the EEG perhaps expresses some universal language, with the brain-wave pattern for "good" words being similar in cultures throughout the world!

UCLA researchers Warren Brown and James March, with Swiss scientist Dietrich Lehman, recently recorded the EEGs of subjects listening to words that sounded the same but had different linguistic functions (such as the "rose," a noun, and he "rows," a verb). When the EEGs were fed into the computers and averaged over all the subjects, it was clear that the brain-wave patterns produced by the words used in different functions (noun or verb) were consistently and dramatically different.[198]

These and other studies have convinced brain scientists today that the constantly changing spatial and temporal patterns of electromagnetic fields are a key to the brain process we call "mind." One such scientist is E. Roy John, director of New York University Medical Center's Brain Research Group. He is engaged in a project to amass and analyze with a computer large numbers of EEG patterns, in the hope of developing precise electrophysiological profiles of a wide variety of brain states. Thus, rather than relying on general diagnoses of such mental problems as "hyperactivity," or "learning disability," using John's technique (called Neurometrics), scientists will be able to compare the subject's EEG to those of normal subjects in the same age range, and, using the immense calculating powers of the computer, to discover immediately the exact location and type of abnormality in the EEG of the subject, allowing for the most specific and beneficial type of treatment.

Extensive research has convinced Dr. John that the energy

distributions in the brain, and their constant fluxes, constitute what he calls a *hyperneuron*. As Dr. Richard Restak describes John's concept, "Rather than something like a queen bee in a hive . . . the hyperneuron is not a 'giant neuron' but an energy process—in fact, the sum total of charges within the nerve cells, glia, and extracellular spaces within the brain. John postulates that consciousness emerges from the 'cooperative interaction of neuronal populations,' which result in hyperneurons. 'The content of subjective experience *is* the momentary contour of the hyperneuron,' says John."[276] And, of course, with the endless flux of the hyperneuron comes the endless flowing of the contents of consciousness.

As various sensory stimuli evoke this overall pattern, or hyperneuron, believes John, it "resonates" with earlier patterns stored away in memory. And just as a plucked violin string tuned to a specific frequency will cause a second violin string tuned to the same frequency to vibrate in resonance, so the specific hyperneuron linked to some past sensory stimulus causes mullions or billions of brain cells to "resonate," and produce a similar electromagnetic pattern that has been stored away in the structure of the individual neurons (in the process we have mentioned earlier, called by neurosurgeon Wilder Penfield "synaptic tendencies").

This resonance effect is, of course, cooperative, and nonlinear (happening not in a series of linearly connected neurons, but in electromagnetic fields generated by the synchronous activity of thousands of millions of neurons), so that even an incoming wave pattern that is merely similar to or hints at a stored pattern will be strong enough to activate that pattern, in the way the first four notes of Beethoven's Fifth Symphony will immediately trigger a richly orchestrated inner "remembering" of the entire work, or in the way a new song with a vaguely familiar line will resonate and call forth stored wave patterns of a different song heard many years ago. This pattern will in turn trigger new resonances; we will remember the person we were dancing with the night we first heard that song, which will trigger a flood of other stored wave patterns, from the smell of a perfume to the faces of friends met that night. Says John, "Consciousness is a property of these improbable distributions of energy in space and time, just as gravity is a property of matter. The neurons are essential to creating the energy pattern, but subjective experience is generated by the pattern itself, not by the individual neurons."[198]

Recall the research proving that words with similar connotations (such as "good" words) give rise to remarkably similar brain-wave patterns (or hyperneurons), and that these patterns are consistent in virtually all normal human subjects: this suggests that causing or creating one such pervasive pattern of flowing electromagnetic fields in the brain could, by means of "resonance," call up closely related brainwave configurations. This has a tremendous significance, since if we could somehow learn to evoke a "good" brain-wave pattern in someone who is in a neutral or negative state of mind, the resonance effect could activate similar stored brain patterns, in turn triggering more resonances in a chain of associations, leading to a series of subjective experiences of things, ideas, memories, or emotions that are all associated with and resonate to the idea of "good." And this brings us back to that colored image of your brain on the television screen of the CAP scan. For those multicolored configurations actually represent brain waves, and it is possible that those changing patterns of colors sweeping across your brain are actual representations of hyperneurons, pictures of universal thought processes in action. In this, the CAP scan is something truly new.

PAC-MAN WITH A CAP SCAN

THE PROBLEM WAS THAT UNTIL THE DEVELOPMENT OF NEW high-powered and incredibly rapid computers, it was difficult merely to make sense of the the constantly changing EEG patterns of a single human's brain, much less to store away somehow the EEG patterns of thousands of subjects, and then compare each of these thousands of EEGs to determine what brain patterns are "normal" in specific situations (e.g., when performing mathematical calculations, when visualizing, when suddenly having a new idea, etc.).

Now, however, a number of scientists have combined breakthroughs in computer science with breakthroughs in electroencephalography and brain science, and come up with several sophisticated brain-mapping devices. Perhaps the CAP scan is the most remarkable of these devices. Psychiatrist Charles Stroebel, Ph.D., M.D., and colleagues at the Institute of Living in Hartford, Connecticut, put together the first CAP scan in 1983. Stroebel has since become director of the Institute for Advanced Studies in Behavioral Medicine, also in Hartford, and has continued to develop, refine, and explore the capabilities of the machine.

The device is capable of processing information from up to twenty electrodes at once, and by means of enormous computerized "number crunching," the CAP scan automatically and instantaneously converts your whole-brain EEG into a multicolor map, and displays it as a cartoonlike image on the television screen, with each type of brain-wave activity represented by a different color. To do this, it is automatically averaging the minute fluctuations of electrical activity picked up by each electrode, discarding the artifacts, the random background noise, and the electrical energy created by the muscles in the scalp. Incredibly, this is all done instantaneously, in "real time," making it possible for you to observe, and therefore to change, your own brain-wave states.

Just the ability to see brain activity in real time opens up an infinity of possibilities for diagnosis and treatment. If you don't like all that red (high-activity beta waves) raging in your right hemisphere, get some of that peaceful light blue (alpha) and dark blue (theta) in there. Like E. Roy John, who has found precise electrophysiological profiles indicative of precise mental functions, Stroebel, through his experiences with the CAP scan, claims that specific brain patterns represent very specific emotions or thoughts, such as obsession, or creativity, or incipient rage. By learning to see these states and alter them, people can not only learn to short-circuit themselves out of unwanted thoughts or emotions but also learn to enter desired states—whether intense logical thinking or transcendent states—at will, by simply altering the colors of the pattern on the television screen; and it can be done with almost the same ease as sending Pac-Man zooming through a maze.

In essence, Stroebel explained to me, the CAP scan has the unique capability of immediately revealing to the user three variables:

BRAIN-WAVE FREQUENCY. The user has an instant visual image of what type of brain waves and what brain-wave patterns he is producing throughout the entire brain. The electrodes, each placed over a particular part of the skull, combine to provide an indication of EEG activity through the whole brain. Each frequency is indicated by a different color: rapid beta waves show up as patches of bright red; slower beta waves are orange; alpha waves are light blue; theta waves appear dark blue; delta waves are deep green. Thus, at a glance, the user can see which areas of his brain are highly active and which are placid, or simply not operating well.

While the values of cultivating the relaxing alpha waves and the memory- and creativity-enhancing theta waves have been frequently pointed out, recent research in brain lateralization suggests that it can also be a valuable talent to be able to alter hemispheric dominance at will. In most people, the left brain is superior in processing verbal material while the right brain shows clear superiority in handling visual/spatial information. Now, studies by neuroscientist David Shannahoff-Khalsa of Salk Institute for Biological Sciences indicate that hemispheric dominance is constantly shifting. Says Shannahoff-Khalsa, "We used the electroencephalograph (EEG) to measure brain waves simultaneously on both right and left sides of the brain. When the brain waves were carefully compared, it became quite clear that one hemisphere dominates for a while then gives way to the other, with each dominating for periods ranging anywhere from twenty-five minutes to two hundred minutes, with an average of about two hours."

Similar conclusions have been reached by other scientists who "tested subjects at regular intervals on verbal (left-hemisphere) and spatial (right-hemisphere) tasks for periods of eight hours and found that when the performance of verbal ability was high, the spatial was low, and vice versa, indicating that the two hemispheres operated out of phase." This discovery, Shannahoff-Khalsa points out, "suggests we can exert more control over our day-to-day mental functioning. For example, certain cognitive functions, such as language skills, mathematics and other rational processes that are thought to be primarily localized in the left hemisphere" might be augmented by "forcibly altering" our cerebral dominance, and in the same way we might "accentuate the creativity that is thought to be characteristic of right-hemisphere dominance," through similar forcible altering.[52]

The problem is that most of us have little idea of which hemisphere is dominant at any given time, and less idea of how to go about "forcibly altering" cerebral dominance. The CAP scan seems to solve this problem, providing us with a clear color image of our brains, so we can instantaneously see which hemisphere is dominant at that time. If the CAP scan reveals that our right hemisphere is bright red or highly aroused while the left is deep blue and green, we know immediately the right hemisphere is dominant. We can then pay attention to all our psychophysiological cues, and get a "gut" feeling for what we feel like, how our minds and bodies function, when the right hemisphere is dominant. Stroebel is convinced that with sufficient CAP-scan practice, the user can actually learn to shift hemispheric dominance virtually instantaneously in order to deal with the task or situation at hand with the most appropriate hemisphere. It would be a powerful leap in the brain power if we were able, for example, to enter an important conference in which we knew all our left-hemisphere talents would be needed and, sensing that we were in a right-hemisphere phase, be able to shift forcefully and quickly into a state of left-hemisphere dominance.

BRAIN SYNCHRONIZATION.   The second variable the

CAP scan reveals instantaneously is the "synchrony" of the brain, i.e., whether both hemispheres are operating together in harmony. In the early 1970s, Stroebel and associates performed a classic series of experiments with large numbers of skilled meditators. They noticed that as the most skilled meditators reached the deepest meditative states, the electrical waves of both hemispheres, usually unrelated, operating at different frequencies and amplitudes, shifted into a single synchronous rhythm. This synchronous rhythm had two components: coherence, and identical phase angle. As Stroebel explained it to me, coherence between the two hemispheres is when both sides of the brain are generating waves of the same frequency. In coherence, he said, "the waves are moving together, but they could be moving exactly out of phase, so you would have two 10-Hz waves, but they could be going positive and negative—one wave at its peak while the other wave is at its lowest point. So you have to calculate the 'phase angle.' When both 10-Hz waves are 'in phase' they are rising and falling together. Coherence plus phase angle permits you then to calculate another index, *synchrony*."

Stroebel's study of brain synchrony convinced him that it is an extremely beneficial state, found only when deep physical relaxation is combined with serenity and mental clarity. Perhaps this rare state, thought the researchers, could explain many of the well-documented beneficial effects of meditation: decreased stress-related hormones in the body, increased physical and mental health, increased ability to deal with stress, increased ability to concentrate, enhanced learning rates. Stroebel found that there was a definite relation between the subjects' experience as meditators and the increase in brain synchrony: the more experienced and skillful the meditators, the more quickly and consistently was brain synchronization produced. But what could be so beneficial about brain synchrony? One answer seemed to be that these meditators were thinking with their whole brains. Unlike most of us, who use only half our brain at a time, activity flickering back and forth between hemispheres, these synchronous thinkers were able to use all their brain power simultaneously.

Since Stroebel's discovery of synchrony, or whole-brain thinking, in the early 1970s a number of other studies have produced evidence that not only is this type of brain activity beneficial, it may well be the natural human brain state. For example, neuropathologist Edward Bird of McLean Hospital's Mailman Research Center, near Boston, has spent years collecting and minutely analyzing human brains donated to his Brain Tissue Resource Center. One study has been to analyze the difference in chemical composition between left and right hemispheres. He cites research indicating that right-handed people with depression have a dramatically lower level of glucose uptake in the left side of their brains (when undergoing PET scans, which measure glucose uptake in the brain). When the depression is treated and disappears, the glucose uptake balances out. Says Bird, "It may be that differences between the two sides of the brain are involved in a number of mental disorders. Maybe in some areas it's normal to have a balance on both sides—*maybe that's what makes us balanced human beings*."[105] (Emphasis added.)

Lester Fehmi, director of the Princeton Behavioral Medicine and Biofeedback Clinic—who works with a multichannel EEG that monitors each of the major lobes of the brain simultaneously and provides a detailed picture of whole-brain activity—also relates hemispheric synchronization to normality or homeostasis. "We spend a lot of time desynchronized: narrow-focusing, objectifying, gripping," he explained to me. "And we don't have in our culture a normalizing model, a way to get that all back to zero again. So large amplitude, in-phase synchrony is the perfect place for rapid normalization. It's the place to go to for rapid healing and normalization of functions."

British physicist C. Maxwell Cade, using an EEG device that visually represents multiple-channel activity from both brain hemispheres (the Mind Mirror—for a description of this machine, see Chapter 11), studied the brain waves of over four thousand people and discovered that as they developed in mental self-regulation, their patterns showed increasing symmetry between the hemispheres. At the highest state, which

Cade calls "lucid awareness," the subject's brain waves were almost invariably symmetrical. Says Cade, "All the unusual abilities that some people are able to manifest (self-control of pain and healing, healing of others, telepathy, etc.) are associated with changes in the EEG pattern toward a more bilaterally symmetrical and integrated form." His research has led Cade to believe "that the 'higher mind,' on the neuropsychological level, was what Carl Jung called transcendent function, and that it was manifested by the integration of left- and right-hemisphere functions in an uninhibited, reciprocal transmission of nervous impulses across the corpus callosum, the great bridge of nervous tissue which unites the two halves of the brain. This, we reasoned further, would to a great extent provide the union of conscious with unconscious mental contents; the integration of the left hemisphere's extraverted, verbal, rational and abstract processes with the right hemisphere's introverted, visual-spatial, synthetic and holistic . . . processes."[66]

Neurologist J. P. Banquet also did EEG studies of meditators, and provided them with push buttons, allowing them to signal when they were at different levels of meditation. He found that when they signaled they were in "deep meditation" or "pure awareness," the two hemispheres of their brains became synchronized: in phase and coherent. He called this state *hypersynchrony*, and concluded that this hemispheric symmetry is the single most outstanding EEG characteristic of "higher" states of consciousness.[17]

Neuroscientist Jerre Levy, of the University of Chicago, an authority in the field of hemispheric lateralization, is also convinced of the value of bilateral symmetry in the brain. "Normal brains are built to be challenged," she says. "They operate at optimal levels only when cognitive processing requirements are of sufficient complexity to activate *both* sides of the brain." Cautioning against popular oversimplifications, such as equating rational thinking with the left brain and creativity with the right, she says, "Great men and women of history did not merely have superior intellectual capacities within each hemisphere. They had phenomenal levels of emotional commitments, motivation, attentional capacity—all of which reflected the highly integrated brain in action."[173]

There seems little doubt that brain synchrony, or whole-brain thought, can promote high levels of mental functioning. There has been only one problem: only experienced meditators seemed to be able to produce the state at will. It is here that the CAP scan represents a breakthrough. Since the scan can gauge synchrony and immediately reveal it to the user, one can simply sit before the television screen, watching one's brain, perhaps using some meditative or self-regulation technique, or simply trying different states of mind and observing how they alter the brain activity on the monitor. If at some point the brain attains bilateral symmetry, one simply "knows" what it feels like, becomes sensitive to the internal cues that signal that the brain is operating in synchrony, and, with sufficient practice, learns to enter this elusive, highly beneficial state in everyday life.

STATISTICAL ABNORMALITIES. The third variable the CAP scan can instantaneously reveal is abnormal brain activity. The computer's ability to store and process vast amounts of information permits it to file away in its memory banks thousands of EEGs. Stroebel has accumulated a multitude of EEGs of "normal" people engaged in various tasks, such as visualizing, or doing mathematical calculations. Then, when someone with an emotional or psychological problem uses the CAP scan, the computer compares that person's EEG with the numerous "normal" EEGs, performing what Stroebel calls "enormous number crunching" to pick out brain areas which are statistically abnormal. The CAP scan displays those abnormal areas on the right of the screen, with the total image of the brain on the left. The subject is then coached by Stroebel in techniques of changing his brain so that the abnormal colors "go away."

Wary of the idea of "normality," I asked Stroebel if there is really so much similarity in the electrical patterns of people's brains when they're performing the same tasks. "Yes," he said, "there's a great deal of similarity, unless they don't think right. Then we start seeing stuff like this," and he gestured to the screen, where he had displayed the image of the brain of a young violence-prone drug abuser. Deep green islands of abnormality glowed out at me from the right side of the screen. Stroebel's strategy with this client would be to guide him through certain relaxation and brain-altering techniques in an attempt to "make the green go away."

In fact, Stroebel originally became interested in developing the machine because he felt that current methods of detecting brain abnormalities simply did not work very well or very accurately. "The vast majority of people with psychiatric and emotional problems have what appears to neurologists to be a normal EEG," Stroebel told me. "So as read by the human eyeball, the sixteen or twenty channels of pens squiggling out these voltages, you just don't see significant things that seem to correlate with psychopathology. So we got interested in using the ability of the computer to process this information and see if there *was* some correlation with psychopathology." After using the machine on large numbers of subjects, Stroebel found that abnormal mental states, such as hyperactivity in children, schizophrenia, obsessions, incipient rage, anxiety, and depression, are immediately apparent when viewed on the CAP scan. "These states are revealed by electrical abnormalities that a typical neurologist would *not* pick up reading an ordinary EEG," he says.

The real breakthrough with the CAP scan is that it allows the subject actually to observe his brain pattern as it is occurring and by observing it to alter it. Says Stroebel, "The big problem up until now was that all the information we get in the CAP scan was available, but it had to be processed and the information was available only long after the fact. Now you can see the state of the brain at the same instant as changes are taking place." By learning to see these states as they occur and to alter them, Stroebel believes, people can not only learn to short-circuit themselves out of unwanted thoughts or emotions but also learn to enter desired states—such as intense concentration, heightened awareness, dreamlike reverie, creativity, or serenity—at will.

BIOFEEDBACK AND THE CREATION OF
IDEAL BRAIN PATTERNS

GRANTED THE CAP SCAN ENABLES YOU TO SEE YOUR BRIAN activity, to see your state of hemispheric dominance or synchronization. But how can simply *seeing* something enable you to change it? The answer must take us into the hazy area of mind-body interaction known as *biofeedback*.

Until two decades ago, one of the most tenaciously held beliefs of Western science was that there are certain parts of the human body we can consciously control—our "voluntary" systems—and others over which we have no conscious control—the "involuntary" systems. Among the involuntary components of our body were thought to be the rhythm and amplitude of our brain waves, blood-vessel expansion and contraction, blood pressure, rate of healing and strength of our immune system, and secretion of hormones.

Then, in the 1960s, sophisticated devices were constructed to measure minute changes in the bodies of laboratory animals. Scientists found that if the minute changes measured by the machines were somehow amplified and "fed back" to the animals, so that when they were performing a desired task, such as making one ear grow hot and the other ear grow cold, they would receive "positive reinforcement," such as a pellet of food or a blast of electrical stimulation to their pleasure centers, then the animals were able to learn to control virtually every part of their bodies—even those long beeved to be "involuntary"—and could learn this control quite rapidly.[235, 236, 89]

Scientists wondered what would happen if humans were hooked up to these devices, and instead of being rewarded with a food pellet, were rewarded by a flashing light, a clicking, or some other clear signal. Early experiments by psychophysiologist Joe Kamiya, of Langley Porter Neuropsychiatric Institute of the University of California Medical Center, involved monitoring subjects' brain waves, and Kamiya found that within an hour most subjects could learn to manipulate their supposedly involuntary brain waves and generate large quantities of alpha waves. Oddly, the subjects could never explain how they were able to generate alpha waves; in fact, if they "tried" to do it, alpha waves disappeared. All they could say was that they just somehow "knew it" when they were in alpha.

As research progressed, biofeedback scientists found that, in the words of biofeedback researcher C. Maxwell Cade, "if one is enabled physically to observe in one's self some biological happening of which one is not normally aware, for example, the presence of what is called the alpha rhythm in one's brain waves, then one can be trained to control that happening." Biofeedback, says Cade, is simply using mechanical means to amplify certain internal cues and make us aware of them. "Since one cannot control that of which one is unaware, biofeedback can be said to provide the means to become aware—acutely aware—of ourselves, and thereby to gain the possibility of self-control." Using sophisticated EEG monitors, Cade trained thousands of people to enter very specific brain-wave patterns—measured mixtures of beta, alpha, theta, and delta. Yet significantly, like Kamiya's subjects, who could never explain how they created alpha waves but "knew it" when they were doing it, Cade's subjects learned not through being taught any specific mind-control technique but by monitoring real-time feedback, in the form of flashing lights indicating their brain-wave patterns.[66]

As scientists found they could "feed back" a signal monitoring not just alpha waves but *any* psychophysiological event that could be measured, they found, to their growing astonishment, that each of these events could be brought under control. The essential factor was that the signal feeding back the information gained from monitoring that function under question had to be presented to the subject in "real time." That is, if one was trying to learn to generate alpha waves and the signal indicating that alpha waves were being created was not processed and given by the biofeedback machine until five minutes—even five seconds!—later, then no self-regulation learning took place. Otherwise, whatever internal processes that could be monitored in real time could be regulated.

The surprising conclusion was that the ancient distinction between voluntary and involuntary components of the human system had no basis in fact. Simply being made aware via immediate, real-time biofeedback of "involuntary" psychophysiological states enabled subjects to alter those states: they could lower blood pressure, increase or decrease the temperature of their hands, make their hearts beat faster or slower, increase or decrease the acid secretions of their stomach or alter the the thickness of their stomach linings, and change the levels of various hormones in their system, reducing harmful stress-related hormones and increasing pleasurable relaxation-related hormones. In fact, it seemed that given the right type of feedback, humans can exercise control over *every cell in their bodies*.

Researcher John Basmajian, for example, discovered that when his subjects were enabled to monitor the firing of a *single specific neuron* called a single motor unit neuron, they quickly learned to fire off these individual cells in complex, consciously controlled rhythms.[22] If through biofeedback techniques humans could somehow locate and control a single cell in the billions of cells that compose the human body, would it not be possible to exercise similar control over those networks of neurons that seem to grow more or less active according to the type of electromagnetic waves sweeping and swirling through the human brain? Could it be possible to construct a biofeedback device that monitored the electromagnetic *patterns* formed in the brain—patterns which as we have seen are possibly identical with perceptions and thoughts, patterns which may represent consciousness? And could it be that by observing *in real time* the electrical patterns of our brain, our *hyperneurons*, we could alter them, and in altering them alter our consciousness?

And if, as research indicates,

—certain brain-wave patterns form around words with similar connotations (such as the "good" words), and these patterns are similar for virtually all the subjects,

—and certain brain-wave patterns are evoked by specific

linguistic forms (such as noun/verb differences evoked by "rose" and "rows"), and these patterns seem to have a universal validity,

— and certain brain-wave patterns indicate, or perhaps *are*, specific and powerful emotional states, thoughts, perceptions,

— then isn't it logical to assume that by using a biofeedback machine that provides the user with a real-time image of his own brain-wave patterns, providing the user with "internal cues" of the electromagnetic fields sweeping through his brain, the user of such a machine can actually alter his brain-wave patterns into others, changing perhaps from anger to love, from anxiety to serene tranquillity, from agitation to deep undistracted concentration, and from rejecting the input of new information to a readiness to absorb, process, and store in long-term memory large amounts of new information? That is, shouldn't such a brain-wave-pattern biofeedback machine increase your ability to learn, to create, to think?

Stroebel believes this is the case. "The power of the brain to reprogram itself is *enormous*," he observes, "particularly when you set up a motivational structure for people to do it." Recalling his now-classic EEG study revealing the existence of brain-wave synchronization in moments of deep meditation, Stroebel told me, "Now that we've got the CAP scans available, they're infinitely superior to that old EEG stuff in terms of raw information. Now we can put the electrode cap on you, sit you down in front of the image of your brain on the television, compare that brain pattern with the pattern synthesized from the patterns of many people in one of these desired states, and simply say, 'Get some of that red out of there, and move more of that blue over here,' and after a while, you find your brain doing something that you're not even aware you're controlling, and there you are in some kind of higher state of consciousness. It's an exciting time to be alive," he marveled. "We're finally getting tools that may be smart enough to let us study what's going on in our brains! I say 'may be,' because the brain perpetually amazes me in terms of all the things it's able to do if it's properly motivated."

PUTTING THE TOOLS IN THE HANDS OF THE PEOPLE

A NUMBER OF MACHINES THAT PROVIDE PICTURES OF THE brain have been developed in recent years, including computerized axial tomography (CAT scan), positron emission tomography (PET scan), and the nuclear magnetic resonance (NMR) scan. However, these machines are so enormously expensive (the NMR and PET scans each cost over $2 million, the CAT scan about $750,000) than even well-equipped hospitals are often balking at such major investments. In contrast, the CAP scan is relatively inexpensive, and growing less expensive with the increasing sophistication of computers. The key to getting the CAP scan into real-time operation is something called an array processor. Says Stroebel: "A year ago it alone cost some $30,000; now it's come down to under $500 for a card that fits in the back of the Apple."

Convinced of the machine's value not only for diagnostic and therapeutic purposes but also for those who want to alter their consciousness and enhance their creativity, Stroebel is determined to make the system as inexpensive as possible. "I'm committed to making this machine affordable," says Stroebel, "so it can be in the office of anyone who's dealing with people with emotional problems, or people who want to improve their creativity, break writer's block, and so on." For this reason, Stroebel is not interested in commercial production or marketing of the computer software that operates the program, but rather wants to keep it in the public domain. "People should understand," he emphasizes, "that they can buy a small personal computer, a Biocomp system, a couple of extra boards, and a software disc that's in the public domain, and be up and running CAP scans for a total investment of well under $20,000." For those who already own computers, the cost would be much less.

One drawback of the more expensive scanners, according to Stroebel, is the possibility of harmful side effects, since they involve shooting the brain with X-rays, injecting radioactive substances or xenon gases into the brain, or subjecting the brain to incredibly powerful magnetic forces. The machines have come into use so recently that no one knows what the long-term effects might be. The CAP scan, however, is completely noninvasive—you need only don a simple cap. "The intriguing thing," says Stroebel, "is that it's virtually impossible for people to do damage to themselves with biofeedback."

THE TRAINING-WHEELS EFFECT

PERHAPS THE MOST EXCITING POTENTIAL USE OF THE CAP scan is not as a therapeutic device, but as a tool for those interested in learning ways of enhancing their mental powers and learning to produce desired brain states such as deep relaxation combined with intense mental alertness, concentration, whole-brain synchronization, and enhanced verbal, mathematical, visual/spatial, or creative skills. Stroebel has found that many of his patients, after several sessions of watching the color representation of their own brain activity on the screen, as Stroebel coaches them in different techniques and strategies for changing their brain activity to the desired pattern, seem ultimately to learn what the desired brain state "feels" like, much as the early alpha-feedback subjects quickly learned to produce alpha without really knowing how they did it, but simply by "knowing" when it was happening.

Once the patient learns how to attain the desired brain state by feel, he can then transfer this learning into the real world. Stroebel compares the CAP scan to bicycle training wheels— the beginner needs the support offered by the wheels until he has learned the difficult art of maintaining balance on two wheels. After that, the training wheels are no longer needed. The implications are immense: once a seeker of enhanced brain function has learned what that state feels like by observing and experiencing the changing patterns of his brain on the television screen, he might then be able to produce that same state at will in real-world situations, from taking an exam to maintaining mental alertness during an athletic competition.

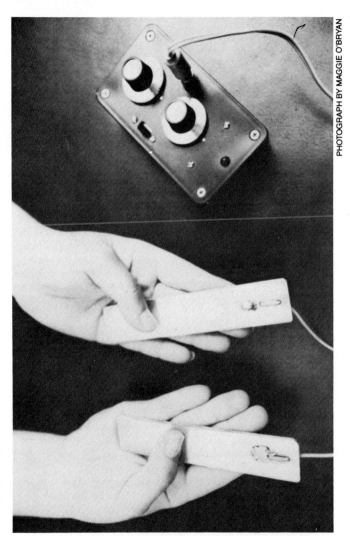

Joseph Light's simple TENS (Transcutaneous Electrical Nerve Stimulation) device is made from "about nineteen dollars' worth of parts from Radio Shack." Many users report that at certain frequency settings, the instrument can increase alertness and concentration, and produce mild euphoria.

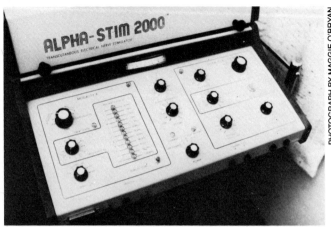

About the size of a typewriter, the Alpha-Stim 2000 uses state-of-the-art electronic circuitry and computer technology to deliver an "individualized" waveform, one that automatically adjusts to the varying resistance of the area being stimulated. Some evidence suggests that use of the device for transcranial stimulation can result in enhanced mental functioning.

This subject is watching the activity of his own brain on the video monitor (at right). The electrodes on his head continuously relay brainwave activity to the computer via "light link" (infrared ray) telemetry. The video image shows a top view of the brain, with the ears on either side, front of brain at top, rear of brain at bottom. (The assortment of biofeedback devices in the background are not a part of the CAP Scan.)

Developer of the CAP Scan, Dr. Charles Stroebel, demonstrates another of the device's modalities: real-time biofeedback in the form of visual images that indicate heart rate, pupil size, and skin temperature. On top of the video monitor is the Biocomp module that receives information via infrared rays emitted by electrodes attached to the subject.

One CAP Scan setting provides a real-time image of the activity of the whole brain on the left of the screen, while only parts of the brain exhibiting "abnormal" activity are shown on the right of the screen; the subject can use self-regulatory techniques to eliminate the abnormal brain activity. This picture shows the brain of a chronic drug abuser; sections on right are green (representing delta-wave activity, usually associated with sleep or coma). Thus, the image indicates that sizable areas of both hemispheres are in an abnormally sleeplike or comatose state.

The two separate arrays of lights on the screen of the Mind Mirror represent brainwave activity in the separate brain hemispheres. The pattern of lights on the screen in this photo indicates that the subject is in a state of passive awareness—bilateral symmetry, with most activity in the beta range, little activity in alpha and theta, and significant delta activity.

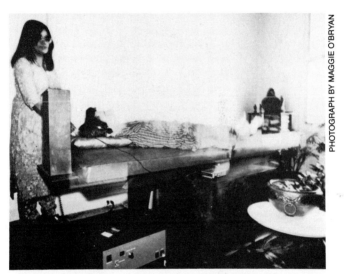

Therapist Chinmayee Chakrabarty demonstrates the Graham Potentializer. The box near the subject's head generates an electromagnetic field through which (as the blurring indicates) the subject is continuously revolved.

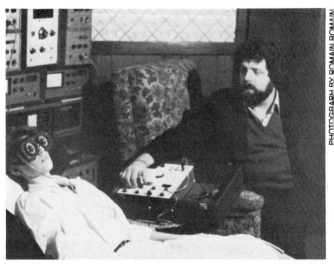

Denis Gorges, inventor of the Synchro Energizer, observes the subject and adjusts the device to the appropriate settings. (The assortment of biofeedback equipment in the background is not a part of the Synchro Energizer.)

The controls on the console of the Synchro Energizer allow the user to select a virtually infinite number of combinations of frequencies, volumes, intensities, sounds, heart rates, and modes (such as alternating or simultaneous stimulation of hemispheres).

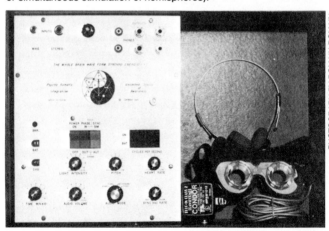

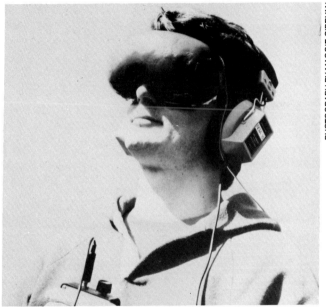

The opaque goggles of the Tranquilite give the user a stylish "human fly" look appropriate for all occasions. Indirectly lit from within, the goggles present a featureless visual field called a *ganzfeld*, while the compact pink noise generator provides a steady auditory stimulus that drowns out external sounds. The device thus serves as a sort of portable sensory isolation chamber.

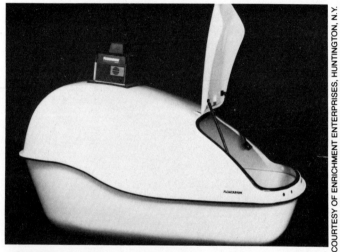

Research has proved that floating induces deep relaxation, heightens suggestibility, and sharply increases the floater's ability to learn new information. Many types of information, from languages to techniques of athletic performance, can be effectively presented in visual form using videotapes. Combining floating with video input can provide an unparalleled opportunity, for accelerated learning. This tank, the Floatarium, is one of a variety of commercially available models that provide an optional video monitor.

And one wonders, if specific brain patterns do in fact represent specific mental states—thoughts, perceptions, visions —would it be possible to hook up men and women who possess truly original, creative minds—our great scientists, philosophers, artists—and allow them to observe their brain patterns fluctuating and flowing until, for perhaps just a fleeting moment, they have a new idea—the Eureka event!—or feel that their minds are working at their best, and then freeze and store that fleeting brain pattern in the computer? And would it then be possible to instruct the computer to consider that pattern "normal," so that you or I could sit down, put on the electrode cap, and watch our brain patterns, at first full of "abnormalities," but then, slowly, as we move the red from here to there, change the green patches to blue, slowly find ourselves reaching that "normal" state which is the human mind at its peak? And our brain having attained the same brain pattern as the great artist, the great scientist, the great philosopher, what then?

Says Stroebel, "We normally use only a very small amount of our brain, probably less than 5 percent." By allowing us to watch the workings of our own brains, the CAP scan can open up that *terra incognita* of the unused 95 percent, and perhaps teach us to boost our brain power enormously. "I can only speculate on what's ultimately going to be possible,' says Stroebel, "but I think the CAP scan opens up a *whole new dimension*."

11

GAZING AT YOURSELF: THE MIND MIRROR

I FIRST MET JOSEPH LIGHT IN THE MIDTOWN NEW YORK OF-fices of a popular magazine. I'd recently read a book, *The Awakened Mind: Biofeedback and the Development of Higher States of Awareness*, in which British physicist-psychologist C. Maxwell Cade described his experiments with a new machine called the Mind Mirror, and I had heard that Light was a U.S. distributor for this device. According to Cade's book, the Mind Mirror's unique method of measuring the EEG allowed users to observe their brain waves in such a way that they were able to ascend through a "hierarchy of states of consciousness." This upward progression led from deep relaxation through states of deep meditation and hemispheric synchronization. Here most EEG biofeedback training stops, considering this state to be the most beneficial. However, Cade claimed that using the Mind Mirror one could learn to pass into an even higher state of what he called "lucid awareness," or "awakened mind," in which subjects can open their eyes, walk around, hold conversations, read and understand literature and works of considerable difficulty and complexity, solve mathematical problems in their heads, intentionally induce desired emotional states, all without disturbing the state.[66] This sounded to me like some sort of ideal mind-enhancement device, and I craved to try it, of course. Whatever else it might be, it sounded like fun.

I called Joseph Light and he offered to give me a demonstration. We agreed to meet at the offices of the magazine, so that my friend, an editor there (the same one who a few weeks earlier had skeptically put on the Synchro-Energizer and immediately begun to hear chanting monks and all sorts of other bizarre audio hallucinations), could also try out the device. Light arrived at the offices, a somewhat ethereal soul with abundant blond curls and an elfin twinkle in his eye that seemed to imply that he might indeed be the sort of fellow who had several secret and interesting things up his sleeve. We retired to a small alcove, where he proceeded to set up the Mind Mirror. For a device with such a formidable reputation, it came in a small package—about the size of a small briefcase. When the briefcase was opened, it revealed an assortment of dials and buttons surrounding a central display screen made up of fourteen lines, each line consisting of a string of about thirty lights. The fourteen lines were divided in half. As Light explained, each of the fourteen lines represented a specific brain-wave frequency. The fourteen lines on the left would display the activity of the left hemisphere, the lines on the right, the right hemisphere. At the bottom, the lowest line represented the brain-wave frequency of 0.75 hertz—in other words, deep deep delta, the slowest brain waves. As the lines moved upward, they represented higher frequencies. Specifically, the lines moved from the deep delta of 0.75 Hz through higher delta frequencies (1.5, 2.75 Hz), into the theta range (4.5, 6.0), to alpha (7.5, 9, 10.5, 12.5), and into the increasingly rapid beta waves (15, 19, 24, 30, and 38 Hz).

The editor arrived, and since he had gone first the last time with the Synchro-Energizer, we agreed it was my turn to go first. Light began hooking me up to the machine. This was quick and simple, and consisted of putting one electrode against my left and one against my right occipital lobe (i.e., the back of my head). These electrodes were held in place with a Velcro headband. The machine was turned on, and behold! the lights on each of the fourteen channels, both right

183

and left, lit up and began moving back and forth in a confusing display. Light told me to try to center myself, and most of the lights retreated toward the center of the machine. What was going on?

Light explained that each row of lights, called light-emitting diodes (LEDs), indicated the amplitude, or strength, of the brain wave I was emitting at that specific frequency. The closer to the center the lights came—that is, the fewer the number of LEDs which were lit up—the smaller was the amplitude of that specific brainwave frequency. The longer the lines became—that is, the more LEDs which were lit up—the more powerful was the amplitude of my brain wave at that frequency.

I was puzzled—I had thought that at specific points in our brains, such as those directly beneath the electrodes, our brains were emitting a single frequency, such as alpha or beta waves. But the Mind Mirror seemed to be showing lights flashing in and out on each of the fourteen channels, from low delta up to high beta. "I don't understand," I said, "how my brain can be creating all these frequencies at the same time and in the same place." At the instant I asked the question, the LEDs in the upper-left beta all shot out to the left in a flurry of activity.

"You see," said Light, "your brain just now engaged in a burst of high beta activity in your left hemisphere—the hemisphere involved in rational, detail-oriented thinking. Simply considering the question caused the activity, and you saw the activity of your thinking registered in that characteristic pattern."

Still, the question remained unanswered; the editor and I remained puzzled, so Light led us through a course in elementary electroencephalography. "What's unique about the Mind Mirror," he said, "is that all other EEGs, whether clinical or experimental, work on the principle that they place an electrode on a specific location on the scalp, and they display the frequency of the highest voltage that they pick up at that location, and everything else is filtered out. So, for example, if they were to place an electrode on your occipital lobe, as I've done with you, all it would display, if they had set it to focus on, let's say, a frequency of 8 hertz, which is low alpha, would be the amount of 8-hertz activity going on at that spot. All it would be telling you is that 8 hertz is the *dominant* voltage or the frequency of the highest voltage that they're picking up on that spot.

"Let me give you an analogy," said Light. "Now wherever you are in your home, you have the frequencies of thousands of radio and television stations—these waveforms are passing right through your room all the time. If you were to take a weak radio and turn the dial, you would find that some stations come in very weak and others strong. What traditional EEGs do is display only the frequency of the strongest radio station. What the Mind Mirror does is take in fourteen of these, not just the strongest station; and it processes and displays them—the entire frequency spectrum—in a logical, easily understood pattern, and it does it all in real time.

"The problem with traditional EEGs is that many electroencephalographers do not understand the limits of their equipment. So when they set their machine to measure, say, 8-hertz activity at a certain place in the brain, they assume that 8 hertz is the *only* frequency in voltages being generated by the brain at that point. But that's not true. With the Mind Mirror, on the other hand, you can put an electrode on the scalp on the same point on the occipital lobe, and it will display fourteen frequencies and voltages from that single point. The brain simultaneously produces *many* frequencies and voltages. What they're doing with traditional EEGs is filtering out everything and only taking in the highest voltage, and then displaying that frequency."

Light described how he had taken the "MM" to a research institution and demonstrated it to a highly respected electroencephalographer. The researcher, who had about $350,000 worth of EEG equipment, was fascinated and said, according to Light, "Well, let's see what we can do with our equipment."

"And with all his hundreds of thousands of dollars' worth of sophisticated equipment," said Light, "they were unable to duplicate the display capabilities of the MM. Now I'm not implying that the MM outperforms $350,000 worth of equipment, because it doesn't—there are functions that traditional clinical EEG equipment has that the MM cannot even come *close* to producing. But what I'm saying is that for the purpose of measuring altered states, or types of cognition, or consciousness-raising, or to determine what the best meditation technique is, I've never seen anything that can come close to the MM. The reason is that the electroencephalographers have been programmed to believe that there is only one frequency and voltage being generated at that one point. And that's not true at all.

"There's so much potential here; if designers of equipment would become aware of this, aspiring young electronics engineers designing biomedical equipment they could come up with some phenomenal equipment, as far as EEGs go. Because right now everything that's available is basically primitive. Just electroencephalography itself is primitive."

to rage about like mad in high beta frequencies in my left hemisphere, while the rest of my brain seemed to be doing nothing. Obviously, I was trying very hard to think in a logical way.

All right, I thought, let's take this mirror for a test drive. For the next fifteen minutes or so, I attempted to sit calmly, watching the light patterns change on the screen, as Light suggested different techniques, including slow breathing, breath holding, repeating a mantra, visualizing various images, and simply trying to empty my mind. At times I would find my brain producing large-amplitude alpha waves in both hemispheres, and at those times I felt very calm, very alert—I knew exactly what was happening around me—and yet my brain was empty. It was an exhilarating feeling. At times I produced large amounts of theta waves, and during these periods I drifted off into a sort of dream state in which vivid images that were totally unrelated to what was going on flashed through my mind. Frequently I became totally frustrated, and the beta lights at the top of the screen went wild.

I began to be able to see the array of lights on the screen as

186

distinct patterns, two wavering lines of more or less brain activity, sometimes with both hemispheres totally out of sync, other times with both hemispheres balanced, when the pattern would take on a beautiful symmetrical form. Once the machine fell into a perfect coke-bottle form—narrow at the top, indicating little or no beta activity, bulging in the mid-alpha range, narrowing a bit where alpha descends into theta, flaring again in low theta, and disappearing completely in delta, the bottom of the bottle.

"That's it," said Light (causing the pattern to immediately disappear), "a perfect 'level four' state—what's typically known as deep meditation. Beyond that is what the machine's developer, Maxwell Cade, calls 'the fifth state,' lucid awareness, the awakened mind. What it consists of is that strong alpha-theta pattern, with the addition of activity in the beta range of 16 to 18 hertz. It combines all the calm, detached inward and outward awareness of level four, but what is unique is that it is *coexistent with thought processes*." This is the state I had heard of, in which people can walk about in what seems to be their normal consciousness, except their brains are operating at a level far superior to normal consciousness, and they are able to perform complex mental and physical tasks.

Later, rereading Cade's book, I found that this fifth state was in virtually every case "bilaterally symmetrical, that is, showing the same amplitude and frequencies in both brain hemispheres." In his studies of several hundred people who were able to attain this fifth state (most after having gone through a number of training sessions with Cade), he found that, as is often typical of biofeedback, the subjects were quickly able to learn how to enter this state in their everyday lives: the training-wheels effect. In every case, according to Cade, the attainment of the fifth state was perceived by the subject as extremely beneficial, with each subject feeling as if his or her mind had reached a higher level of integration, with accompanying increases in mental powers and an unmistakable reorientation toward life. Said one man in his fifties, "In this very relaxed state in which the mind is still working on an

187

intellectual level, other faculties are being brought in as well. The meaning isn't forced on one, but I was able to grasp quite intuitively the inner meaning of what was being taught, and not through a process of ratiocination." Other subjects reported that their attainment of the fifth state was accompanied by bursts of creativity, euphoria, and mystical feelings of being at one with the universe.

I took this all with a grain of salt—like all such highly motivated groups, Cade's subjects had a stake in finding that this thing they had expended time and effort in learning how to do was something valuable and beneficial. And his sampling of subjects was self-selected as well—anyone with the type of mind that might have found the fifth state boring, irritating, confusing, or frightening would have dropped out of the Mind Mirror training groups long before learning how to attain the fifth state (if they had ever joined the training group in the first place). But granted that Cade's several hundred subjects didn't constitute a legitimate controlled study, still, it seemed that something unusual was happening to them when they got their brain waves into this configuration Cade called the fifth state.

I was reminded of Prigogine's idea of dissipative structures, and wondered if perhaps by "boosting" the brain into high-amplitude-brain-wave patterns that have never been experienced before, the Mind Mirror might be increasing fluctuations within the brain to such a degree that the brain was spurred to reorganize at a higher level of internal order, resulting in an increase in coherence, complexity, and intercommunication between neural networks.

"This fifth state," I asked Light, "do you mean that by using this machine I could reach that level?"

"It's a learning process," said Light. "You see the pattern of your brain and by trying different techniques, you see how they alter the pattern. Depending on your natural mental state, you begin to see your pattern change more or less rapidly. For example, you can take an individual who has never meditated in his life and hook him up to the Mind Mirror, and have him sit there with his eyes closed, and discover his basic EEG pattern, and then give him a mantra and *immediately*, within seconds, he'll show a dramatic change in brainwave patterns.

"You can also determine how many years a person has been meditating. Generally when a person first starts meditating, the alpha range is typically between 8 and 13 hertz. So new meditators, as shown on the Mind Mirror, when they're producing alpha it will be at 12.5 hertz. But someone with more experience, when they're producing alpha it will be at 7.5 hertz. Also, people who've been meditating for a longer period of time seem to produce a wide band of alpha, so they produce alpha at 12.5, 10.5, 9, and 7.5 hertz—in other words, they're producing powerful alpha throughout the entire alpha spectrum. You can tell an awful lot about meditation using the Mind Mirror. I've hooked up yogis to this device, and other people who have tremendous mental control, astonishing abilities to manipulate their brain waves, and it would be dramatically displayed on the Mind Mirror. They would sit down, and bang, they're in the fifth state. Generally, it's people who are meditating, practicing yoga, even tai chi. I've wired up people that practice tai chi and told them to do a centering exercise, and suddenly everything becomes synchronized between the right and left hemisphere and with their *eyes open* they begin to produce the pattern—fifth state."

"Can it be learned?" asked the editor.

"Yes. The truth is, you're probably familiar with it—it is probably the state that all highly talented people are in when they're doing what they do best and working at their highest level, whether it's doing mathematics, playing basketball, dancing, or doing Zen meditation." I immediately was reminded of Mihaly Csikszentmihalyi's description of the state of flow, and wondered if perhaps flow was just another term for this state of whole-brain integration through symmetry and synchronization—if perhaps that third baseman who makes an instinctive diving stab at a blinding line drive, the athlete who seems to be playing effortlessly, fluidly, at the peak of his game, if people engaged in what Maslow calls peak experiences, were spontaneously synchronized. I also immediately began wondering how it would be possible to hook up something like the Mind Mirror to people involved in these experiences and see what was going on in their brains.

"According to Cade," Light was saying, "maybe 8 percent of all people immediately recognize it as a state they've experienced naturally. Also, another 8 percent or so can be taught to enter this state with just a minimal amount of training. For others it might take longer, but the Mind Mirror is like a constant visible example, right there in front of you. The machine does nothing to change your consciousness; you're doing everything. It just creates a feedback loop. It enhances or accelerates your ability to learn to meditate, and gives you a positive reinforcement that something indeed is taking place and changing—you can see the alterations in your brain state instantaneously.

"How I used the Mind Mirror was to make a list of about fifty various meditative techniques. Now the machine can be patched into a cassette tape recorder, so you can use it and then play it back and see it displayed on the screen. So I sat with my eyes closed and went through the various techniques, and chose a couple for me which I found created a dramatic change in my brain-wave pattern. That's how I was able to select my personal types of meditation."

It seemed somehow improper to inquire if Light's efforts had lifted him into the fifth state, so, as the editor was visibly eager for his chance at the machine, I asked Light if he could give me one final demonstration of how the machine could help me alter my brain.

"All right," said Light. "Now I want you to begin slow breathing, slow, even, about two or three times a minute. . . . Now, add a mantra—any mantra will do. Keep the two going at once, the breathing and the mantra." As I did so I saw my pattern bulge out into a beautiful abundance of alpha and theta waves.

"Now," said Light, "imagine energy, a stream of light, coming out of your right eye, entering your left eye, running around the hemispheres, coming out your right eye, back into your left, and just keep that stream of energy flowing. Do the breathing, the mantra, and the energy flow, all at once." This produced quite a bit of fluttering around in my right beta channels.

"This is weird," I said.

"Now," said Light, "add a fourth thing. You might enhance it if you start a body rhythm, just start swaying back and forth a little bit. That's right. All four at once." I did this for a while. It must have been quite a while, since on my tape recording of the session there is a long period of total silence.

During that silence I cannot say what happened, except that it seemed as if a flood of light poured into the top of my head and goose bumps raised up all over me, my entire body feeling as if it were vibrating minutely but at an incredible frequency. What I felt was power. I felt as if I could tear the building apart and fly down Park Avenue.

"Look at that," said the editor in a low voice, and I opened my eyes and looked. Bulging alpha, bulging theta, all symmetrical, and beta waves nailed to the wall on both sides, and at the instant I looked, it all disappeared into a random pattern.

CHECKING OUT GOD ON THE EVENT LIGHT

AS HE REMOVED THE ELECTRODES FROM ME AND APPLIED THEM to the editor, Light explained how, after training more than

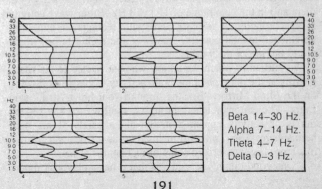

Beta 14–30 Hz.
Alpha 7–14 Hz.
Theta 4–7 Hz.
Delta 0–3 Hz.

four thousand people using the Mind Mirror, Cade had been able to identify five major characteristic patterns, each representing a specific mental state. The five typical patterns (represented below in Figure 2) are:

1. High beta activity in the left hemisphere, with little other significant brain activity. This is characteristic of outward-directed attention, or mental activity such as verbal, linear, logical thinking. The subject is attempting to "understand" or maintain control.

2. Symmetrical alpha rhythms. This is the classic "alpha state" investigated by early biofeedback researchers. The subject who produces this pattern is calm, alert, yet with no ideas or images.

3. Alpha blocking. The subject is in a state of passive awareness—the high beta activity indicates alertness, but the equally strong theta and delta activity show the subject is deeply relaxed. Information from other researchers suggests this state might be associated with heightened suggestibility and the ability to assimilate large amounts of information.

4. Symmetrical alpha and lesser-amplitude theta. This is the typical state of "meditation." The subject is calm, intensely aware of both inner and outer realities, yet detached from both. This is the state of one who has activated the "relaxation response."

5. The awakened mind; lucid awareness; the fifth state. Very-high-amplitude alpha waves, lesser-amplitude activity in theta and in the beta range of 16 to 18 Hz. Brain-wave activity is synchronous. It is associated with feelings of euphoria, heightened mental powers, creativity, the ability to be "in the world but not of the world."

We turned to watch the editor, who sat riveted to his chair, peering at the patterns of his brain activity, ebbing and flowing on the Mind Mirror. "Breathe through your left nostril," said Light. The editor breathed through his left nostril and sudden bursts of activity appeared in the alpha bands of his right hemisphere. Then, mindful of his duty as a salesman for this machine, Light described some of its features to me.

"One good thing," he said, "is that it has a playback mode.

You can tape your session and play it back later, so if you're working by yourself, you can store the information on an ordinary cassette tape and play it back on the visual display later, to see what was working for you. Which brings up another feature, what's called an 'event light.' So, for example, you may be by yourself and experimenting with various meditative techniques, and, say, ten minutes into your practice you see God or something of that sort, you could push that little button, and see how that subjective feeling corresponds to your brain-wave patterns. Then, of course, you would want to practice to try to duplicate that brain-wave pattern, on the assumption that the same unique brain-wave pattern would produce something similar to the original experience."

And again I wondered, as I had with the CAP scan, if these fleeting patterns of electromagnetic energy are synonymous with specific states of mind, if every possible brain state in the world has its own specific hyperneuron or configuration of energy flows through vast networks of neurons, and if we can immortalize certain heightened states by means of "event buttons" or "fifth-state patterns." Is it possible that thoughts and perceptions exist, pure, precise electromagnetic configurations that don't care *whose* mind they exist in, like Platonic ideals, so that, given sufficient practice, we can reproduce them in ourselves, and in fact transfer them from one person to another in the form of tape cassettes or computer discs? Is it possible that we may someday be able to take selected brain-wave configurations home with us on a cassette tape, like teenagers taking home their favorite record, jack one of them into our Mind Mirror, put on our electrodes, and then practice and practice until we can ease our brains into the same patterns produced by our greatest minds working at their peak? The brain, says NIMH neuroscientist Candace Pert, is just a "wet little minireceiver of collective reality." A radio that can be tuned to any frequency. The question is, what programs do we want to hear? What programs are we capable of hearing? What programs are possible?

The editor, experimenting, had put on his Walkman playing the latest rock hit. "Look at this," he cried. As the music blasted into his ears, every light on the right side of his brain was nailed to the wall, nothing on the left. Total blowout of the right hemisphere. "That's interesting!" he cried. It really was.

12

TUNING THE BRAIN WITH SOUND WAVES: HEMI-SYNC

IT IS LATE NIGHT IN THE HEART OF THE DOWN-TO-EARTH 1950s. The man has been feeling strange recently, with bursts of vibrations pulsing through him like a painless electric shock. Now, as he lies beside his sleeping wife, the vibrations have come again. To take his mind off the frightening sensations, he concentrates on the pleasure he will have the next day while soaring in his glider. Suddenly he finds his shoulder pressed against a hard surface. Thinking he has somehow fallen out of bed, he reaches back and feels the surface—peculiar yet familiar. He turns and sees he is floating against the ceiling, bouncing a bit each time he moves, like a balloon. Startled, he rolls over and peers down in the dim light, seeing two figures sleeping in his bed. One is his wife. What an odd dream, he thinks. Curious to see whom he might dream to be in bed with his wife, he peers more closely at the sleeping man. The recognition is stunning and chilling—the man on the bed is himself. . . .

Now, in mid-1985, I am stretched out in the total darkness of an isolation cubicle as stereo headphones send eerie, throbbing sounds into my ears. The pulsing tones seem to resonate through my whole body like a painless electric shock, and my body feels profoundly, pleasantly, and strangely relaxed. The relaxation is strange because it seems to have been imposed on me. It is not the gradual easing away of body tensions that accompanies the usual sort of relaxation, but a noticeable drop, as if I had been floating on the ocean's surface and then gently but ineluctably been sucked downward and found myself resting comfortably on the ocean's floor, a hundred feet down. I am aware that this is a state that has somehow been created in me by the sounds on the tape I am hearing. I seem to be falling asleep.

As I am about to drift off, the low throbbing on the tape alters subtly. A higher, humming pulse has been superimposed on the lower throb. It's as if I've been lolling somewhere, gazing idly into the distance, nothing on my mind, eyes unfocused, when suddenly I realize that something has been happening in my field of vision, and instantly my eyes focus. Now with that same feeling of snapping to alertness, my brain has become intensely clear, sharp, while my body remains totally relaxed. I seem to have left my body behind and am pure brain, alert, energetic, capable, concentrated. From somewhere I hear a bizarre snorting. Curious, I try to discover where the noise is coming from. It comes again, and with a start, I realize the noise is my own snoring. My body is asleep but my mind is totally awake. Over the throbbing tones in my earphones a voice tells me that it is time for me to try to leave my body by "rolling out" of it like a log. What? Suddenly I remember, I am at the Monroe Institute of Applied Sciences, back in the remote hill country of central Virginia. The friendly voice urging me to leave my body is that of the institute's founder and guiding light, Robert Monroe, the same man who once found himself bouncing against his ceiling like a balloon, and who in the nearly three decades since then has journeyed while still *in* his body from hard-driving corporate executive to mind-expansion guru with his own high-tech ashram. And thereby hangs a tale. . . .

THE WELL-TRAVELED BUSINESSMAN: GOBLINS AND ASTRAL SEX

HAD BOB MONROE BEEN A SCIENTIST, THAT FIRST BODILESS journey might have seemed so "subjective" that he would have dismissed it as mere hallucination. If he had been a more introspective man, he might have seen it as the product of some inner turmoil or past trauma and engaged in agonized soul searching, or run straight to a psychoanalyst. If he had been more spiritually inclined, acquainted with occult lore, he would have immediately recognized that he was having a well-known phenomenon called an "out-of-body experience" (OOBE), and he would probably have given himself to the rare pleasures of astral traveling with little curiosity about the causes, the significance, and the practical uses to which this phenomenon might be put in the "real" world.

Fortunately, Monroe was a self-reliant, pragmatic, and curious self-described "orthodox business executive . . . well grounded and active in the material world," who operated on the principle "if it works, use it." So he set out to explore this "Second State" in much the way Lewis and Clark and other early adventurers explored the New World, pushing into the unknown in mingled terror and wonder, making detailed notes, observing all things with a fresh and innocent eye, and wondering above all how the heck this stuff could be put to practical use.

Monroe claims he quickly learned how to use the vibrations to "unhook himself from the physical with ridiculous ease," and found he could pass through walls and journey through the real world. He "visited" friends and other townspeople, and his observations, carefully noted in his journals, of what they were talking about, doing, wearing, invariably turned out to be true. While invisibly visiting one friend Monroe impishly pinched her, and the next day she had a black and blue mark in that very spot, but had no idea where it had come from.

Monroe next found he could "unhook from local traffic and

travel the interstate," journeying to realms other than the everyday world we perceive. One such realm or "locale" Monroe claims he frequented was a hallucinatory place inhabited by ghosts, the astral bodies of sleeping humans, and nasty little gremlins who rode him like a horse. Another locale seemed to be an antimatter duplicate of our physical earth world. At times he was assisted by spirit "Helpers," who'd appear unexpectedly and seemed to be guiding him toward greater wisdom. Monroe's account of his travels, *Journeys Out of the Body*, jam-packed with parasitic goblins and dead humans, astral sex, scary tips into mind-boggling other dimensions, and practical tips on how to get out of your body, all told with wry humor, quickly became a cult sensation with its publication in 1971, and has been through many printings. Whatever their "real" explanation, Monroe's trips made for splendid reading.

SOUND SORCERY: COMING TO YOU OVER THE AIRWAVES

MONROE'S ADVENTURES SOON HAD UNEXPECTED SIDE EFfects. Never a particularly religious man, he now felt a new sense of spiritual peace. His OOBE's had convinced him that all humans survive physical death, and he now had no doubt that our "reality" is only a small part of a vast spectrum of energy systems existing outside the time/space framework. His encounters with the Helpers convinced him that learning to leave physical reality behind could give us the knowledge to evolve into beings of greater wisdom and higher pleasures. He came to believe that everyone is capable of entering the Second State, and that if all people learned how to master the technique, they would be released from their fear of death, which he believed is at the root of most human problems.

Determined to find a way of teaching others to journey out of their bodies at will, Monroe began tinkering around with ways of bombarding the brain with sounds. His instinctive use of sound to influence the brain was only natural. After all, he'd spent his life manipulating sound waves in a variety of ways. During his long career as a radio and TV jack-of-all-trades, he had created, written, directed, produced, and even composed orchestral underscore music for over four hundred programs, and had climbed to the post of vice-president of programs and director of the Mutual Broadcasting System before going his own way to become owner and president of a group of radio stations and a cable-TV corporation with stations throughout Virginia and North Carolina. As he told me, "Sound has been my main world."

He knew his own OOBEs had been triggered by vibrations and reasoned that if he could somehow cause others to resonate to the same vibrations, they would also have OOBEs. Since it was known from EEG studies that certain brain-wave frequencies (such as alpha, theta, etc.) accompanied certain mental states, Monroe intuitively assumed that the physical vibrations he experienced had something to do with the electrical activity of the brain.

Both brain waves and sound waves are measured in Hz or cycles per second, and Monroe made another intuitive leap, assuming that brain-wave activity could be altered and indeed controlled or "driven" by rhythmic sound waves. If he could just discover the brain-wave frequency that triggered OOBEs, all he would have to do would be to zap the brain with sound waves of the same frequency and the brain would begin to vibrate sympathetically at the same frequency. Presto: instant liftoff into astral realms.

Through the 1960s and early 1970s, Monroe explored the effect of sounds on the brain and discovered that he could indeed produce a driving or *entrainment* of brain waves. Like a crystal goblet resonating to a pure tone, the brain resonated when bombarded with pulsing sound waves, an effect Monroe patented in 1975, calling it a *frequency following response* or FFR. The problem was that while brain-wave frequencies are slow (mostly less than 30 hertz), the human ear is incapable of hearing sounds of much less than 40 hertz.

While Monroe was pondering this problem in his small laboratory in Virginia, Dr. Gerald Oster, a biophysicist at

Mount Sinai School of Medicine in New York, was also investigating the effects of sound waves on the brain. He discovered that pulsations called *binaural beats* occurred in the brain when tones of different frequency were presented separately to each ear. Binaural beats are based on an effect we've all experienced. If two tuning forks of slightly different pitch are struck at once, they produce a sound that waxes and wanes in a pulsing wah-wah-wah sound or *beat*. The rapidity of the beat equals the difference between the two frequencies. For example, a tuning fork with a pitch of 400 hertz and another of 404 hertz, when struck simultaneously, will produce a beat frequency of 4 hertz.

Oster and Monroe independently investigated this beat phenomenon, replacing tuning forks with electronic oscillators, which provide tones whose frequency, purity, and intensity can be precisely controlled. When two oscillators tuned to different frequencies are combined and sent through a loudspeaker, or sent through two separate loudspeakers and mix in open air, they produce a very precise beat that can be heard with both ears or with one ear. Such beats are called *monaural beats*. However, as Oster wrote in 1973, "A quite different phenomenon results when stereophonic earphones are used and the signals are applied separately to each ear. Under the right circumstances beats can be perceived, but they are of an entirely different character. They are called binaural beats. . . . Binaural beats require the combined action of both ears. They exist as a consequence of the interaction of perceptions within the brain."[251] In other words, when stereophonic headphones are used and signals are sent separately to each ear—signals of 400 and 404 hertz, for example—one ear hears only the 400-Hz signal, the other hears only the 404-Hz signal; but somehow the sounds are blended *inside the brain* and set up a binaural beat frequency of 4 Hz. That is, the 4-Hz beat frequency, never an actual sound but only a frequency difference between two actual sounds, is "heard" within the brain itself, created by both brain hemispheres working simultaneously. As a result, the entire brain becomes entrained to the internal beat and begins to resonate at 4 hertz.

Monroe realized that this solved the problem of how to get the brain to respond to sounds at frequencies far below the hearing threshold. If the brain can "hear" beat frequencies that are too slow to be actually heard by the ear, such as a 4-Hz beat frequency, then it should follow that the brain will respond to that beat frequency with a frequency following response—the brain should become entrained to the internal beat and begin to resonate sympathetically at 4 hertz. In thousands of subsequent experiments, using an EEG to monitor the brain waves of people hearing different signals in each ear, he verified that he could indeed entrain or drive brain waves using binaural beats. But in the process of solving that problem, he had stumbled onto something that he suspected might be of even greater significance. For most amazingly, the entrainment or frequency following response did not take place only in the area of the brain responsible for hearing, or only in the left or right hemisphere: the *entire brain* resonated, the waveforms of both hemispheres becoming identical in frequency, amplitude, phase, coherence. What Monroe had discovered was a technique for producing a state of equilibrium and unity between the brain's two hemispheres.

I HEAR A SYNCHRONY

WITH THE 1960s' DISCOVERY THAT THE BRAIN'S HEMISPHERES operate independently and in different modes, scientists quickly realized the implications: human brain activity is predominantly focused in one hemisphere at a time, with dominance moving back and forth between hemispheres according to the type of task being performed, or in cycles ranging from a half hour to three hours. But what would happen, they wondered, if we could use all our brain power simultaneously, both hemispheres functioning equally and cooperatively? The answer came in the early 1970s when EEG studies of the brain waves of experienced meditators revealed that in deep meditative states, brain waves shifted from the usual asymmetrical patterns, with one hemisphere dominant, into a balanced state of whole-brain integration, with the same brainwave frequencies throughout, the state called hemispheric synchronization.

The scientists noted that this rare phenomenon accompanied deep tranquillity, flashes of creative insight, euphoria, intensely focused attention, and enhanced learning abilities. But sadly, they also noted that only experienced meditators seemed able to create the state at will. But now here was Monroe, zapping people's brain with sounds and with the ease of fine-tuning a radio, boosting them into a state of hemispheric synchronization. Instant meditation!

Intentionally induced bilateral synchronization was startling enough in itself, but its implications were even more revolutionary. Other scientists who had been studying synchronization found that when it occurred in their subjects, it could have any dominant frequency. It seemed impossible to predict, let alone control, the dominant brain-wave frequency in which the state of synchrony took place. However, Monroe's technique enabled him to do so. If he wanted to put a subject into a synchronized brain state in the theta range, for example, then he could send a signal of 400 hertz through one ear and 404 hertz through the other. The binaural beat would then predictably cause the whole brain to resonate in the theta range frequency of 4 hertz.

This was exciting stuff. Scientists had long known that specific brain-wave frequencies produced predictable mental states, ranging from the mental arousal of beta, through the relaxation of alpha, through the memory-triggering, creative theta, to the deep sleep of delta. Now Monroe could determine brain-wave frequencies simply by selecting the proper binaural beat. That meant it was possible to produce, at will, unified brain-wave patterns in both hemispheres, thus evoking desired physiological and mental states simply by twisting a selector knob: brain tuning! Dial up some serenity!

To test this, Monroe made a tape that would induce a very slow (delta) binaural beat frequency in the brain, and when he played it to hundreds of subjects, they promptly fell asleep. A tape to induce theta waves caused the subjects to produce not only theta brain waves but the "theta state." That is, not only did the subjects produce synchronized theta waves as measured on an EEG, they invariably emerged from the experience reporting all the mental phenomena associated with the theta state, such as vivid hypnagogic imagery, creative thoughts, integrative experiences, and spontaneous memories.

Monroe made extensive EEG tests of the effect of specific beat frequencies on brain waves. As the experimental results accumulated, he realized he had come up with something truly new and dubbed the process "Hemi-Sync." Exploring the uses of Hemi-Sync, Monroe found that by sending the brain a series of different signals superimposed upon each other, he was able to hold a subject at any state of arousal ranging from deepest unconsciousness, to REM (dreaming) sleep, to semi-sleep, and on upward through intense concentration and one-pointed fixation into high-anxiety states of intolerable arousal. By mixing the various signals in a suitable sequence, Monroe could induce mental events of unusual intensity—for example, he could first send the subject very slow, relaxing signals, and then overlap them with a fast signal that would ordinarily be too nerve-wracking, and produce a state in which the subject was physically deeply relaxed but mentally extremely alert and lucid. Following this same recipe, Monroe found that by dropping the body into a state of profound sleep and then triggering a wakeful awareness with a combination of extremely rapid beta signals, he was able to induce the body vibrations and other sensations that led, for many of his subjects, to those mysterious mental events known as out-of-body experiences.

AMPING UP THE BRAIN: LIGHT BULB INTO LASER

Through many years of experimentation, Monroe and a group of friends he called the Explorer Team, worked in Monroe's small lab, patiently exploring and noting the mental and physical effects (particularly brain-wave frequency, amplitude, and synchronicity as indicated by EEG) of various beat frequencies, and comparing them to the effects of other sound inputs, such as selections by Mozart, Bach, popular and rock music, and simple rhythmic beats at a variety of tempos. "You can't imagine how boring it is," Monroe told me, "to sit there hour after hour, waiting to get hooked up to the instruments and get them adjusted right and then listen to some tone that maybe won't have any effect on you at all." Out of the thousands of possible frequencies that could be produced, they were able to discover some fifty-three that had positive and strong effects on the human brain.

One thing they noticed was that when the brain was responding to a specific beat frequency, the amplitude of the brain wave at that frequency increased dramatically: not only did Hemi-Sync induce hemispheric synchronization, it also caused both hemispheres to work more powerfully in the desired frequency. Psychiatrist Dr. Stuart Twemlow of Topeka, Kansas, notes: "In our studies of the effect of the Monroe Tape system on brain waves, we have found that the tapes encourage the focusing of brain energy (it can be measured as with a light bulb, in watts) into a narrower and narrower 'frequency band.' This focusing of energy is not unlike the yoga concept of one pointedness. . . . As Focus 10 [or the "mind-awake body-asleep" state] counts down, there is a gradual increase in brain-wave size, which is a measure of brain energy or power." Twemlow suggests that "the tape system encourages the recruitment of neurons in the brain to focus their attention on a single task, whether that be to reduce tension on the muscles, to improve sleeping, or control pain."

This idea of focusing energy into a narrow frequency band calls to mind the laser (light amplification by stimulated emission of radiation). The laser is able to concentrate or intensify energy enormously—the laser beam carrying less energy than it takes to boil an egg is so focused it can sear through a thick metal plate like butter. Laser light gains its power from the fact that it is both coherent (i.e., the light waves are in phase or synchronization) and pure (the waves are all of the same wavelength), unlike the ordinary light bulb, which produces light waves that are not coherent (the atoms produce energy randomly), so that even when the light bulb is focused it still produces only an irregular stream of photons: even the most intensely focused ordinary light bulb won't burn through a steel plate. If hemispheric synchronization produced by binaural beat frequencies can indeed make the brain's waves more coherent and pure, then perhaps, like the laser, the focused brain can gain access to a whole new realm of powers and capabilities.

Though Monroe had begun his research with the goal of inducing OOBEs, the results of his experiments with Hemi-Sync made it clear that the process had a much wider range of applications, including the increase or enhancement of a variety of brain and mind functions, including focusing of attention, suggestibility, problem solving, creativity, memory, and learning. Using a combination of Hemi-Sync frequencies with spoken suggestions and guided visualizations, Monroe proceeded to put together a library of tapes with specific applications, including sleep induction, pain control, accelerated healing, rapid psychiatric treatment, enhanced learning, improved tennis and golf.

By the late 1970s, partially as a result of a series of successful Hemi-Sync workshops conducted by Monroe at Esalen Institute in California and in other organizations concerned with human growth and evolution, the word was beginning to get out. Something new was happening in Virginia. Robert Monroe was using sounds to induce OOBEs and alter consciousness in remarkable ways. And the world (or at least that part of the world interested in OOBEs and altered consciousness) began to beat a path to his door. In response to the increasing interest, Monroe expanded his modest sound laboratory into a combination educational and research organization called the Monroe Institute of Applied Sciences.

Hidden away on eight hundred acres in the foothills of the Blue Ridge Mountains of central Virginia, the institute is housed in three ruggedly attractive stone-and-timber lodges on the brow of a hill commanding views over the forested hills and valleys. The educational divisions of MIAS consists, in part, of a series of week-long intensive Hemi-Sync training sessions in consciousness expansion. These sessions were highly praised by such influential figures as Elisabeth Kübler-Ross (who claimed to have had an experience that changed her life as she explored higher states of consciousness using Hemi-Sync), and Joseph Chilton Pearce, writer of such books as *The Crack in the Cosmic Egg*, who asserted that with Hemi-Sync Monroe "has developed an astonishingly effective system for breaking through the barriers of enculturation and opening the mind-brain to its natural capacity. The potentials of this training stagger the imagination and challenge our deepest sense of adventure and fulfillment." With such endorsements, the seminars, called Gateway Voyages, became popular not only among professionals in "the mind field," but also among actors, writers, and other creative people. By mid-1985 nearly five thousand people had passed through the Gateway sessions. Since the only prerequisite is $925 for tuition, room, and meals, just about anyone who's interested can attend. The research division of MIAS consists of a laboratory specially equipped for inducing, recording, and studying out-of-body journeys and travels "beyond space and time." Participation in this division is limited to those who have a knack for that sort of thing.

ENCOUNTERS IN THE BLACK CUBE: EGYPTIAN NECROMANCY, ENERGY TUBES, THE GANDHI CLUSTER, AND A VIEW OVER BAGHDAD

"THROUGHOUT HISTORY," SAYS BOB MONROE, "THE DRIVING force of human civilization has been the search for other intelligent beings. In fact, contact and communication between humans and other intelligent beings has been the content of all human religious systems." Scorning such search tools as the huge radiotelescopes now scanning the universe ("like trying to gauge whether there's intelligent life on earth by measuring and studying the exhaust fumes of their autos," he laughs), Monroe prefers to conduct the probe by "going out and searching for artifacts, other forms of life" in the out-of-body state, when one is no longer hindered by the physical body and its requirements, or by the limitations of space-time reality.

This search seems to be the central purpose of the research division of MIAS, particularly that group of skilled OOB travelers known as the Explorer Team. For several years these voyagers have been "conversing" with a variety of intelligent energy forms, and attempting to answer the perennial question, What's the purpose of human life? (The answer so far, Monroe hints, is to "graduate" from human, space-time reality, which unfortunately is hard to do—"we're all 'human' junkies, because human life is addictive in the worst way," says Monroe. How does one graduate from earth? Like a rocket, says Monroe, one must "attain escape velocity." How to do this? One way is to "lighten the load factor" by jettisoning harmful baggage, such as uncontrolled emotions; another way is to develop what Monroe calls *agape* or "super-love"— the cosmology a striking space-age version of ancient gnosticism.)

Well, I'm one of that paltry and diminishing number of people with nary an inkling of having a past life, an out-of-body experience, or a close encounter with a flying saucer, and I remain unconvinced that the Great Pyramid is a coded message from extraterrestrial beings. I am skeptical about this stuff. And yet, and yet, I find it intriguing, almost embarrassingly so, for a supposedly hard-headed journalist like me. So, though I'd signed up for the week-long Gateway Voyage (only for research purposes, of course) when I was offered the chance to arrive four days early to observe a dozen Explorer sessions in which three of the institute's most skilled explorers would communicate with nonhuman species and report on realities outside the space-time continuum, I jumped at the chance. Wouldn't you?

On my first visit to the lab I was introduced to a petite middle-aged blond woman with a whispery southern-rural twang, who went by the name IMEC. Eyes round as saucers, reticent to the point of shyness, she seemed like a little backwoods girl who had stumbled into some puzzling new world, though this was to be her seventy-sixth Explorer session. She climbed into a black cube the size of a small garage, a state-of-the-art sensory deprivation chamber, containing a water bed, lined with copper shielding to prevent any electromagnetic radiation from affecting the sensitive instruments or the explorer's mental state, and standing on four thick legs, each one buried in a bed of sand to eliminate the effects of any earth tremors. After IMEC was hooked up to devices (including a Mind Mirror) to monitor brain waves, galvanic skin response (a reliable indicator of arousal or deep relaxation), and her electromagnetic field, the door of the cube was shut, sealing her into total darkness and silence. At the control panel, the monitors and I donned headphones through which we could hear IMEC's breathing, and waited while she played a Hemi-Sync signal specifically designed for explorers—a very slow, relaxing beat in the theta range overlayed by an extremely rapid beat of over 200 hertz.

Suddenly a loud voice intoned "Good afternoon," and IMEC was no longer with us, having been replaced by the "entity" known as Friend. The monitors had explained that IMEC is that type of explorer known as a "channel," who allows some other energy form to temporarily enter her body and communicate directly with other humans. Now here was Friend, speaking in a deep, forceful, authoritative voice, quite unlike that of mild IMEC in intonation, vocabulary, and accent, and reminding me of a pompous philosophy professor I once had.

Friend's first order of business was to welcome me, and ask if I had any questions. I was still stunned by the transformation I'd witnessed, and the skeptic within me was wondering if this was somehow being staged for my benefit. I came up with a question, but in the confusion I forgot to turn on the microphone as I asked it. The tape of this session confirms that my question is a long, silent gap. So I was startled when, without having heard my question, Friend quickly responded to it with a detailed answer. (Even more disquieting, in succeeding sessions with IMEC, whenever I began to formulate a question, Friend interrupted his disquisition to answer my question before I could even put it into words.)

Harald Wessbecher, a young German architect, psychic, and healer, was the next explorer. Ordinarily outgoing, affable, brimming with confidence and charm, he too underwent a striking transformation in the cube. After a long silence, the monitor called his name and a small, childish voice, seemingly far away, breathless with awe or fright, answered hesitantly. "Try to contact a high source of information" instructed the monitor. As he did so, we observed the instruments—the galvanic skin response altered with extraordinary speed, and for the first time I witnessed what Bob Monroe claims is one of the most striking and important criteria for determining when someone is undergoing a dramatic shift in consciousness, such as having an OOBE: the body's polarity, or electromagnetic field, simply reverses itself. This shift, according to Dave Wallis, former aerospace engineer and now technical director of the institute laboratory, "is like taking out your battery, turning it upside down, and putting it back in. It's mind-boggling! What does it mean? Who knows?"

In the black cube, Harald had unexpectedly gotten trapped in the psychic nets of a nasty past life he spent as a magician-necromancer in ancient Egypt who sacrificed humans to absorb their life-power. Finally escaping this past life he decided to investigate the "mysteries of materialization." After cruising about a bit he reported that "what I can see is like a network of energy streams that cross-link with each other in a very tight net. Any individual existing now in the spacetime network—humans, plants, animals—sends out these energy streams, and they interweave like a multidimensional cobweb. I see these streams, they are like tubes of energy, and when these cross-points occur, materialization occurs." Suddenly Harald's voice took on the excitement of a small boy watching fireworks. "When you look at a person, these energy streams —they're a bright glowing sparkling red color—flow out of the body in all directions, from every cell, so it's a very wild sight!"

After the session I asked Harald whether these events were

true OOBEs or simply products of his imagination. He said, "You think, it's so wild! But maybe the fact that it *is* so wild makes it more believable, simply because it's so strange that you think, I would never ever be able to think of this myself!" He shook his head in bemused contemplation, and said, "The entities do what they want to do!"

Through over a dozen sessions, the Explorers brought back information that was never less than fascinating, and yet my inner skeptic began to chafe and to wonder, "Well, how can any of this stuff be verified?" Then Virginia psychic Terri Pope, after channeling information from the "Gandhi Cluster" (a gathering or admixture of many nonphysical intelligences, apparently including the spirit or energy of Gandhi) about the future of the human race (great evolutionary changes in store, including bigger feet and more ambidextrous and nimble hands), was given a test in remote viewing (the ability to "see" some distant place whose location the viewer does not know). Given an "address" consisting only of degrees, minutes, and seconds of latitude and longitude, Terry was told: "Move your consciousness to that point and when you are there, report your perceptions."

This was her first attempt at remote viewing, and after a moment she reported that she "saw" a highway running by a stream, near an old red brick building that was part of a "historical area or park" linked to some "revolutionary period." It was near a village of "tightly packed houses." Later the transcript of her viewing was compared to the actual site (which was known only by one person, who was not present at the session), a monument to men killed in a revolution, standing near Baghdad. Close by it was a highway flanked by a stream and a village of tightly packed houses, and the monument was very old, of red brick, and part of a historic park.

Were the explorers truly speaking with energy clusters and traveling beyond space and time? After four days of sessions I still had no idea; but it was clear that they truly *believed* that they were, and that, as evidenced by unique EEG patterns (extraordinary synchronization as shown by the Mind Mirror), reversals of polarity, and quick shifts in galvanic skin response, something extraordinary was happening in their minds and bodies. But of course, reasoned the skeptic within me, these were carefully selected people, with clearly demonstrated predispositions for this kind of experience. Even with the boost of the Hemi-Sync tones, I said to Bob Monroe, voyages into such bizarre alternate realities were not possible for normal people like me, who had never shown any psychic bent. "It's easy," said Bob. Then he laughed. "You'll see."

THROUGH THE GATEWAY: LUST IN LIMBO, PSYCHIC SWORDSMANSHIP AND THE WHITE LIGHT

EVERY FEW WEEKS A GROUP OF TWENTY PEOPLE ARRIVED AT the institute for a week-long training session in "developing, exploring and applying expanded states of consciousness." I had expected my fellow participants to be other-worldly types, space cadets with a penchant for the esoteric and occult, but as the individuals arrived—among them a sales analyst, a schoolteacher, a university librarian, an actress, a sailboat skipper, a business-management student, a political organizer, and a psychologist—I found them to be firmly grounded in *this* world, urbane, and intellectually curious. Most of them, like me, had never had an OOBE or other psychic experience. All of us were eager to get out and kick our astral heels a bit in the nonphysical realms.

From the start it was clear that the program would use a number of techniques known to help loosen one's connection to ordinary reality and intensify moment-by-moment experience. We had to give up all watches and clocks, and for the rest of the week we ate when meals were ready, went to bed when we were tired, appeared for conferences when a bell rang, all without reference to hours or minutes. There were no daily papers, magazines, radios, or televisions to distract us with news from earth. Participants used no alcohol or drugs.

Isolated from civilization (we never left the institute grounds), we soon lost track not only of what day it was, but of the fact that there was a world out there at all.

The main cause of this shift in awareness seemed to be our almost continuous exposure to Hemi-Sync tapes. A customized sleeping-listening alcove—called a Controlled Holistic Environmental Chamber (or CHEC unit), with walls shielded against noise and electromagnetic radiation, fresh air and negative ions pumped in, headphones, and a heavy black curtain to draw across the entry and eliminate all light—was built into each participant's room. We slept in our CHEC units with pulsating Hemi-Sync tones played under the sounds of ocean surf through stereo speakers, and awakened to a lively song energized with rapid Hemi-Sync tones. Before breakfast we did some tai chi and stretching while Hemi-Sync played over the speakers in the conference room. Throughout the day we alternated between listening to Hemi-Sync tapes (each about forty-five minutes) in our CHEC units and gathering in the conference room to discuss our experiences and to prepare for the next. Each day we listened to about seven Hemi-Sync tapes, each one taking us progressively farther away from ordinary consciousness into "expanded awareness."

These virtually constant Hemi-Sync experiences seemed to have a cumulative effect. Since you were so cut off from ordinary reality, with no baseline against which to measure your own shifting perceptions, this effect crept up on you. During one coffee break about the third day I was standing on the deck of the lodge, gazing out across the meadow to the dense forest and hills beyond, and suddenly noticed that I wasn't seeing the scene in a usual way—instead each individual leaf was clear, sharp-edged and bright, each tree ringed with vibrant radiant fields of energy that seemed to flash, the whole swatch of landscape a glowing and vibrating interplay of countless fields of green. When I turned to the fellow next to me and tried to explain, he smiled, wide-eyed. "Yeah," he nodded with relief. "I'm glad you see it too."

Robert Monroe described the seminar to me as a training system to help participants "break through the fear barrier" and move to progressively higher levels of consciousness. He compared the process to making clearings in a vast jungle, making a cozy camp in the middle of the great unknown inhabited by wild beasts, going progressively deeper and deeper into the jungle, until the paths and clearings become familiar. We participants felt this progression as a sense of increasing confidence, and increasing competence with the tools we were provided. To start with, we were shown a variety of tools for helping us leave behind ordinary reality. These included the use of a mental "energy conversion box" into which we could put all potential distractions and mundane concerns before departing on our journey (including thoughts of sex—Monroe laughingly told us his greatest obstacle in the early days of his OOBEs was that when he got out of his body he was frequently overcome with an irresistible desire to make love with his wife, and impulsively dived back into his physical self to satisfy his passions), and a deep-breathing/chanting technique called "resonant tuning," to make us more aware of and open to the influence of sound vibrations. Next we were taught to move with the changing Hemi-Sync beats to Focus 10, a state of "body asleep, mind awake." Quickly the ritual of using the energy conversion box, resonant tuning, and sinking back into Focus 10 became familiar and comforting.

Next we moved to Focus 12, a state where "conscious awareness is expanded beyond the limits of the physical body." Here we practiced using such tools as the "Energy Bar" (an all-purpose device that I visualized as being much like the laser swords wielded by Luke Skywalker and Darth Vader), and explored techniques of self-healing, problem solving, and exploring nonphysical realities. Soon we were able to move quickly to Focus 15, a state of "no time," where we experimented with moving into the past and future, as well as attempting to communicate with non-material beings. As we gained confidence, we were guided through the levels above 15, each level associated with an energy pattern of a different color, until we soared into the pure white light of Focus 21, the "bridge from human to nonphysical realities." Along the way we practiced different ways of getting out of our bodies (including such tried and true techniques as the "log roll," the "backward somersault," and ever-popular "upward float"), and some of the participants claimed they were able to glide free the first time, hover over their bodies, and wander through the lodge. Those who remained locked in their too solid flesh weren't too disappointed, since by now it was clear what Bob Monroe meant when he had told us the first night that OOBEs were not the goal of the program, but "only one of many ways to use the energies discovered in expanded states of consciousness." Monroe emphasized that "there are in fact many many more *useful* ways to use that same energy that creates the out-of-body state."

While we made our voyages alone, we soon discovered that we were part of a group experience: all the solitary hours in the dark seemed to sensitize us to others. As the group assembled after each tape, we discussed our experiences, and profited from each other's discoveries. For example, during our first jump into the "no time" of Focus 15, one man visualized a large "time-speed selector dial" that could be adjusted so that he could stay in Focus 15 for what seemed like many hours but was in "real time" only a few minutes. This was clearly a valuable tool, and many of the rest of us quickly made it a part of our own Focus 15 experiences. We frequently ran into each other during our trips to other levels. One woman told the group she had met me at Focus 12, clad in armor, riding a white horse, with a baby in my arm, and during my next journey I encountered myself as that same knight, discovering that the baby in my arms was myself as an infant, while a third member of the group later told me she witnessed the encounter. This communal sharing enriched and energized our experiences, eliminating any doubts we might have had about the value or reality of our experiences: wild things were happening to everybody, and the excitement was infectious. By the end of the week we were not only friends, but had intimate knowledge of each other's deepest desires, fantasies, and fears. Through some strange alchemy everyone seemed to have changed in dramatic ways, and again, we were each other's witnesses of transformation.

BUT DOES IT REALLY WORK?

Back home after the Gateway Voyage, I noticed some aftereffects. A lifelong insomniac, I now was sleeping more deeply and regularly. The Hemi-Sync tapes I brought back with me were very effective, especially just after I woke up or before falling asleep. Even without using tapes the training wheel effect obtained: I was able to enter Focus 10, 12, and 15 in some ordinarily stressful situations, with happy results; but it was much harder to get to the states beyond Focus 15 without the boost provided by the high-frequency tones on the tapes (none of the tapes beyond Focus 12 is available for home use). And few of my voyages had the astonishing richness of imagery and event as the experiences at the institute.

This was understandable: after all, at the institute I had listened to the tapes in a sensory deprivation cocoon for many hours every day; for comparison, imagine the mind-altering effects of simple meditation, if you meditated in total darkness for seven or eight hours every day. Add to this the amplifying effect of being in virtually constant contact with twenty other people going through similarly disorienting experiences, and living in a place of such uncanny pastoral beauty, and you have a sure-fire recipe for powerful spiritual events. Looking back, I had no doubt that some extraordinary things had happened to me and to the other members of the group. But how much of what happened was caused by the Hemi-Sync technique? I was eager for some facts, scientific evidence.

Much of the evidence available comes from members of the institute's professional division—physicians, psychologists, educators, scientists, therapists, and others throughout the world who are busily investigating and documenting the effects of the Hemi-Sync techniques in their own areas of specialization.* Among research published or distributed

*There are now more than fifty Hemi-Sync tapes available for home use, including tapes intended to increase concentration, improve your golf or tennis game, put you to sleep, reduce pain, relax you, enhance your memory, and instruct you in the use of a variety of tools and techniques for self-improvement. "Waves of Change" is a

through the institute thus far are studies indicating that Hemi-Sync has striking effects in helping alcoholics and drug addicts, increasing learning abilities of handicapped, retarded, autistic and emotionally disturbed children, improving vision, reducing pain during and after surgery, enhancing creative thinking and problem-solving abilities, facilitating accelerated learning, stimulating recovery from stroke, boosting mental-motor skills, and dramatically improving classroom learning.

LEARNING WITH THE WHOLE BRAIN

AMONG THE MOST INTERESTING STUDIES ARE SEVERAL IN THE area of accelerated or enhanced learning. A study by psychologist Dr. William Schul, who used a speech compressor to present oral information at a rate of one thousand words per minute, demonstrated that Hemi-Sync significantly increased the subjects' ability to hear and remember the information presented.[301] A study at the U.S. Army's Defense Information School at Fort Benjamin Harrison concluded that students there using Hemi-Sync had a 77.8 percent improvement in mental-motor skills, as well as reductions in stress and improvements in self-control, personal motivation, and performance.

Educator Devon Edrington, of Tacoma Community College, has been exploring the uses of Hemi-Sync for learning since 1978. In a recent paper he wrote that he has employed Hemi-Sync with college students "in four major areas: (1) enhancement of cognitive learning; (2) enhancement of mental imagery; (3) promoting creativity; (4) allaying anxiety. All of these uses depend upon focusing attention, which is accomplished by providing auditory stimuli at frequencies which induce the brain into an appropriate state while simultaneously

series of six albums, each containing six cassettes, that provides a systematic guide to the entering and exploring states of "expanded" consciousness—in many cases these tapes are identical to ones used at the Monroe Institute for the Gateway Voyages. The first of these albums, *Discovery*, is the best introduction to Hemi-Sync and guide to reaching Focus 10. Cost: $59.95.

synchronizing the hemispheres . . . to eliminate hemispheric rivalry."

Edrington and several colleagues have used Hemi-Sync at Tacoma Community College in such courses as philosophy, ethics, speech, psychology, drawing, creative writing, and Spanish. In a study of two sections of a psychology class, both sections were taught by the same person, both sections contained twenty-four students, and composition of the groups was random. Both groups heard the same lectures, read the same books, took the same tests. The control group simply heard the lectures. The other group heard the lectures against a background of Hemi-Sync prepared by Robert Monroe specifically to increase learning, memory, and attentiveness. The Hemi-Sync group scored higher than the control group on all tests, and when all tests were combined, the Hemi-Sync group scored an average of 10.19 percent higher, which, Edrington notes, ". . . By most grading standards, translates into at least one letter grade higher."[94]

Tacoma public schoolteachers Jo Dee Owens, impressed with Edrington's study, began using Hemi-Sync in grade school and high school classes with great success. The method was observed by the Tacoma public schools research and evaluation division, which concluded that Hemi-Sync had extraordinary effects, including boosting "independence and cooperation," attention, and creativity, as well as enhancing cognitive learning. Since then, Edrington has designed a Hemi-Sync synthesizer that produces Hemi-Sync signals and automatically mixes them with music or other sounds from a tape deck or turntable, so the sound composite can then be sent through stereo headphones or external speakers. Since the signal produced by the device is always twenty decibels below the amplitude of the music or voice being played, the Hemi-Sync beat remains inaudible. The device can be set to produce a number of signals, including theta mixed with delta for deep relaxation, pure theta for visualization and affective (or "feeling") learning, theta mixed with delta and beta for attention focusing and cognitive learning, and theta mixed with beta for a combination of visualization and affective learning with attention and cognitive learning. As a result of the work of Edrington and Owens, the synthesizer is now being used for learning enhancement in many public school systems, including Tacoma, Boise, Idaho, and Nelson County, Virginia. Hemi-Sync is also in use in many institutions of higher learning, including Brown University Medical School, the University of Hawaii, the University of North Carolina, the University of Kansas Medical School, and the U.S. Army language schools. (The synthesizer is also available for personal use and is sold through the Monroe Institute.)

Encouraged by the success of Hemi-Sync in learning enhancement, Edrington determined to analyze just what effects the technique had on brain waves. His study is the most rigorous, carefully conducted, and therefore most scientifically impressive exploration of Hemi-Sync undertaken thus far. After placing subjects in a neutral environment (a bed in a darkened, quiet room), Edrington played them a variety of sound stimuli through stereo headphones, including Hemi-Sync at a frequency of 4 hertz (theta), pink noise, music, rhythmic pulses without Hemi-Sync, silence, and combinations of the stimuli. The findings were striking: in response to the 4-Hz Hemi-Sync, the subjects showed an enormous increase in production of theta brain waves, and the theta range "exhibited an increase in amplitude from base to test readings in every subject, in nearly every test cut. In other words, every subject displayed consistent and strong theta entrainment." This entrainment came only in response to the Hemi-Sync stimulus. In addition, the measurement of hemispheric synchronization indicated that 87 percent of the subjects showed significant increases in synchronization. The study, Edrington told me, leaves no doubt that Hemi-Sync has a direct and significant entrainment and synchronizing effect on the brain.

IN THE MAGIC RANGE: BICYCLE TRAINING WHEELS OR THE DOG'S HIND LEG?

THE SIGNIFICANCE OF EDRINGTON'S FINDINGS BECOMES clearer when considered in the light of related findings by other scientists. Biophysics authority Dr. Gerald Oster, who conducted the seminal studies of the effects of binaural beat frequencies mentioned earlier, has found that the brain does indeed respond by becoming entrained to the difference between the two frequencies. More, he finds that beat frequencies of 4 to 6 hertz (the theta area used in the Hemi-Sync tapes) are in what he calls "the magical range." As he told me, "I mean that frequency range has some contemplative character to it, very comfortable and interesting." Binaural beats in that range, he says, have a "terrifically calming effect." Before ascribing extraordinary beneficial effects to this he feels there must be more research, but he has no doubts that the use of binaural beats can have a consciousness-altering effect, and concludes that "as far as putting you in a relaxing mood, I tell you, it's something!"

Probably the foremost authority on hemispheric synchronization is Dr. Lester Fehmi, director of the Princeton Behavioral Medicine and Biofeedback Clinic, who observes brain waves by using multichannel EEG monitors that provide an image of whole-brain activity. Fehmi confirms that hemispheric synchronization and brain-wave entrainment can be induced by binaural beats. His extensive research indicates that this state is quite beneficial. As he told me: "There's a whole-brain sensory integration going on. It's as if you become less self-conscious and you function more intuitively. . . . The scope of your awareness is widened a great deal, so that you're including many more experiences at the same time." Fehmi also believes that a combination of low frequency binaural beats with high-frequency beats—what Monroe used for his "body asleep, mind awake" states—could lead to a situation in which you "could carry the thread of a logical and a narrow, objective kind of awareness, so that you could have that living inside of this whole-brain integration, diffuse oceanic experience."

Biofeedback and brain-wave authority Dr. Elmer Green of the Menninger Foundation, Topeka, Kansas, and co-author of *Beyond Biofeedback*, agrees with Fehmi on the potentials of brain synchronization ("To me it represents a *learning* state"), and is convinced that increased amplitude in the theta range is uniquely beneficial, producing "integrative experiences" and "new and valid ideas or syntheses of ideas" that spring "by intuition from unconscious sources."

The research of these scientists seems to support the claims Bob Monroe makes for the physical and mental benefits to be gained from the hemispheric synchronization and increased amplitude of theta waves produced by the Hemi-Sync process. However, both Green and Fehmi have some reservations about Hemi-Sync. Says Fehmi, "It's a real effect, but it doesn't teach you how to get there. It's like a pill in a way— you don't know how the pill works, you don't know how this audio driving works. And you may end up somewhat refreshed, but if you had the option to get on a device that would allow you to learn to create the permissive conditions for the creation of this synchrony, then you'd be in much better shape, because then you could apply that anywhere without the tools and begin to learn how to function in everyday activity while doing that. I'm interested in self-mastery, and those other approaches aren't consistent with that."

Green agrees: "What we're trying to do is not *drive* the brain but to help people learn how to get control of their *own* brains: controlled synchrony without any outside driving.... They tried to train a dog to get control of its central nervous system by lifting the dog's leg. That's 'driving' the central nervous system. And they lifted this dog's leg ten thousand times, and it didn't learn anything! But when they shocked him so he moved the foot himself, he learned in about five sessions. In other words, passive driving I don't think accomplishes much. It's only when the volition is involved, and you *want* to do something, either to escape or to accomplish something, that you really learn something. A lot of people took LSD and had interesting experiences and then what did they do for the rest of their lives? Nothing. Because they never learned any skills."

Bob Monroe responds to such criticisms with his claim, based on experiences with thousands of subjects, that "specific Hemi-Sync states can be learned and reestablished with the original stimulus," the "bicycle training wheels effect." Asks Green, "Has anybody ever researched that? Where're the data?" Once again, we witness the confrontation between the mind-machine explorers, with their ebullient optimism, and their faith in gut feelings and "anecdotal evidence," and the pure scientists, with their innate skepticism and their demands for hard data and irrefutable proof.

Green, who is acquainted with Monroe and the Gateway program, tossed me questions: "You can't deny that the people who go through Gateway have very real experiences. But how much of it depended on their expectations? It hasn't been researched. And since expectations and the placebo effect are *so powerful*, there's no way of knowing. A lot of people can put themselves into a trance just by lying down and listening to sounds like white noise. Until you separate it from all the other things, how much do you know is due to the Hemi-Sync and how much is due to the setting? The setting there is very very impressive. You go into this place and you lie on the water bed, you go through all the procedures, very impressive, they tell you in advance all the different levels and everything. How in the heck could anybody do that, even if they didn't have any Hemi-Sync, and not have some experiences? I'm not saying Hemi-Sync doesn't do it; I'm saying where's the research? Because I'm a natural born skeptic. It's hard for me to believe anything, especially if there aren't any data. If people go there because they like what they're experiencing, that's fine. Nothing wrong with that. Except that it may not be true that it's caused by one thing or another."

Edrington's recent research provides a partial answer to Green's questions: clearly Hemi-Sync does have significant mind-altering effects. But as Green pointed out the uncertainties, I had an image in my mind's eye of Bob Monroe talking with a group of us at the institute. I had asked why, if OOBEs provided real information about the real world, there was such a lack of verifiable studies in which subjects traveled out of their bodies to, say, San Francisco, and read information printed on a paper there, and returned with that information. Monroe laughed. "The thing is, out-of-body travel between here and San Francisco is like traveling through a gray foggy muss. It's not too comfortable. So how many times can you travel out-of-body to San Francisco before it gets boring? It really *is* boring! So why would you want to do that when the bright lights and all the excitement and adventure are waiting up there in the upper realms? That's your proper home. That's the place to be. How you gonna keep 'em down on the farm, when they can get up inere to the bright lights? Scientists set up their experiments, and as soon as the subjects get out of their bodies," Monroe laughed, and sailed his hand upward, "good-bye! and ffft! they're gone."

And then, as he frequently did when one of us would ask a question that demanded hard evidence, proof, certainty, he held up his hands, thumb tips together, and presented us with what he called "the mirror." "Don't take my word for it, don't believe anything *I* say," he insisted. "You want the answer? Here's the mirror. You have the tools now. Go find out yourself."

There's no doubt more research needs to be done. Meanwhile, there's a certain amount of research that can be done by almost anyone. The goal of the research is to answer certain questions: do the binaural beats of Hemi-Sync produce an altered state of consciousness in the user? Is this state experienced as beneficial, useful, or pleasant? Can one learn to produce these states at will? It's not like experimenting with genetic manipulation or radioactive material, requiring billions of dollars' worth of equipment and advanced degrees in microbiology or nuclear physics. Nor does it require belief in OOBEs, whatever they may be, or in Bob Monroe's arcane gnostic gospel about the spiritual values of "graduating" from physical reality to higher planes, no matter how charming and exotic those beliefs may be. All that's required is a bit of curiosity and a tape player with headphones. You can do the research at home, alone, in your spare time. The tools are available. Go find out for yourself.

13

PACEMAKER FOR THE BRAIN: THE SYNCHRO-ENERGIZER

DURING THE PERIOD I SPENT LIVING ALONE ON THE MOUN-tainside, I spent a lot of my time staring into the fire. I'd piled up some rocks in front of the lean-to for a fireplace, and would pass the evenings sitting on a log, gazing at the flickering flames, the multicolored embers shading from deep red to pure white. In a sort of semitrance, I observed images and sometimes whole scenes that were quite realistic—cities rising out of deserts, marching armies, a group of nuns strolling arm in arm, monkeys swinging from tree to tree. I knew that these things weren't really there, but I also knew that I would not be seeing them if I weren't staring into the fire. Somehow the shifting, flickering lights were stirring up visions inside my head. At times I would feel cut free from time—not a twentieth-century person, but simply a human, staring into the same fire humans have stared into for hundreds of thousands of years, seeing the same things. I got a powerful sense of how mysterious fire must have been to our ancient ancestors, and how entertaining—what need did they have for television when they had this constant source of images?

The knowledge that a flickering light can cause visual hallucinations, then, is something humans have known since the discovery of fire. Modern science, of course, has tried to analyze this phenomenon, and has conducted its experiments with light sources more sophisticated than fire. The great neuroscientist W. Gray Walter carried out a series of experiments in the 1950s in which he used a stroboscopic device to send rhythmic light flashes into the eyes of the subjects at frequencies ranging from ten to twenty-five flashes per second. He was startled to find that the flickering seemed to alter the brain-wave activity of the whole cortex instead of just the areas associated with vision. Wrote Walter, "The rhythmic series of flashes appear to be breaking down some of the physiologic barriers between different regions of the brain. This means the stimulus of flicker received by the visual projection area of the cortex was breaking bounds—its ripples were overflowing into other areas." The subjective experiences of those receiving the flashes were even more intriguing: "Subjects reported lights like comets, ultra-unearthly colors, mental colors, not deep visual ones."

One thing that was happening, Walter realized, though it did not explain the curious visual effects, was that the flickering lights were causing the EEGs of the subjects to change and take on the rhythm of the flashing light. This phenomenon had already been widely noted—almost from the moment the brain-wave patterns of the EEG were first recorded in the late 1920s researchers had realized that photic (light) stimulation could alter the EEG. In 1934, scientists established not only that the EG pattern could be changed by repetitive visual stimulation at a known frequency, but also that the brain would would quickly respond by falling into the same frequency. This effect, known as *entrainment* or *photic driving,* is the visual equivalent of the audio-frequency-following response stumbled onto by Robert Monroe and others who subjected the brain to rhythmic sounds and found that the brain's EEG pattern would assume the frequency of the sound.

In the 1960s, some British artists and American writer William Burroughs read of Walter's experiments, were fascinated by the reports that visual entrainment at certain frequencies apparently caused visual hallucinations, and put together a simple device to make use of it. They called it the Dreammachine. As one of the inventors described it in the rousingly apocalyptic terms appropriate to that psychedelic era:

> The Dreammachine . . . is a pierced cylinder, which whirls around a light source to produce stroboscopic "flicker" over the closed eyelids of the viewer. "Flicker" at precise rates per second produces radical change in the "alpha" or scanning rhythms of the brain as shown by electroencephalographic research. Subjects report dazzling lights of unearthly brilliance and color, developing in magnitude and complexity of pattern as long as the stimulation lasts. When the flicker is in phase with the subject's alpha rhythms he sees extending areas of colored pattern which develop throughout the entire visual field, 360 degrees of hallucinatory vision in which constellations of images appear. Elaborate geometric constructions of incredible intricacy build up from multidimensional mosaic into living fireballs like the mandalas of Eastern mysticism or resolve momentarily into apparently individual images and powerfully dramatic scenes like brightly colored dreams. . . . "Flicker" is a threshold experience of induced experience produced by altering the speed of light to accommodate the maximum range of our alpha rhythms. "Flicker" creates a dazzling multiplicity of images in constantly altering relationships which makes the "collages" and "assemblages" of so-called "modern" art appear utterly ineffectual and slow. Art history is no longer being created. Art history as the enumeration of individual images ended with the direct introduction of light as the principal agents in the creation of images which have become infinitely multiple, complex and all-pervading. The comet is Light.[64]

Scientific interest in the flicker effect increased during the 1960s, and then blossomed in the early and middle 1970s with a burst of independent studies by researchers around the world.[9,53,74,111,163,242,257,275,360,374,379] These reports repeatedly confirmed that rhythmic flashing lights rapidly entrained brain waves. However, the researchers went beyond mere verifying of photic entrainment and investigated what effects this photic entrainment might have on the subjects. What they discovered was surprising, exciting, and suggested that photic stimulation could be a powerful tool for improving the functioning of the mind and body. In independent studies, researchers discovered that:

—at certain frequencies (particularly in the alpha and theta range), the rhythmic flickers could alleviate anxiety during the period of stimulation;

—subjects who had received such stimulation reported long-lasting and substantial reductions in their anxiety;

—at those same frequencies, the flashing light induced in the subjects a state of deep physical relaxation and mental clarity;

—by using photic stimulation it was possible to "train" the brain to modify its EEG frequency;

—after such training the verbal-ability and verbal-performance IQ of the subjects was increased;

—at certain frequencies (again, in the alpha and theta range), the flashing light increased the hypnotizability and the suggestibility of the subjects;

—flickering lights could bring the two hemispheres of the brain into a state of greater coherence or synchronization;

—such coherence between the hemispheres is related to increased intellectual functioning;

—in children up to the age of about fourteen, the most commonly produced frequency is theta, while for adults, the most commonly produced frequency is beta—that is, the percent of theta in the normal EEG decreases and the amount of beta increases as an individual grows into adulthood—and thus by entraining adults' brain waves at a theta frequency it is possible to return an adult to a freer, more childlike mental state, characterized by vivid spontaneous mental imagery and imaginative, creative thinking.

This flurry of studies about photic driving of the brain waves was going on at the same time as other researchers were discovering the existence of hemispheric synchronization and realizing that it was a state associated with a variety of benefits, such as deep relaxation, euphoria, and enhanced creativity and intellectual functioning. At the same time other researchers, such as Oster and Monroe, were finding that binaural-beat frequencies had a driving or entrainment effect on the brain (the frequency-following response), and that by using these phased sound waves it was possible not only to induce hemispheric synchronization, but to select the frequency at which such synchronization took place simply by altering the beat frequency. And, at the same time, other researchers were discovering that certain types of electrical stimulation of the brain, using devices such as the TENS, could alter the electrical activity of the brain, and in doing so could alter the neurochemical activity of the brain, producing a variety of beneficial effects, including relaxation, pain reduction, and heightened mental functioning.

HERETIC, PITCHMAN, PIONEER FOR SCIENCE

ONE PERSON WHO WAS PAYING CAREFUL ATTENTION TO THESE separate developments was a Cleveland, Ohio, psychiatrist and medical researcher, Dr. Denis Gorges. Since each modality—flickering light, pulsating sound, vibrating electromagnetic impulses—could clearly alter brain-wave patterns and induce hemispheric synchrony, what would happen, he wondered, if all the modalities were combined? Already experienced in biofeedback training, electroencephalography, and electronics, Gorges set out to create such a machine. He devised stroboscopic goggles with a series of small lights encircling each eye, and hooked them to a control console that allowed the user to adjust the intensity of the flashes and select any frequency from 1 to 30 Hz (that is, from slow delta to rapid beta) simply by turning a knob.

To this he added stereo headphones, also attached to the console, enabling the user to select a variety of sounds (heartbeat, surf, variable tone, metronome) at any desired intensity. Using sophisticated computer circuitry, Gorges was able to interlock the auditory and visual pulsations into a synchronous relationship, so that as the flashes slowed down or speeded up, grew brighter or dimmer, the sounds kept pace. Gorges also expanded the potentials of the combination of photic driving and binaural beats by enabling the user to select four separate modes of delivering the signals to the brain: the pulses can be delivered simultaneously to both eyes and ears, alternated between the eyes and the ears, or alternated between the left eye and ear and the right eye and ear, or they can cross-stimulate the right ear and left eye together alternated with the right ear and left eye.

To top it off, the console of the device generates a low-frequency, low-power (under 1 gauss) electromagnetic field that pulses at the same rate as the visual and auditory stimuli, to stimulate the brain and alter its electrochemical activity. Surely, Gorges thought, with all these different types of brain stimulation combined, this thing should be a veritable steamroller of a mind machine!

As he experimented with the device, Gorges found that its effect exceeded his expectations—the combination of phased sound, flashing lights, and electromagnetic energy boosted the powers of hemispheric synchronization and controlled EEG patterns into a whole new realm. Subjects not only rapidly went into a state of deep whole-body relaxation and hemispheric synchronization, but also reported that the machine induced a kaleidoscopic stream of brilliant and emotionally charged images. Frequently users experienced vivid scenes with an extraordinary quality of "being there," or visions that metamorphosed into a storylike string of connected scenes or images. At times the scenes were long-forgotten childhood events, at times they were astonishing "mind movies." Users also reported frequent Eureka events and flashes of creativity. And in many cases, the relaxation and sense of being mentally energized lasted for several days after using the device.

Gorges patented the machine, dubbed it the Synchro-Energizer, and began to market the device to health professionals, educators, research institutes, and private individuals around the world. Citing his own clinical and experimental uses of the machine, and preliminary studies done by several other researchers and clinics, Gorges claimed the machine was capable of increasing intelligence, sharpening perceptions, intensifying visualizations, improving both short-term and long-term memory, accelerating learning, increasing creativity, facilitating the retrieval of unconscious memories and images, stimulating holistic problem-solving, reducing the effects of childhood-formed inhibitions, and "permanently enhancing the efficiency of one's brain." "This thing," Gorges grandly proclaimed, "is absolutely the most significant application of modern technology to increasing the abilities and functions of the human mind."

Well now. Earlier I mentioned that many of the mind-machine makers, while keeping one foot in the scientific arena, also have their other foot firmly planted in the market-place. Gorges is perhaps the prototypical example. A burly bear of a man, with a thick black beard and bushy hair, given to flapping his eyebrows as he excitedly expounds upon the powers of his device, he can at times seem to be what one writer called "a real-life portrayal of the mad scientist in a Saturday matinee movie." Others, after witnessing his high-powered rapid-fire sales pitch, have compared him to the fast-talking patent-remedy salesman with the traveling medicine show from that other Saturday matinee movie. For me, the movie character he most resembles is one of those genial, delightfully quirky Frank Capra heroes, powered by a kind of innocent and unshakable optimism, convinced he has invented a machine that can benefit all mankind: "Mr. Gorges Goes to Town." As he extols the virtues of his wonder machine he positively exudes enthusiasm. His words pour out so fast you can hardly take them in. As he mentions this study and that study, and describes how one stimulation mode produces "hemispheric alertness," another produces "cross-stimulation, and peripheral expansion with total external awareness," and another produces "profound internal awareness and centralized fixation," you almost forget that, in fact, no real hard-science studies of the machine have been conducted at all.

Medical researcher Dr. Gene W. Brockopp, who has used the Synchro-Energizer extensively, puts it this way in a recent paper about the device: "Although it is mentioned in some of the promotional literature that research has been done on the synchro-energizer, no research reports are available. Anecdotal information on various individuals who have used the machine is available but nothing even approaching the level of an adequate case study is available at the present time. . . . To the author's knowledge, there is no compiled base of theoretical, experimental, or clinical data on the synchro-energizer."[56]

To Gorges, such criticisms are simply too piddling to deal with. Of *course* there isn't sufficient hard scientific evidence to support his claims—but studies like that take a lot of time and a lot of money. Let the machine speak for itself. It works! As he proudly told me, "I've *always* been a heretic and a rebel." Painstaking research holds little interest for him, he said. "I'm interested in *results*!" When asked about the long-term effects of regular use of the Synchro-Energizer, Gorges cries, "Long-term effects? Long-term effects? Who knows about long-term effects? I don't. Nobody knows about long-term effects. This is a new machine, a new technology. Even the doctor doesn't know about long-term effects. . . . It's exciting to be a pioneer for science."[139]

Gorges's enthusiasm for his device is mighty, and he is mightily persuasive. And I can understand his enthusiasm, having seen a number of people, laughing up their sleeves, sit down in crowded and noisy rooms and put on the goggles and headphones, turn on the machine, and within seconds slip into deep trances or states of glowing euphoria. One hardheaded skeptic donned the Synchro-Energizer and went into a twenty-minute trance so deep that when he came out of it he claimed that only a minute had passed and absolutely nothing had happened to him, and nothing would convince him otherwise until Gorges produced a Polaroid shot of him sitting slumped over in the chair, wearing the Synchro-Energizer and a blissful smile. I have seen the harried editor I mentioned previously put on the machine and immediately begin hearing chanting monks, angelic choirs, and strange boogaloo blasting on his mental radio waves, and I remember his first words after coming out of his trance and taking off the goggles: "I've got to have one of these things for myself!"

So I can understand Gorges's enthusiasm and his eagerness to get this thing into the mass market. The thing really does work. (In fact, I have to point out that the machine can be so powerful and mind-boggling that it is uncomfortable for some people: nearly a sixth of the subjects who tried the machine in one experiment found the experience unpleasant.) There's no doubt that Gorges's gizmo can do something extraordinary. The question is, what is it doing? I decided to consult a few health professionals who had more experience in using the device.

TWILIGHT LEARNING AND CHILDHOOD FLASHBACKS BY FLICKERING LIGHTS

THE FIRST PERSON I SPOKE WITH WAS ONE OF THE FOREMOST biofeedback authorities in the world, Dr. Thomas Budzynski of the Behavioral Medicine Associates clinic in Denver. Budzynski and several associates had issued a "report" on the Synchro-Energizer in 1980, while he was with the Biofeedback Institute of Denver. According to the report, all of the staff members of the institute participated in at least five sessions using the device. "Results ranged from production of drowsy, hypnagogic-like states (with theta frequency used), to vivid, holograph-like images. At times, images from childhood were experienced." When staff members began using the device with clients, the results were "quite encouraging."

According to the report, the device was effective at producing "a sensation of detached relaxation." The staff found that the machine was very useful as a "Hypnotic Facilitator," and that "employing the 3–7 Hz range, we found that clients easily entered the hypnotic state." Also striking was the way the machine acted as a "Facilitator of 'Unconscious Retrieval.'" Staff members tape-recorded the clients' intermittent verbal description of the imagery they were experiencing, and transcriptions of this material would then be used by the therapist in the next session. According to the report, "Often this material provides valuable insight into unconscious processes relevant to the problem. The therapeutic process would appear to be accelerated by this procedure." Perhaps most interesting was the staff's use of the device to accelerate and enhance the user's ability to learn and remember new material, a process the report calls "twilight learning." Says the report: "Twilight learning implies that the client is presented with auditory material while in a twilight or hypnagogic [theta] state. The Synchro-Energizer can produce such a state after a period of 10 or 15 minutes. Auditory material was then presented starting with very low level and slowly building to a comfortable listening volume. The material is absorbed in an uncritical fashion, thus circumventing certain resistances present in the fully conscious state."

The report also noted that the lower frequencies (3–6 Hz) "seem to allow the subject to recall past childhood events with a high degree of 'being there' quality." When they monitored the EEG patterns of subjects, they found that the S/E "drives the appropriate EEG frequencies after a 5–10-minute delay time." Citing the need for serious scientific study of the machine, the report tentatively concludes that both "the absorption of near-threshold verbal material" and the "Facilitation of Retrieval of Unconscious Material" may indeed be enhanced by use of the S/E.[350]

When I spoke to Budzynski over five years after this initial report, he emphasized that no really solid research had been done yet with the S/E, but he still remained impressed with the device. "What the machine can do," he said, "is promote a brain-wave state which is one of relaxation, at the simplest level—people report that they feel pretty relaxed and pretty good. It seems to have a tranquilizing effect for individuals who are quite anxious and high-strung. It tends to quiet them down for three to four days after a session. And eventually, with perhaps ten or twelve sessions, it seems to produce a longer-lasting effect—they feel more peaceful, more calm. It may be accomplishing a sort of integration of sorts. People do report a lot of childhood visual flashes or scenes that come to mind. Then we integrate that with therapy. They talk about what they saw and experienced while using the Synchro-Energizer, and we weave that into our psychotherapy program, and it does seem to be very useful for getting at some of these early and forgotten memories."

When asked whether any EEG tests showed that the subject's brain waves became entrained to the rhythm of the S/E, he said there was evidence that "when you use the theta frequencies eventually there's an increase in theta energy. So there probably *is* some entrainment taking place. Not in everyone, but in some individuals. It seems that some people are more willing to allow the machine to train their brain waves than are others. I suspect it's because it produces a slight feeling of vulnerability as it tends to pull you toward a theta state. Some people resist that and some go along with it."

What about the use of the machine for "superlearning"? Budzynski agreed that this was one area where the device could be potentially quite effective. "We combine the machine with subliminal tapes and certain guided image tapes," he said. "These tapes are then used to promote positive kinds of mental processes. The machine enhances the absorption of the material. I definitely would say the machine increases suggestibility." Budzynski pointed out that his studies have shown that the theta state in combination with a strengthening of right-hemisphere functioning enormously increases the ability to learn. (Or, as he had said on another occasion, "Get access to the right hemispheres of individuals very quickly and keep them in that state, and that's where a *lot of work gets done very quickly.*" In this theta, or twilight, state, he said, the brain "has these properties of uncritical acceptance of verbal material, or almost any material it can process.")[59] Since the S/E is a powerful tool for putting even anxious people into this receptive state, Budzynski suggested, it could, if used appropriately, dramatically boost one's learning abilities.

Budzynski did add a cautionary note, saying he would be wary of recommending the machine for general use, because since the machine was such a powerful facilitator for the emergence of unconscious material, there was always a possibility that frightening or repressed material might emerge for which the user was not prepared. He also warned that anyone with a history of seizures could use the machine only under medical supervision.

I spoke next with Dr. Roman Chrucky, Medical Director of the North Jersey Development Center in Totowa, New Jersey, who had been using a Synchro-Energizer extensively in his practice. His observations supported Budzynski's: he too found that the machine had a very strong relaxing and calming effect ("It acts as a tranquilizer," he said, "and the effect seems to last two or three days. Usually you see the maximum change a day or two after they use the machine"); he too noted that the device "enhances and speeds up hypnotic induction" and enhances suggestibility ("When the client is using the Synchro-Energizer he's very receptive, so using it is a great way of introducing suggestions for changes the individual wants to go through, changing habits—stop overeating, quit smoking, and so on").

But as we talked, Chrucky kept returning to one aspect of the S/E which he felt was most intriguing: enhanced creativity. "A lot of people spontaneously told me that they've felt much more creative when they're using it," he said. "I've found that using the theta frequency I get that kind of response on myself as well, increased creativity."

Dr. Gene W. Brockopp, the Buffalo, New York, medical researcher I cited earlier, found that the S/E had very dramatic effects on many subjects and set out to discover what sort of scientific studies had been done that would cast some light on how the device worked. After finding that there were no solid studies of the S/E itself, he reviewed the work that had been done in areas that were directly relevant and summarized the research in a paper, "Review of Research on Multi-Modal Sensory Stimulation with Clinical Implication and Research Proposals." Among the areas he examined were research on photic and auditory stimulation of the brain, on consciousness and hemispheric differentiation, on EEG patterns and personality variables, and on the behavioral effect of induced stimuli patterns. Using this available research and combining it with his own research and clinical experiences with the S/E, he then made a number of tentative conclusions about the effectiveness of the S/E.

One of his findings was that "coherence of the high-frequency EEG output of the hemispheres is apparently related to increased intellectual function or related to the quality of intellectual functioning." Thus, if the S/E is in fact creating hemispheric coherence of high-frequency EEG output in users, it could very well lead to increased intellectual functioning. Another finding, that "when a brain-wave state is experienced, learned, and practiced over a period of time, it is resistant to habituation (weakening), at least in the short term," could explain why the machine seems to have a cumulative effect, so that after a series of experiences with the S/E users seem to find it easier to enter the desired brainwave state at will.

Exploring the clinical implications of the available research, Brockopp surmises, "The energizer may not 'energize' the brain but actively induce a state of deactivation in which the brain is passive, but not asleep; awake, but not involved with the 'clutter' of an ongoing existence. If this is true, then it may be a state in which new cognitive strategies could be designed and developed."

Citing studies indicating that children spend much of their time in a theta state, Brockopp speculates that the S/E, through its "entrainment of the theta wave . . . may result in the recovery of early childhood experiences. . . . Also, increasing theta decreases the ability of the person to be vigilant and therefore may result in the person expressing ideas without the monitor of the more thoughtful brain processes being active. Information obtained from their earlier state is then available for evaluation and understanding by those more thoughtful and cognitive brain processes and therefore may be resolved, releasing the person from past traumas." This return to childhood thought patterns and increased access to previously unconscious ideas may explain why so many users of the S/E report that the device frequently triggers vivid childhood memories, and acts as what Budzynski calls a "facilitator of unconscious retrieval." (And, like Budzynski, Brockopp points out that the theta state induced by the S/E may, for some people, "have the undesirable side effect of precipitating or enhancing early memory patterns that the person may not be able to integrate into their personality without professional assistance." Further, Brockopp concludes, "Individuals who are tightly organized or compulsive and who need to maintain their sense of vigilance will respond to the energizer either by experiencing discomfort or by going to sleep and thereby bypassing the conflict.")

Noting that "there is some correlation between functional brain-wave state and personality pattern," Brockopp suggests, "If we can help a person to experience different brain-wave states consciously through driving them with external stimulation, we may facilitate the individuals' ability to allow more variations in their functioning through breaking up patterns at the neural level. This may help them develop the ability to shift gears or 'shuttle' and move them away from habit patterns of behavior to become more flexible and creative, and to develop more elegant strategies of functioning."[56]

This idea that breaking up patterns at the neural level can lead to more flexibility and creativity brings us back to Prigogine's concept of dissipative structures. We can speculate that when the brain, a dissipative structure, is subjected to a high degree of stimulation by the S/E, its fluctuations or perturbations are too great to be handled by the existing structure (i.e., neural patterns), and it must abandon that structure and reorganize at a higher, more coherent, more flexible level, with a greater degree of communication between its neural components. Thus, the S/E may be forcing the brain to "escape to a higher order," which would explain the frequent reports by users of enhanced creativity, intellectual functioning, and so on. In this sense, the S/E could be seen as a tool for forcing the brain to evolve and grow, much in the way that the enriched environment caused the Berkeley rats of the Rosenzweig experiments to grow in brain size and intelligence.

In summary, it's clear that while Gorges's claims for his machine may not be totally supported by direct scientific evidence, there are a lot of indirect and anecdotal indications that the device can be a powerful tool for mental growth (with his characteristic modesty, Gorges claims it helps users "to do exactly what 30 years of meditation will teach, only do it in a matter of minutes"). Gorges has always contended that if he could get the machine into widespread use, the scientific studies would follow, and this seems to be happening. There are now over a dozen solid scientific studies of the device under way, including research projects at the University of Illinois at Champaign-Urbana (sports performance, gerontology), the University of Iowa (education and accelerated learning), the University of Alberta (four departments, including pharmacology and psychology), the University of California at San Francisco Dental School (pain reduction and relaxation), San Francisco State (substance abuse), Medical College of Ohio (stress reduction), the University of British Columbia, and the University of California at San Diego.

Several researchers with knowledge of electronics have criticized the S/E's high price (it now sells for about $5,000), claiming that they could put together a similar device that would be somewhat less expensive. Many individuals may find that they can get a more limited but still striking auditory-visual stimulation effect at less cost by using Robert Monroe's Hemi-Sync tapes in conjunction with a stroboscopic flash machine (several of these devices, which emit flashes at variable frequencies including alpha and theta, are available at relatively low cost from biofeedback-equipment dealers), or simply by making their own Dreammachine or "flicker box." (One way to do this is to cut out a series of appropriately placed holes in a large piece of cardboard, tape the cardboard into a large cylinder, place the cylinder on end atop a record turntable, and hang a light bulb inside the cylinder; as the turntable spins, one then gazes at the cylinder, and the light is seen in flickers as each hole in the cardboard cylinder passes in front of one's eyes. It is essential that the holes be spaced in such a way that the flicker occurs at the desired frequency; e.g. for alpha, on a turntable spinning at 33⅓ rpm, there would have to be about fifteen to twenty holes, for theta, about eight to twelve, evenly spaced around the cylinder.)

Gorges responds to criticism of the S/E's cost by pointing out that with its four different stimulation modes, selection of sounds, adjustable pitch, and independently adjustable sound and light frequency and intensity, the device has a virtually infinite number of settings. He emphasizes that he has spent years developing and perfecting the device, at his own expense, and that developmental costs are included in the price tag. If and when he begins production of the instrument on a larger scale (there are now over a thousand S/Es in use), he will be able to reduce the costs. He also says that he is continuing to work on improving the machine, and claims that he should soon be able to make an S/E as small as a pack of cigarettes, with miniature speakers similar to those of hearing aids and goggles as light as ordinary eyeglasses. Other plans include a smaller, less expensive unit that can interface with a computer, so that users can plan their own brain-wave frequency switching sequences, setting up in advance what states of consciousness they want to pass through and in what sequence. "They could go from a state of profound relaxation, into one of heightened awareness, into one designed to maximize job performance or learning. . . . The possibilities really are unlimited," says Gorges, always ebullient, always enthusiastic. "We're only now scratching the surface of what the human brain can do."[139]

Granted the machine's therapeutic valve for those suffering from chronic pain, anxiety, learning disabilities, and so on, it's more interesting to contemplate what might happen if the device came into widespread use among normal, healthy people. I can see it now: thousands of people easing through the city streets, jogging in the parks, eating hot dogs, making love, with little S/E units clipped to their waists like Walkmans, eyes encircled by flickering lights, placidly synchronizing their brains. Public S/Es are everywhere—bars, doctors' waiting rooms, airports, office and factory lounges, public toilets—like miniature jukeboxes for the mind. Put on the goggles and headphones and tune up a ten-minute selection, maybe a blast of creativity, some down-home tranquillity, a bit of jazzy dendritic growth, a classical transcendence opus, or an action-packed mind-movie thriller. And perhaps now and then, gazing into the computerized high-tech flicker, someone will have an odd sensation of déjà vu, a dizzying feeling of being sucked back a half million years, and catch a momentary glimpse of hulking apelike shadows dancing against the wall of a cave, an image of woolly mammoths, saber-toothed tigers, the glittering eyes of the other members of the clan gathered around and gazing into the mysteries of the flickering fire.

14

THE PLEASURES OF MERELY CIRCULATING: THE GRAHAM POTENTIALIZER

At first glance it could be any sunny Manhattan apartment—potted plants, bright print fabrics, a cot at one side of the room. Unprepossessing, cozy, and surprising to me, since I have come in search of an electromechanical therapeutic apparatus that, according to one study, could catapult me into a dramatic "alteration of states of consciousness" that results in "increased relaxation, inner peace, tranquillity, significant personal insights and mystical experiences," as well as such physiological benefits as "reduction of pain, relief of stress symptoms, relief from insomnia . . . accelerated healing of cuts and burns, and improvement of neurological disorders." The device is known as the Graham Potentializer, a name I savor, since whenever I have mentioned it to people in conversation, they have assumed the name is "the Grand Potentializer," a wonderfully majestic and appropriate sort of title for a machine with such great reputed powers. I have expected to find some hulking, arcane electromechanical apparatus surrounded by banks of complicated electronic devices.

"This is it," says the woman who operates the device, and gestures toward the cot. Then I notice that the cot has an enclosed motor under it, a large box at the head, and a metal

240

bar that looks something like a TV antenna at the foot. It doesn't look like much. But in fact, the operator explains, the device is unique, combining several forms of energy—motion, sound, and an electromagnetic field—to stimulate the brain and body, giving the user what inventor David Graham, a Canadian electrical engineer, calls a "transfusion of energy." Among the common benefits Graham claims "streamlined neural response of the brain (a measurable factor of intelligence), acceleration of learning and expansion of mental capacity."

Powerful claims. I feel a sense of anticipation as the operator tells me to take off my shoes and socks and lie down on the device. I place my bare feet against the metal antennalike device, which it turns out is a ground. The box at my head, I am told, generates a low-voltage, pulsating electromagnetic field (the electromagnetic field is produced by a sine-wave generator of 125 Hz producing a mild 1.5 to 2 volts in the hemispheric copper headpiece). The operator places me so that my head is several inches away from the headpiece, so, with my feet grounded, my entire body will be surrounded by the electromagnetic field.

DON'T MEAN A THING IF IT AIN'T GOT THAT SWING

As I LIE BACK, THE OPERATOR PLACES STEREO HEADPHONES ON my ears and then turns on a motor beneath the cot. The entire cot begins to move in a circle—the cot itself does not tilt, and my body remains level, as I rise and fall rhythmically, moving through a counterclockwise circle. The movement is smooth, gentle, and feels very good—it makes about ten revolutions per minute, fast enough so I can feel myself moving, but slow enough that the movement is soothing. As my body moves through the upward arc of the circle I feel a slight sensation of heaviness similar to the feeling you get in an ascending elevator. On the downward swing I feel just a bit lighter; it is like the feeling you get in a descending elevator. These feelings are accompanied by a subtle sort of sloshing first to one side, then to the other, as the machine moves through the circle. It is as if I were reclining lengthwise on the seat of a rapidly revolving Ferris wheel, except in this case the radius of the Ferris wheel is only about five inches.

The music coming into my ears is very relaxing, and as I lose self-consciousness, I become most aware of the motion. I'm reminded of, and find myself reexperiencing, childhood train trips when I slept in Pullman berths, enjoying the delicious sensation of rocketing through the night, lulled by the clickety-clack and rocking motion of the train. I recall vividly how much I enjoyed swinging—reading on the frontporch swing, swinging in an old tire hung from a tree branch, pumping on the playground swings until I was swinging so high my heels pointed to the sky. Even as babies we are deeply soothed by gentle rocking, in a cradle or our mother's arms. Perhaps we have an evolutionary tendency to swing, inherited from the millions of years our ancestors spent swinging through the treetops.

Deeply relaxed, I try to feel the electromagnetic current passing through me, but can't. However, I notice that my mind is filled with bright images and scenes; the visualizations take the form of energy flowing through me—at one point I see myself standing under a waterfall, which is pouring into the top of my head and passing out my feet, and the waterfall is light, energy.

When the machine slowly revolves to a stop I realize forty-five minutes have passed, though it seems to have been only a few minutes. I am so relaxed I don't want to open my eyes. I want more. As I stand up, I notice a pleasant tingling in my fingertips and toes, a sensation of energy, and a feeling of mental clarity. This is surprising, since I have been suffering from a terrible case of the flu, had a sore throat, and the day before had undergone some dental surgery. Now I feel great. Remember the placebo effect, whispers a voice in my head.

In the following weeks I use the machine frequently and find the positive effects seem to stay with me; for several days after using the device I feel refreshed, and seem to work better, think more effectively, and feel surprisingly energetic and calm. Was it possible that something so childishly simple as moving around in circles could have such powerful beneficial effects? I asked the machine's inventor, David Graham, to explain how it worked.

MOTION AND THE MIND: LOOP-THE-LOOP LEARNING

THE MOST IMPORTANT ELEMENT OF THE GRAHAM POTENTIA-lizer (GP), said Graham, was the rhythmic, circular motion. This rotating motion, he claimed, affects all the body fluids. These fluids, which compose about 90 percent of our body volume, are rhythmically stimulated and sloshed about by the movement, giving us a gentle and soothing all-over body massage, a massage that takes place within our body's organs and tissues. The motion has a particularly potent influence on the liquids in the vestibular system of our inner ear, the place where signals originate that tell us what position our body is in, where we're located in space, whether we are moving or not, and if so, how fast and how much.

Imbedded in the semifluid gelatinous membrane of the inner ear's otolith organs are millions of tiny hair cells. When we sit motionless, these hair cells sense gravity alone; movement (backward, forward, up, down) causes the hair cells to shift. In reaction to the movement or gravity, the hair cells send signals directly to the cerebellum, a large lobe sitting atop the brainstem at the lower back part of the brain. A second element of this internal orientation system consists of three tubes in the inner ear called the semicircular canals. These snail-shaped tubes contain a fluid that moves about within the canals whenever we tilt or rotate our heads. The signals generated in these canals are also sent directly to the cerebellum.

The cerebellum, one of the most primitive parts of our brain (i.e., the earliest to evolve), determines and regulates movement, balance, equilibrium, and other motor activities. It has a rich network of connections with both the limbic system (that part of the brain containing the hypothalamus, hippocampus, and other centers concerned with such things as emotions and learning—the places where James Olds and others have attached electrodes to stimulate the "pleasure" and "pain" centers are in the limbic system) and to the neocortex, or thinking cap.

The motion of the GP, according to Graham, stimulates the sensitive hair cells and semicircular canals of the inner ear; since the rhythmic rotation is a movement to which most of us are unaccustomed, and is a continuous motion, the stimulation is not only much different but much greater than the type of stimulation we usually experience in our inner ear. The nerve endings in the inner ear respond by sending out an enormous amount of electrical signals to the cerebellum, which processes them and passes on more signals to the limbic system and neocortex. Thus the rotating motion triggers increased neural activity in all parts of the brain: in a real sense, you could say that the motion "exercises" the brain, stimulating neurons in a new way and sending signals through neural networks that have never been used before. "It's very seldom that we adults get out of a standing or sitting vertical position," Graham told me, "except when we swim or sleep." He pointed out that children, on the other hand, have an innate love of vestibular stimulation, eagerly spinning around in circles until they fall over in dizzy euphoria, turning cartwheels and somersaults, rolling down hills, revolving on merry-go-rounds and Ferris wheels, blasting the nerves in their inner ear with the ecstatic sensory overload of a roller-coaster ride.

As we get older and more dignified, the number of somersaults and cartwheels we perform diminishes dramatically. Why, many of us go for days without rolling down a hill or spinning like a top a single time. Most of us even give up break dancing. The result is similar to what happens to other parts of the body we don't use or exercise enough: if you don't use it you lose it. Slowly our vestibular system grows stiff, accustomed to only a few orientations, and as the connections linking inner ear to the cerebellum to the limbic system and neocortex become narrowed down to this small range of variability—neural pathways become habitual, etched into our brains like deeply rutted roads—experiences outside the normal range can become unpleasant, nauseating, or even frightening. Compare the reactions of children and normal adults when the small plane they're flying in does a sudden steep turn or dive, when they're on a roller coaster, or while sailing on a tossing sea.

Well, you might say, so what? So we no longer get our pleasures by spinning ourselves around in circles, we're adults, we have more important things to do than the loop-the-loop, and we take our pleasures in more sophisticated ways. And this, essentially, is the question I asked David Graham. Granted, I said, children like to spin and stimulate their vestibular systems in various ways. And granted, your device does seem to have this vestibular-stimulation effect. And granted, it is very pleasurable. But there are lots of pleasurable experiences. What is it about this specific one that makes it valuable?

"It's very simple," Graham said. "Vestibular stimulation is relayed through the cerebellum to other parts of the brain; that is, the millions of nerve endings in your inner ear respond to movement with electrical responses that are carried throughout the brain, triggering an enormous amount of neural activity. This neural activity is of an uncommon sort, not only stimulating many different parts of the brain, but causing the neurons to forge new connections. So what the rotation is really doing is 'exercising' the brain—altering and increasing the flow of neuroelectricity and neurochemicals to large areas of the brain. The first thing this kind of vestibular stimulation does is bring a dramatic increase in your motor and learning capabilities. In other words, the 'exercise' has a brain-building effect, just as physical exercise has a bodybuilding effect.

"In fact," Graham said, "there have been a number of studies in recent years that clearly show that movement, simple movement, is absolutely essential to brain growth. Movement is like a nutrient: if we didn't consume the right kind of nutrients, we would not be healthy and there would be no brain growth; and in the same way as nutrients, movement is a key to brain growth."

What you're claiming, I said, is that somehow the GP can not only exercise your brain and make you smarter—increase learning capabilities—but also stimulate actual brain growth. Graham agreed, and cited some of the studies of the relationship between movement, enhanced learning abilities, and brain growth. I later took a look at the published reports of some of this research. Perhaps the most striking have been a series of studies conducted since the mid-1970s by neuroanatomist David Clarke of Ohio State University College of Medicine. Clarke conducted his research with groups of children; some groups were normal, some were handicapped, suffering from Down's syndrome (mongolism), cerebal palsy, or hyperkineticism. Clarke would put the children in a chair specially designed to spin around in circles at precisely controlled rates. This spinning was "designed to have maximum effect on the semicircular canals of the inner ear." Clarke reported, "Normal children who received spinning 'treatments' developed balance and coordination more rapidly than those not treated. Palsied infants showed improvement in the control of head, neck and trunk, in coordination of the extremities and in maintaining equilibrium.... Down's syndrome children showed rapid motor development in comparison to a control group. Their percentage of gains was nearly comparable to that of the normals."[75]

Neuropsychologist James Prescott, of the National Institute of Child Health and Human Development, in Bethesda, Maryland, also believes that "the brain's vestibular-cerebellar pathway, which regulates balance by sensing gravity, plays a major role in the development of normal social behavior" as well as brain development. According to Prescott, "The lack of movement, by depriving the vestibular-cerebellar system of stimulation, may be the critical factor in social withdrawal." And Prescott describes studies showing that lack of movement leads to a "brain abnormality—a loss of dendritic connections in the cerebellum."[325] That is, the lack of movement leads not only to social or psychological changes, but to actual physiological deterioration of brain neurons. There are indications that the reverse is also true: increased vestibular stimulation leads to a gain of dendritic connections and other types of brain growth.

THE CASE OF THE MOVING AND NONMOVING MONKEY MOTHER MODELS

BOTH CLARKE AND PRESCOTT CLAIM THAT THEIR INVESTIGAtions of movement were inspired by the famous experiments conducted in the 1950s and early 1960s by psychologist Harry Harlow of the University of Wisconsin. In those studies, infant monkeys were deprived of their mothers. Some of them were raised in isolation, with no opportunity to touch or play with other monkeys. Others had a cloth- or fur-covered surrogate mother, which was bolted to the floor and motionless. Within three months, these young monkeys were severely impaired, apparently schizophrenic. They would sit in a corner and rock back and forth (as some mentally retarded children do); when put in with other monkeys, they could not relate to them, and were unable to function sexually. They had frequent violent outbursts. Many who read of the study concluded that it simply demonstrated that schizophrenia was a result of inadequate mothering. Harlow disagreed, and showed that a group of monkeys raised in a cage with siblings but no mother still developed normally.

The researchers were puzzled—what could be the specific cause of the monkeys' mental disturbances? In some way, sensory deprivation had caused the damage, but what sensory input is crucial to proper brain development? Sight, sound, touch? One of Harlow's colleagues, Bill Mason, decided to raise one group of monkeys with their mothers, a second group with a surrogate mother (a bleach bottle covered with fur and bolted in place), and a third group with the same surrogate mother (fur-covered bleach bottle), except that this mother was hooked to a motor that would swing it back and forth, so that it would bat the baby monkeys around, and when the monkeys clung to it, it would swing them vigorously. The results were striking: the monkeys that were raised with the stationary surrogate mother developed the same deprivation problems as those monkeys raised in total isolation, while the ones raised with the movable surrogate mother developed normally.[276] Clearly, the crucial factor in the development of normal brains and normal social abilities was *movement*.

THE MOTION OF EMOTION

THE SECOND KEY TO THE MIND-ALTERING EFFECTS OF THE GP is the mild 2-volt electromagnetic field that encompasses the user's body. This field, according to Graham, interacts with and alters the body's own natural electrical field. Human electrical fields, known as "bioelectric" or "electrodynamic" fields, are as yet not fully understood, but have in recent years become the subject of an enormous amount of scientific interest and study (as late as the 1960s there were only a handful of studies published on bioelectricity, while by the early 1980s over six thousand studies were being published on the subject each year). Researchers now believe this bioelectric field pervades the entire body, providing integration and direction for biological functions including growth, healing, and brain activity.

One of the foremost investigators of bioelectric fields has been Robert O. Becker, whose experiments led him to hypothesize the existence of what he called a "primitive data-transmission system." Further research led him to observe: "We found that the potentials are organized into an electrical field, represented by lines of force, which roughly parallels the pattern of the nervous system."

Becker surmised that this primitive data-transmission system was the key not only to healing and regeneration of tissues and organs, but also to alterations in states of consciousness. Since the flow of the bioelectric current within the body was definitely not within the nervous system itself,

Becker searched for the source and structure of the bioelectric network that, his research proved, pervaded the entire body. One interesting explanation was the ancient Chinese theory of acupuncture, which holds that a basic energy known as *Chi* flows through the entire body along a series of pathways or meridians. Imbalances in these pathways can cause illness (mental or physical), and such illnesses can be prevented or cured by sticking needles at precise points along the meridians to alter and harmonize the Chi energy. Recent research showed that applying specific electrical currents at these sites had the same effect as inserting acupuncture needles. Becker was intrigued by the fact that the acupuncture system seemed to parallel in many ways the bioelectric system he was attempting to map. He tested the electrical properties of the acupuncture meridians on a large number of subjects and concluded: "Electrical correlates have been established for a portion of the acupuncture system and indicate that it does have an objective basis in reality."[260]

This conclusion takes on added meaning in light of a number of recent studies proving that one of the results of acupuncture, whether using needles or electric current, is a steep rise in the levels of endorphins in the body. This explains the pain-reducing and anesthetic effects of acupuncture. But as we noted earlier, endorphins perform many functions aside from pain relief, including boosting certain types of memory and learning. And although there have been no studies yet measuring the effect of electrical stimulation on peptides other than endorphins, it makes sense to assume that electrical stimulation can boost levels not only of endorphins but of other peptides as well. Thus, electrical stimulation of the body's electrical field, it must be assumed, can have a variety of profound, long-lasting effects on body and mind, emotions and behavior.

Says Becker: "We are dealing here with very fundamental mechanisms integral to the workings of the central nervous system. In the early 1960s, I had the idea that consciousness might be related to the existence of a direct current. Every alteration in a state of consciousness might be associated with a shift in the amount of current. Depressing the flow of current, for example, would decrease excitability, and increasing DC would cause arousal. Animal experiments corroborated this theory." Becker concludes that "there's something like an underlying state that works according to the principles of solid-state physics. This state would be influenced by perturbations in relatively small fields, particularly in certain frequencies."[27]

Becker's ideas have been confirmed by the work of physician W. Ross Adey of the Brain Research Institute at UCLA, who has studied the "effects of weak electric and electromagnetic fields on the behavior of man and animals." Adey has discovered that such fields have very significant effects on behavior and that such effects must be approached in a holistic manner; he concludes "[that] the brain is an organ uniquely constructed of vast numbers of excitable elements and that it may be subtly influenced in ways that have no counterpart in liver, muscle, or kidney. . . . We may therefore anticipate that responsiveness to weak electromagnetic fields in cerebral tissue is a manifestation of collective properties of its numerous cellular elements, which may not be discernible in the separate behavior of isolated elements."[5]

In Adey's description of the collective properties of the brain in response to weak electromagnetic fields, we can see a connection with our earlier discussion of the brain as a dissipative structure, and recall Dr. William Bauer's conclusion that "in summary, the mechanism of tissue interactions with electromagnetic fields may be as follows: an electromagnetic field of the correct magnitude and frequency causes a 'perturbation' or repositioning of the molecular plasma membrane of cells. This in turn may influence membrane enzyme systems by favorably altering stereoscopic configurations of molecules in much the same manner as a chemical catalyst holds molecules in the correct orientation for chemical reactions. . . . In other words, an electromagnetic field may act in the same way as a hormone upon the cell membrane."[25]

The proper electromagnetic field, that is, may have the effect of increasing the fluctuations or perturbations in the brain's structure, causing the brain to alter its internal organization and to "escape to a higher order," reorganizing with a greater degree of coherence and complexity, and with a greater amount of communication between its components (i.e., individual neurons, neuronal networks, and various brain structures, such as the cerebellum, parts of the limbic system, the neocortex, etc.). This brain change might be experienced as an Aha! or Eureka event. However, as Bauer points out, because of its catalytic effect on brain cells, the electromagnetic field can act in the same way as a hormone. Hormones, as we know, are chemicals secreted by endocrine glands (e.g., the thyroid, the pituitary) that provide a signal to a target organ or organs; these signals are often very long-lasting, and control slow but vital processes, such as growth, reproduction, regeneration, maturation, and aging. Thus, Bauer's statement suggests that an electromagnetic field of the proper amplitude and frequency can not only dramatically alter the brain's activity, but change its structure as well, causing it to grow and increase in complexity and coherence. And perhaps such fields may act as catalysts or hormones, turning on some innate but as yet undiscovered capability of individual neurons to regenerate.

Kenneth Pelletier, of Langley Porter Psychiatric Institute and the University of California School of Medicine, San Francisco, sums up the implications of the recent flood of discoveries about the effects of electromagnetic fields:

> It is becoming increasingly clear that psychological processes produce detectable variations in the electrical and biochemical activity of the entire central nervous system. Minute electromagnetic potentials appear to govern basic biological functions manifested in recovery from injury as well as regeneration. Biological processes can be influenced directly by manipulation of these electrical potentials through electrical stimulation. . . . Perhaps [Becker's primitive data-transmission and control system] is the link between human consciousness and its influence on the endorphin and enkephalin response. . . . Understanding of this link may make it possible systematically to direct consciousness to regulate these internal electrical and biochemical processes, in a manner analogous to the now common practices of clinical biofeedback.[260]

David Graham alludes to these ideas in describing how the electromagnetic field generated by his Potentializer works. "The whole principle of drugs," he told me, "is that they put a substance into your brain that in effect changes the chemistry of the brain, which in turn changes the electrical activity of the brain. Unfortunately, drugs are not only synthetic substances that can be harmful, they also are hard to get through the blood-brain barrier to the small but specific area of the brain where you intend them to have their effect; instead, they tend to bludgeon the whole brain. My hypothesis for a new model of medicine is the bioelectric. That is a two-way process. You can, if you know how, externally change the electrical activity in the brain or body, which in effect will change the chemical production of the brain or the chemical composition of the body. This is what the Potentializer does."

Is it possible the GP could stimulate brain cells to regenerate? "As you know," said Graham, "most scientists still contend that neurons can't regenerate. Well, I don't believe it. I think that under the right conditions brain cells *can* reproduce themselves, just like the other cells of our body. A number of recent studies are demonstrating this." Perhaps the most stunning of the studies Graham was referring to was the pioneering work of Clarence Cone of the Cell and Molecular Biology Laboratory of the Veterans Administration Hospital Center, Hampton, Virginia. Working for NASA, Cone discovered that it was possible to stimulate neuron regeneration by means of "direct electromagnetic changes across the cell surface."[78] Cone's discovery, patented by NASA, has been confirmed by scientists working in other laboratories.[241] Also, it has recently been reported by Fernando Nottebolm and colleagues at Rockefeller University that the neurons in the brains of birds go through cycles of death and regeneration, thus contradicting the long-standing belief that no neurons are formed after infancy. Nottebohm hopes to demonstrate this same neural-regeneration phenomenon in human brains, with the goal of learning to induce growth of new neurons after brain damage. If neurologists provide the right conditions, says Nottebohm, "they might stimulate the growth of new neurons and new neural connections and enhance recovery of brain function" in those with brain injuries.

Graham pointed out that one of the most common therapeutic uses for the GP is with brain-damaged children, such as those suffering from Down's syndrome (mongolism). A number of independent studies have shown that when these children are treated with the GP, they show striking improvements in many areas, including intelligence, awareness, and language. One study by Harvey Grady, Director of Research at the A.R.E. Clinic, Phoenix, detected "expanded mental ability" and significant "neurological growth" in one Down's syndrome sufferer using the GP; in a twenty-two-month period, the subject's "neurological development," according to Grady, "increased from 39 percent to 48.2 percent of average. . . . In this case it appears that [Graham Potentializer] therapy catalysed an acceleration of easily measurable physiological and neurological growth rates. . . ."[128] Is it possible that such neurological growth is in fact stimulated by the GP? In what parts of the brain did this growth occur—dendritic length? glial cells? neurons? Is this growth matched by actual neural regeneration in the brain? And if the GP can actually trigger brain neurons to regenerate in a brain-damaged subject, can it have the same growth-boosting effect on people with healthy brains? These are questions that Graham couldn't answer with any certainty, since he has not been able to do any research into the effects of the GP on neural growth or regeneration. "I can't prove it now," said Graham, "but I have a feeling that when all the facts are in we'll find that this machine can slow down aging, as well as enhance our healing and immune systems, by stimulating regenerative processes."

ELECTRICAL HUMANS ON AN ELECTRICAL EARTH

IF THE IDEA OF SURROUNDING YOUR BODY WITH AN ENVELOPE of electromagnetic energy seems a bit weird, then you must keep in mind that, as Graham told me, "the earth is continually emitting an electrical field. This natural field varies from 100 to 15,000 volts per meter, and all the scientific evidence indicates that the field is beneficial to all living organisms. Unfortunately, as we humans have learned to alter our environment with steel and concrete, we have unwittingly screened out much of the Earth's natural electrical field. Now, research has shown that when humans are cut off from the earth's natural electromagnetic fields, they start to show a whole lot of physical and behavioral abnormalities. They can do this in a laboratory, by putting someone inside an enclosure surrounded by metallic shields that totally cut off any electromagnetic energy; this enclosure is called a Faraday cage. They've discovered that when the earth's natural field is taken away, people react with such symptoms as fatigue, drowsiness, boredom, lethargy, irritability, and so on. But what's happened now, particularly in big cities, is that humans have shut themselves in what are basically just huge Faraday cages —the big buildings of steel and concrete screen out the earth's natural fields.

"Not only have we cut ourselves off from the natural fields of earth," said Graham, "but we've also surrounded ourselves with an incredible variety of artificial fields, many of which we are now discovering can have disastrous effects on the human mind and body. Among these harmful fields that we're constantly exposed to are powerful transmissions from radio and TV towers, from high-tension electrical wires that crisscross the country, and from household appliances like microwave ovens, TV sets, and computers. They've discovered that this electromagnetic pollution or 'electronic smog' has all sorts of deleterious effects on humans, including causing stress, cancer, tumors, depressing the immune system, and a variety of mental and behavioral disorders."

The Potentializer, however, according to Graham, produces a very mild field (less than 2 volts) at a frequency (125 Hz) that he claims is beneficial. The field, says Graham, "interacts with your own natural electrical field, balancing and strengthening where needed. In effect, an energy transfusion occurs. Your brain enjoys a highly effective exercising that improves its neural responses. In one case, a university student registered a 25 percent jump in his neural efficiency quotient after just one fifteen-minute session of the Potentializer."

(There are still questions about the safety of some electromagnetic fields. Says Dr. Becker, "Please caution your readers not to go out to an electronic-parts store and try to build something that will mend bones or grow hair or whatever else. It is now known that there can be very dangerous side effects from electromagnetic energy." As an example, Dr. Wendell Winters of the University of Texas in San Antonio reported in 1984 that five strains of human cancer grew 600 percent faster in one day of exposure to a 60-Hz field—the same frequency as our electric power lines, to which we're constantly exposed.)[140]

ROTATING FIELDS AROUND FIELDS

THE GP'S ELECTROMAGNETIC FIELD, SAID GRAHAM, IS A KEY element of the device; however, his studies have revealed an interesting point. By itself, the field has a small but noticeable effect on subjects. Subjects who were put on the machine and merely rotated without the electromagnetic field being turned on were affected more strongly than those who were exposed to the field without the motion. However, when the two elements of motion and electromagnetic field were combined, the statistics showed that the effects on the subjects soared. "The two together," said Graham, "have a sort of synergistic or catalytic action, so the effect really takes off."

The idea that combining motion with electromagnetic energy has a "potentiating" effect makes sense when you remember that it is a combination that is quite natural. Says Graham, "As human beings we live on a rotating earth, and move through its electromagnetic field. This may well be the native condition that develops human consciousness."

Humans generate and are constantly radiating their own natural electrical field. The earth also has a natural field. As humans rotate around the earth, then, in essence each individual's field is being rotated around another field. Says Graham, "If you take a look at how electricity is generated, it always involves motion. You spin a couple fields around each other, and without the spinning you can't generate electricity. The Potentializer is very similar. Without the motion, nothing much happens. But when you revolve your field around the machine's field, some sort of interaction takes place, and some sort of energy is created, just as two electrical fields spinning around each other generate electricity. What you get is what I call an energy transfusion.

"Really, the machine is just accelerating natural processes. When you lie down to sleep at night, the earth rotates and you travel around with it, and you're moving through the earth's magnetic field. When you wake up, you're refreshed. This is what happens on the machine. Except that when you sleep, you only traverse a portion of the circle during the night, while the machine takes you around in a lot of little circles."

So, I asked, each time you go around on the machine you're simulating a revolution of the earth? "Exactly," said Graham, "and this is what stimulates intellectual growth. Look, the human brain is full-grown and basically complete at seven years of age, but it doesn't reach full growth in terms of intellect or consciousness—that is, in its ability to learn— until sixteen or later. During those intervening years, what has happened is that you've lain down a lot more nights being stimulated by the earth's magnetic field and the spin of the earth. Now that's exactly what the machine does—you simulate that on a small, accelerated scale."

Well, this all seemed to me to be pretty speculative, or what some might even call incipiently crackpot stuff. Graham claimed that rotating in a proper electromagnetic field brought increased intelligence and intellectual growth. As far as I knew there was no way to prove or disprove this. But Graham also claimed that his machine brought increased intelligence and intellectual growth. If he had evidence of this, then did it really matter what caused this brain enhancement? I asked him what proof he had that the GP did indeed alter consciousness and increase intelligence in some measurable way.

He provided me with a series of EEG studies he had done, involving thirty subjects over a total of 215 sessions. In these controlled studies, he analyzed a number of brain-wave characteristics that EEG authority (and developer of Neurometrics) E. Roy John has identified as "the most sensitive indicators of brain functioning." Among these indicators are the average brain-wave frequency, the amount of alpha waves, and the phase relationship between the right and left hemispheres (i.e., the degree of hemispheric synchronization). Dr. J. P. Ertl, a highly respected Canadian psychologist best known for his pioneering research into the relationship between IQ and brain-wave activity, developed a special EEG to measure these "sensitive indicators" identified by Dr. John. Ertl also designed the machine to measure what is known as the *neuro-efficiency quotient* (NEQ). As Ertl has discovered through extensive training, the NEQ, which essentially measures the brain's assimilation speed, correlates extremely closely with intelligence as measured by IQ testing. The idea that you can measure intelligence physiologically has immense implications, since such tests could determine "pure" intelligence, unlike present IQ tests, which are all to some degree contaminated by cultural biases (favoring certain educational, racial, social, or family backgrounds).

The results of Graham's study, using Ertl's EEG system, were striking. The Potentializer caused increases in the production of alpha waves. The subjects also showed decided shifts in hemispheric dominance (resulting in a balancing or synchronization of the two brain hemispheres). And, most intriguingly, the machine definitely enhanced the NEQ: Ertl's research indicates that the average NEQ, corresponding to an average IQ of 100 to 120, is generally between 15 and 18. The statistics cited in the study show that the Potentializer "moves neuro efficiency towards 20 to 21. This level is 3 to 4 points higher than that found in the average population, which would correspond to a general increase in neuro efficiency of approximately 25%. Neuro efficiency, like evoked potential response, is highly correlated to IQ. The [Graham Potentializer] may well increase native intelligence."[129]

257

After reviewing the data, brain-wave analyst Ertl concluded that the machine "definitely does something beneficial to the brain waves . . . a solid change was induced in the basic brain-wave parameters." Ertl writes, "I can state that the hypothesis that the [Graham Potentializer] does nothing to brain waves must be rejected by anyone familiar with scientific methodology. The changes in EEG parameters were of great magnitude, consistent, highly significant statistically. . . . I am satisfied that the EEG changes observed were caused by the [GP]. The possibility of changing spectral characteristics of brain waves without drugs or surgery may have enormous potential benefits."

Significantly, the study also showed that while the electromagnetic field by itself and the revolving motion by itself both had some influence on brain waves (motion being more powerful than the field), the combination of motion and field was far more effective in significantly altering brain waves, thus providing statistical proof of the synergistic or potentiation effect of field and motion. (This study was completed before Graham added the third element to his device, sound; however, as we have seen in the chapters dealing with the brain-wave-altering effects of sound waves, all evidence suggests that the addition of relaxing sounds should increase the effectiveness of the device.)

Although the machine has had virtually no publicity, increasing numbers of medical professionals throughout the United States and Canada have made it an integral part of their treatment programs. The owners are mostly physicians, psychiatrists, psychologists, educators, and chiropractors, with a sprinkling of ministers, counselors, and interested scientists. Although they can only describe their own perceptions of the effects of using the device, I found that their experiences support Graham's assertions. Users and therapists consistently and independently reported that the device rapidly induced deep relaxation, reduced or eliminated stress or symptoms of stress, relieved pain, induced positive attitudes and emotions, expanded learning abilities, increased intelligence, creativity, and problem-solving abilities, and improved gross and fine motor functioning and coordination.

One typical owner is Chinmayee Chakrabarty of Montefiore Hospital in the Bronx. A psychotherapist, Chakrabarty uses the GP in her private practice, and told me, "It's a powerful machine, believe me. I've seen it have extraordinary effects again and again. It's had a truly powerful effect in my personal life." Invariably, she says, the machine produces "dramatic reductions in pain," and quickly makes the user "calm and deeply relaxed." She points out (as do other users) that "it really opens people up. All sorts of material comes floating to the surface. This is extremely helpful in most cases, enabling people to discover in themselves emotions, ideas, and memories they had not been aware of. However, there are certain people I would not put on the machine—people who are on the borderline, who might not be able to deal with some of the emotions and memories revealed to them on the machine."

When I asked her what she found to be the machine's most common and most powerful effect, she had no hesitation. "Mainly in improving clarity of thinking—it focuses the mind, helps you to see yourself and your problem from a new perspective. If I had to describe it in one word, I'd call it a 'defogger.' It clears away all sorts of confusion and seems to help integrate reason and emotion. It also produces a great increase in energy—you think and work more productively, because your mind has this new vitality and clarity."

One of the most interesting informal studies of the Potentializer was conducted by bioelectricty authority Joseph Light. As mentioned earlier, Light has done much investigation of the Mind Mirror; in his research he has found that heightened states of consciousness, in which the subject experiences great mental clarity and focus, increased creativity, euphoria, and expanded awareness (what inventor Maxwell Cade calls the "awakened mind"), produced a characteristic brain-wave pattern on the Mind Mirror. Light proceeded to hook up some twenty-five subjects to the Mind Mirror, had the subjects try different mind-altering techniques (such as meditation, slow breathing, and self-hypnosis) and devices (such as TENS), and observed which were the most effective in making the subjects produce the characteristic "awakened mind" pattern on the Mind Mirror. "It was surprising," Light told me, "but I found that the Potentializer was far and away the most effective in producing this deep meditative state of all the techniques and devices I tried. It really works."

15

GAZING HARD INTO THE VOID: TRANQUILITE

THE BULGING BLUE GOGGLES MAKE YOU LOOK LIKE A CROSS
between the Fly and the Creature from the Black Lagoon. I
pull them over my face and find that they glow inside with
diffuse indirect lighting, presenting my eyes with a seamless,
featureless field of radiant restful turquoise. Next I put on the
stereo headphones. They are attached to a cigarette-pack-sized
box which is generating a gentle, rhythmic noise—external
sounds are totally blotted out, and I hear only a pulsating
liquid gurgling. Combined with the pure blue, the soothing
murmur stirs memories of diving in the warm clear waters off
the Caribbean coast of Central America: I am drifting about
twenty feet down, facing upward, ears singing as the water
sweeps past them, heavy from the increased water pressure,
and above me the blue sky seen through the water forms a vast
and perfect azure dome.

I very quickly become deeply relaxed. No—I can't tell if
it's quick or not, since I've lost my sense of time. I am bulging and dopey with a pleasant lassitude, and feel like closing
my eyes, but remember that I have been instructed to keep my
eyes open. Usually I can only keep my eyes open a short
while before I become uncomfortable and have to blink, but
now the blue is so restful and I am so relaxed that my eyes are

motionless, eyelids at rest, almost as if I'd been mesmerized. Colorful visions flash across my mind's eye, and I observe them for a while, like a surreal movie at a private screening. I suddenly wonder whether my eyes are open or closed; I could probably find out, I think, but who cares? It's too much effort. Soon I have forgotten that there are other people in the room watching me . . . that there is even a room out there . . . that anything exists except this wonderful, serene blueness . . . a glowing universe of blueness. And then the blueness disappears, and there is . . . nothing.

The disappearing act is the result of gazing into what psychologists call a *ganzfeld*, a word meaning "homogenized field," coined by the German scientists who pioneered the technique in the 1930s. Those psychologists immersed experimental subjects in a dense, uniform fog and discovered that the subjects reacted as if they were in a sensory-deprivation environment. Later, in the 1940s and '50s, influential psychologist Donald Hebb performed a series of experiments in which subjects were actually deprived of most external stimulation, and what visual stimulation they did receive came through translucent goggles that diffused the dim light and kept them from seeing any shapes or forms. As a result of this monotonous stimulation, the subjects experienced altered states of consciousness characterized by hallucinatory hypnagogic images, intense emotions, and much freer association of ideas. Hebb theorized that the brain required not only continuous input but a continuously *changing* input to maintain normal awareness.

A number of scientists, intrigued by Hebb's work, wondered what would happen to the brain if it received a uniform (i.e., unchanging) visual input. Recalling the earlier studies of the ganzfeld, these researchers decided to investigate the effects of the ganzfeld on the brain. To create the necessary patternless visual field, they cut Ping-Pong balls in half, put the split halves over the eyes of subjects, and directed a beam of light at the white hemispheres. The investigators found that a strange thing happened. After a short period, the subject reported a total absence of visual experience—what they called "blank-out." Research psychologist Robert Ornstein of Langley Porter Neuropsychiatric Institute reports that blank-out "was not merely the experience of seeing nothing, but one of not seeing, a complete disappearance of the sense of vision. . . . During 'blank-out' the observers did not know, for instance, whether their eyes were open or not."[249]

Other scientists decided to investigate this blank-out effect in another way, by presenting the eyes of their subjects with a "stabilized retinal image." Normally, our eyes are in constant motion, and we never look at anything steadily for a prolonged period of time. As we observe the things around us, our eyes move about in sweeping arcs, and even when we try to fix our attention on some object our eyeballs jitter involuntarily. Normally, then, whatever we are seeing is kept in constant motion on our retinas, stimulating different cells from moment to moment. To eliminate this constant visual movement, the scientists constructed an apparatus consisting of a tiny image projector mounted on a contact lens in the eye of the subject. Whatever direction the eyeball turned, the lens, and thus the projector, also moved; the retina was presented with an unchanging "stabilized" image. But after a few minutes of peering at this inescapable image, the subjects were startled: the image disappeared!

The researchers concluded that "continuous uniform stimulation resulted in the failure of any kind of image to be produced in consciousness." Very strange. The researchers traced the stimulus, and found that it was definitely received by and passed through the retina, but then somewhere in the central nervous system the stimulus simply disappeared! They concluded that these periods of continuous stimulation "indicated a functional similarity between continuous stimulation and no stimulation at all." Well, this was surprising stuff—who could have predicted that the human brain would react to no stimulation and continuous stimulation in exactly the same way? And what did it all mean?

HAVING YOUR HEAD IN THE CLOUD
OF UNKNOWING

A FEW CHAPTERS BACK I SUGGESTED THAT ONE OF THE EARLI-
est methods our primitive ancestors used for self-entertain-
ment and exploring the contents of their own minds must have
been by peering into the flickering lights of campfires, allowing the rhythmic flashes to alter and augment their own brain-
wave rhythms. One thing the ganzfeld experiments have
proved is that a monotonous, constant, unvarying light can be
just as entertaining and mind-revealing as rhythmic flickers.
But again, while scientists talk about "discovering" the ganzfeld technique, it's clear that the blank-out effect is something
humans have known about and made practical use of for mil-
lennia, and most likely for millions of years.

Every culture that has ever existed has used some technique for restricting awareness to a single, unchanging source
of stimulation for a more or less lengthy period of time. In
different cultures and different situations, this restriction of
attention is used for a variety of purposes: to attain a state of
ecstasy, gain spiritual insight, escape pain and suffering, obtain new wisdom, enhance creativity, gain access to special
mental and physical powers, improve health or alleviate sickness, become one with the universal force, increase sensory
acuity, cleanse the doors of perception, become a better
hunter, and so on.

The specific techniques used are many. Buddhists concentrate on their breathing, first counting each breath without allowing their attention to wander, and after having succeeded
in this, focusing totally and exclusively on the *process* of
breathing. After learning this elementary type of concentration, or "one-pointedness" of mind, students of Zen are given
a paradoxical or logic-busting riddle, called a koan (such as
"What is your face before your parents' birth?" or "The flag
doesn't move, the wind doesn't move, only your mind
moves"), and instructed to focus their one-pointed attention on

it intensely, unceasingly, and for long periods of time. One way of focusing attention widely used in yoga is the monotonous repetition (aloud or silently) of a sonorous word or phrase known as a *mantra*—you are to concentrate on the mantra, such as Om, to the exclusion of everything else. Other common yogic practices include *tratakum* or "steady gaze," in which you fix your concentration on some external object, such as a vase, a flower, a rock, a candle, or a mandala (a specially constructed visual image, such as a circle, a cross, or a star, that draws your attention toward the center). Yogis also gain the desired one-pointedness of mind by focusing on sounds, both internal sounds, such as heartbeats, breaths, and subtle noises of the inner ear, and external sounds, such as the monotonous sound of a waterfall, rushing river, wind through trees, or rain. Some sects of Sufis, known to us as the whirling dervishes, effectively restrict their focus of attention and reach states of heightened awareness by monotonous, repetitious dancing in circles. The ancient Egyptians reportedly achieved altered brain states by staring at the sun, developing the ability by first peering through a small peephole, then staring through progressively larger and larger holes until they could stare directly into the full sun without damaging their eyes.

This striving for blank-out through monotonous stimulation has also been a key element in our Western, Judeo-Christian tradition. Hebrew scholar Gershom Scholem points out there are records of such practices at least as far back as the second century B.C., during the time of the Second Temple, when the practitioner would sit with his head between his knees, chanting the name of a magic seal. The unknown Christian mystic who wrote the fourteenth-century book *The Cloud of Unknowing* advised those who sought wisdom to repeat a simple word, such as "God" or "love": "Choose whichever one you prefer, or, if you like, choose another that suits your taste, provided that it is of one syllable. And clasp this word tightly in your heart so that it never leaves it no matter what may happen. . . . with this word you shall strike down thoughts of every kind and drive them beneath the cloud of forgetting."

Jesus often seems to refer to the focusing of attention as a spiritual practice, as in this passage about having a "single eye:" "The light of the body is the eye: therefore when thine eye is single, thy whole body is full of light. . . . If thy whole body therefore be full of light, having no part dark, the whole shall be light, as when the bright shining of a candle doth give thee light."

These diverse traditions and practices are based on the same central element: intentionally restricting awareness to a single, monotonous process, so that attention is totally withdrawn from ordinary thought and external activities. And while the practices and traditions are diverse, they all seem to lead to the same state of consciousness. Eastern traditions often speak of it as the "void," "emptiness," or "nothingness." Western mystics speak variously of "the cloud of unknowing," the "mysterious darkness wherein is contained the limitless Good, a void, other than solitude" (Augustine Poulain), the "annihilation of memory" (St. John of the Cross). Psychologists, of course, call it "blank-out," and they can make it happen by putting sliced Ping-Pong balls over your eyes, or fitting you with clever contact lenses equipped with tiny projectors. And now, thanks to the stimulating effect of the American marketplace, some inventive entrepreneurs have put together a bug-eyed Rolls-Royce of consumer ganzfelds known as the Tranquilite.

All these devices and techniques for restricting attention are based on a property of human physiology. As Robert Ornstein explains it, "One consequence of the way our central nervous system is structured seems to be that if awareness is restricted to one unchanging source of stimulation, a 'turning off' of consciousness of the external world follows." This is an important and often misunderstood point. Often people who pride themselves on being level-headed or who have a strong opinion of what is "proper" behavior find it hard to take seriously the claims of enhanced mental and physical powers made by various meditative techniques simply because the techniques themselves seem so bizarre, exotic, or just plain silly, laden with mumbo-jumbo, blue smoke, and mirrors.

But, as Ornstein points out, the dervish dancing, concentration upon arcane symbols, riddles about the sound of one hand clapping, whining chants, and other meditative techniques "are not deliberately mysterious or exotic but are simply a matter of practical applied psychology."[239] That is, all these techniques are simply making use of a quirk of our nervous system to alter our awareness—it's not the methods that are mysterious, but what happens in the brain as a result of them.

FIDDLING WITH THE VOLUME-CONTROL KNOB IN YOUR BRAIN

THE KEY TO TURNING OFF OR BLANKING OUT SEEMS TO BE A special formation about the size of your little finger deep within the core of the brain, the *reticular activating system* or RAS. This formation at the top of the brainstem has two component parts, both of which have widespread connections to all other parts of the brain. One part controls our level of arousal; the other part controls and directs our attention. The part that controls arousal can be compared to the volume knob on a radio: it takes sensations that are entering the brain and turns them up or turns them down. This part also controls the level of arousal of the brain's electrical rhythms: when we are in deep sleep, the RAS has slowed our brain waves down to 1 or 2 cycles per second—delta or "slow-wave" sleep. When the RAS decides to arouse us, the brain waves speed up and we awaken into normal consciousness. When the RAS causes us to become extremely aroused, the brain waves become even more rapid, and we experience highly excited mental states that can be very uncomfortable, such as anxiety or panic.

The second component of the RAS controls selective attention. If the arousal control is like the volume knob of a radio, this part is like the selector knob: it "tunes in" whatever it has determined is important or meaningful, and allows us to ignore all the vast amounts of sensations and information that are pouring into our brain every moment but are of no immediate interest to us. It is this part of the RAS that enables a mother to sleep through a booming thunderstorm and awaken to her baby's cry, that allows us to ignore the constant pressure and friction on our skin from our clothing but feel the touch of a mosquito on a single hair of our arm, that permits us to concentrate on reading a book in a busy train station, oblivious to the activity around us. One of the principles by which the RAS seems to determine what is important or of interest is novelty: if some stimulus is new or unexpected, the RAS directs our attention to it, even if "it" is simply an absence of something (as parents suddenly notice a silence from the room where their children are playing). On the other hand, even if a stimulus is extremely strong, the RAS will turn our attention away from it if it is something expected or to which we have become accustomed (as people living beside airports or busy highways soon stop hearing noises which are loud enough to drive visitors to distraction).

What seems to happen when we are presented with a ganzfeld (or put on the Tranquilite) is that the part of the RAS that controls arousal is presented with external sensations that are unchanging, without pattern and apparently without "meaning." Thus, the RAS turns our arousal level down. EEG tests of people using the ganzfeld technique (and the Tranquilite) prove that arousal does indeed go down: the brain's electrical activity slows down as the brain waves get bigger (higher amplitude) and slower (lower frequency), falling into the alpha and theta range. As a result, we become deeply relaxed, and our brain-wave activity becomes more balanced and synchronized between the hemispheres.

At the same time, that part of the RAS that directs our attention perceives that the sensations arriving from outside are unchanging, monotonous, patternless, meaningless. Since it values novelty, it finds nothing of interest or importance in the external sensations, and shifts our attention away from the external sensations to our internal world. Just as the people who live by the airport don't hear the deafening jetliner, we no longer "see" the white light of the ganzfeld: blankout has occurred. Since there is no information coming in from outside, our internal sensations seem much more powerful and notice-able. Images, ideas, memories, emotions that would have been drowned out by sensations coming in from outside now become clear and vivid, just as the stars, which are over-powered and rendered invisible by the bright sun during the light of day, sparkle brilliantly on dark moonless nights.

ON THE BENEFITS OF BLANK-OUT

IN RECENT YEARS THERE HAS BEEN AN EXPLOSION OF RE-search into the effects of various meditative and conscious-ness-altering techniques, using sophisticated radioimmuno-assays to measure the level of many neurochemicals, sensitive monitors of functions such as galvanic skin response, muscu-lar tension, and oxygen consumption, and computerized EEGs producing extremely exact measurements of the brain's elec-trical activity, including such things as neuro-efficiency quo-tient (NEQ), average evoked potential, and brain-wave activity. While there are innumerable methods that have been used to induce the blank-out characteristic of meditative states, ranging from dervish dancing to chopping wood to running to counting breaths, scientists have found that all have the same key effects on the mind and body. Among those effects are many that clearly increase the mental capabilities of the subject. Among the proven results of deep meditation are:

—*Stress reduction*. Levels of stress-related biochemicals such as adrenaline and cortisol are dramatically decreased; blood pressure and heart rate also decrease (as we have seen earlier, numerous studies have indicated that stress hinders learning, thinking, creativity; several recent studies have proved that high blood pressure also leads to a decline in in-telligence as measured by various IQ and performance tests; this decline is probably related to a decreased supply of oxy-gen and other blood-carried nutrients to the brain, because of the constriction of brain capillaries caused by the elevated blood pressure).

—*Deep relaxation*. Muscular tension, oxygen consumption, and skin conductivity (measures of physical and mental tension and arousal) all decrease. A wealth of studies (including the "superlearning" research of Georgi Lozanov and the "twilight learning" research of Thomas Budzynski) have shown that the brain is able to absorb, process, and store far more information while the body is in a state of deep relaxation than when it is tense.

—*Altered brain-wave activity*. Brain waves change from the high-frequency/low-amplitude beta waves of normal consciousness to the much-lower-frequency and higher-amplitude alpha and theta waves. Evidence indicates that these slower, more powerful brain waves are related to increased access to memories, enhanced creativity, and boosted efficiency in speed of processing information and reacting to incoming stimuli (neuro-efficiency quotient). Such states of increased fluctuation in the brain's structure increase the capacity of the brain to grow and evolve, to "escape to a higher order" of coherence, complexity, and more effective and enriched inter-neural communication.

—*Hemispheric synchronization*. The electrical activity of the brain's two hemispheres becomes coherent, in phase, effectively fostering a state of whole-brain consciousness, in which both brain hemispheres work together, integrating two different modes of thinking (verbal and visuo-spatial; analytical and synthesizing) and producing gains in certain types of mental functioning.

—*Increased powers of attention*. EEG tests can measure attention by observing the amount of habituation subjects show to various stimuli, such as a click. Subjects in normal consciousness quickly become habituated to stimuli, while those in the blank-out meditative state maintain high levels of attention.

—*Improved reaction time*. Studies show that habitual meditators react to an external stimulus at least 30 percent faster than nonmeditators; and when tested after a period of meditation, meditators improved another 15 percent while nonmeditators, after relaxing for the same period of time the meditators meditated, were 10 percent worse.[103]

—*Increased sensory acuity.* Meditators report that after meditation the world seems fresher, the colors more intense, sensual pleasures more delightful. Studies of meditators show dramatic increases in visual acuity; other studies have proved that meditation lowers the auditory threshold for discrimination of frequency and amplitude.[103]

Periods of deep meditation have been found to improve mental functioning in numerous other ways (improvement of self-image and self-confidence, enhanced creativity, and improved memory, among others). The evidence for the benefits of meditation is by now so overwhelming that even the most traditional and conservative educators, therapists, scientists, artists, business executives, athletes, and health-fitness professionals accept the fact that meditation can be extremely useful and productive, and many are eagerly exploring ways of integrating certain meditative practices into their lives. Unfortunately, many have discovered this is not easy to do.

One problem is that to enter the blank-out state that seems to be the key to meditation's benefits, you must first become deeply relaxed. Ours is a society in which the ability to become deeply relaxed has not been valued very highly. In fact, several scientists have concluded that a large percentage of us have never experienced true deep relaxation in our lives! When told to become relaxed, we do some sort of "letting go" and then claim we've relaxed; but testing of muscular tension with an electromyogram (EMG) shows that even when "relaxed" most of us are still wracked with tensions—tensions that have become so much a part of us that we're not even aware of them. So, for most of us, true relaxation is something we must learn; and to learn deep relaxation takes disciplined effort and time. Sadly, self-discipline is a quality that many of us find in short supply; and time, well, who has time these days to spend an hour every day simply learning how to relax? Time is money, right?

The next problem is that even after you've learned to relax, you still have to learn to focus your attention to such a degree that you get the blank-out effect. Again, this takes effort, practice, time, discipline. Several studies have shown that the

271

majority of people who attempt to learn how to meditate abandon their efforts within months (just as the majority of people who take up jogging soon give it up). There's no doubt, it's not easy. Many people find that it takes months of determined meditating before they are successful in getting into the authentic meditative state. And even dedicated meditators often are fooling themselves—one study of long-time meditators showed that a significant number of them who claimed to be in deep meditation were not; their brain indicators showed that they were merely deeply relaxed, without the strong alpha-theta waves and brain synchronization that characterize true meditation.

As Ornstein points out, "The problem of reaching this state [of blank-out] in the usual way, say the spokesmen of the disciplines of meditation, is that ordinary means are inefficient, that men usually concern themselves with irrelevant dimensions, that the subjective state desired is not often produced by the ordinary means themselves, and that, if produced, its aftereffects do not persist."[239]

The moral is that while meditation may be desirable, it's a hard row to hoe, and large numbers of people will find it too much trouble to go through for reputed benefits that seem far away. But wait. As we've seen earlier, meditation works by taking advantage of a quirk in our nervous system—when we focus our attention on an unchanging input, our consciousness reaches a point of blank-out, in which we experience what is variously called the void, nothingness, infinity, timelessness, satori, samadhi, one-pointedness, the annihilation of memory, peace. What if there were some device or technique that would reliably and quickly induce this blank-out state, something anyone could use? Why then, if it produced the blank-out state that is the key to the benefits of meditation, surely such a handy gizmo would produce the same benefits as meditation, except without all the discipline, time, and mystic mumbo-jumbo required for meditation. As we've seen, the various methods and techniques used to induce meditative states, whether dervish dancing, chanting, breathing, breath counting, or symbol contemplation, are of no importance or value *in themselves*, but only as ways of making use of that blank-out quirk of the brain. A device or machine that could induce that blank-out state in just a few minutes would simply be a more efficient, more effective meditative technique.

Now many who look on various meditative techniques as valuable in themselves, who see meditation as a type of religious or spiritual discipline, would scoff at the idea that a machine could put just about any jerk into deep meditation. It all seems somehow sacrilegious to them. But the point is that the goal of all the meditative techniques, which is reaching that blank-out experience of the void, is not an inherently religious goal. Rather it is a goal that has to do with obtaining the benefits mentioned above: a high level of mental clarity, increased intelligence and creativity, improved reactions, keener attention and concentration, deep relaxation, better coordination, intensified sensory acuity. These benefits of meditation *can* be directed toward spiritual or religious ends, but they can just as easily be used for playing tennis, writing better poetry, mastering the piano, handicapping the horses, memorizing lines for a play, doing math homework, or intensifying your sexual experiences.

If an inexpensive little machine can get you to that place in a few minutes, instead of requiring daily efforts for weeks or months to reach the same place, then most of us will opt for the machine. Granted, the meditators who claim that there are benefits to be gained from the discipline and experiences involved in the long effort to master meditation are right. In the same way, if I were to walk from New York City to Los Angeles, it would take me months, but I would learn from the experience. But if my true goal were to get to Los Angeles, then I would probably decide to fly, and get there the same day. Yes, I will miss the excitement of passing through Des Moines and Tucumcari, but then again, I will be in L.A. doing whatever it is that must be done while the walker is still shuffling through Union, New Jersey.

Which brings us back to this blue bug-eyed ganzfeld derivative known as the Tranquilite. As the device's designer, Charlie Rush, said to me when I removed the goggles after my first experience, "One of the first people to test this unit was an experienced meditator. He'd been in a Zen monastery and had spent hours meditating every day for many years. And when he took it off he looked at me and said, 'Instant meditation!' He used it quite a bit, and said that it took him to the same place as meditation did, but was faster, and made it easier to get into meditation when he wasn't really in the mood, or when he was tense."

No argument there. Gazing at the glowing blue field, I quickly became deeply relaxed; at some point after not too many minutes I would experience blank-out, a period that was immensely pleasant and restful. At times this state would be interrupted by dreamlike images or sudden ideas plopping into the blankness like smooth pebbles into a still pond. And after I removed the goggles, it seemed as if the volume knob on my senses had been turned up—colors rich, saturated, intense, sounds full and weighty.

SHUTTING DOWN THE ROBOT

"IF THE DOORS OF PERCEPTION WERE CLEANSED EVERYTHING would appear to man as it is, infinite. For man has closed himself up till he sees all through narrow chinks of his cavern," said William Blake. One reason for the brighter colors and sharpened senses we experience after meditation is rooted in the same phenomenon that the Tranquilite uses to create a blank-out in our senses: habituation. Because the stimulus is unchanging, our brain soon becomes habituated to it, the RAS decides it is of no importance or interest, and the stimulus is blanked out; we no longer experience it at all as our attention turns elsewhere, seeking significance. But in just this way we are constantly becoming habituated to innumerable components of our daily lives. Sights, sounds, feelings, or ideas that may have aroused our interest at first quickly become old stuff; when we first learn to drive a car it seems that there is so much to pay attention to, but soon we can find ourselves driving for hundreds of miles without being aware of it, like robots or automatons; the blue of the sky, the world that surrounds us, ordinary things become like the unchanging ganzfeld, and our brain becomes habituated, our RAS decides they are of no importance or interest, and we experience a blankout of these ordinary things. But then, in deep meditation, the external world is truly blanked out: the ordinary things disappear, we experience a short but total vacation from the world. The robot is turned off. And when we return it is as if we were seeing things with eyes that have been refreshed, sensing with perceptions that have been scrubbed clean.

Like most of the other designer/manufacturers of mind machines I encountered, Charlie Rush is a bit of a maverick. He came to create the Tranquilite almost by accident, and as a by-product of his own driving personal interest in finding effective ways of exploring his mind. "For a long time I've been intrigued with the idea of creating a bridge between Eastern esoteric thought and Western technology," he told me. "I knew the states the esoteric masters taught about were real, and I knew that there must be ways to attain them using modern technology. I read Dr. Lilly's work on sensory deprivation and the flotation tank, and was eager to try that out, but I didn't know if there were any of those tanks around. Then I discovered the studies of the ganzfeld effect. I tried a lot of ganzfeld experiments on myself. I used to do intense ganzfeld sessions for eight hours at a time, trying in a sense to replicate some of Lilly's isolation-tank experiments. I found that I felt exhilarated and very relaxed as a result of these experiments. At the same time I was doing these experiments I was also using an alpha-theta biofeedback machine, and I discovered that the ganzfeld would enhance the production of theta tremendously —made it much easier to go into that state, with all the hypnagogic imagery and so on.

"At first I would just cut a Ping-Pong ball in half and put the pieces over my eyes, with a light shining on them. But I found I was getting a lot of distraction—light leaks, discomfort from sharp edges. So I started fiddling around, contouring the Ping-Pong pieces so they'd fit. I made a wire frame so that everything was comfortable and adjustable. I found I was designing something new. Then I discovered the work of Robert Monroe. I went and spent some time at the Monroe Institute, and was impressed with his use of sounds to alter consciousness. So to enhance the effectiveness of the ganzfeld, I decided to add sound. At first I would turn the stereo so that it was between FM stations, making just a hissing—that's basically a white noise. It cut off all other external sounds, adding to the constant, unchanging ganzfeld stimulation. But I found that white noise can get to be anxiety-producing after a while, while what's called 'pink noise'—which is white noise that's been put through a number of acoustic filters to take out or reduce certain frequencies—is more flat and relaxing. I had an expert in psychoacoustics put together this pink-noise generator." What were the component sounds? I asked. When I put on the device, I seemed to hear water—the rushing waves combined with an echoing dripping noise, like water dripping rhythmically off a stalactite in a cave. But a friend of mine swore that the sound she heard was wind rushing through the leaves of a tree.

"It's all in your head," Charlie Rush said, laughing. "Your mind deprived of its normal sensory input will start to create on its own. It's just a pink noise, featureless, unchanging. Your mind is what's altering it. At different times I've had people say it sounds like a rainstorm, a train, a factory, waves breaking on the shore—the same person hearing all this, and the sound does not change. I've had people for whom it conjured up the feelings and imagery of being in the middle of a symphony orchestra, or all of a sudden they feel as if they're out in the middle of the wilderness, with crickets and frogs going.

"Anyway, after that I found out that different-colored ganzfelds would have different psychological effects. I tried about thirty different shades of pink and found a couple that are very calming. Red, I discovered, is pretty powerful, and gives you a very euphoric high. Blue is probably the most relaxing. So by this time I decided to put all these different elements together into a unit that would be portable and that would allow the colors to be changed. Everyone who tried it was really excited about it. I had some cancer patients use it, people who were in really intense pain, and they had quite remarkable pain reductions. I've had friends who were virtually on the verge of suicide, and I put the Tranquilite on them for an hour and it reduced their anxiety. They wanted one of their own. This is when I realized that I should try to produce this thing and sell it. So I put in my patent application and decided to try and get this thing on the market.

"In the last year," said Rush, "I've been trying this out on a lot of different people, and the results have been quite encouraging, and quite varied. For example, there's an artist who has used it a lot, who gets a lot of intense, spontaneous images. She started bringing back these images, and now she's begun to put them on canvas—very densely layered. She's strongly influenced by M. C. Escher, and she calls her work 'Impossible Space.' She says the Tranquilite allows her to really get out there and explore 'the spaces between the spaces.' Another artist uses it as what she calls a 'thinking cap.' She says that while she's wearing it she can organize her entire week in advance. One businessman, who works in a very high-pressure situation, puts it on now and then for just five minutes in the midst of work, and says he gets deeply relaxed even in a busy room. Also, he claims it frees his stream of consciousness, loosens up his thinking a bit, and that helps him take new approaches to problems and think more creatively. It's being put into use in a drug and alcohol rehabilitation center, to help the patients relax and explore their thoughts. Some people are using it for accelerated learning—they are able to absorb information better when wearing the device. Overall it seems to have the effect of being a brain booster."

THE HUNGRY AND EXPLORATORY BRAIN

ONE EXPLANATION FOR THE APPARENT MIND-STIMULATION EFfect of the device can be found in the work of brain researcher Jerzy Konorski. In his book *Integrative Activity of the Brain*,

Konorski concludes that the essential function of the brain is to act as a survival mechanism; this survival orientation operates in all levels of the brain, from individual neurons through neural networks up to the mind as a whole, and it seems to take two basic forms: "searching behavior" and "exploratory behavior." Searching behavior is directed toward a specific need or goal—sex, food, warmth, power, security. Exploratory behavior, on the other hand, has no specific goal; it is based on an innate need to continue experiencing, receiving information, absorbing stimuli. Konorski claims, "These stimuli are almost as necessary for . . . well-being as is food or water." The way we receive these stimuli is through our information-receiving systems (eyes, ears, and so on); and the information we receive in the form of stimuli is like a nutrient, "nourishing" our neurons. But when such stimulation is lacking, our neurons, neural networks, minds, develop "stimulus hunger." This hunger, according to Konorski, activates an "exploration system" in the brain.[189]

By eliminating most external stimuli, the ganzfeld and Tranquilite activate the brain's exploration system, causing the brain to reach out actively, hungry for meaningful stimulation. So when images, ideas, emotions, suggestions, sensations arise, the stimulus-hungry brain seizes on them, explores them, and values them more highly than it would if it were in its usual goal-oriented searching behavior; we perceive them as having extraordinary significance and intensity. In the same way, when we receive information from the outside world, in the form of suggestions, learning tapes, and so on, our brains, driven by stimulus hunger, are extraordinarily receptive to the information. Information that might ordinarily be quickly forgotten, because it has to compete with a variety of other stimuli, is now absorbed totally and becomes a permanent part of our memory. The result is the "superlearning" effect mentioned by Charlie Rush.

PSYCHIC POWERS BLOSSOM IN THE VOID

A CENTRAL IDEA THIS BOOK HAS BEEN EXPLORING IS THAT CERtain machines or devices might stimulate the brain and cause it to operate more effectively and coherently, calling into play powers and capabilities (such as whole-brain thinking through hemispheric synchronization, enormously accelerated learning, enhanced powers of self-regulation, and highly intensified sensory acuity) that might ordinarily lie dormant. Many have proposed that humans have a whole array of powers and capabilities that lie dormant and whose very existence is hotly denied by many scientists. These powers are what have been called "psychic" powers, or "psi", and include such things as telepathy, telekinesis, precognition, out-of-body experiences, and clairvoyance or "remote viewing."

Whether these phenomena exist or not is an interesting question, but not one which can be dealt with in this book. However, it's significant that those who argue for the existence of psi generally claim that it is an innate human capability, something we all possess and could, with proper training, develop. Biologist Lyall Watson, for example, citing new evidence that the glial cells have electrical properties, acting like transistors to magnify electrical signals many thousands or millions of times, points out that this could explain the phenomenon of telepathy: "Theoretically, there is no reason why we should not be able to detect messages coming from similar organisms many miles away . . . and perhaps even from transmitters on the other side of the planet."[364]

Just supposing for the sake of argument that humans do have psychic abilities, it makes sense that the source of these abilities would be the brain (it's hard to imagine sending telepathic messages from, say, the liver or the kneecap). If psychic abilities are an innate power of the brain, then it also makes sense that these abilities could be boosted by the right kind of stimulation, just as our brain's electrical waves, hemispheric synchronization, and ability to absorb information can be increased by stimulation. That is, if these machines really do enhance brain functioning, then they should enhance psychic abilities.

And in fact, many of those with the most experience in using these devices claim that they do. In my interviews with the makers of these mind machines and with those who make frequent use of the machines, psychic experiences have been a recurring topic. It's been my intention to keep this book on a solid scientific foundation, exploring aspects of brain growth and mind enhancement for which there is real evidence. So I never asked anyone about psi or psychic experiences. And yet, time and again, with no prompting, people I was interviewing would suddenly launch into a tale about how they left the body while hearing Hemi-Sync tapes, or communicated telepathically with a spouse while on the Synchro-Energizer, or went for strolls on a Vermont farm with a deceased friend while on a Graham Potentializer in New York City. Well, yes, yes, of course there are a lot of explanations for such things —they're dreams caused by deep relaxation, hallucinations resulting from the unusual energy flows through the brains, hypnagogic images emerging from the theta state, and so on. But in general, there is no evidence.

In the case of the ganzfeld (and by extension the Tranquilite) there is some real evidence, solid enough to warrant mention. One of the foremost psi researchers in the United States is Charles Honorton, director of the Psychophysical Research Laboratories in Princeton, New Jersey. After early studies under the tutelage of the pioneer of scientific psi research, J. B. Rhine of Duke University, Honorton began his own work nearly twenty years ago in the dream laboratories of Brooklyn's Maimonides Hospital. After a careful study of virtually all the available literature, he concluded that most psi experiences occurred when the body was in a state of deep relaxation and the mind was largely cut off from sensory input—during hypnosis, trance states, sleep, and meditation. He decided that if he could put people into the ideal state of deep relaxation and reduced sensory input, he might increase their psychic abilities. The best way to do this, he found, was to put the subjects into a ganzfeld chamber (a small soundproof room in which the subject sits in a comfortable chair, wearing earphones, with a bright light shining on halved Ping-Pong balls placed over the eyes).

By now more than a thousand men and women have participated in these ganzfeld psi experiments. According to Honorton, psychic phenomena have occurred in half the studies. An experiment is considered to be successful—i.e., to demonstrate evidence of psi—if the subject answers correctly twenty times more often than would be expected by pure chance. Since Honorton's ganzfeld subjects have been successful in 50 percent of the experiments, this is considered to be statistically highly significant.

16

ADRIFT ON THE GREAT LAKE OF UNKNOWING: THE FLOTATION TANK

At some point in the last chapter, in examining how an unchanging environment or stimulus can cause a subject to experience a turning-off or blank-out of the external world, with all sorts of beneficial results, the alert reader will have wondered, "Well, why go through all the trouble of creating an unvarying stimulus or ganzfeld to capitalize on a quirk of the central nervous system and put the user into a state of blank-out; why not just skip the intermediate step and put the user into a total blank-out right from the start?"

The answer is that such a blank-out device does exist. Known as a flotation tank, it not only is an enormously effective tool for enhancing mental functioning, but is by far the most intensively researched, well documented, and widely used of all the devices mentioned in this book.

THE CASE OF THE INCREDIBLE DISAPPEARING BODY

Although modern flotation tanks make use of sophisticated technology, the way they work is quite simple. Essentially, the tank is an enclosed container about the size of a closet turned on its side. The vessel contains a shallow pool of warm water (about ten inches deep) in which over eight hundred pounds of Epsom salts have been dissolved, creating a solution so dense—far more buoyant than the Dead Sea or Great Salt Lake—that anyone who lies back in the water bobs on the surface like a cork. When the door is closed the tank is totally dark. This complete absence of external visual stimulation is something most of us never experience in ordinary life situations, since even in the darkest rooms, or on the darkest of nights, with our eyes tightly closed, we still receive some ambient light. In the tank, it is impossible to tell whether your eyes are open or closed. Immediately, that is, you are in a visual blank-out.

Since your ears are underwater and stopped with plugs, there is also an almost total absence of external sounds, another experience with no counterpart in ordinary life situations. With this turning off of both sight and sound, the float tank matches the blank-out effect created by the unchanging ganzfeld and pink noise of the Tranquilite. However, the tank goes beyond this by restricting stimuli reaching other senses as well. The warm water of the tank is maintained at a constant temperature of about 93.5 degrees, which is equal to the body's temperature at the skin surface—there is no feeling of either warmth or cold, so that you soon lose any sense of separation between skin and water, and the boundaries of your body seem to dissolve, effectively creating a blank-out of the sense of touch, pressure, friction, and other skin sensations.

Another sensation floating turns off is the usually ever-present pressure of gravity. In the words of the tank's inventor, neurophysiologist Dr. John Lilly, "You're free of gravity; you don't have any more of those gravity confrontations that you do all day long. Finding where gravity is, and in what direction, and computing how you can move and not fall takes up about 90 percent of your neural activity. As soon as you start floating you're freed of all the gravity computations you've been doing all the time, so you find you have a whole vast piece of machinery that was being used for something else and you can now use it for your own purposes. . . . It's as if you are somewhere between the moon and the earth, floating, and there's no pull on you. As soon as you move, of course, you know where you are, but if you don't move your environment disappears and, in fact, your body can disappear."[203]

The tank, then, uses technological means to quickly, easily, reliably, and safely produce the turning off of the senses that all the meditative techniques such as breath-counting, chanting, repetition of mantras, and focused gazing strive for but so rarely attain. Even first-time floaters find that within minutes they are suspended weightlessly, without a body, in a total black, silent void.

And unlike meditative techniques, which are so numerous and have so many variables that it is difficult to subject them to large-scale, objective, controlled, repeatable scientific studies, the flotation tank is a controlled and unchanging environment, ideally suited for scientific research. Attempts to study meditation often must compare groups of subjects engaged in specific meditative techniques with control groups who are (usually) simply sitting quietly. But as we have seen, it is often hard to tell if meditators are truly in an authentic meditative state. However, when using the tank, there can be no doubts which group is floating and which is not. The result is that float-tank research produces those things so dear to the scientific heart—hard data, value-free statistics, replicable objective studies. As a consequence, there has been a surge of flotation-tank research in recent years by large numbers of scientists interested in the workings of the human mind, including cognitive psychologists, neuroendocrinologists, educators, and psychiatrists. These researchers have produced a comparatively large body of information about the effects of flotation and sensory deprivation. Among their findings:

STRESS REDUCTION. Events which disturb our body's natural equilibrium or *homeostasis* are stressful, and as we've noted earlier, stress impairs our ability to think clearly. One study of schoolchildren cited above shows that children suffering stress scored 15 percent lower on IQ tests than children experiencing low stress.[340] Elevated blood pressure also clearly lowers mental performance. Other studies have demonstrated that stress causes dramatic reductions in ability to think coherently or creatively, and to perform movements requiring skill and dexterity.

So it's of enormous importance that a large amount of research, particularly several series of studies at the Medical College of Ohio,[106] Lawrence College,[330] St. Elizabeth's Hospital in Appleton, Wisconsin,[29] and the University of British Columbia,[345] demonstrate that floating has a dramatic stress-reduction effect. Among the findings are that periodic floats reduce heart rate, oxygen consumption, and the levels of stress-related biochemicals in the bloodstream, including cortisol, ACTH, lactate, and adrenaline. The studies show that floating not only reduces these biochemicals during the float period, but also keeps the levels low for days and in some cases weeks after the float session. Because of an apparent vasodilatory effect (that is, blood vessels and capillaries are caused to relax and dilate), floating not only reduces high blood pressure but speeds and increases the flow of blood, with its oxygen and other nutrients, to all parts of the brain. We can speculate that this increased flow of blood to the brain enhances mental functioning and assists in building new brain tissue and nourishing neurons, leading to greater dendritic length, increased richness of dendritic connections, and increased thickness and weight of the neocortex. An enriched flow of blood is essential to protein synthesis, and since recent findings by neuroscientists have shown that memory formation is dependent on protein synthesis in the brain, we can also speculate that this blood-enrichment effect of floating enhances memory formation.

INCREASED TOLERANCE FOR STRESS. All of us are able to withstand or resist certain levels of stress, but for each of us the level at which stress becomes disruptive is different. In the words of Yale biochemist Philip Applewhite, "The hypothalamus brain program that recognizes stress when it comes in over the nerves is certainly a source of variability. Some people may feel stressed when not much has happened to them; they have a low tolerance for stress. For others it may take considerably more stress before the hypothalamus identifies it as such; these people have a high tolerance for stress."[8] That is, the hypothalamus acts as a *homeostatic mechanism*, acting to help the body maintain its equilibrium in the face of external stress. Some people's homeostatic mechanism is much more sensitive to stress, that is, some people's homeostatic mechanism has what is called a lower "set point."

In light of this, it's significant that studies by neuroendocrinologist John Turner and psychologist Tom Fine at the Medical College of Ohio indicate that floating not only significantly reduces the levels of stress-related biochemicals, but also has what Turner and Fine call a strong "maintenance effect"—the lowering of the stress biochemicals continued for many days after the subject's last float. This has led them to conclude that floating can "alter the set points in the endocrine homeostatic mechanism so that the individual would be experiencing a lower adrenal activation state. It would essentially be associated with a greater degree of relaxation."[358]

This is striking, since it means that the beneficial effects of floating are not just temporary, but alter the metabolism, (or homeostatic set point), essentially damping down the fight-or-flight response. This means that levels of pressure that might once have disrupted your ability to think clearly and perform effectively will seem less stressful after floating. That is, *floating is a way of increasing our tolerance for stress.*

DEEP RELAXATION. We all know instinctively that peak mental performance flows from relaxation, since our descriptions of peak moments of mental clarity and creative flashes emphasize effortlessness, fluidity: problems that we have strained over for months suddenly resolve themselves in a moment of release, and we say, "Why didn't I see it before —it's so easy!" By comparison, those who are mentally struggling are a study in muscular tension—they writhe in their chairs, grimacing, contorted. Also, as we've seen, studies of "twilight learning" or "superlearning" show that we are best able to assimilate new information and think clearly when we're relaxed.

But good relaxation is hard to find. Relaxation techniques such as Progressive Relaxation, Autogenics, and meditation take effort and discipline, with no assurance of success. In fact, many authorities now believe that most of us have never experienced complete relaxation in our lives, so we have no real conception of what it feels like, and no idea of how to cause our bodies to create that state.

In the warm Epsom salts of the float tank, however, free from the tug of gravity, your muscles naturally unfold like Chinese paper flowers in water, growing supple and pliant. Several studies have used an electromyograph (EMG), which measures muscular tension, to compare groups who simply floated with groups of nonfloaters who relaxed by using various relaxation techniques. In every study floaters quickly became far more deeply relaxed than the nonfloat groups. Significantly, this reduction in tension persisted, according to one study, for up to three weeks after a float.

In fact, all evidence indicates that floating actively and automatically triggers the mirror image of the fight-or-flight response, the *relaxation response*. This reflexive response includes reductions in heart rate, blood pressure, alterations in brain-wave activity, muscular relaxation, decreased oxygen consumption, decreases in stress-related biochemicals, and increased secretions of biochemicals that fill the body with a sense of well-being, pleasure, safety, and mental clarity. If the fight-or-flight response is one of spending energy and acting, the relaxation response is one of saving energy and thinking. Research indicates that floating activates this healthful response effortlessly. According to Fine and Turner of the Medical College of Ohio: "These [other relaxation] techniques have the individual elicit relaxation utilizing some internal strategy with or without external feedback as to the success of the strategy. In contrast [flotation tank] relaxation utilizes an environment to induce relaxation with the individual passively experiencing the process. . . . The controlled repeated experiences of this effortless passive relaxation provided by the [tank] may provide an advantage over these other methods requiring a trial and error approach to the deep relaxation state."[106]

PUMPING ENDORPHINS.   In their continuing inquiries

into the psychobiological effects of floating, Fine and Turner found that a session in the tank dramatically reduced pain and often induced a feeling of mild euphoria. They experimented further, using subjects who suffered from severe chronic pain. The results were exciting. Fine told me that "virtually all of our chronic pain patients have said that during the flotation period they have lost awareness of their pain." Wondering what this pain-relief mechanism might be, they set up a double-blind experiment in which one group received the endorphin antagonist naloxone. The other group received only a placebo. The study showed that 100 percent of the subjects were able to tell whether they had received the endorphin blocker or not. The implications are that floating stimulates the body to release endorphins, and that the increased levels of endorphins caused by floating are the cause of the pain reduction and feelings of euphoria. As we have seen earlier, endorphins are intimately related with a variety of brain-mind functions, including memory and learning. It's possible that by stimulating our natural reward systems, increased endorphin levels might assist in putting floaters into an ideal state for learning.

INCREASED THETA PRODUCTION. Partially as a result of the deep relaxation floating induces, floaters experience an increased production of theta waves. One study by Gary S. Stern of the University of Colorado at Denver found that "the significant effect of floating . . . indicates that individuals who had floated in the isolation tank for one hour significantly raised their theta level."[334] The intriguing and mysterious theta state, on the threshold between the conscious and the unconscious, is characterized by vivid, unpredictable imagery, spontaneous memories, Eureka moments when creative ideas and solutions to problems appear suddenly, and feelings of serenity, euphoria, and peace. It is also, as indicated by studies such as those of biofeedback expert Thomas Budzynski of the University of Colorado Medical Center, a "twilight" state when the brain "has these properties of uncritical acceptance of verbal material, or almost any material it can process. What if you could cause a person to sustain that state, and not fall asleep?" askes Budzynski. "I believe flotation tanks are an ideal medium for doing that."

INCREASED ACCESS TO THE RIGHT HEMISPHERE. Research also indicates that floating increased the power of, or increases the floater's access to, the right brain. Thomas Budzynski, who is engaged in EEG measurement of the hemispheres under varying conditions, asserts "In a float condition, left hemisphere faculties are somewhat suspended and the right hemisphere ascends in dominance." Or, Budzynski says more bluntly, "The right brain comes out in that float tank and says 'Whoopee!'" Budzynski, with many other brain researchers, believes that this increased access to the faculties of the right hemisphere can lead to enhanced learning abilities. Says Budzynski, "Get access to the right hemispheres of individuals very quickly, and keep them in that state, and that's where a *lot of work gets done very quickly.* We get at this same place with float techniques, 'twilight learning', subliminal processing, hypnosis, all of these."[59]

HEIGHTENED SUGGESTIBILITY. There is now overwhelming evidence that floating enormously increases suggestibility; that is, whatever information you receive while in the tank, whether in the form of suggestions made silently to yourself or as audio or visual information presented to you while floating, is accepted fully. In part, this is due to the altered brain-waves states mentioned above—increased theta, greater direct access to the right hemisphere, and hemispheric synchronization.

Another explanation is the "stimulus hunger" effect—in the absence of external stimulation, the RAS "turns up" the brain's volume control and the brain becomes "hungry" for information. So when it's given a message, it accepts it totally. Another explanation is that the part of the brain in charge of reality testing, critically evaluating incoming information, is turned off in the restricted stimulation environment of the tank, so messages can bypass the usual censor or filter and enter directly into the subconscious. In fact, Dr. Lloyd Glauberman, a New York City therapist with many years of experience in the use of hypnosis, who is now using float tanks equipped with in-tank speakers for training athletes and altering behavior patterns, told me that "the float tank is much more powerful than hypnosis—simply floating, without inducing a trance, makes you more suggestible than hypnosis." Studies at the University of British Columbia and elsewhere indicate that these in-tank suggestions have a unique "maintenance effect," retaining their power for months and, in several studies, years.

VISUALIZATION.   Scientists estimate that well over 90 percent of the brain's energy is expended processing external stimuli—visual and tactile information, gravitational forces, and so on. Freed in the tank of external responsibilities, the mind turns inward, and subtle mental processes which are ordinarily drowned out in the clamor of external stimuli gain remarkable force and clarity. One of these is internal imagery.

The ability to create and manipulate internal imagery, called visualization, is one of the most powerful learning techniques at our disposal, increasing our ability to solve problems by "seeing" them in a new way, increasing our ability to remember by associating nonvisual information with visual cues, and, perhaps most important, enabling us to vividly rehearse or experience events mentally. Many studies have shown that an image held vividly in the mind tends to be perceived by the subconscious and the body as being real. Visualizing yourself skillfully performing some action, whether delivering a speech, hitting a perfect tennis backhand, or solving some problem, can be as effective as actually performing the action: mental images produce real physical and mental effects. The problem is that most of us find it hard to visualize performing a feat with the kind of total concentration and clarity necessary to convince our body it's actually happening.

In the tank, however, you are free from all distractions and light. According to Dr. Glauberman, "Your ability to visualize is much more powerful while you're floating than it is even in hypnotic trance. Imagery seems more real, more dreamlike. Most of the time you're actually *in* the experience."

Dr. Rod Borrie, a New York City cognitive therapist who

guides his clients through in-tank visualizations to help them increase learning, improve athletic and work performance, and change behavior patterns such as smoking and overeating, explains the effect in terms of information theory. "The brain," he says, "can process only about seven bits of information at one time. Complex movements, such as athletic movements, are made of far more than seven bits of information at a time. Visualization puts all those bits in one chunk, like putting together a bunch of random letters, which would be impossible to remember, so they form a single word, which can be easily remembered. While floating, you put many actions together into a total image, so when the time comes to actually perform, the entire action is 'remembered' as a single image."

Just how real this "memory" can be is attested to by javelin thrower David Schmeltzer of the New York Pioneer Track Club, who uses in-tank visualization to "watch" himself throwing perfectly. Recently, he surpassed his personal record by several feet, and recalls, "When I released the javelin on that day it was like déjà vu. At the point of release, I said, 'I *know* this throw, I've thrown this throw before!'"

The power of previsualization is not limited to relatively short actions, but can be used to rehearse mentally or "program" yourself for enormously complex situations with virtually infinite variables. For example, Bob Said, a former Grand Prix sports-car champion, who has led two Olympic bobsled teams and five U.S. World bobsled teams, described to me how he clearly visualized every foot of the bobsled run as he floated each morning while training for the 1984 Winter Olympic trials. "In the sled," he said, "you know where you want to be in each corner but often you find yourself someplace else. So you try to visualize all the different ways you can get into each corner, so that when you get into the corner you're already programmed for coming out." In sports, as in many life situations, we need to act rapidly, almost automatically. But too often we're paralyzed by the need to stop and think. For Said, the "muscle memory" that comes from repeated visualization frees him from that need: "If you have to *think* a reaction in the sled, even if you have the world's fastest reactions, you're too slow. The 'cleaner' you are, the faster you are. I'm definitely sharper from floating, but it's not a sharpening of abilities so much as it's allowing one's abilities to function the way they're supposed to, by getting rid of the clutter."

According to Borrie, who has worked with Glauberman in training a number of top-flight athletes by using in-tank visualization, "Every athlete we're working with who has competed has set a personal record. And they keep on setting them. It's just a very, very powerful tool." "Phenomenal," agrees Glauberman, "and it hasn't even begun to be tapped yet." They both emphasize that such learning through visualization is not limited to athletic performance—mental rehearsals like those of Said can be equally effective in complex situations such as performing surgery, giving a speech or presentation, or performing a role in a play or ballet.

ENHANCED LEARNING AND CREATIVITY. The close relationship between learning and visualization is pointed up by a recent large-scale, rigorously controlled study at Texas A&M, where chemistry professor Thomas Taylor tested two groups on their ability to learn and think. One group listened to specific lessons while relaxed in a dark room, the other while in the tank. Afterward, the groups were hooked up to an EEG and tested on how much they had learned. The learning was evaluated on three levels of increasing difficulty: simple memory or rote learning; the ability to apply the information to new situations and problems; and "synthesis thinking," the ability to combine the ideas learned in new and creative ways.

The results were startling. The float group learned significantly more than the nonfloat group on every level; but most important, as the degree of difficulty and complexity of the learning tasks increased, the superiority of floaters over nonfloaters increased sharply. Concluded Taylor, "There's no question that the [float] group learned more, but where they learned is the most important point. People who floated learned at a different cognitive level. The results showed that the more difficult the concept, the bigger the difference in the performance of the two groups."

Interestingly, Taylor had tested the subject groups to see which were "visualizers" and which were "verbalizers" and concluded: "When the same learning records are analyzed on the basis of persons who are basically 'visualizers' versus those who are primarily 'conceptualizers' (nonvisual thinkers), a greater degree of learning occurred in the visual than in the nonvisual group." While the number of visualizers in both groups was equal, Taylor noted that the float group appeared to visualize better than the nonfloat group. The EEGs indicated that the float group also produced significantly higher amounts of theta waves, which are associated with strong mental imagery. In summary, visualization enhances learning at all levels, floating increases visualization, floating's enhancement of learning ability increases as the complexity and difficulty of the material being learned increases, and floating sharply increases the ability to think creatively and synthetically.[357] Floating seems to enhance mental functioning and open pathways of interaction between mind and body in so many ways that researcher Tom Fine of the Medical College of Ohio has called it "a breakthrough tool in psychobiology."

TANKS FOR THE MEMORIES: USING THE TANK FOR LEARNING

STUDIES LIKE THE ONE AT TEXAS A&M HAVE CONVINCED many scientists and educators that the tank can be a potentially revolutionary tool for accelerated learning, and tanks are now being used for that purpose at schools, universities, and over 250 float centers throughout the United States, Canada, Europe, and Japan. As research and popular use increase, it's becoming clear that the float tank can be used to enhance learning in a number of ways.

IN-TANK LEARNING. The most obvious method of using the tank is to profit from the deep relaxation, increased theta waves, heightened suggestibility, and increased ability to process information induced by floating and present the floater with the information to be learned while he or she is actually in the tank. This can be done with simple self-suggestion or visualization, the user choosing appropriate messages and images much as is done in ordinary self-hypnosis. Virtually all float tanks being produced today are equipped with in-tank speakers, so that floaters can record the information they wish to acquire on an audio tape to be played to them while they float. Users have reported excellent results in learning everything from new languages to prepping for law, medical, and real estate exams. Language students, for example, have reported that they are able to acquire several hundred new words in a single one-hour session, with a retention rate of almost 100 percent.

Most tank manufacturers now sell tanks with video monitors attached, so that floaters can relax until they are in a suitably receptive state, then turn on color videocassettes of visual material to be learned. Most commonly used thus far are commercially produced tapes of professional athletes playing at the peak of their form, demonstrating sports that include golf, tennis, running, downhill and cross-country skiing, racquetball, auto racing, soccer, baseball, basketball, football, sailing, and bowling. In a golf or tennis tape, for example, each type of swing is reproduced dozens of times for repetitive visual and sensory stimulation. The images are enhanced by sound—the solid sound of the club or racquet hitting the "sweet spot"—and computer-enhanced sequences that electronically highlight the flowing physical movements. Float-tank research at Stanford University indicates that watching such perfect performances has a "modeling" effect, causing you to absorb the movements in what has been called *muscle memory programming,* so that when you climb out of the tank the actual feel of the movements has been assimilated by your body. Watching a one-hour cassette is thought to be the equivalent of many hours of ideal physical practice.

Many athletes have made their own tapes. Professional football player Rafael Septien, a field-goal kicker for the

Dallas Cowboys, is one example. Each day he climbs into the tank and watches images of himself kicking perfect field goals. He credits this use of floating with helping him become an All-Pro kicker. "There's no doubt the tank is powerful," he told me. "They say that practice makes perfect, but actually it's *perfect* practice makes perfect. That's what you visualize in the tank—perfect practice." Other tapes have used the modeling effect to help train surgeons, musicians, salespeople, performers, visual artists, teachers, scientists, and business executives—whatever can be presented visually can be effectively presented to a floating learner. Says one maker of such training tapes, "Through recent advances in the neurological sciences, computerization, and solid-state sensing devices it is now possible to electronically transfer skills encoded on video software to the human nervous system." The possibilities of combining sight and sound seem virtually limitless and are only beginning to be explored.

POST-FLOAT LEARNING.   One of the most widely noticed effects of floating is a feeling of mild euphoria, mental clarity, and sensory acuity that lasts many hours, even days, after leaving the tank. The euphoria can be explained by the continuing deep relaxation and the increased flow of endorphins and perhaps other peptides. The mental clarity is largely due to the alteration in brain waves—slower frequency, higher amplitude, more hemispheric synchronization—that studies indicate also continues long after emerging from the tank. The sensory acuity—floaters speak of finding colors brighter, richer, more saturated, of seeing more sharply, hearing more clearly, having intensified senses of touch and smell —seems to have come from having allowed the senses to take a short vacation. They return to the world refreshed, having been what psychologist Arthur Deikman calls "deautomatized," with their doors of perception cleansed. As an example of how floating can sharpen the senses, consider recent research indicating that after only one minute of total darkness the eye's sensitivity to light increases ten times; after just twenty minutes it increases six thousand times; and after forty minutes—less time than most people spend in a flotation session—the eye reaches its limit of sensitivity to light, becoming about 25,000 times more sensitive than before the exposure to the darkness.[214]

This enhancement of mental and physical functioning makes the hours after a float ideal for learning of all sorts, since the mind is extremely receptive to external information, yet still in a somewhat free-floating state that is conducive to imaginative and creative thinking. Many floaters find that it is in the hours after a float that they find themselves discovering solutions to problems or being seized with new ideas, and often notice that this is a time when reading, studying, listening to music, and so on are particularly rewarding and productive.

PRE-FLOAT LEARNING. While I was interviewing floaters one man mentioned to me a "strange experience" he had while learning Dutch. On one occasion he went in for a float immediately after his lesson. For various reasons he didn't have any time in the next few days to review the lesson, but when he went in for his next lesson, he found that he had virtually total recall of the last lesson, and his instructor remarked that he must have studied very hard in the interim. He felt that somehow the float had subconsciously solidified the information in his brain. Was this possible? he wondered.

Shortly after that I was reading some reports of sensory-restriction research and read of a study in the early 1960s in which researchers read a lengthy passage from Tolstoy's *War and Peace* to two groups of subjects. They did not tell the subjects to remember this passage; in fact, it was just one of a number of events that occurred prior to the experiment. The subjects did not expect a retest. One group was a control group, and went about its normal activities; the other group spent a period in a sensory-restriction chamber. After twenty-four hours the two groups were retested. The researchers found that while there was a significant drop in retention for the control group, there was *none* for the experimental subjects. In fact, the sensory-deprivation group remembered *more* after twenty-four hours than at first! In interviewing the subjects, the researchers found that none of them had expected a retest, and only one had reported that he had even thought about the passage from *War and Peace* during the interim. The researchers dubbed this the "reminiscence effect." Somehow, simply being in a state of sensory restriction caused an increase in memory.[382]

A recent series of experiments has cast more light on this curious reminiscence effect. Subjects were given information, then one group consumed several ounces of alcohol—not enough to cause inebriation, but enough to put the subjects into a relaxed and somewhat euphoric state. The control group consumed no alcohol. When the two groups were later retested, it was found that the alcohol group had significantly greater recall of the information.

How to explain this? Well, scientists now agree that there are at least two types of memory, generally known as short-term memory (STM) and long-term memory (LTM). When we are aware while driving of how many cars are behind us and how close they are, this is information being held in STM —ten miles down the road we will have forgotten it. When we look up a phone number and hold it in our minds for a few moments required to make the call, this too is the STM at work. STM, in short, deals with information we need to hold in our minds temporarily, but which is quickly forgotten. On the other hand, there is another type of information that can be held in consciousness just as fleetingly as, say, that telephone number, but can become so permanent that it can be recalled with absolute clarity a lifetime later, such as the memory of some brief event observed momentarily by a child but remembered ninety years later. This is information that has passed into LTM.

Studies using drugs that inhibit protein synthesis in the brain have proved that short-acting electrochemical changes in the brain represent STM while protein synthesis in the brain is necessary for LTM. When drugs that inhibit protein synthesis in the brain are given soon after subjects learn something, the information is forgotten—that is, it never makes it into LTM.

However, when the drugs that inhibit protein synthesis are given more than an hour after the learning, the information is not forgotten, which means it has already become a part of LTM. In other words, information passes into LTM—protein synthesis takes place in the brain—during the hour or two after the information is received.[281]

One type of protein synthesis in the brain is structural growth: the growth of dendrites, formation of new dendritic spines and synapses. As we have seen, this type of protein synthesis was first detected by Mark Rosenzweig, Marian Diamond, and their colleagues at UC Berkeley. They found that rats exposed to enriched environments exhibited heavier and thicker cortical layers, composed of larger neurons, more glial cells, longer dendrites, and more dendritic connections. Later studies have shown that even a few minutes of environmental enrichment are sufficient to cause permanent brain growth; that is, a brief experience of stimulation can result in protein synthesis. A study by William Greenough of the University of Illinois has shown that rats trained to run a maze show dendritic growth immediately after the training. That is, *brain growth is a specific response to learning*.

Learning and long-term memory can occur only when protein synthesis takes place in the brain. Protein synthesis in the brain (growth of dendrites and axons, increase in number of glia, increase in number and richness of dendritic connections) is a direct result of learning. That is, brain growth facilitates learning and memory on the one hand, and learning and memory lead to brain growth on the other hand. Memory and learning, in other words, cannot be separated from physical brain changes. Rosenzweig and colleagues proved that environmental enrichment leads to physical brain growth and increased memory and learning. Now we see that physical brain growth is essentially identical with the process of learning and increasing memory stores. To use Prigogine's terms, as energy enters the system in the form of new information or experiences, it can only be incorporated by means of actual change in the structure and organization of the system, that is, by brain growth. If something happens to stop this brain growth, such as administering a drug to inhibit protein synthesis, the new information that has entered the system will disappear, be forgotten. However, if sufficient time is allowed for this protein synthesis to take place, permanent changes will have taken place in the brain, and the information will be a part of long-term memory.

To return to the "reminiscence effect" noted by sensory-deprivation researchers, we can surmise that this effect results from the fact that after being given the information, the sensory-restriction group was removed for a period from new sensory input, from things that would compete with the information for long-term memory. Similarly, the alcohol group remembered more because in their slightly tipsy state they turned their brains off to potential new information to be remembered, thus giving the original information sufficient time to "solidify."

It seems clear that this reminiscence effect can be put to good use by floaters. Whatever information they want to put into their long-term memory should be studied immediately prior to entering the tank (or should be presented via video or audio tapes during the early part of the float). The period of sensory restriction that follows—ideally at least an hour—should allow time for the necessary protein synthesis to occur in the brain to permit the information to become consolidated and committed to long-term memory.

Also, a number of float-tank studies have made it clear that floating has a vasodilatory effect, relaxing the tiny capillaries that carry blood into and throughout the brain. This results in a greater supply of blood to the individual neurons in the brain. Since blood carries the nutrients essential for protein synthesis, increased blood flow to the brain can only enhance protein synthesis. In the words of Dr. Arnold Scheibel, professor of medicine at UCLA and an expert on brain growth, "if there is a bottom line, it is that no neuron is healthier than the capillary that supplies it. And we have a very strong feeling that in the capillary supply system is the story of the maintenance or the slow decline" of the brain.[49] The vasodilation that takes place while you are floating, then, facilitates brain growth, which means that by increasing blood flow to the brain floating can facilitate learning and the formation of long-term memory.

It should be clear that to a greater or lesser degree, all the factors that make the float tank such a powerful tool for enhancing intellectual functioning—deep relaxation, alteration of brain waves, focusing of attention, heightened suggestibility, increased protein synthesis in the brain—are present in the other devices mentioned in this book. Thus, the techniques mentioned for using the tank as a learning-enhancement tool can also be applied in conjunction with the other devices. For example, you could easily prepare audio cassettes with information to be learned, then play them to yourself while using the Graham Potentializer, the Mind Mirror, the Synchro-Energizer, or the Tranquilite. Similarly, you could profit from the reminiscence effect by studying material you wish to make a part of your permanent memory prior to or during use of any of the other devices.

In fact, there is evidence that in some cases combining two or more of the devices can lead to a greater increase in mental powers than can be obtained through use of a single device. For example, in one recent study, psychotherapist Dr. Deborah Ann Baker measured the effects of simple flotation on the enhancement of creativity and problem-solving and compared the results with a group who heard Hemi-Sync tapes while floating. The tests showed that in every characteristic measured, including ability to become deeply relaxed, ability to concentrate, feeling increased energy, experiencing a dreamlike state while floating, and problem-solving, the combination of floating with the Hemi-Sync tapes was far more powerful and effective than simple floating.[16] I suspect that future studies will show this same potentiating effect resulting from the combining of other devices mentioned in this book. It would be interesting to see for example, the effects of watching your brain-wave patterns on a Mind Mirror while floating, or wearing the Synchro-Energizer while on the Graham Potentializer. The potential combinations seem limited only by the imagination of the user, and suggest that the ultimate mind machine is still to come.

17

THE EVOLUTIONARY BRAIN

THE SCIENTISTS MENTIONED AT THE BEGINNING OF THIS BOOK insist that we are now in the midst of a revolution. It is not just a scientific revolution, but a revolution in our assumptions about human capabilities and potentials, in how we understand what it means to be human, to think, to value, to learn. As we've seen, the key to this revolution has been the recent breakthrough to a fuller, though still incomplete, comprehension of the complexity and elegance of the electrochemical processes taking place in our brains.

Behavior, cognition (how information from the environment enters a person and is processed so that it can affect actions), character, all the things that compose an individual's personality or sense of self, were once thought to be almost wholly the result of mysterious drives, tendencies, and attitudes that were themselves rooted in past events and forces, such as a mother who was too protective, a depressed father, or a too-pushy older sibling. A person's character was thought to be set by the experiences one had by the age of six, and intelligence was assumed to be determined by heredity. But now it's becoming clear that our behavior, attitudes, moods, personalities, thoughts—including sexual preference and desires, hunger, fear, happiness, pain, sleep, memories, creativ-

302

ity, and imagination—all are the result of interactions between specific neurochemicals and receptors on the surfaces of our neurons. Says neurochemist Candace Pert of NIMH:

> Behavior isn't such a mysterious thing. I think it emanates from microcircuits of electrons flowing from one neuron to another. What we're working on now is connecting up neurochemical facts—the brain's "juices"—with circuit diagrams of the brain. Circuit diagrams are what people called neuroanatomists have been concerned with for years—the actual interconnections of the neurons, the wiring of the brain. What's happening now is we're learning which neural pathways secrete endorphins and which secrete other neurojuices. There's no doubt in my mind that one day—and I don't think that day is all that far away—we'll be able to make a color-coded map of the brain, with blue for one neurochemical, red for another, and so on. . . . We'll be able to describe the brain in mathematical, physical, neurochemical, and electrical terms, with all the rigor of a differential equation.[367]

Pert's confidence recalls the then controversial statement made more than a decade ago by experimental psychologist David Krech of UC Berkeley, an early collaborator with Mark Rosenzweig in experiments with rats raised in enriched and impoverished environments. "I foresee the day," said Krech, "when we shall have the means, and therefore, inevitably, the temptation, to manipulate the behavior and the intellectual function of all people through environmental and biochemical manipulation of the brain."[65]

Today Krech's prediction has been fulfilled, as psychiatrists and other medical professionals routinely manipulate the emotions, behavior, and intellectual functioning of their patients with scores of psychoactive drugs that mimic the actions of natural neurotransmitters or peptides.

If the upheavals in neuroscience can be called a revolution, then one of the researchers who helped fire the opening shot is Pert, who in 1973, working with Solomon Snyder, discovered the opiate receptor. In the wake of this discovery came the discovery of endorphins and many other peptides, as well as the discovery of several dozen types of brain receptors, uniquely shaped molecular "keyholes" designed to receive natural brain chemicals which have not yet been discovered. Among the receptors that scientists have found are several types of benzodiazepine receptors (drugs such as Valium and Librium are benzodiazepines), which apparently play a key role in sleep, relaxation, and anxiety. The discovery of these receptors suggests that humans are capable of secreting a brain chemical—"natural Valium" or a "mellow molecule"—that acts to reduce anxiety and muscular tension, without the fatigue, confusion, and other side effects associated with the synthetic drug.

Other receptors have been found that are activated by the street drug PCP, or Angel Dust, indicating that we probably secrete our own natural Angel Dust. Why would we have brain juices to make us weird and crazy? Says Dr. Frederick Goodwin of the NIMH, "They might be there to promote the breakdown of normal channels of thought, to allow revelry, dreaming, and imagination."[152] If scientists are able to locate and activate our natural Angel Dust peptide, they may enable us to trigger our imagination and creativity at will.

Dr. Wallace Mendelson of the NIMH has developed a Valiumlike substance that soothed and relaxed laboratory rats, as expected. But EEG readings showed that while physically mellow, the rats were highly alert mentally. Speculates Mendelson, "We may have hit on an altered state of animal consciousness." This combination of deep physical relaxation with mental alertness has been compared to meditation. Could the drug lead to a human "meditation pill?" Says Mendelson, "Calling this meditation is still pretty speculative, but if it does happen, it will be within the next five years."

California drug designer Alexander Shulgin has been experimenting with drugs that he claims can enhance imagination and creativity and sharpen the perceptions. Says Shulgin, "A number of materials I have been working on are amplifiers of specific senses that will enhance the visual, the interpretive color sense, or the auditory acuity, without blanketing the entire body with intoxication and confusion." Describing how his creativity drugs work, Shulgin claims, "It's as though you had a neurological capability wired into the brain—something that Ma Bell has tucked away in her computer and you just have no way of dialing in because the neurotransmitters are not at hand, they are not mobilized, they are suppressed, or something is amiss. The drug catalyzes it." He predicts, "The time will come when we'll separate all our senses and capabilities—the visual from the auditory, the tactile from the sense of smell as well as wit, intellectual capability, creativity—and enhance them with drugs."[65]

Other researchers are experimenting with a variety of "memory pills" that stimulate learning and memory by binding to receptors in the brain's memory centers. As neuroscientists continue to find new receptors, many predict that the number of receptors will soon be in the hundreds.

While brain chemicals have already revolutionized psychiatric treatment and promise to enhance mental functioning in normal, healthy people, many don't see drug-induced alterations in consciousness as an altogether happy prospect. Brain drugs are not now and will probably never be fully accepted as a daily part of a natural, healthy human life. For many, the mere fact that they are synthetic, made from laboratory chemicals, makes them suspect. "There is no social, scientific, or medical apparatus for optimizing normal human behavior," says Dr. Arnold Mandell, biochemical psychiatrist and developer of new drugs. "I think it will take decades because there is no aegis in our society for introduction of performance- or life-improving drugs. Under whose aegis could we administer a creativity drug, for instance? It isn't that you're sick, so no doctor can give it to you. There is a wall against all this work."[65]

Since the chemicals are drugs, they will (unless there are extraordinary changes in our society) remain controlled substances, dispensed only by prescription. As Nathan S. Kline, pioneer in the mind-drug field, once pointed out, "The real problem in the field of psychopharmaceuticals is not so much the creation of new classes of drugs, but determining who shall make the decisions as to when they should be used, on whom, and by whom." Where there are restrictions, there are those who will ignore the restrictions to make money. As sophisticated laboratory equipment grows more portable, and as mind-enhancing drugs such as memory pills become more easily synthesized, underground chemists will distribute these drugs through the black market. As is the case with black-market drugs today, some of these substances will be imperfectly made, tainted, and potentially dangerous.

In addition to these problems, there is the basic fact that the substances are *drugs*. Very few people are willing to inject substances directly into the brain or cerebrospinal fluid, so the drugs must be injected into the bloodstream or taken orally. As a result, much of the drug does not make it into the brain through the filter of the blood-brain barrier; this portion is carried to other parts of the body, where it can have a variety of often harmful side effects. Those drugs that do make it into the brain often not only go to that spot of the brain where they act in the way the user desires, but are circulated throughout the brain, stimulating unrelated areas and causing such side effects as fatigue, weakness, agitation, and confusion.

LEARNING AND EXPERIENCE AS A DRUG: IT'S ALL IN YOUR MIND

SAYS CANDACE PERT, "OUR DRUGS ARE STILL VERY CRUDE." She predicts that soon scientists will have an array of very sophisticated drugs that are more specific and controllable in their effects. But even so, she admits, drugs may not be the answer. "It's all in the mind anyway," she says. "Perhaps what this is telling us is that drugs can never be as subtle as our own neurochemicals, which can be released in one spot and not another. Drugs assault the whole brain at once. Who knows, the future psychiatric treatment may consist of auto-hypnosis, meditation, exercise, diet modification, and so on. . . . Drugs are just analogues of our own internal chemicals anyway, and there's evidence that life events prompt the release of neuro-chemicals."[367]

Other scientists agree that in the end, techniques for stimulating our own neurochemicals naturally are preferable to drugs. "A drug is merely a very fast, very accessible catalyst," says drug inventor Shulgin. "A drug does nothing but catalyze what can be catalyzed in many other ways." Brain researcher James McGaugh of UC Irvine, a pioneer in the area of memory-enhancing drugs, says, "The drugs don't do anything that cannot be done by providing more experience."[65]

Experience. The word brings us back to the experiments conducted by Mark Rosenzweig, Marian Diamond, David Krech, Edward Bennet, and others, showing that rats raised in enriched environments developed different brains than did rats raised in normal or impoverished environments. Their brains were physically larger—thicker cortex, more glial cells, larger and more complex neurons, longer dendrites, more dendritic spines, larger postsynaptic area. Their brains had different levels of key neurotransmitters and other neurochemicals. And when tested for memory, learning, and other types of intelligence, the rats from the enriched environments were far superior. In the words of Marian Diamond, "The main factor is stimulation. The nerve cells are designed to receive stimulation."[225]

Stimulation somehow caused the rats to release brain chemicals—their own, natural juices regulating things like learning, memory, and the brain growth (i.e., protein synthesis) associated with (and essential for) learning and the formation of long-term memory. Stimulation, or to use the word favored by McGaugh, "experience," acted like a drug in the brain. Stimulation/experience altered brain chemistry with extraordinary quickness (remember William Greenough's experiments showing the formation of new nerve connections within seconds of stimulation/experience), by sparking the release of the brain's natural learning and memory peptides and neurotransmitters.

There can be no doubt about this. Certain types of experiences or stimulation or environmental influences can cause the release of beneficial and desirable brain chemicals. Several thousand studies of meditators, for example, show that this technique for altering the input to the brain can bring dramatic changes in brain chemistry and result in improvements in a variety of mental functions, including memory, IQ, neuro-efficiency quotient, and creativity. A number of studies indicate that running or jogging can cause the brain to release large amounts of endorphins. In addition to medication and exercise, Pert mentions autohypnosis and diet modification as other ways of altering neurochemical levels. Simply smiling or laughing, a recent study shows, is a quick way to boost levels of some juices.[297]

There is also evidence that novel experiences, such as learning to play a new musical instrument or studying a new language as an adult, cause changes in brain chemistry and structure. In science it has often been noted that many original thinkers are "late bloomers," who have changed fields in middle age. Examples are Francis Crick, who started his career as a physicist and only in his thirties shifted his focus to molecular biology and helped discover the structure of DNA, Leo Szilard, who became a biologist as he approached fifty, Wilhelm Ostwald, a Nobel laureate in chemistry who shifted to mathematics and devised the first mathematical theory of color at age fifty-nine, and Louis Pasteur, who developed the germ theory of disease when in his forties. Szilard and Ostwald have recommended that those interested in continued intellectual growth make use of this "novice effect," by abandoning their area of expertise or specialized research every five or ten years and exploring a new problem or area that is fascinating but about which they are virtually ignorant. Subjected to a novel barrage of experiences and stimulations, the brain is forced to grow, to make new neural connections, to forge new chemical pathways, to retain its youthful plasticity, to see the world with fresh eyes.

With this in mind we can see one reason for the growing interest in mind machines of the sort we have looked at in this book. They are effective devices for presenting humans with concentrated bursts of experiences and stimulations of the type that cause the brain to release or step up production of the brain chemicals associated with pleasure, learning, memory, and creativity. They are the technological equivalent of the super-enriched environments that researchers found could, in a few minutes, stimulate brain growth that was equal to the amount of brain growth it took a month to achieve in an ordinary enriched environment.

They are machines, yes, but in a real way they are quite natural, since they work by causing the body to release its own natural chemicals and speed up its natural growth process. That is, they act like drugs, but they are not drugs. They are nonintrusive, using only flickering lights, a moving cot, an unvarying light, phased sound waves, a buoyant salt-water solution in a dark chamber—unlike drugs, synthetic substances that can bring harmful side effects. Like drugs, they can act rapidly, powerfully, and without any effort on the part of the user. But unlike drugs, the machines allow the intensity and amount of stimulation to be controlled by the user, and the user can at any time simply choose to end the experience, while drugs take many hours and sometimes days to be neutralized and excreted from our bodies.

O BRAVE NEW WORLD

FOR MANY OF US, THE IDEA OF MACHINES THAT INFLUENCE THE mind brings a deep sense of chill, vaguely threatening: we think of cold steel, mindless, lifeless, inhuman, and dehumanizing. Deep Luddite longings grumble within us, fears of brainwashing or control by a machine-assisted totalitarian state. We visualize vast dormitories or prisons or hospitals filled with row upon row of motionless zonked-out humanoids hooked up to humming machines and receiving their infusions of bliss. It's the stuff of a million science fiction novels and films. Big Brother Is Watching You.

There's no doubt certain devices can be used for purposes of mind control. Just as there's no doubt certain machines, some of which are described in this book, can be used to enhance mental functioning. The question becomes, what distinguishes a potentially beneficial device from a potentially dangerous one?

One answer, I think, is found in the orientation the device

makes you take toward your own body and mind. Machines can intensify your awareness of your body and mind, or they can actively distract your awareness. They can turn your attention inward, allowing you to explore your own physical and mental capacities and expand your store of authentic experiences, or they can capture your attention, steal your consciousness, and direct it toward things which are not you, entertaining displays full of sound and fury but signifying nothing. They can, by increasing your awareness of your capabilities and being responsive to your guidance and desires, empower you and help you gain authority and control over your life, or they can, by hooking you into a device over which you have no control, turn you into a passive receiver. They can increase and intensify your perceptions, senses, and feelings by bringing you into intimate contact with yourself, or they can override and crush those perceptions and feelings by imposing upon you the opinions, experiences, and perceptions of others. Machines that increase our knowledge of ourselves, that expand our powers, enrich our minds, increase our personal freedom, can be called "tools of authenticity" (from the Greek *authentes*: "one who does anything with his own hand"). The experiences they give us are real, genuine, true, trustworthy, authentic. Such machines, by making us more familiar with ourselves, can teach us to trust ourselves more. In this way they can enhance our own strength as individuals.

On the other hand, some machines obviously decrease our awareness of ourselves, bodies and minds. For example, most television. There is growing evidence that television, for the most part, literally lives up to its name as a "dumb box" or "boob tube," causing the brain to actually decrease its sensitivity and alertness, reduce its levels of learning- and memory-inducing neurochemicals, decrease brain-wave amplitude, diminish its richness of neural connections. That is, television seems to be a mechanical counterpart to the impoverished environment which caused rats to develop with shrunken brains and reduced intelligence.

Another question we must answer when evaluating the potential benefits or dangers of a mind-influencing device is:

who is in control? It is a characteristic of all devices used for mind control that they are controlled by people other than the users. Those who want to use such devices to exercise control over others are careful to keep the devices out of the hands of the users. One example is the possession of nuclear weapons. As long as only one nation has control of such devices, they can be used to exercise power over other nations. If, however, such devices become easy to make, relatively inexpensive, and widely available, so that almost any nation that wants to can construct them, then they lose much of their value and effectiveness as control devices. Similarly, network television, because it is so enormously expensive to produce, is almost totally controlled in the United States by a few powerful and wealthy corporations. The "users" of network television—that is, the people who watch regularly—have no means of controlling what they see except by changing channels to another virtually identical show. The stimulations or experiences the users receive are not specifically directed toward them, but molded to be acceptable to scores of millions of people.

On the other hand, tools that increase our intelligence and awareness, that stimulate our brains and enrich our minds, are those which can be effectively controlled by individual users, and manipulated to fit the user's particular individual needs and interests. This means that the user must have direct access to the machine. It is important, then, that the devices be widely available, and inexpensive enough so that they can be owned or rented by private individuals. The machines described in this book are all available, selling at prices that make them accessible to almost everyone. With such devices owned or used by so many people, operated and controlled by the users, it is impossible to conceive of a way they could be used for purposes of mind control or brainwashing.

Machines that distract us from what is real are machines that can decrease our self-assurance, our ability to think independently, originally, freely. By doing so these machines become tools that diminish us, make us more susceptible to control by others, even by totalitarian systems. This technology of alienation is one which is a real threat to our world today, and one we should oppose vigorously. One effective way to oppose this authoritarian, deadly technology is the proper use of the technology of growth, the machines of mind enhancement and authenticity, the tools that increase our awareness of ourselves, and by doing so lead us to an increased awareness that all of us are one.

EVOLVING BRAIN, EVOLUTIONARY MIND

THE VIEW OF EVOLUTION THAT IS BECOMING INCREASINGLY ACcepted today is that of "punctuated equilibrium." Unlike the classical Darwinian view, which held that species evolved very slowly by means of a series of minor changes that took place over millions of years, this new theory sees evolution as a series of sudden transitions or evolutionary leaps, separated by long periods of relative stability. According to this theory, a species can exist for millions of years with little evolutionary change; then, in a short period of time and with surprising rapidity (and usually as a result of major environmental changes or upheavals), the species changes dramatically, leaping suddenly to a distinctly higher evolutionary level. This theory is supported by the evidence, since the fossils we have found tend not to show a smooth progression from one species to another, but instead to be a lot of similar fossils for one species, and another lot for the species that it seems to have evolved into, with almost no fossils falling in between.

This view of evolution accords quite well with Prigogine's theory of dissipative structures. We know that the structure of a life form will tend to maintain internal organization and coherence by dissipating entropy into the environment. Environmental changes will cause energy fluctuations, which will be absorbed or damped by the structure; a species will be able to survive a slight climatic change, say, a minor temperature drop, by altering its behavior patterns, migrating, and so on. But when the environmental change is major, the fluctuations are too great to be absorbed and dissipated by the existing structure, and the structure will reach the "bifurcation point," where it must transform itself radically or be destroyed. This sudden transformation, reorganization, or escape to a higher order is the evolutionary leap.

Today we are living in a time of major environmental upheaval. Among the unprecedented transformations taking place right now is our new ability to manipulate molecular biology, altering genes, creating completely new life forms. Advances in computer technology give us the capacity to store and process with lightning speed inconceivably vast amounts of information; calculations that would have taken decades to complete are now performed almost instantaneously; discoveries that would never have been made now emerge from the ability to combine, compare, and interrelate large quantities of information from a variety of sources. Atomic physicists are now able to transform some elements into others, to create new elements by altering nuclear structure with their powerful particle accelerators—in other words, to alter the very nature of matter or "reality." With communication satellites, television, interconnected computers, and a network of telephones that covers the entire earth, humans are now able to communicate with virtually any other member of their species; no longer a collection of tribes and races separated by distance and ignorance, we are becoming one, a global village, a single vast network in which information and energy are transmitted through all parts in a complex interweaving of energy flows, very much like the constant patterns of electrochemical impulses sweeping through the brain. The world has become a single planetary brain, with each of us as a neuron.

These unprecedented upheavals as well as others in such areas as industry, chemistry, agriculture, the exploration of space, medicine, technology, transportation, and education are combining and feeding off each other, in a process of increasing acceleration. As systems theorist and student of evolution John Platt writes:

> Jumps by so many orders of magnitude, in so many areas, with this unprecedented coincidence of several jumps at the same time, and these unique disturbances of the planet, surely indicate that we

are not passing through a smooth cyclical or acceleration process similar to those in the historical past. Anyone who is willing to admit that there have been sudden jumps in evolution or human history, such as the invention of agriculture or the Industrial Revolution, must conclude from this evidence that we are passing through another such jump far more concentrated and more intense than these, and of far greater evolutionary importance.[290]

Humans are experiencing this environmental change as increased fluctuations or perturbations, an increased influx of energy that can no longer be absorbed by the old structure. We are at a bifurcation point, in the process of reorganizing at a higher level of complexity, diversity, interconnection, and organization. That is, we are in the midst of an evolutionary leap: either we must escape to a higher order, or be destroyed.

The evolutionary struggle for survival continues, though today humans face more serious threats to their survival as a species than ever before. For several million years, early humans struggled against wild beasts, hunger, disease, cold. Those who were the "fittest" survived to pass their genes along through their offspring. Today, we face the possibility that our entire species can be eradicated as a result of our own mistakes. In addition to the threat of nuclear destruction, we are challenged by environmental pollution, overpopulation, widespread hunger and famine, and destructive ideologies such as nationalism and political or religious fanaticism. The humans who are "fittest" to survive these challenges are not necessarily those who are physically strongest or most powerful, but those who are the most imaginative, intelligent, adaptive, and capable of developing strategies to ensure their survival and the survival of the species. The problems can no longer be solved by physical force or strength. The problems demand mental solutions. To survive, humans must develop new mental capabilities. In other words, the evolutionary leap which we are now making is taking place in our brains.

In the past, evolution has been a process of genetic accident—various random mutations appear, of which certain prove to be successful, enhancing the creature's ability to survive. Today, for the first time, humans have the opportunity to take control of their own evolution. If evolution involves the development of new mental powers, stimulating the brain to new levels of achievement, then the machines we have looked at in these pages, which can enhance mental functioning and stimulate richer and denser neural interconnections in the brain, might be seen as evolutionary tools. The fact that these machines can be controlled and altered in ways determined by the user presents us with a unique situation: now humans can consciously direct their own development.

Seen in this way, the process of evolution becomes goal-oriented, teleological; now the process involves not only surviving, but developing toward desired goals. Given the right type of machine, one could theoretically choose to develop those capabilities associated with the left hemisphere of the brain, by stimulating the left brain at the expense of the right hemisphere; the result might be the development of extraordinary powers of serial, linear, verbal, abstract thought. Similarly, one could choose to stimulate the development of the right hemisphere, leading to the development of a passionate and emotionally charged personality with rich powers of visualization and intuition.

Of course, these extreme examples are not advisable or desirable. But once we have accepted the idea that humans now have the capability of choosing and directing their own mental evolution, many questions arise. What should be the goal of human evolution? What type of mental development should we stimulate? What kind of creature should we desire to become? What sort of life is worth living?

THE LAST FRONTIER

WE HAVE SEEN THAT MANY NEUROSCIENTISTS TODAY NOW look upon the brain as "the last frontier." But new frontiers always seem to turn up. Beyond each frontier lies another.

But if the brain is not the *last* frontier, it is certainly a frontier. It has all the things that make a frontier so interesting—mysteries, strange inhabitants, legends and myths, vast unexplored areas, possibilities for adventure, heroism, self-discovery, self-transformation, new wisdom, and sudden unimaginable wealth. Our exploration of this frontier has only begun. We are now at a crucial and decisive moment—a moment comparable to that period when the explorers from the Old World were suddenly beginning to get an inkling that this New World they had stumbled onto was something far greater than they had ever imagined, a world of incalculable riches.

It was at that point, and for centuries thereafter, that those explorers and their descendants made a decision about how this New World, the last frontier, should be explored, exploited, and developed. They sought gold, enslaving and destroying millions of Indians in their search. They sought land, power, and wealth, and to get it they struggled not only with the Indians but among themselves.

What direction will our exploration and development of the brain frontier take? The exploitative, destructive course we took in the exploration of our geophysical last frontier, the American West? Or a new type of exploration that benefits the entire race, the whole earth, and potentially the universe? We are at the point Arthur Clarke called *Childhood's End*—when we can leave behind the long childhood of our species and evolve into a new type of human, not driven by childish angers, impulses, and desires, but inspired by a mature vision of human potentials, an adult wisdom. The question is, what type of adult will we grow into?

Some social critics have condemned varieties of mental exploration and growth as essentially narcissistic—selfish, private, individual, inward-directed, ultimately antisocial. But it is becoming evident that the development of the human brain is an essential evolutionary step. Human survival may well depend on our ability to increase our mental powers and develop new strategies for overcoming our present crises. So mental enrichment, brain stimulation, and the exploration of our mind's potentials are not self-serving or escapist, but rather social acts, and part of a potentially beneficial, history-determining social process—one which can widen our knowledge and help determine the future of the race.

BACK TO THE FERRIS WHEEL

ALL THIS STUFF ABOUT MENTAL EVOLUTION NOTWITHSTAND-
ing, probably the main reason folks make use of these devices
is that they make people feel good. In my talks with frequent
users of the machines I found that most of them are less interested in the findings of controlled experiments than in having
fun and feeling fine. The time is right for machines of this
sort; in the next few years they will become increasingly popular.

One reason for this is that our national obsession with
physical fitness continues to grow. And the logical next step
after physical fitness is mental fitness. The mind machines can
be seen as the brain-training counterpart to the sleek Nautilus
and Universal machines, the ergometers and rowing devices
and cross-country ski contraptions. It's not hard to imagine
serious brain athletes getting their gray matter in shape by
pumping peptides and neurotransmitters while yelling "Feel
the burn!" Everyone will join a chic skull spa, equipped with
all the popular mind machines. After work they can drop by
for a quick session on the Synchro-Energizer followed by a
stiff workout on the Graham Potentializer and finishing up
with a head-to-head competition on the Mind Mirror—the
winner is the one who produces the highest amount of hemispheric synchronization. After the workout they can hang
around the spa and, like weight lifters comparing biceps or
runners bragging of their marathon times, compare their
neuro-efficiency quotients, talk about how many IQ points
they've gained since joining the spa, and brag about their ability to produce high-amplitude theta waves at will.

Add to this craving for fitness our long-standing American
love affair with machines and our determination to feel good
at all costs, and you've described a culture that could take to
mind machines as easily as it has to computers and cars. I can
see it clearly: coin-operated Alpha Stims in cocktail lounges,
laundromats, taxis. Drop the coin in the slot for a quick jolt to
juice up your neurons and get those endorphins flowing.

TENS-powered truck drivers, rolling the highways with electrodes humming inside their socks. Rows of blissful grade-schoolers going round and round doing naptime loop-the-loops on their Graham Potentializers. Diplomats taking a break from the summit talks to slip into their Tranquilites for a bit of ganzfeld peace. Naked intellectuals muttering in the darkness, discussing the world economy while bobbing contemplatively side by side in huge flotation "think tanks." A gaggle of ad writers gathered around the conference table, each one wearing a Synchro-Energizer, the entire group flickering at the same rhythm, hearing the same phased sound waves; "Yes," cries one, "now we're on the right wavelength!"

AFTERWORD

READERS FAMILIAR WITH COMPUTERS, AND THEIR 10 AND 20 megabyte hard disks, where "mega" means million, might have visualized a megabrain as some Hydra-headed creature with multitudinous brains. In fact, mega comes from a Greek work meaning *great, mighty, extended, powerful*. The Megabrain state is something we've all experienced, those moments when our brain seems to become great, mighty, powerful, extended.

We call these Megabrain states by many names: peak experiences, Eureka events, aha! moments, illumination, flow, the awakened mind, satori, bliss, brilliance, mastery, insight, synthesis, and so on. We enjoy this state so much we would gladly be in it as often as possible. Unfortunately, it is not easy to enter the state, and throughout history many techniques have been devised to allow disciplined users to enter the Megabrain state. These techniques include various mystic practices, yoga, meditation, chanting, and so on.

It has been a central idea of this book that recent neuro-scientific discoveries have determined that the state is characterized by some very clear and easily recognized patterns of brain activity, that is, physical correlates of the brain states the mystics, meditators, monks, and masters only knew by experience, and could only define vaguely and teach inexactly. This book has explored the idea that there are certain devices that can help shift the brain into those patterns of activity that characterize the Megabrain state (such as brainwave activity in the slow or theta range, hemispheric synchronization, and so on).

As Writer Colin Wilson has pointed out, "Once we understand the basic techniques, we can achieve the peak experience as predictably as a good athlete can achieve the high jump." And writer Robert Anton Wilson, discussing the "robot cycles" humans seem trapped into repeating, claims that, "When the accumulated facts, tools, techniques and gadgets of neuro-science—the science of brain change and brain liberation—reaches a certain critical mass, we will all be able to free ourselves from these robot cycles." Perhaps we are now reaching that critical mass.

In the short time since the publication of the hardcover edition of *Megabrain* there have been a number of important developments. Among notable advances in the use of the devices mentioned in the book, the most gratifying to me involves the linking of two mind-empowering tools. It was described to me by Dr. Charles Stroebel, developer of the CAP Scan. "There has been a really exciting and significant development," he told me recently, "and it's a direct result of *Megabrain*. Just by coincidence you put the picture of the CAP Scan on the same page with the photo of the Alpha Stim. I became interested in the possibilities you explore, in your suggestion that the combining or linking of various of the mind machines could have a potentiating effect, and decided to couple the Alpha Stim and the CAP Scan. The effects have been very dramatic: I use the TCET mode of the Alpha Stim while the people are hooked up to the CAP scan and it quickly alters and normalizes their brainwave activity.

"I now think that this coupling will allow us to work successfully with severely depressed people. Many of my clients are severely depressed. The abnormal EEG patterns show up very clearly on the CAP Scan." However, as Stroebel explained it, for traditional biofeedback to work, the subject must be self-motivated, must have a feeling that the effort involved will ultimately pay off—i.e. that sitting there attempting to alter the colored patterns of brainwave activity showing on the CAP Scan monitor will make them feel better in the long run. Unfortunately, severe depressives are often so bogged down in feelings of despair, hopelessness, and fatigue that they lack the necessary self-motivation, or the ability to look at things "in the long run," to try to alter their brainwave patterns.

"But now," says Stroebel, "when I hook these depressives up to the Alpha Stim while they're watching their brainwave activity on the CAP Scan, they can actually see how their EEG normalizes, and can feel the difference it makes. I think this could be a breakthrough in the treatment of depression. It's tremendously exciting, and it's a direct result of *Megabrain*."

Toward the end of Chapter 9 I suggest that the proper type of electrical stimulation of the brain could "activate your brain's learning pathways and enhance your ability to think," which would mean that certain electrical stimulation devices "could be used as practical tools to increase learning." However, I pointed out that as yet no hard scientific evidence of such electrical learning enhancement existed. Several experts in bioelectricity and electromedicine, having read that chapter, decided to perform such experiments, and as this is being written a number of studies are underway. One such study has already been completed: Richard Madden of the School of Electromedical Sciences of the City University of Los Angeles has found that subjects attached to an advanced electrical stimulation device using the transcranial mode (TCET) showed "improved learning" of various motor-mental skills compared to a control group that received no electrical stimulation.

Also in recent months several new tools for enhancing brain functioning have become available or have come to my attention. Some of the most fascinating of these devices:

THE BRAIN WAVE BIOFEEDBACK SYNCHRONIZER. For nearly 20 years one of the most innovative and influential researchers in biofeedback EEG has been Lester Fehmi, director of the Princeton Behavioral Medicine and Biofeedback Clinic. As I mentioned earlier in this book, Dr. Fehmi was among the first to discover the crucial importance of brainwave *synchrony* (see Chapter 6).

Early in his research he found that people could easily learn to control brainwave activity (increasing and decreasing amplitude and producing various brainwave frequencies, such as alpha) by means of biofeedback. However, he noted, the EEG biofeedback devices only used electrodes placed over one or two of the brain's major lobes (occipital, parietal, frontal, and left and right temporal). The biofeedback subjects, he discovered, were learning how to control brainwave activity, *but only in the area or lobe of the brain that was being monitored by the EEG electrode*. In other words, while individual lobes of the brain might be brought into synchrony, other areas of the brain might be unaffected, functioning asynchronously.

Also, while the EEG could determine whether brainwaves from separate lobes were of the same frequency, they could not provide information about whether the brainwaves were *in phase* (two waves are "in phase" when they are rising and falling in synchrony; they are "out of phase" if even though they are rising and falling at the same frequency one is rising while the other is falling). This was important, since Fehmi had discovered that "phase synchrony among the lobes is observed to enhance the magnitude and occurrence of the subjective phenomena associated with alpha and theta."

What was needed, Fehmi realized, was a multi-channel phase-sensitive biofeedback EEG—one that would simultaneously monitor all the major lobes of the brain, comparing brainwave activity at those lobes to see if that activity was not only at the same frequency but also in phase. Like other biofeedback EEGs, such a device would provide biofeedback to the user in the form of a tone or a light, but unlike the others, it would only signal when the user was in a state of whole-brain, in-phase synchrony—a state that research indicates is associated with a variety of benefits, including increased concentration, memory, learning, relaxation, and decreased anxiety and stress (says Fehmi, "synchrony represents the *maximum efficiency of information transport* through the whole brain"). Such a device would enable users to learn very quickly to enter extraordinarily productive states of consciousness.

Fehmi built the device, THE BRAIN WAVE BIOFEEDBACK SYNCHRONIZER, and uses it in his research and clinical work, as well as making it available to others. While the most sensitive model has ten channels (providing information from all parts of the cortex), Fehmi has now perfected a 5-channel model that he believes is just as effective, providing phase sensitive readings from the four major lobes of the brain. "In some ways," Fehmi told me, "having this thing is as good as having your own personal Zen master."

The device can be set to provide biofeedback signals not just for brainwave synchrony at one frequency (e.g. 10 Hz, or alpha) but also to pick up various subharmonics and harmonics of the frequency. For 10 Hz, for example, the device could also be set to pick up synchronous brainwaves at the harmonics of 20 Hz and/or 40Hz, that is, signals in the mid- and high-beta range. This is exciting, since there is evidence that synchrony at these harmonics can have significant effects. Fehmi gave as an example a tennis player who, by learning to produce whole brain synchrony not just in the alpha range but also in the high beta range of 40 Hz, could dramatically improve his reaction time. Since synchrony means the "maximum efficiency of information transport," Fehmi pointed out, "if you speed up that clock—synchrony at 40 Hz instead of just at 10 Hz—then the information transfer is even faster."

COMPUTER BREAKTHROUGH. Imagine that while you are sitting at your computer working with a word processing program, consulting a data base, or analyzing your financial situation, something in the computer is stimulating your brain, making you smarter, more creative. Such a program is now being produced. It is called BREAKTHROUGH!, and the guiding spirit behind the software package's creation, engineer physicist/visionary Orest Bedrij, tells me that the program is inspired by and based on many of the neuroscientific discoveries explored in *Megabrain*—that what passes for normal thinking engages only a tiny fraction of the brain's real capacities, that increasing brain power involves forging new neural pathways and creating denser, more complex neural networks, that this neural enrichment can be produced by "environmental enrichment," i.e. increasing certain types of brain stimulation, and that creative insights, Eureka events, or *breakthroughs* are the result of this kind of increased stimulation.

While still in his twenties Dr. Bedrij was IBM technical direction at the Jet Propulsion Laboratory of the California Institute of Technology, where he was responsible for the development, programming, and integration of the computer complex that controlled the first soft landing on the moon. He later founded several compaies that pioneered the development of LSI (large scale integrated chips) computer memory systems. He is a leading thinker in the field of pure physics concerned with the search for Einsteins "unified field theory," and his small gem of a book, *One*, describes eloquently "The unity of mankind and time, space, matter, gravity and energy."

With a strong personal as well as scientific knowledge of the vast potential of the human being, Dr. Bedrij explained to me, he felt it was essential to get the tools for tapping this potential out of the ivory tower and into the marketplace, out of the laboratory and into the workplace. Thus Breakthrough!, which is being marketed not only to individuals but also to major corporations, educational institutions and governmental agencies. Breakthrough's design is unlike the "expert systems" currently in vogue—systems that emulate intelligence and thus "do the thinking," for the user. Instead the program seeks to trigger and enhance the user's own intelligence—to "leverage brainpower," and serve as a "mind catalyst," in Bedrij's words. "Others are trying to give too much responsibility to the PC," says Dr. Bedrij. "It's the mind of man that's creative. We want to *stimulate* that creativity, not simulate it."

An "integrated package," Breakthrough! brings together eight different problem-analyzing or "idea management" environments and text editors offering ways of triggering and amplifying thoughts and accelerating learning, and allowing users to input facts, questions, partial solutions, and intuitive insights into a problem or decision, so that, as Bedrij says, "even as the user is consciously using the program to solve a problem, the various catalysts are stimulating his unconscious mind in what we call 'Breakthrough-thinking.'"

Among the components of the program are a variety of "thought-triggering stimuli," including an innovative "flashing window rotation" feature. What this means is that the computer monitor can flash windows containing words, sentences, phrases and questions while the user is working on a task. The user can select the number of windows (one to five simultaneously), the size and location of the windows (e.g. from tiny boxes at the corners of the monitor screen, to large sections covering some or all of the text on the monitor), the flashrates of the windows (from thousandth of a second flashes too fast to register on the conscious mind, but still capable of having subliminal effects, to longer durations), and the intervals between flashes.

The various windows can be programmed to contain information selected randomly from a "library" or large database of thoughts and questions from books, seminal thinkers and other leading reference sources. Also, you can create your own selection of window prompts from a personalized directory file of ideas, questions, affirmations, or partial solutions.

This flashing window feature works to increase learning and creativity in a variety of ways. For example, cognitive psychologists have found that greatest retention of new information results from "spaced" rather than "massed" practice— i.e. from small units of information presented with resting time between each unit, such as the flashing windows. Numerous studies have proven that multiple repetitions of material to be learned dramatically increase retention. Also, there is evidence that rehearsal of information in short-term memory, such as with the electronic flashcard process, increases the chances that the information will be transferred to long-term memory. Further, numerous recent studies have proven that multi-image presentations of information and ideas (such as using split-screen, or Breakthrough's multi-window feature) increase retention and facilitate learning.

In addition, we have all sensed that new or creative ideas are often the result of fusing thoughts or bits of information that have not been linked in such a way before. With the flashing window feature, you can be working on a task on your computer, such as writing a manuscript, or talking on the phone, while simultaneously four or five flashing windows are presenting random combinations of facts, thoughts, questions, suggestions and so on, all registering in some way—peripherally or subliminally—on your mind; and at some point, two or more of these ideas may suddenly rattle together in your mind and strike sparks, leading to a flash of insight, a new idea.

The Breakthrough! program has an enormous range of features, but some that should make sense to *Megabrain* readers include a moving background pattern on the monitor to slow brainwave activity into the more creative alpha range, and audiotapes of music in the 55–65 beats per minute range to increase relaxation and heighten awareness. Interestingly, cognitive psychologist Diane Kramer, who has studied the Breakthrough! program, links its effectiveness as a "motivator and enhancer" of learning, problem-solving, decision-making and creativity to Dr. Mihali Csikszentmihalyi's concept of *flow states*, which we've discussed in Chapter 5. With its flashing windows and multitasking environment, allowing the user to regulate the amount of mental input, challenge, or stimulation, Dr. Kramer points out, Breakthrough! "facilitates the 'flow state,'" in which the mind functions effortlessly, with peak efficiency, and the user feels invigorated, alert, totally focussed on the task at hand.

RETURN TO THE ELECTRICAL WHEATFIELDS OF THE BRAIN

A RECURRENT THEME OF THIS BOOK HAS BEEN THE EXISTENCE of human "bioelectric" fields or systems (a system that works, as Robert O. Becker concludes, "according to the principles of solid-state physics," and is "influenced by purturbations in relatively small fields, particularly in certain frequencies"), and the extraordinary responsiveness of the mind and body to types of electricity.

A second theme has been the difficulty for scientists exploring new fields, fields on the cutting edge, like bioelectricity, to obtain recognition (and funding) by the scientific establishment. In Becker's words, bioelectricity "is the most important area of medical research today," presenting the possibility of "a quantum jump in medical technology." However, he points out, "we have the electrical . . . technology and we have the evidence. But we don't have the funding. . . . The establishment is too busy cutting and burning and charging huge fees to do it, while thousands continue to suffer."

Thus it was an event of great importance when many of the leading researchers in the field of bioelectricity gathered recently in Los Angeles for a Congress of Bio-Energetic Medicine that included lectures, seminars and workshops. The speakers were highly respected scientists, and virtually all were from Europe, where bioelectric research is far in advance of the U.S.

One reason for the growing interest in bioelectricity among scientists and laypeople alike has been the work of one of the featured speakers at the Congress in Los Angeles, Dr. Bjorn Nordenstrom, professor of radiology at Karolinska Institute, Stockholm, and former Chairman of the Nobel Assembly, which chooses the Nobel laureates in medicine. Dr. Nordenstrom has caused excitement in medical and scientific circles around the world with his recent book, *Biologically Closed Electric Circuits*, in which he describes his research, particularly his "discovery" of a "heretofore unknown universe of electrical activity in the body—the biological equivalent of electric circuits."

As a recent article on Nordenstrom in *Discovery* summarizes his findings, "In the body electric, the circuits are switched on by an injury, an infection, or a tumor, or even by normal activity of the body's organs; voltages build and fluctuate; electric currents course through arteries and veins and across capillary walls, drawing white blood cells and metabolic compounds into and out of surrounding tissues. This electrical system works to balance the activity of internal organs and in the case of injuries, represents the very foundation of the healing process. . . . It is as critical to the well-being of the human body as the flow of blood."

Of course readers of this book will be aware that Nordenstrom's "discovery" is one of those that scientists so often make of things that have long been known, and documented by such scientific freethinkers as Robert O. Becker. However, Nordenstrom's work seems to have awakened the medical-scientific establishment to the importance of these biological electrical systems, which means more funds for research and, we hope, more research and advances in the field of bioelectricity, including the areas we have been investigating in this book.

In addition to talks and demonstrations by Dr. Nordenstrom, speakers at the Congress of Bio-Energetic Medicine included West German physicist Dr. Fritz Popp, whose work involves the activity of photons in biological systems (says Popp, "There are a lot of indications in physics of a serious basis of holistic medicine"); Drs. Jean-Claude Darras and P. De Vernejoul of France, whose experiments proved the transport of bioelectric energy along the acupuncture meridians (they injected acupuncture points with a radioisotope while doing high speed CAT Scans) making possible devices to moniter acupuncture pathways for use in diagnosis and treatment; Dr. Peter Guy Manners of England, who has long been investigating the effects of sound, light and color on the human body, and who described his system of applying audible sound directly to the body for healing (the body operates at natural harmonic frequencies, says Dr. Manners, and each organ or structure has its own sonic field due to the molecular agitation taking place within the organ, and any change in the body's harmonic pattern causes pain and disease; by tuning to the resonant pattern of the particular organ, detection—and correction—of imbalances is possible); and English physicist Dr. C.W. Smith, who described his findings pointing toward the significance of electromagnetic radiations as a source of "coherent excitation" for living systems, and demonstrated the effects of electromagnetic fields on allergy-sensitive subjects.

The work of these and other scientists goes far toward advancing our understanding of how some of the devices we have explored in this book can have such profound effects on the brain. Some of the technology they have developed will soon become available (or, in several cases, is already available) in this country. In the meantime, a number of other devices have come onto the market that, by influencing the "universe of electrical activity in the human body," show some evidence of producing beneficial effects on the brain.

PULSTAR. For over fifteen years inventor Michael Hercules worked as an aerospace engineer, specializing in biomedical electronics and vibration analysis on the Landing Excursion Model for the NASA moon shots. He also served as Test Conductor for the Titan I project. "During this time," he told me, "I became interested in the research revealing the many benefits of meditation (such as the boosting of intelligence, improved healing, and stress reduction), and decided to construct a mechanical aid to help meditators overcome difficulties in reaching deep meditative states."

Keying on the Russian Electro-Sleep Machine that had aroused great interest some years ago, Hercules altered and streamlined it, and came up with what is now known as the Pulstar, a device he claims "subliminally teaches control of brain-wave frequency by propagating an electronic signal through the brain." The device is about the size of a small book, with an on-off switch, a knob to control the intensity of the signal (which is in the 5 to 20 micro ampere range—well below the limits set by the FDA), a white noise generator (according to Hercules this buffers the electronic pulse wave and makes it more acceptable to the brain), and a frequency selector knob, which allows you to choose any frequency from 6 Hz (in the Theta range) up to 14 Hz (low Beta). Four electrodes are held against the skull with a headband.

The user selects an appropriate frequency (the inventor's research has led him to recommend certain frequencies for specific goals or states: e.g. 12 Hz for "centering," relaxation and mental stability; 10.5 Hz for healing of the body, extreme relaxation; 7.5 for inner awareness with a sharp sense of focus and attention, guided meditation, creative thinking; and 6.3 Hz for accelerated learning and increased memory). Then, when the signal is turned on, the user feels a mild pulsing. At this point, says Hercules, "the brain locks onto and falls into step with the frequency selected." This entrainment, according to EEG analysis done by Hercules, "takes place throughout the entire cerebral cortex and puts both brain hemispheres into synchronization."

Hercules notes that the device produces what we have called the Bicycle Training Wheels Effect: "As a teaching device, its main purpose is to directly instruct the user how to duplicate the desired frequency at will. Once a particular frequency has been learned, the machine is no longer required."

While users report that the device is effective for a variety of uses, including accelerated learning, stress reduction, creativity enhancement, meditation, athletic or fitness training, sleep reduction, and pain control, one of the most intriguing areas is that of healing and cellular regeneration. Several medical and scientific research organizations are investigating the effects of Pulstar in these areas, and there are indications that at certain frequencies the device stimulates the release of growth hormone and speeds the healing and growth of cells.

Hercules offers himself as an example of the Pulstar's powers in this area. In 1986 he suffered a severe stroke that, as a result of the destruction of brain cells, totally paralyzed his left side. "It was thought I might be permanently paralyzed," he told me. "I used the Pulstar, and went from bed to wheelchair to walker to cane to almost total recovery in five weeks." When I talked with him about six months after the stroke, Hercules was preparing to go off to Mexico for scuba diving. Recovery from such extensive destruction of neurons clearly involves substantial rewiring and other structural changes in the brain, establishing new routes of neural communication. Hercules claims, and there is some evidence to bear out his claims, that the Pulstar can stimulate such brain growth.

THE BRAIN TUNER.   One of the most highly respected figures in the field of electromagnetics is Dr. Robert Beck, an engineer/physicist who has invented a neuro electrical stimulator called The Brain Tuner that is arousing great interest. Unlike adjustable devices that deliver relatively simple waveforms at frequencies selected by the user, the Brain Tuner is said to emit 256 simultaneous frequencies—what the distributor calls "all known beneficial frequencies for the natural stimulation of the brain's neurotransmitters." (According to the secretive Dr. Beck, this is made possible by the device's unique integrated circuits, containing some 50 transistors and 4 diodes, that produce "nested modulations of short-duration rectangular non-linear waves in pulsed bursts. Very short risetimes insure harmonic output at beneficial spectral 'windows.'") Thus, in a complex intermingling of frequencies, the device seems to be capable of stimulating the brain to pour out an electrochemical cocktail.

The device seems to be a step beyond the "Black Box" of Dr. Margaret Patterson that gained attention several years ago when a variety of rock stars such as Peter Townshend and Keith Richard used it to overcome addictions to heroin, alcohol, and other drugs. The Brain Tuner itself has been used successfully to treat addictions (and relieve withdrawal symptoms) involving cocaine, heroine, alcohol, and tobacco. Among the results noted most commonly by users are stress reduction, raising of stress tolerance levels, alleviation of depression and anxiety, normalized sleep patterns, reduced sleep requirement, more REM sleep, more vivid and lucid dreams, improvement of both short term and long term memory, improved concentration, and increased energy levels. The device is quite simple to use—two electrodes are applied to acupuncture points in the hollows just beneath the earlobes. The electrodes are plugged into a console smaller than a pack of cigarettes. A single knob turns the device on and adjusts the intensity of the stimulation, which feels like a mild, pleasant tingling. During the period of use (about 40 minutes) many people note a mild euphoria, and a sensation of increased mental energy and clarity. These effects can linger for hours and in some cases days. Thus far there has been little rigorous scientific exploration of the brain tuner.

THE MAGNETIC MOOD PACER II. One technique of electrical stimulation that has aroused great interest among scientists in recent years is the use of pulsed electromagnetic fields (PEMF). Used by increasing numbers of orthopedic surgeons to combat such common bone diseases as osteoporosis and "ununited" fractures (broken bones that won't heal), PEMF also seem to have the property of entraining or "pacing" the body's cells by activating sensitive neuronal receptors.

When these PEMFs are tuned to frequencies in the human EEG range, they seem to actually entrain the brainwaves of many people. One such device now available is the MAGNETIC MOOD PACER II, designed by Dr. Bob Bech and his associate Ed Skilling. Unlike the neuro electric stimulation devices, the Mood Pacer does not require electrodes attached to the head or body. In fact, the field produced by the pacer—a wireless, battery-powered box about the size of a bar of soap—can be effective several feet from the device. However, while virtually everyone is affected by direct electrical stimulation, it seems that only about 35% of subjects tested are sensitive to magnetic brainwave pacing.

We have already discussed the possible benefits of entraining brainwaves, throughout the whole brain. It should be noted that the Mood Pacer II pulsates—and entrains brainwaves—at a frequency of 7.83 Hz. This is also the pulse rate of the earth-ionosphere cavity, also known as the "Schumann resonance." This has been found to be one of those "window" frequencies that appear to have a wide range of beneficial effects on human beings, ranging from reports of enhanced healing to accelerated learning. When a biological system vibrates at this frequency, it can be said to be in a state of resonance or entunement with the planet's own magnetic frequency, and it is perhaps this rhythmic unity with what has been called the earth's "natural brainwave" that produces such profound effects. In addition to entraining brainwaves, the magnetic pulse generator seems to have other benefits. In recent years our civilization has immersed itself in a dense electromagnetic "smog" of conflicting electromagnetic interference and man made radiation "noise," including microwave and radar, causing our cells to lose contact with many of the natural micropulsations and electromagnetic fields (see

Chapter 14). Research has proven that this electromagnetic pollution can have a wide range of harmful effects. But magnetic pacers can apparently act as a countermeasure to this environmental electromagnetic pollution. Although the signal strength of the pacer is slight (only milliwatts, or thousands of a watt) there seem to be mechanisms in living tissue, such as long-chain liquid-crystal dipoles that exhibit superconductive characteristics, that allow the PEMFs to override the destructive environmental electromagnetic noise pollution. Because the device is close to the user's body, its weak signal overrides much stronger sources at a distance.

Several other PEMF generators are now available in the U.S., including the AS-50 (or the larger, more versatile clinical model known as SOMA-MAG) which provides 12 distinct modes of electrical wave forms, including positive, negative and bi-phasic magnetic energy. One wave form is an audible pure tone selected from a frequency spectrum of 397 to 665 Hz; a second wave, an inaudible 10.6 Hz (alpha) signal is superimposed on the audible carrier. This combination of sound with pulsating magnetic fields is claimed to increase the effectiveness of the device (I can only report the manufacturer's claims, since I have not yet experimented with this device myself, and have seen no scientific studies verifying its effectiveness). The AS-50 and SOMA-MAG are far more sophisticated and flexible than the tiny Mood Pacer II, but also carry steep price tags and seem designed for therapeutic applications.

It should also be noted that while I refer frequently in this book to the Alpha-Stim, it is not the only advanced microelectronic neuro-stimulator in use. Another device, called the Electro-Acuscope 80, has been widely praised, has underdone rigorous scientific testing, and seems quite effective in inducing the same sort of deeply relaxed, lucid, alert, mildly euphoric state as the Alpha-Stim when used in the transcranial mode. An even newer instrument, the My-O-Matic, is now coming into use. Designed by Thomas Wing, DC, a fourth generation acupuncturist, it emits what has been called an "electrically stimulated tidal wave," a wave-form so unique Wing has succeeded in gaining a patent on it. It seems to be able to flow through hitherto unbreakable skin resistances with ease, filling cells with harmonious, low-intensity vibrations. While "official" use of these devices is mostly confined to easing pains and speeding healing, many are exploring their effects on a variety of mental functions.

CAVEAT. I cannot emphasize too much that bioelectricity is still a new field, and that the effects of electricity on cells is still not completely understood, in many cases, in fact, is quite mysterious. It *is* known, however, that at certain frequencies, electrical stimulation can be harmful, causing, for example, increased growth of cancerous cells. Also, as I've noted earlier, electrical stimulation devices can present dangers to individuals with some physical conditions, such as some heart problems and epilepsy. I spoke about these devices with electromagnetics expert Preston Nichols. He has no doubts about the profound mind-enhancing effects such devices can have, and the great potential benefits they offer. But, he asked me, "Who's to say what frequencies are beneficial, what harmful? Let's see the research. Granted, there's a lot of evidence that some of these frequencies have very specific effects, but do we know *all* the ones that are harmful? We can't know the long term effects, since nobody's observed the effects over a period of many years. I think all this is fascinating and important, and I'm involved in the research myself, but there's just so much we don't know."

HYPNO-PERIPHERAL PROCESSING. One of the variety of ways flotation can boost learning abilities is by dramatically increasing the floater's receptivity to new information. Recently, New York psychologist Dr. Lloyd Glauberman (whose work with training athletes I described in Chapter 16), in collaboration with neuropsychologist Dr. Phil Halboth, has developed a new way of using the hyper-receptivity induced by floating: he has created a series of extraordinary audio tapes specifically designed to be heard while in the flotation tank. The tapes use state-of-the-art digital recording technology, and incorporate the latest research in information processing, and differences in brain hemispheres, to present messages stimulating rapid and dramatic behavioral change, in a technique Glauberman and Halboth call HYPNO-PERIPH-ERAL PROCESSING.

Once in the tank and wearing stereo headphones, you hear calm voices, against a background of stately, soaring synthesizer music, gently guiding you into a deeply relaxed state. Then the soundtrack divides and you hear a separate voice in each ear, each voice narrating a different fairy-tale-like story —charming tales of wizards, magic cities, intergalactic zoos, mystic shoemakers and dream machines. "The simultaneous input overloads the conscious mind," says Glauberman, "because there is simply too much information to process consciously," Unable to focus on either story, your conscious mind seems to let go or turn off.

Using the hypnotic techniques of Milton Erickson, with elements of neurolinguistic programming, Glauberman and Halboth have loaded the tales with a variety of powerful suggestions, though the suggestions are couched in indirect terms and seemingly simply part of the story, so that they go undetected. Also, since the mind can at best focus on one of the stories (and usually gives up and stops paying conscious attention altogether), most of the stories themselves, and the hidden messages they contain, bypass the consciousness entirely, entering the unconscious mind.

To top off this barrage of informational overload, yet another series of suggestions has been imbedded in the tapes by an imaginative combining and interweaving of words and phrases from the two separate sound tracks in such a way that they can only be perceived peripherally by the combined functioning of both brain hemispheres.[1]

---

[1] As this is being written at least one HPP tape is being distributed and others recorded in a new recording technique called BIOPHONIC SOUND. Developed from an earlier technique called "Holophonic Sound," it produces tapes with such uncanny clarity that the *Brain/Mind Bulletin* has called it "extrasensory sound," and a "magical experience" that allows you to "hear sound in space as well as in time." The recording technique is based on the physiology of the human brain, and (says the Bulletin) "triggers intriguing sensory associations." Indeed, listening to these tapes give you an eerie sense of "being there," almost as if you are inside of the sounds, which adds to the effectiveness of the messages Glauberman and Halboth have devised. Glauberman tells me that ultimately the entire series of HPP tapes will be available in Biophonic Sound.

Thus far Glauberman and Halboth have created tapes for many purposes (including weight loss, stress management, improved time management and reduction of smoking and drinking, among others). Most of their clients float once a week while listening to the appropriate tapes. In a recent informal study of these subjects, Glauberman and Halboth discovered that the combination of the tank and the tapes "had a definite and profound impact on everyone." I personally have tested many of these tapes out on a variety of individuals and have been impressed with their effectiveness.

Often, the responses to the tapes were unexpected. "One man was coming to me for depression," says Glauberman. "A few days after listening to a tape, he came to me with excitement and told me that the panic attacks he had whenever he came into New York had abruptly disappeared. Well, he'd never even told me he was having these attacks! I looked over the peripheral messages on the tape he'd listened to and found that one of the tales mentions offhandedly that the central character, who is exploring a magic city, 'felt comfortable now in the city.' Apparently the man's subconscious had felt the need for that change and had somehow opened itself up to that specific message from the tape! This suggests that an unconscious scanner is at work to select indirect hypnotic or peripheral messages that have meaning for the person's life."

Both therapists agree that the tank seems to be essential for the tapes to have their full transformational effects. Says Halboth, "the combination of the peripheral tapes with floating is a 'double-whammy,' far more powerful than either modality alone. My clinical observations leave no doubt," he says, "that the tank intensifies the effectiveness of the tapes enormously. It seems to me to produce the effects of long-term therapy in a very short time." (However, I have found that when used in combination with other devices described in *Megabrain*, such as the Synchro Energizer, the Hemi Sync tapes, the Tranquilite, and the Graham Potentializer, the tapes seem as effective as when heard in the float tank. This suggests that the key is not the specific tool used, but rather "altered state" produced by the tool—the extraordinary receptivity to information and to behavioral change [or "reimprinting"] that accompanies the theta state, and the increased secretion of learning-linked neuropeptides that take place in that state.)

SUPERLEARNING AND BREAKING ADDICTIONS IN THE TANK.   Since I wrote Chapter 16 on how the flotation tank can be used as a superlearning tool the results of a remarkable and potentially revolutionary study have been released. The use of flotation can be "uniquely effective" in the treatment of addictive behaviors, according to Dr. Henry Adams, of the National Institute of Mental Health, and head of the alcoholism research programs at St. Elizabeths Hospital, Washington, D.C.

As he studied the field of alcoholism treatment, Adams told me, he found it "something of a scandal"—billions of dollars were being spent investigating a variety of treatments, but none of them really worked—"they produced almost no changes in actual alcohol consumption levels," Adams points out, "and no clinical proof that they are effective." Adams noted that a primary characteristic of those with addictive behavior patterns (such as alcoholism, drug abuse, smoking, obesity, and compulsive gambling) is a high level of what he calls *arousability*—they react more strongly (are more sensitive) to environmental stimulation than ordinary people; events undisturbing to most might seem unbearably stressful to people with high arousability, causing them to attempt to reduce their arousal, experienced as tension or anxiety, by consuming psychoactive substances.

Adams found that the characteristics of high arousability—high levels of fast EEG brain wave activity and a deficiency of slow or theta-level brain wave activity; tension, excitability and so on—were the very characteristics that flotation eliminated or reduced. At the same time Adams had noted another consistent effect of flotation, "stimulus hunger". Says Adams, "stimulus hunger renders subjects far more open and receptive to meaningful communication. Thus messages presented to subjects experiencing floating-induced stimulus hunger produce far greater impact than the same messages presented to

337

subjects in normal environments. Normally, what you have is millions of stimuli coming in all the time, interfering with the learning process. In flotation virtually all of the stimulation is eliminated, so that if you use those circumstances to present some kind of message, whether it's a videotape of sports training or a verbal message about drinking or smoking, there's no interference with the learning process, so you have an *enormously* enhanced efficiency in learning. The word 'superlearning' is quite accurate!"

Adams set up a study using an isolation chamber to see if the combination of sensory restriction with brief, taped anti-alcohol messages would do what no other technique has yet done: actually reduce alcohol consumption. The results, in both a pilot and a follow-up study, have been more impressive than he had thought possible: after a single chamber session, in which they heard only a five-minute message about alcohol, the subjects showed a decrease in alcohol consumption of 55% after two weeks, and most impressively, reversing the usual process in which change as the result of therapy tends to diminish in effectiveness over time, this decrease in consumption grew to 61% after six months!

Also impressive was the fact that even the group that experienced the single chamber session alone, with no message, showed 47% decreases in consumption after six months—an astonishing testimony to the effectiveness of simple arousal reduction. The untreated control groups showed no such decreases—in fact, they *increased* their alcohol consumption.

The use of such chambers (including flotation tanks) concludes Adams, is "the only technique ever shown by controlled studies to be effective in reducing alcohol consumption for extended periods of time. It is clinically effective, simple, easy to apply in treatment and prevention settings, and free of significant risks, hazards, and medical side effects. Its use should be seriously considered by all personnel involved in alcohol and substance abuse."

Although Adams used isolation chambers in his studies, he is now pursuing his researches using flotation tanks, convinced that the "chamber is slower and less potent than flotation. It probably takes at least 2½ to 3 hours in the chamber to produce most (but not all) of the changes induced by an hour of flotation." Floating, Adams emphasizes, "differs from all current treatment and prevention techniques in that it quickly and consistently lowers arousal to comfortable levels, thereby accomplishing the same psychological and physiological effects which substance abusers seek from psychoactive chemicals." Most importantly, it "is not a hypothetical laboratory phenomenon, but a viable, tested technology."

FOR MORE INFORMATION

MANY OF THE DEVICES DESCRIBED IN THIS BOOK CAN BE PURchased or leased. There are many commercial facilities, such as flotation centers, stress reduction centers, health clubs and so on, where it is possible to have a session or a series of sessions with some of the Megabrain devices. Many therapists and medical practicioners use one or more of these tools in their practice and will allow people to use the devices without entering into "treatment." There are periodic workshops, seminars, and "Megabrain Adventures" that take place throughout the country, providing hands-on experience with many devices.

For information about where the Megabrain devices may be used or purchased, about locations of workshops and seminars, and about new developments in the field of mind enhancement technology, write to:

MEGABRAIN
P.O. BOX 1059
COOPER STATION
NEW YORK, NY 10276

BIBLIOGRAPHY

1. Abbata, D., et al. "Beta-endorphin and Electroacupuncture." *Lancet*, December 13, 1980.
2. "An Active Voice for Glia." *Science News*, November 3, 1984.
3. Adam, J. E. "Naloxone Reversal of Analgesia Produced by Brain Stimulation in the Human." *Pain*, Vol. 2 (1976), pp. 161–66.
4. Ader, R., ed. *Psychoneuroimmunology*. New York: Academic Press, 1981.
5. Adey, W. Ross. "Introduction: Effects of Electromagnetic Radiation on the Nervous System." *Annals of the New York Academy of Sciences*, Vol. 247 (1975), pp. 15–20.
6. Agras, W. S., M. Horne, and C. B. Taylor. "Expectations and the Blood-Pressure-Lowering Effects of Relaxation." *Psychosomatic Medicine*, Vol. 44 (1982), pp. 389–95.
7. Andreasen, Nancy C., M.D., Ph.D. *The Broken Brain: The Biological Revolution in Psychiatry*. New York: Harper & Row, 1984.
8. Applewhite, Philip B. *Molecular Gods: How Molecules Determine Our Behavior*. Englewood Cliffs, N.J.: Prentice-Hall, 1981.
9. Aranibar, A., and G. Pfurtscheller. "On and Off Effects in the Background EEG Activity During One-Second Photic Stimulation." *Electroencephalography and Clinical Neurophysiology*, Vol. 44 (1978), pp. 307–16.
10. Ashford, B. "To Flash or Not to Flash: The Use of Intermittent Photic Stimulation During Hypnotic Induction, a Preliminary Report. *Australian Journal of Clinical and Experimental Hypnosis*, Vol. 10 (1982), pp. 3–11.

BIBLIOGRAPHY

11. Assagioli, Roberto. *Psychosynthesis*. New York: Viking, 1971.
12. ———. *The Act of Will*. New York: Viking, 1973.
13. Atkinson, Richard C., and Richard M. Schiffrin. "The Control of Short-Term Memory." *Scientific American*, August 1971.
14. Azima, H., and F. J. Cramer. "Effects of Decrease in Sensory Variability on Body Scheme." *Canadian Journal of Psychiatry*, Vol. 1 (1956), pp. 59–72.
15. Bailey, Ronald H., et al. *The Role of the Brain*. New York: Time-Life Books, 1975.
16. Baker, Deborah Ann. "Effects of REST and Hemispheric Synchronization Compared to Effects of REST and Guided Imagery on the Enhancement of Creativity in Problem-Solving." Faber, Va.: Monroe Institute of Applied Sciences, 1985.
17. Banquet, J. P. "EEG and Meditation." *Journal of Electroencephalography and Clinical Neurophysiology*, Vol. 33 (1972), pp. 449–58.
18. ———. "Spectral Analysis of EEG and Meditation." *Journal of Electroencephalography and Clinical Neurophysiology*, Vol. 35 (1973), pp. 143–51.
19. Barabasz, Arreed F. "Restricted Environmental Stimulation and the Enhancement of Hypnotizability: Pain, EEG Alpha, Skin Conductance and Temperature Responses." *The International Journal of Clinical and Experimental Hypnosis*, Vol. 2 (1982), pp. 147–66.
20. Barfield, A. "Biological Influences on Sex Differences in Behavior." In Michael S. Teitelbaum, *Sex Differences*. Garden City, N.Y.: Anchor Press, 1976.
21. Basmajian, John V. *Muscles Alive: Their Functions Revealed by Electromyography*. Baltimore: Williams & Wilkins, 1962.
22. ———. "Control and Training of Individual Motor Units." *Science*, Vol. 141 (1963), pp. 440–41.
23. ———, ed. *Biofeedback—Principles and Practice for Clinicians*. Baltimore: Williams & Wilkins, 1979.
24. Bauer, William, M.D., M.S. "Electrical Treatment of Severe Head and Neck Cancer Pain." *Archives of Otolaryngology*, Vol. 109 (1983), pp. 382–83.
25. ———. "Neuroelectric Medicine." *Journal of Bioelectricity*, Vol. 2, Nos. 2 and 3 (1983), pp. 159–80.
26. Becker, R.O., and Marino, A.A. *Electromagnetism and Life*. Albany: State University of New York Press, 1982.
27. "Becker's New Biology: Living Things in E/M Fields." *Brain/Mind Bulletin*, Vol. 8 (1983), No. 11.
28. Beisser, A. R. "Denial and Affirmation in Illness and Health." *American Journal of Psychiatry*, Vol. 136 (1979), pp. 1026–30.

29. Belden, Allen, and Gregg Jacobs. "REST in a Hospital-Based Stress Management Program." Paper delivered at first International Conference on REST and Self-Regulation. Denver, Colorado, March 17, 1983.

30. Belson, Abby Avin. "New Focus on Chemistry of Joylessness." *New York Times*, March 15, 1983.

31. Benson, Herbert. *The Relaxation Response.* New York: Morrow, 1975.

32. ———. *The Mind/Body Effect: How Behavioral Medicine Can Show You the Way to Better Health.* New York: Simon & Schuster, 1979.

33. ———, et al. "Historical and Clinical Considerations of the Relaxation Response." *American Scientist*, July–August 1977.

34. ———, and R. K. Wallace. "Decreased Drug Abuse with Transcendental meditation: A Study of 1862 Subjects." *Congressional Record*, 92nd Congress, 1st Session, June 1971.

35. Bentov, Itzhak. *Stalking the Wild Pendulum: On the Mechanics of Consciousness.* New York: Dutton, 1977.

36. Bernhardt, Dr. Roger, and David Martin. *Self-Mastery Through Self-Hypnosis.* Indianapolis: Bobbs-Merrill, 1977.

37. Bexton, W. H., W. Heron, and T. H. Scott. "Effects of Decreased Variation in the Sensory Environment." *Canadian Journal of Psychology*, Vol. 8 (1954), pp. 70–76.

38. "Bilateral 'Synch': Key to Intuition?" *Brain/Mind Bulletin*. Vol. 6 (1981), No. 9.

39. Blackwell, B. "The Endorphins: Current Psychiatric Research." *Psychiatric Opinion*, October 1979.

40. Blakemore, Colin. *Mechanics of Mind.* Cambridge: Cambridge University Press, 1977.

41. Blakeslee, Sandra. "Clues Hint at Brain's 2 Memory Maps." *New York Times*, February 19, 1985.

42. Blakeslee, Thomas R. *The Right Brain.* New York: Doubleday, 1980.

43. Bloom, Floyd. "Neuropeptides." *Scientific American*, October 1981.

44. ———. "The Endorphins: A Growing Family of Pharmacologically Pertinent Peptides." In *Annual Review of Pharmacology and Toxicology.* Palo Alto, Cal.: Annual Reviews, Inc., 1983.

45. Borrie, Roderick A., and Peter Suedfeld. "Restricted Environmental Stimulation Therapy in a Weight Reduction Program." *Journal of Behavioral Medicine*, Vol. 3 (1980), pp. 147–61.

46. "Brain Electric Therapy Helpful to Cocaine Addicts." *Brain/Mind Bulletin*, Vol. 9 (1984), No. 14.

47. "Brain 'Glue' Mimics Neurons." *Brain/Mind Bulletin*, Vol. 10 (1984), No. 1.

48. "Brain Peptide Vasopressin Offers Clue to Depression." *Brain/Mind Bulletin*. Vol. 4 (1979), No. 1.
49. "Brain Research Enjoying an Explosion of Interest." *Los Angeles Times*, January 25, 1984.
50. "Brain 'Self Renews' in Response to Chemical Injections, Activity." *Brain/Mind Bulletin*, Vol. 7 (1982), No. 9.
51. "The Brain." *Scientific American*, September 1979, entire issue.
52. "Breathing Cycle Linked to Hemispheric Dominance." *Brain/Mind Bulletin*, Vol. 8 (1983), No. 3.
53. Bridgwater, Gary, Clifford Sherry, and Thaddeus Marcynski. "Alpha Activity: The Influence of Unpatterned Light input and Auditory Feedback." *Life Sciences*, Vol. 16 (1975), pp. 729–37.
54. Briggs, John P., Ph.D., and F. David Peat, Ph.D. *Looking Glass Universe: The Emerging Science of Wholeness*. New York: Simon & Schuster, 1984.
55. Brody, Jane E. "Emotions Found to Influence Nearly Every Human Ailment." *New York Times*, May 25, 1983.
56. Brockopp, Gene W. "Review of Research on Multi-Modal Sensory Stimulation with Clinical Implications and Research Proposals." Unpublished manuscript, 1984.
57. Budzynski, Thomas. "Biofeedback and the Twilight States of Consciousness." In G.E. Schwartz and D. Shapiro, eds., *Consciousness and Self-Regulation*, Vol. 1. New York: Plenum, 1976.
58. ——. "Tuning in on the Twilight Zone." *Psychology Today*, August 1977.
59. ——. "A Brain Lateralization Model for REST." Paper delivered at first International Conference on REST and Self-Regulation, Denver, Colo., March 18, 1983.
60. ——, and K. Peffer. "Twilight State Learning: The Presentation of Learning Material During a Biofeedback-Produced Altered State." *Proceedings of the Biofeedback Research Society*. Denver: Biofeedback Research Society, 1974.
61. Buell, S. J., and P. D. Coleman. "Dendritic Growth in the Aged Human Brain and Failure of Growth in Senile Dementia." *Science*, November 16, 1979.
62. Burr, H.S. "The Meaning of Bioelectric Potentials." *Yale Journal of Biological Medicine*, Vol. 16 (1944), p. 353.
63. ——. *The Fields of Life*. New York: Ballantine, 1972.
64. Burroughs, William S. *The Job*. New York: Grove, 1974.
65. Bylinsky, Gene. *Mood Control*. New York: Scribner, 1978.
66. Cade, C. Maxwell, and Nona Coxhead. *The Awakened Mind: Biofeedback and the Development of Higher States of Awareness*. New York: Delacorte Press, 1979.
67. Calvin, William H., Ph.D., and George A. Ojemann, M.D. *Inside*

the Brain: Mapping the Cortex, Exploring the Neuron. New York: New American Library, 1980.

68. "Canadian Study Frames New Right/Left Paradigm." *Brain/Mind Bulletin*, Vol. 8 (1983), p. 7.

69. Cannon, Walter B. *The Wisdom of the Body*. New York: Norton, 1932.

70. Capra, Fritjof. *The Turning Point: Science, Society, and the Rising Culture*. New York: Simon & Schuster, 1983.

71. Carrington, Patricia, Ph.D. *Freedom in Meditation*. New York: Anchor Press, Doubleday, 1978.

72. Carter, John L., and Harold L. Russell. "Changes in Verbal-Performance IQ Discrepancy Scores After Left Hemisphere EEG Frequency Control Training: A Pilot Report." *American Journal of Clinical Biofeedback*, Vol. 4 (1981), pp. 66–67.

73. Cheney, Margaret. *Tesla: Man out of Time*. New York: Dell, 1983.

74. Ciganek, L. "The EEG Response (Evoked Potential) to Light Stimulus in Man." *Electroencephalography and Clinical Neurophysiology*, Vol. 30 (1971), pp. 423–36.

75. Clarke, D.L. "Vestibular Stimulation Influence on Motor Development in Infants." *Science*, Vol. 196 (1977), pp. 1228–29.

76. Collins, Glenn. "A New Look at Anxiety's Many Faces." *New York Times*, January 24, 1983.

77. ———. "Chemical Connections: Pathways of Love." *New York Times*, February 14, 1983.

78. Cone, Clarence, and C. M. Cone. "Induction of Mitosis in Mature Neurons in Central Nervous System by Sustained Depolarization." *Science*, Vol. 192 (1976), pp. 155–58.

79. Cooper, L., and Milton Erickson. *Time Distortion in Hypnosis*. Baltimore: Williams & Wilkins, 1954.

80. Corrick, James A. *The Human Brain: Mind and Matter*. New York: Arco, 1983.

81. Cousins, Norman. "Anatomy of an Illness (as Perceived by the Patient)." *New England Journal of Medicine*, Vol. 295 (1976), pp. 1458–63.

82. ———. *The Healing Heart: Antidotes to Panic and Helplessness*. New York: Norton, 1983.

83. Csikszentmihalyi, Mihaly. *Beyond Boredom and Anxiety: The Experience of Play in Work and Games*. San Francisco and London: Jossey-Bass, 1975.

84. Davis, Joel. *Endorphins: New Waves in Brain Chemistry*. Garden City, N.Y.: Dial Press, 1984.

85. Dawkins, Richard. *The Selfish Gene*. Oxford: Oxford University Press, 1976.

86. Deikman, A. J. "Deautomatization and the Mystic Experience."

Psychiatry, Vol. 29 (1966), pp. 324–38.

87. ——. "Experimental Meditation." *Journal of Nervous and Mental Disorders*, Vol. 136 (1963), pp. 329–73.

88. Diamond, M.C., B. Lindner, R. Johnson. E.L. Bennett, and M.R. Rosenzweig. "Differences in Occipital Cortical Synapses from Environmentally Enriched, Inpoverished, and Standard Colony Rats." *Journal of Neuroscience Research*. Vol. 1, pp. 109–19.

89. DiCara, Leo. "Learning in the Autonomic Nervous System." *Scientific American*, January 1970.

90. ——, ed. *Recent Advances in Limbic and Autonomic Nervous System Research*. New York: Plenum, 1973.

91. Dossey, Larry, M.D. *Space, Time & Medicine*. Boulder, Colo.: Shambhala, 1982.

92. Driscoll, R. "Anxiety Reduction Using Physical Exertion and Positive Images." *Physiological Record*, Vol. 26 (1976), pp. 87–94.

93. Eccles, John C. *The Understanding of the Brain*. New York: McGraw-Hill, 1977.

94. Edrington, Devon. "A Palliative for Wandering Attention." Unpublished manuscript, 1984.

95. Eliade, Mircea. *Yoga: Immortality and Freedom*. Princeton, N.J.: Princeton University Press, 1969.

96. "Endorphin Link to Pain Relief Is Confirmed." *Medical World News*, February 19, 1979.

97. "The Endorphins—the Body's Own Opiates." *Harvard Medical School Health Letter*, January 1983.

98. "Endorphins Trigger Isolation-Tank Euphoria." *Brain/Mind Bulletin*, Vol. 9 (1984), No. 4.

99. "Evidence Sheds New Light on Prior Right/Left Assumptions." *Brain Mind Bulletin*, Vol. 8 (1983), p. 7.

100. Fehmi, Lester F., and George Fritz. "Open Focus: The Attentional Foundation of Health and Well-Being." Somatics, Spring 1980.

101. Ferchmin. P.A., and V.A. Eterovic. "Four Hours of Enriched Experience Are Sufficient to Increase Cortical Weight of Rats." *Society for Neuroscience Abstracts*, Vol. 6, p. 857.

102. ——. "Forty Minutes of Experience Increase the Weight and RNA of Cerebral Cortex in Periadolescent Rats." Unpublished manuscript.

103. Ferguson, Marilyn. *The Brain Revolution*. New York: Bantam, 1975.

104. ——. *The Aquarian Conspiracy*. Los Angeles: Tarcher, 1980.

105. Finder, Joseph. "Dr. Bird's Brains." *Omni*, November 1983.

106. Fine, Thomas H., and John W. Turner, Jr. "Restricted Environmental Stimulation Therapy: A New Relaxation Model." Unpublished manuscript.

107. Flood, J.F., E.L. Bennett, A.E. Orme, and M.R. Rosenzweig. "Relation of Memory Formation to Controlled Amounts of Brain Protein Synthesis." *Physiology & Behavior*, Vol. 15 (1975), pp. 97–102.

108. Flood, J.F., G.E. Smith and A. Cherkin. "Memory Retention: Potentiation of Cholinergic Drug Combinations in Mice." *Neurobiology of Aging*, Vol. 4 (1983), pp. 37–43.

109. "'Focusing': Useful Tool in Producing Insight, Creativity." *Brain/Mind Bulletin*, Vol. 3 (1978), No. 17.

110. French, J. D. "The Reticular Formation." In *Physiological Psychology: Readings from Scientific American*. San Francisco: W. H. Freeman, 1975.

111. Fukishima, Takanori. "Application of EEG Interval-Spectrum Analysis (EISA) to the Study of Photic Driving Responses: A Preliminary Report." *Arch. Psychiat.*, Vol. 220 (1975), pp. 99–105.

112. "Gary Lynch: A Magical Memory Tour." *Psychology Today*, April 1984.

113. Gatchel, Robert J., and Kenneth P. Price, eds. *Clinical Applications of Biofeedback: Appraisal & Status*. New York: Pergamon, 1979.

114. Gazzaniga, M. S. *The Bisected Brain*. New York: Appleton-Century-Crofts, 1974.

115. ——, and J. E. Le Doux. *The Integrated Mind*. New York: Plenum, 1978.

116. Gendlin, Eugene T., Ph.D. *Focusing*. New York: Everest House, 1978.

117. Gilula, Marshall F., M.D. "Protocol for 1981 Synchro-Energizer Study: Multiple Afferent Sensory Stimulation (MASS) as a Tool for Investigating Clinical Neurological Problems and Pure Noetic Research Methodology." Unpublished manuscript, 1980.

118. Glasser, William. *Positive Addiction*. New York: Harper & Row, 1978.

119. Gleick, James. "Exploring the Labyrinth of the Mind." *New York Times Magazine*, August 21, 1983.

120. Globus, A., M.R. Rosenzweig, E.L. Bennett, and M.C. Diamond. "Effects of Differential Experience on Dendritic Spine Counts." *Journal of Physiological and Comparative Psychology*, Vol. 82 (1973), pp. 175–81.

121. Glueck, Bernard C., and C. F. Stroebel. "Biofeedback and Meditation in the Treatment of Psychiatric Illness." *Comprehensive Psychiatry*, Vol. 16 (1975), pp. 303–21.

122. "Glutamate May Be Key to Memory Formation." *Brain/Mind Bulletin*, July 30, 1984, p.1

123. Goldstein, Avram. "Thrills in response to music and other stimuli." *Physiological Psychology*, Vol. 8 (1980), No. 1

124. Goleman, Daniel. *The Varieties of Meditative Experience*. New York: Dutton, 1977.

125. ———. "The Aging Mind Proves Capable of Lifelong Growth." *New York Times*, February 21, 1984.

126. Goodman, David M., Jackson Beatty, and Thomas B. Mulholland. "Detection of Cerebral Lateralization of Function Using EEG Alpha-Contingent Visual Stimulation." *Electroencephalography and Clinical Neurophysiology*. Vol. 48 (1980), pp. 418–31.

127. Gould, Stephen Jay. "Genes on the Brain." *New York Review of Books*, June 30, 1983.

128. Grady, Harvey. "Electromechanical Therapy of a Child with Down's Syndrome: A Report of a Case." *Journal of Holistic Medicine*, Vol. 4 (1982), No. 2.

129. Graham, David. "The Effects of the Electromechanical Therapeutic Apparatus on the Electrical Activity of the Brain." Unpublished manuscript, undated.

130. Green, Elmer, and Alyce Green. *Beyond Biofeedback*. New York: Delacorte, 1977.

131. Guillemin, Roger. "Peptides in the Brain: The New Endocrinology of the Neurone." *Science*, Vol. 202 (1978), pp. 390–402.

132. ———, and Roger Burgus. "The Hormones of the Hypothalamus." *Scientific American*, November 1972.

133. Haber, Ralph. "How We Remember What We See." *Scientific American*, May 1970.

134. Hales, Dianne. "Psycho-Immunity." *Science Digest*, November 1981.

135. Hall, Stephen S. "The Brain Branches Out." *Science 85*, June 1985.

136. Hampden-Turner, Charles. *Maps of the Mind*. New York: Macmillan, 1981.

137. Harner, Michael. *The Way of the Shaman*. New York: Harper & Row, 1980.

138. Harth, Eric. *Windows on the Mind: Reflections on the Physical Basis of Consciousness*. New York: Morrow, 1982.

139. Hartmann, Thom. "The Synchro-Energizer: A Patented Device to Control Brain Waves." *Popular Computing*, November 1984.

140. Harvey, Ruth S. "The Miracle of Electromedicine." *National Institute of Electromedical Information, Inc. Digest Bulletin*, Winter 1985.

141. Hatterer, Dr. Lawrence J. *The Pleasure Addicts*. Cranbury, N.J.: A. S. Barnes, 1980.

142. Heath, Robert G. "Interview." *Omni*, April 1984.

143. Hebb, Donald. *Organization of Behavior: A Neuropsychological Theory*. New York: Wiley, 1961.

144. Henry, James P. "Present Concept of Stress Theory," in *Catechol-*

amines and Stress: Recent Advances, ed. Earl Usdin, Richard Kve-
triansky, and Irwin Kopin. *Developments in Neuroscience*, Vol. 8.
New York, Amsterdam, and Oxford: Elsevier North Holland, 1980.

145. Heron, Woodburn. "The Pathology of Boredom." *Scientific Ameri-can*, January 1957.

146. ———. "Cognitive and Physiological Effects of Perceptual Isolation."
In *Sensory Deprivation: A Symposium*, ed. P. Solomon. Cambridge:
Harvard University Press, 1961.

147. "'Higher' brain reorganization may accompany insight." *Brain/
Mind Bulletin*, Vol. 3 (1978), No. 6.

148. Hooper, Judith. "Plastic Brains." *Omni*, November 1981.

149. "Hormone Aids Memory, Learning." *Brain/Mind Bulletin*, Vol. 8
(1983), No. 7.

150. "Hormones Tied to Heart Ills." *New York Times*, October 24, 1982.

151. Hosobachi, Y., J.E. Adams, and R. Linchintz. "Pain Relief by
Electrical Stimulation of the Central Gray Matter in Humans and Its
Reversal by Naloxone." *Science*, Vol. 197 (1977), pp. 183–86.

152. "How the Brain Works." *Newsweek*, February 7, 1983.

153. Hughes, J., et al. "Identification of Two Related Pentapeptides from
the Brain with Potent Opiate Antagonist Activity." *Nature*, Vol. 258
(1975), pp. 577–79.

154. Hutchison, Michael. "Tanks for the Memories." *Village Voice*,
July 13, 1982.

155. ———. "Isolation Tanks: The State of the Art." *Esquire*, August
1983.

156. ———. *The Book of Floating: Exploring the Private Sea*. New York:
Morrow, 1984.

157. ———. "The Synchro-Energizer: Letting a Black Box Meditate for
You." *Esquire*, February 1984.

158. ———. "Exploring the Inner Sea." *New Age Journal*, May 1984.

159. ———. "The Plugged-In Brain." *New Age Journal*, August 1984.

160. ———. "Mapping the Brain for Peace of Mind." *Esquire*, November
1984.

161. ———. "One Man, One Float." *Esquire*, November 1984.

162. Iversen, Leslie L. "The Chemistry of the Brain." *Scientific Ameri-can*, September 1979.

163. Iwahara, Shinkuo, Setsuko Noguchi, Kuo Man Yang, and Oishi
Hiroshi. "Frequency Specific and Non-specific Effects of Flickering
Light upon Electrical Activity in Human Occiput." *Japanese Psy-
chological Research*, Vol. 16 (1974), pp. 1–7.

164. Jacobs, Gregg, Robert Heilbronner, and John M. Stanley. "The Effects of Short-Term Flotation REST on Relaxation: A Controlled
Study." Paper delivered at first International Conference on REST
and Self-Regulation, Denver, Colo., March 18, 1983.

165. ——. "The Effects of Sensory Isolation on Relaxation." Unpublished paper.

166. Jacobson, Edmund, M.D. "Imagination of Movement Involving Skeletal Muscle." *American Journal of Physiology*, Vol. 91 (1930), pp. 567–608.

167. ——. "Evidence of Contraction of Specific Muscles During Imagination." *American Journal of Physiology*, Vol. 95 (1930), pp. 703–12.

168. ——. *Progressive Relaxation*, rev ed. Chicago: University of Chicago Press, 1938.

169. ——. *You Must Relax*, rev. ed. New York, Toronto, London: McGraw-Hill, 1962.

170. Jaffe, Dennis T., Ph.D. *Healing from Within*. New York: Knopf, 1980.

171. Jantsch, Erich. *The Self-Organizing Universe*. New York: Pergamon, 1980.

172. Jaynes, Julian. *The Origins of Consciousness in the Breakdown of the Bicameral Mind*. Boston: Houghton Mifflin, 1976.

173. "Jerre Levy: Human Brain Built to Be Challenged." *Brain/Mind Bulletin*, Vol. 8 (1983), No. 9.

174. Jevning, R. "Meditation Increased Blood Flow to Brain in UC Study." *Brain/Mind Bulletin*, Vol. 4 (1979), No. 1.

175. John, E. Roy, and R.W. Thatcher. *Functional Neuroscience*. Hillsdale, N.J.: Lawrence Erlbaum Associates, 1976.

176. Jonas, Gerald. *Visceral Learning*. New York: Viking, 1973.

177. Kall, Robert. "Mind Scanner." *Omni*, February 1984.

178. Kammerman, M., ed. *Sensory Isolation and Personality Change*. Springfield, Ill.: Charles C. Thomas, 1977.

179. Kandel, Eric R. *Cellular Basis of Behavior: An Introduction to Behavioral Neurobiology*. San Francisco: Freeman, 1976.

180. ——. "Small Systems of Neurons." *Scientific American*, September 1979.

181. Kasamatsu, A., and T. Hirai. "Science of Zazen." *Psychologia*, Vol. 6 (1963), pp. 86–91.

182. Katchalsky, A., L.E. Scriven, and R. Blumenthal, eds. "Dynamic Patterns of Brain Cell Assemblies." *Neuroscience Research Program Bulletin*, Vol. 12 (1974), pp. 1–195.

183. "The Keys to Paradise." *Nova: Adventures in Science*. Boston: Addison-Wesley, 1982.

184. Kinsbourne, Marcel. "Sad Hemisphere, Happy Hemisphere." *Psychology Today*, May 1981.

185. Koestler, Arthur. *The Act of Creation*. New York: Macmillan, 1964.
186.——. *The Ghost in the Machine*. New York: Random House, 1967.

187. ——. *The Roots of Coincidence*. New York: Random House, 1972.

188. Kolata, Gina. "Molecular Biology of Brain Hormones." *Science*, Vol. 215 (1982), pp. 1223-24.

189. Konorski, Jerzy. *Integratiive Activity of the Brain: An Interdisciplinary Approach*. Chicago: University of Chicago Press, 1967.

190. Koob, George F., and Floyd E. Bloom. "Behavioral Effects of Neuropeptides: Endorphins and Vasopressin." In *Annual Review of Physiology*, 1982. Palo Alto, Cal.: Annual Reviews, Inc., 1982.

191. "Lack of Endorphins in Alcoholics Can be Corrected." *Brain/Mind Bulletin*, Vol. 9 (1984), No. 8.

192. Legros et al., "Influence of Vasopressin on Memory and Learning." *Lancet*, January 7, 1978.

193. LeCron, Leslie M. *Self Hypnotism*. Englewood Cliffs, N.J.: Prentice-Hall, 1964.

194. Lenard, Lane. "Visions That Vanquish Cancer." *Science Digest*, April 1981.

195. Leonard, George. *Education and Ecstasy*. New York: Dell, 1968.

196. ——. *The Ultimate Athlete*. New York: Viking, 1975.

197. ——. *The Silent Pulse*. New York: E. P. Dutton, 1978.

198. Lerner, Eric J. "Why Can't a Computer Be More Like a Brain?" *High Technology*, August 1984.

199. Lester, Henry A. "The Response to Acetylcholine." *Scientific American*, February 1977.

200. Levine, J. B., N. C. Gordon, R. T. Jones, and H. L. Fields. "The Narcotic Antagonist Naloxone Enhances Clinical Pain." *Nature*, Vol. 272 (1978), pp. 826-27.

201. Lewis, Mitch. "Sprots Injuries: A Case Study." *International Electromedicine Institute Newsletter*, Vol. 1 (1984), No. 2.

202. Lilly, John C., M.D. *The Center of the Cyclone*. New York: Julian, 1972.

203. ——. *The Deep Self*. New York: Simon & Schuster, 1977.

204. ——. *The Scientist*. New York: J. B. Lipponcott. 1978.

205. ——. "Interview." *Omni*, January 1983.

206. ——, and Jay T. Shurley. "Experiments in Solitude, in Maximum Achiievable Physical Isolation with Water Suspension, of Intact Healthy Persons." In *Psychophysiological Aspects of Space Flight*, ed. B. E. Flaherty. New York: Columbia University Press, 1961.

207. Llaurado, J.G. *Biologic and Clinic Effects of Low-Frequency Magnetic and Electric Fields*. Springfield, Ill.: Charles C. Thomas, 1974.

208. Lord, J.A.H., et al. "Endogenous Opioid Peptides: Multiple Agonists and Receptors." *Nature*, Vol. 267 (1977), pp. 495–99.

209. "Low-Level Direct Current Through Brain Affects Mood." *Brain/Mind Bulletin*, Vol. 2 (1977), No. 2.

BIBLIOGRAPHY

210. Lozanov, Georgi. *Suggestology and Outlines of Suggestopedy.* New York: Gordon & Breach, 1982.

211. Lumsden, Charles J., and Edward O. Wilson. *Promethean Fire: Reflections on the Origin of Mind.* Cambridge: Harvard University Press, 1983.

212. Lynch, Dudley. "Creative Flashes from the Twilight Zone." *Science Digest,* December 1981.

213. Lynch, Gary, and Michel Baudry. "The Biochemistry of Memory: A New and Specific Hypothesis." *Science,* Vol. 224 (1984), pp. 1057–63.

214. McAleer, Neil. *The Body Almanac.* New York: Doubleday, 1985.

215. McAuliffe, Kathleen. "Brain Tuner." *Omni,* January 1983.

216. Maccoby, Eleanor E. *The Development of Sex Differences.* Palo Alto, Cal.: Stanford University Press, 1966.

217. McEwan, Bruce S. "Interactions Between Hormones and Nerve Tissue." *Scientific American,* July 1976.

218. McGaugh, J. L., ed. *The Chemistry of Mood, Motivation and Memory.* New York: Plenum, 1972.

219. MacLean, Paul D. "Contrasting Functions of Limbic and Neocortical Systems of the Brain and Their Relevance to Psycho-physiological Aspects of Medicine." *American Journal of Medicine,* Vol. 25 (1958), pp. 611–26.

220. ——. "New Findings Relevant to the Evolution of Psychosexual Functions of the Brain." *Journal of Nervous and Mental Disease,* Vol. 135 (1962), pp. 289–96.

221. ——. "The Paranoid Streak in Man," in *Beyond Reductionism,* ed. Arthur Koestler and J.R. Smythies. Boston: Beacon, 1969.

222. ——. *A Tribune Concept of the Brain and Behavior.* Toronto: University of Toronto Press, 1973.

223. Maier, W. J. "Sensory Deprivation Therapy of an Autistic Boy." *American Journal of Psychotherapy,* Vol. 25 (1970), pp. 228–45.

224. Maranto, Gina. "The Mind Within the Brain." *Discover,* May 1984.

225. "Marian Diamond: A Love Affair with the Brain." *Psychology Today,* November 1984.

226. Maslow, Abraham. *Motivation and Personality.* New York: Harper, 1954.

227. ——. *Towards a Psychology of Being.* Princeton, N.J.: Van Nostrand, 1962.

228. ——. *Religions, Values, and Peak Experiences.* New York: Viking, 1970.

229. ——. *The Farther Reaches of Human Nature.* New York: Viking, 1971.

230. Mayer, D. J., D. D. Price, and A. Raffil. "Antagonism of Acupuncture Analgesia in Man by the Narcotic Antagonist Naloxone."

Brain Research, Vol. 121 (1977), pp. 360–73.

231. "Memory Enhancement Shown in New Human Studies." *Brain/Mind Bulletin*, Vol. 3 (1978), No. 18.

232. Meredith, Dennis. "Healing with Electricity." *Science Digest*, May 1981.

233. Millay, J. "Brainwave Synchronization: A Study of Subtle Forms of Communication." *The Humanistic Psychology Institute Review*, Vol. 3 (1981), pp. 9–40.

234. Miller, Jonathan. *States of Mind*. New York: Pantheon, 1983.

235. Miller, Neal. "Learning and Performance Motivated by Direct Stimulation of the Brain." In *Electrical Stimulation of the Brain*, ed. D. Sheen. Austin: University of Texas Press, 1961.

236. ——, and Leo DiCara. "Instrumental Learning of Urine Formation by Rats; Changes in Renal Blood Flow." *American Journal of Physiology*, Vol. 215 (1968), pp. 677–83.

237. "'Mind Mirror' EEG Identifies States of Awareness." *Brain/Mind Bulletin*, Vol. 2 (1977), No. 20.

238. Mollgaard, Kjeld, Marian C. Diamond, Edward L. Bennett, Mark R. Rosenzweig, and Bernice Lindner. "Quantitative Synaptic Changes with Differential Experience in Rat Brain." *International Journal of Neuroscience*, Vol. 2 (1971), No. 2, pp. 157–67.

239. Naranjo, Claudio, and Robert E. Ornstein. *On the Psychology of Meditation*. New York: Viking, 1971.

240. Neher, Andrew. "Auditory Driving Observed with Scalp Electrodes in Normal Subjects." *Electroencephalography and Clinical Neurophysiology*. Vol. 13 (1961), pp. 449–51.

241. "Neuron Regeneration in Lab Promising for Cancer, Aging." *Brain/Mind Bulletin*. Vol. 1 (1977), No. 13.

242. Nogaway, Tokuji, et al. "Changes in Amplitude of the EEG Induced by a Photic Stimulus." *Electroencephalography and Clinical Neurophysiology*, Vol. 40 (1976), pp. 78–88.

243. "Of Human Bonding: Social Attachment, Alienation." *Brain/Mind Bulletin*, Vol. 5 (1980), No. 12.

244. O'Leary, Daniel S., and Robert L. Heilbronner. "Flotation REST and Information Processing: A Reaction-Time Study." Paper delivered at first International Conference on REST and Self-Regulation, Denver, Colo., March 17, 1983.

245. Olds, James. "Pleasure Centers in the Brain." *Scientific American*, Vol. 195 (1956), pp. 105–16.

246. ——. "The Central Nervous System and the Reinforcement of Behavior." *American Psychologist*, Vol. 24 (1969), pp. 707–19.

247. ——. *Drives and Reinforcements: Behavioral Studies of Hypothalamic Functions*. New York: Raven, 1977.

248. Ornstein, Robert E. *On the Experience of Time*. New York: Penguin, 1969.

249. ——. *The Psychology of Consciousness*. San Francisco: Freeman, 1972.

250. ——, ed. *The Nature of Human Consciousness*. New York: Viking, 1974.

251. Oster, Gerald. "Auditory Beats in the Brain." *Scientific American*, September 1973.

252. Ostrander, Sheila, and Lyn Schroeder, with Nancy Ostrander. *Superlearning*. New York: Delacorte, 1979.

253. Oyle, Irving, M.D. *The Newr American Medicine Show: Discovering the Healing Connection*. Santa Cruz, Cal.: Unity Press, 1979.

254. ——. *The Healing Mind*. Millbrae, Cal.: Celestial Arts, 1979.

255. Paasch, Hope. "Wet Behind the Ears, but Learning Fast: Study Shows Floating Good for Students." *Texas A&M Battalion*, August 12, 1982.

256. ain: Placebo Effect Linked to Endorphins." *Science News*, September 2, 1978.

257. Peacock, Samuel M. "Regional Frequency Sensitivity of the EEG to Photic Stimulation as Shown by Epoch Averaging." *Electroencephalography and Clinical Neurophysiology*, Vol. 34 (1973), pp. 71–76.

258. Pelletier, Kenneth R. *Mind as Healer, Mind as Slayer*. New York: Delacorte, 1977.

259. ——. *Toward a Science of Consciousness*. New York: Delacorte, 1978.

260. ——. *Longevity*. New York: Delacorte, 1981.

261. Penfield, Wilder. *The Mystery of the Mind*. Princeton: Princeton University Press, 1975.

262. "People Can Outgrow Low IQ." *Brain/Mind Bulletin*, Vol. 7 (1982), No. 15.

263. Persinger, M.A. *ELF and VLF Electromagnetic Field Effects*. New York: Plenum, 1974.

264. Petrenko, E.T. "Effect of Flashes on Spectral Composition of Brain Potentials and Biomechanical Efficiency of Equilibrium." *Human Physiology*. Vol. 8 (1982), pp. 64–68.

265. Pfurtscheller, Gert, Pierre Buser, Fernando H. Lopes da Silva, and Hellmuth Petsche. *Rhythmic EEG Activities and Cortical Functioning*. Amsterdam: Elsevier/North-Holland Biomedical Press, 1980.

266. *Physiological Psychology: Readings from Scientific American*. San Francisco: Freeman, 1971.

267. Pines, Maya. *The Brain Changers: Scientists and the New Mind Control*. New York: Harcourt Brace Jovanovich, 1973.

268. Pomeranz, B. "Brain's Opiates at Work in Acupuncture." *New Scientist*, Vol. 6 (1977), pp. 12–13.

269. "Pre-Birth Memories Appear to Have Lasting Effect." *Brain/Mind Bulletin*, Vol. 7 (1982), No. 5.

270. Presman, A.S. *Electromagnetic Fields and Life*. New York: Plenum, 1970.

271. Prigogine, Ilya. *From Being to Becoming*. San Francisco: Freeman, 1980.

272. ——, and Isabelle Stengers. *Order Out of Chaos: Man's New Dialogue with Nature*. New York: Bantam, 1984.

273. "Prigogine's Science of Becoming." *Brain/Mind Bulletin*, Vol. 4 (1979), No. 13.

274. "Rats Can't Learn Without Aid of Norepinephrine." *Brain/Mind Bulletin*, Vol. 5 (1980), No. 2.

275. Regan, D. "Some Characteristics of Average Steady-State and Transient Responses Evoked by Modulated Light." *Electroencephalography and Clinical Neurophysiology*, Vol. 20 (1966), pp. 238–48.

276. Restak, Richard M., M.D. *The Brain: The Last Frontier*. New York: Doubleday, 1979.

277. Reston, James, Jr. "Mission to a Mind." *Omni*, July 1984.

278. Rogers, M., D. Dubey, and P. Reich. "The Influence of the Psyche and the Brain on Immunity and Disease Susceptibility: A Critical Review." *Psychosomatic Medicine*, Vol. 41 (1979), pp. 147–64.

279. Rose, Steven. *The Conscious Brain*. New York: Knopf, 1975.

280. Rosenblatt, Seymour, M.D., and Reynolds Dodson. *Beyond Valium: The Brave New World of Psychochemistry*. New York: Putnam, 1981.

281. Rosenzweig, Mark R. "Experience, Memory, and the Brain." *American Psychologist*, April 1984.

282. ——, Edward L. Bennett, and Marian C. Diamond. "Effects of Differential Environments on Brain Anatomy and Brain Chemistry." In J. Zubin and G. Jervis, eds., *Psychopathology of Mental Development*. New York: Grune & Stratton, 1967.

283. ——. "Brain Changes in Response to Experience." *Scientific American*, February 1972.

284. Rossi, A. M., P. E. Nathan, R. H. Harrison, and P. Solomon. "Operant Responding for Visual Stimuli During Sensory Deprivation: Effect of Meaningfulness." *Journal of Abnormal Psychology*, Vol. 79 (1969), pp. 188–93.

285. Rossier, J., F. E. Bloom, and R. Guillemin. "Stimulation of Human Periaqueductal Gray for Pain Relief Increases Immunoreactive Beta-Endorphin in Ventricular Fluid." *Science*, January 19, 1979.

286. Routtenberg, Aryeh. "The Reward System of the Brain." *Scientific American*, November 1978.

287. ———, and Rebecca Santos-Anderson. "The Role of Prefrontal Cortex in Intracranial Self-Stimulation." *Handbook of Psychopharmacology*, Vol. 8, ed. Leslie L. Iversen, Susan D. Iversen, and Solomon H. Synder. New York: Plenum, 1977.

288. Rugg, M.D., and A.M.J. Dickens. "Dissociation of Alpha and Theta Activity as a Function of Verbal and Visuospatial Tasks." *Electroencephalography and Clinical Neurophysiology*, Vol. 53 (1982), pp. 201–7.

289. Russell, Peter. *The Brain Book*. New York: Hawthorn, 1979.

290. ———. *The Global Brain: Speculations on the Evolutionary Leap to Planetary Consciousness*. Los Angeles: Tarcher, 1983.

291. Sagan, Carl. *Dragons of Eden*. New York: Random House, 1977.

292. Salk, L. "The Role of the Heartbeat in the Relations Between Mother and Infant." *Scientific American*, March 1973.

293. Samuels, Mike, M.D., and Nancy Samuels. *Seeing with the Mind's Eye*. New York: Random House, 1975.

294. San Martini, P., R. Venturini, G.A. Zapponi, and A. Loizzo. "Interaction Between Intermittent Photic Stimulation and Auditory Stimulation on the Human EEG." *Neuropsychobiology*, Vol. 5 (1979), pp. 201–6.

295. Schmeck, Harold M., Jr. "The Biology of Fear and Anxiety: Evidence Points to Chemical Triggers." *New York Times*, September 7, 1982.

296. ———. "Addict's Brain: Chemistry Holds Hope for Answers." *New York Times*, January 25, 1983.

297. ———. "Study Says Smile May Indeed Be an Umbrella." *New York Times*, September 9, 1983.

298. ———. "Domination Is Linked to Chemical in the Brain." *New York Times*, September 27, 1983.

299. ———. "Explosion of Data on Brain Cell Reveals Its Great Complexity." *New York Times*, March 6, 1984.

300. Schul, Bill D. "Conceptual Discussion of Work Plans." Faber, Va.: Monroe Institute of Applied Sciences. Undated.

301. ———. "Effects of Audio Signals on Brainwaves." Faber, Va.: Monroe Institute of Applied Sciences. Undated.

302. Schultz, Duane P. *Sensory Restriction: Effects on Behavior*. New York: Academic, 1965.

303. Schultz, Johannes. "The Clinical Importance of 'Inward Seeing' in Autogenic Training." *British Journal of Medical Hypnotism*, Vol. 11 (1960), pp. 26–28.

304. ———, and Wolfgang Luthe. *Autogenic Training: A Psychophysio-*

logic Approach in Psychotherapy. New York: Grune & Stratton, 1959.

305. Searle, John R. "The Myth of the Computer." *New York Review of Books*, April 29, 1982.

306. "Self-Organizing Brain Models Cooperative Action." *Brain/Mind Bulletin.* Vol. 9. (1984), No. 17.

307. Selye, Hans, M.D. *The Stress of Life*, rev. ed. New York: McGraw-Hill, 1976.

308. Shafii, Mohammad, M.D., R. Lavely, and R. Jaffe. "Meditation and Marijuana." *American Journal of Psychiatry*, Vol. 131 (1974), pp. 60–63.

309. ———. "Meditation and the Prevention of Drug Abuse." *American Journal of Psychiatry*, Vol. 132 (1975), pp. 942–45.

310. Silverman, Lloyd. "Unconscious Symbiotic Fantasy: A Ubiquitous Therapeutic Agent." *International Journal of Psychoanalytic Psychotherapy*, Vol. 7 (1978–79), p. 568.

311. ———, F. M. Lachmann, and R. H. Milich. *The Search for Oneness.* New York: International Universities Press, 1982.

312. Simonton, O. Carl, Stephanie Matthews-Simonton, and J. Creighton. *Getting Well Again.* Los Angeles: Tarcher, 1978.

313. ———, and Stephanie Simonton. "Belief Systems and Management of the Emotional Aspects of Malignancy." *Journal of Transpersonal Psychology*, Vol. 7 (1975), pp. 29–47.

314. Sitaram, N., H. Weingartner, Caine, and J.C. Gillin. "Choline: Selective Enhancement of Serial Learning and Encoding of Low Imagery Words in Man." *Life Sciences*, Vol. 22 (1978), pp. 1555–60.

315. Sitaram, N., H. Weingartner, and J. C. Gillin. "Human Serial Learning: Enhancement with Arecoline and Choline and Impairment with Scopolamine Correlate with Performance on Placebo." *Science*, Vol. 201 (1978), pp. 274–76.

316. Sjolund, B.H., and M.B.E. Eriksson. "Electroacupuncture and Endogenous Morphines." *Lancet*, Vol. 2 (1976), p. 1085.

317. Smith, Adam. *Powers of the Mind.* New York: Random House, 1975.

318. Smith, Anthony. *The Mind.* New York: Viking, 1984.

319. "Smuggling Drugs Across the Blood-Brain Barrier." *Science News*, January 2, 1982.

320. Snyder, Solomon H. "Opiate Receptors in the Brain." *New England Journal of Medicine*, February 3, 1977.

321. ———. "A Multiplicity of Opiate Receptors and Enkephalin Neuronal Systems." *Journal of Clinical Psychiatry*, Vol. 43 (1982), pp. 9–12.

322. Solomon, Philip, P. E. Kubzansky, P. H. Leiderman, J. H. Mendelson, R. Trumbull, and D. Wexler, eds. *Sensory Deprivation: A*

Symposium Held at Harvard Medical School. Cambridge: Harvard University Press, 1961.

323. Sommer. Robert. *The Mind's Eye*. New York: Delacorte, 1978.

324. Soulairac, A., H. Hossard, and A. Virel. "The Effect of Electronically Induced Alpha Rhythm on Anxiety States." *Annales Medico-Psychologiques*, Vol. 2 (1977), pp. 704–11.

325. "Spinning Therapy Calms Hyperactivity, Accelerates Physical Development." *Brain/Mind Bulletin*, Vol. 5 (1980), No. 20.

326. Springer, Sally P., and Georg Deutsch. *Left Brain, Right Brain*. San Francisco: Freeman, 1981.

327. Squire, Larry R., and Hasker Davis. "The Pharmacology of Memory: A Neurobiological Perspective." In *Annual Review of Pharmacy and Toxicology, 1981*. Palo Alto: Annual Reviews, Inc., 1981.

328. Staib, A., and D. N. Logan. "Hypnotic Stimulation of Breast Growth." *American Journal of Clinical Hypnosis*, Vol. 19. (1977), p. 201.

329. Standing, Lionel. "Learning 10,000 Pictures." *Quarterly Journal of Experimental Psychology*, Vol. 25, pp. 207–22.

330. Stanley, John M., William D. Francis, and Heidi Berres. "The Effects of Flotation REST on Cognitive Tasks." Paper delivered at first International Conference on REST and Self-Regulation, Denver, Colo., March 17, 1983.

331. Starr, Douglas. "Brain Drugs." *Omni*, February 1983.

332. "Static Brain Models Give Way to Dynamic, Fluid Concepts." *Brain/Mind Bulletin*, Vol. 9 (1984), Nos. 11–12.

333. Stein et al. "Memory Enhancement by Central Administration of Norepinephrine." *Brain Research*, Vol. 84 (1975), pp. 329–35.

334. Stern, Gary S., Ph.D. "Physiological and Mood Effects of Salt Water Flotation Periods." Unpublished paper.

335. Stevens, Charles F. "The Neuron." *Scientific American*, September 1979.

336. Stone, Pat. "Altered States of Consciousness." *Mother Earth News*, March/April 1983.

337. Storfer, Miles David. *A Readers Guide to Brain Research Activities and Their Potential*. New York: Foundation for Brain Research, 1982.

338. ——. *Brain Research: Our Journey Has Begun*. New York: Foundation for Brain Research, 1984.

339. ——. "The Human Memory." *Mensa Research Journal*, Mensa Education and Research Foundation, 1985.

340. "Stress Held Factor in IQ Scores." *New York Times*, May 31, 1983.

341. Stroebel, Charles F., M.D. *QR: The Quieting Reflex*. New York: Putnam, 1982.

342. Suedfeld, Peter. "The Benefits of Boredom: Sensory Deprivation Reconsidered." *American Scientist*, Vol. 63 (1975), pp. 60–69.

343. ——. "The Clinical Relevance of Reduced Sensory Stimulation." *Canadian Psychological Review*, Vol. 16 (1975), pp. 88–103.

344. ——. "Using Environmental Restriction to Initiate Long-Term Behavioral Change." In *Behavioral Self-Management: Strategies, Techniques and Outcomes*, ed. R. B. Stuart. New York: Brunner/Mazel, 1977.

345. ——. *Restricted Environmental Stimulation: Research and Clinical Applications*. New York: Wiley, 1980.

346. ——. "REST: Technique, Treatment, Transcendence." Address delivered at first International Conference on REST and Self-Regulation, Denver, Colo., March 17, 1983.

347. ——, and J. A. Best. "Satiation and Sensory Deprivation Combined in Smoking Therapy: Some Case Studies and Unexpected Side-Effects." *International Journal of Addiction*, Vol. 12 (1977), pp. 337–59.

348. ——, and R.D. Hare. "Sensory Deprivation in the Treatment of Snake Phobia: Behavioral, Self-report and Physiological Effects." *Behavioral Therapy*, Vol. 8 (1977), pp. 240–50.

349. Suinn, Richard M. "Body Thinking: Psychology for Olympic Champs." *Psychology Today*, July 1976.

350. "Synchro-Energizer: Report No. 1." Biofeedback Institute of Denver. Unpublished manuscript, 1980.

351. "Synchro-Energizer and Isolation Tank Research Report." Potential Research Foundation. Unpublished manuscript, 1980.

352. Tallman, John F., et al. "Receptors for the Age of Anxiety: Pharmacology of the Benzodiazepines." *Science*, Vol. 207 (1980), p. 274.

353. Tart, Charles T., ed. *Altered States of Consciousness*. New York: Wiley, 1969.

354. ——. *States of Consciousness*. New York: Dutton, 1975.

355. Taylor, Gordon Rattray. *The Natural History of the Mind*. New York: Dutton, 1979.

356. Taylor, Thomas E. "Learning Studies for Higher Cognitive Levels in a Short-Term Sensory Isolation Environment." Paper delivered at first International Conference on REST and Self-Regulation, Denver, Colo., March 17, 1983.

357. ——, Margaret C. Hansen, et al. "A Study of EEG as an Indicator of Changes in Cognitive Level of Understanding in a Sensory Isolation Environment." Unpublished paper, Department of Chemistry, Texas A&M University.

358. Turner, John W. "Hormones and REST: A Controlled Study of REST-Assisted Relaxation." Paper delivered at first International

Conference on REST and Self-Regulation, Denver, Colo., March 18, 1983.

359. Ungar, Georges. "Biological Assays for the Molecular Coding of Acquired Information." In *Macromolecules and Behavior*, 2nd ed., ed. J. Gaito. New York: Appleton-Century-Crofts, 1972.

360. Vogel, William, Donald M. Broverman, Edward Klaiber, and Karoly J. Kun. "EEG Response to Photic Stimulation as a Function of Cognitive Style." *Electroencephalography and Clinical Neurophysiology*, Vol. 27 (1969), pp. 186–90.

361. Walford, Roy L., M.D. *Maximum Life Span*. New York: Norton, 1983.

362. Walkup, Lewis E. "Creativity in Science Through Visualization." *Perceptual and Motor Skills*, Vol. 221 (1965), pp. 35–41.

363. Walsh, Roger. *Towards an Ecology of Brain*. Jamaica, N.Y.: SP Medical and Scientific Books, 1982.

364. Watson, Lyall. *Lifetide: The Biology of the Unconscious*. New York: Simon & Schuster, 1979.

365. Wauquier, Albert, and Edmund T. Rolls. *Brain Stimulation Reward*. Amsterdam: North-Holland Publishing Co., 1976.

366. Weil, Andrew. *The Natural Mind*. Boston: Houghton Mifflin, 1972.

367. Weintraub, Pamela, ed. *The Omni Interviews*. New York: Ticknor & Fields, 1984.

368. West, Michael A. "Meditation and the EEG." *Psychological Medicine*, Vol. 10 (1980), pp. 369–75.

369. Westcott, M., and J. Ranzoni. "Correlates of Intuitive Thinking." *Psychological Reports*, Vol. 12 (1963), pp. 595–613.

370. Wickramsekera, Ian. "Sensory Restriction and Self Hypnosis as Potentiators of Self-Regulation." Paper delivered at first International Conference on REST and Self-Regulation, Denver, Colo., March 18, 1983.

371. Willard, R. D. "Breast Enlargement Through Visual Imagery and Hypnosis." *American Journal of Clinical Hypnosis*, Vol. 19 (1977), p. 195.

372. Williams, J. E. "Stimulation of Breast Growth by Hypnosis." *Journal of Sex Research*, Vol. 10 (1974), pp. 316–24.

373. Williams, J. T. and W. Zieglgansberger. "Neurons in the Frontal Cortex of the Rat Carry Multiple Opiate Receptors." *Brain Research*, Vol. 226 (1981), pp. 304–8.

374. Williams, Paul, and Michael A. West. "EEG Responses to Photic Stimulation in Persons Experienced at Meditation." *Electroencephalography and Clinical Neurophysiology*, Vol. 39 (1975), pp. 519–22.

375. Wise, Steven P., and Miles Herkenham. "Opiate Receptor Distribution in the Cerebral Cortex of the Rhesus Monkey." *Science*, Vol. 218 (1982), pp. 387–89.

376. Witelson, Sandra. "Sex and the Single Hemisphere: Specialization of the Right Hemisphere for Spatial Processing." *Science*, Vol. 193 (1976), pp. 425–26.

377. Wolpe, J. *The Practice of Behavior Therapy*. New York: Pergamon, 1969.

378. Woolfolk, Robert L., and Frank C. Richardson. *Stress, Sanity and Survival*. New York: Monarch, 1978.

379. Yaguchi, Kiyoshi, and Shinkura Iwahara. "Temporal Sequence of Frequency Specific and Non-specific Effects of Flickering Lights upon the Occipital Electrical Activity in Man." *Brain Research*, Vol. 107 (1976), pp. 27–38.

380. Young, J. Z. *Programs of the Brain*. Oxford: Oxford University Press, 1978.

381. Zaidel, Eran. "Unilateral Auditory Language Comprehension on the Token Test Following Cerebral Commissurotomy and Hemispherectomy." *Neuropsychologia*, Vol. 15 (1977), pp. 1–18.

382. Zubek, J. P., ed. *Sensory Deprivation: Fifteen Years of Research*. New York: Appleton-Century-Crofts, 1969.

383. Zuckerman, M. *Sensation Seeking: Beyond the Optimal Level of Arousal*. Hillsdale, N.J.: Lawrence Elbaum Associates, 1979.

INDEX

361

ABOUT THE AUTHOR

MICHAEL HUTCHISON's writings on neuroscience and the technology of self-transformation have included *The Book of Floating* and numerous magazine articles. His fiction has been awarded the James Michener Prize; his nonfiction has appeared in *Esquire, The Village Voice, Outside, The Partisan Review, New Age Journal*, and other magazines and newspapers. He lives in New York City.